The Politics of Curriculum and Testing

Education Policy Perspectives

General Editor: Professor Ivor Goodson, Faculty of Education, University of Western Ontario, London, Canada N6G 1G7

Education policy analysis has long been a neglected area in the UK and, to an extent, in the USA and Australia. The result has been a profound gap between the study of education and the formulation of education policy. For practitioners, such a lack of analysis of new policy initiatives has worrying implications, particularly at a time of such policy flux and change. Education policy has, in recent years, been a matter for intense political debate – the political and public interest in the working of the system has come at the same time as the breaking of the consensus on education policy by the New Right. As never before, political parties and pressure groups differ in their articulated policies and prescriptions for the education sector. Critical thinking about these developments is clearly imperative.

All those working within the system also need information on policy-making, policy implementation and effective day-to-day operation. Pressure on schools from government, education authorities and parents has generated an enormous need for knowledge amongst those on the receiving end of educational policies.

This Falmer Press series aims to fill the academic gap, to reflect the politicalization of education, and to provide the practitioners with the analysis for informed implementation of policies that they will need. It offers studies in broad areas of policy studies, with a particular focus on the following areas: school organization and improvement; critical social analysis; policy studies and evaluation; and education and training.

The Politics of Curriculum and Testing

The 1990 Yearbook of the Politics of Education Association

Edited by

Susan H. Fuhrman

Center for Policy Research in Education

and

Betty Malen

University of Washington

The Falmer Press

(A Member of the Taylor & Francis Group)

London · New York · Philadelphia

UK   Falmer Press Ltd, 4 John Street, London WC1N 2ET

USA   The Falmer Press, Taylor & Francis Inc., 1900 Frost Road,
          Bristol, PA 19007

First published 1991

**A catalogue of reference for this book is available
from the British Library**

**Library of Congress Cataloging-in-Publication Data
is available on request**

ISBN 1-85000-974-0 cased
ISBN 1-85000-975-9 pbk

Cover design by Caroline Archer

Typeset in 11/12 Bembo by Chapterhouse Typesetting Ltd, Formby, Lancs.

*Printed in Great Britain by Burgess Science Press, Basingstoke
on paper which has a specified pH value on final paper
manufacture of not less than 7·5 and is therefore 'acid free'.*

Contents

Part 3. Systemic approaches to instructional guidance

About the PEA

The Politics of Education Association (PEA) promotes the development and dissemination of research and debate on educational policy and politics. PEA brings together scholars, practitioners, and policy-makers interested in educational governance and politics; is affiliated as a Special Interest Group with the American Educational Research Association (AERA); and meets each spring in conjunction with AERA's annual meeting. The annual membership dues for PEA are $US20.00 (subject to change). Members receive a copy of the annual Yearbook and the *Politics of Education Bulletin*, which includes news on member activities and occasional short scholarly pieces. Membership dues should be sent to Robert Wimpelberg, PEA, College of Education, University of New Orleans, New Orleans, LA 70148, USA.

Acknowledgement

We are extremely grateful to Stacy Gands for her assistance producing this volume. She helped keep us on schedule, she proofread numerous chapters through long nights in her office at the Center for Policy Research in Education, Rutgers University, and was our essential link in contacting authors.

SHF and BM

About the Editors and Contributors

Susan H. Fuhrman is a Professor of Education Policy with a joint appointment at the Eagleton Institute of Politics and the Graduate School of Education, Rutgers, the State University of New Jersey. She directs the Center for Policy Research in Education (CPRE) a consortium of Rutgers, Michigan State University, Stanford University, and the University of Wisconsin – Madison, that is funded by the Office of Educational Research and Improvement, the U.S. Department of Education, to study state and local policies to improve schooling.

Betty Malen is an Associate Professor in the area of Policy, Governance, and Administration at the University of Washington. Her central research interests are education policy and politics. Her most recent work focuses on school-based management as an education reform strategy.

Doug A. Archbald is an Assistant Professor at the University of Delaware. At CPRE, he has co-directed a project on the content and effects of state/district curriculum systems. His other research interests include magnet schools, school choice theory, and performance-based assessment in education.

Eva L. Baker has been the Director of the University of California Los Angeles Center for the Study of Evaluation for the past 13 years, and is a Professor of Educational Psychology at the UCLA Graduate School of Education. Her research commitments include assessment of educational policy, research on the design of new measures in writing and in subject matter, the application of artificial intelligence to educational problems, and the evaluation of high technology in education and training.

Rolf K. Blank is a project Director with the State Education Assessment Center of the Council of Chief State School Officers in Washington, DC. He is directing an effort to build a 50-state system of indicators of the condition of science and mathematics education in elementary and secondary schools.

Danise Cantlon is a graduate student in teacher education at Michigan State University. She is a research assistant for the Center for the Learning and Teaching of Elementary Subjects.

James G. Cibulka is a Professor of Administrative Leadership at the University of Wisconsin-Milwaukee. His specializations include educational politics, finance and policy. He was formerly a Senior Research Fellow at the U.S. Department of Education, where he studied educational restructuring in the United States and Great Britain.

William H. Clune is Voss-Bascom Professor of Law at the University of Wisconsin Law School and Director of the Wisconsin branch of CPRE. His past research on educational policy has included school finance, school law, implementation, special education, and public employee interest arbitration. His present research with CPRE concerns the effects of graduation requirements and other student standards, school site autonomy, and regulation of the curriculum.

David K. Cohen is Interim Dean of the School of Education and John A. Hannah Distinguished Professor of Education and Social Policy at Michigan State University. He has studied the effects of schooling, various reforms of teaching, the evaluation of educational experiments and large-scale interventions, and the relations between research and policy. His current research at CPRE and the Center for the Learning and Teaching of Elementary Subjects concerns relations between teaching practice and policy.

Donald Freeman is Associate Dean of the College of Education at Arizona State University in Tempe. A senior researcher with the Center for the Learning and Teaching of Elementary Subjects, Freeman has studied the content of the elementary curriculum and the influence of various factors, including policies, textbooks, and teacher convictions, on that content.

Ivor Goodson is a Professor of Education at the University of Western Ontario and is General Editor of the Education Policy Perspectives Series that publishes this Yearbook. He has written extensively on the social construction of the curriculum.

R. J. S. 'Mac' Macpherson is a Senior Lecturer in the Department of Administrative, Higher and Adult Education Studies and Sub Dean of the Educational Administration program at the University of New England, New South Wales, Australia. He publishes in the areas of systemic and policy reform, the curriculum of Educational Administration, organization theory and research methodology.

Jennifer O'Day is a research assistant at the Center for Policy Research in Education at Stanford University, where she is a fourth-year doctoral student. She has co-authored articles on research on teaching, teacher education, teacher policies, and the policies and practice of grade retention in the USA.

Janice Patterson is a former CPRE Senior Research Fellow at the University of Wisconsin-Madison. She has researched the effects of education reform on academically at-risk high schoolers as well as computer education policy and computer use in schools.

Andrew C. Porter is Director of the Wisconsin Center for Education Research and a Professor of Educational Psychology at the University of Wisconsin-Madison. His research spans the areas of research on teaching, education policy analysis, student and teacher assessment, and psychometrics, especially the problem of measuring change. At CPRE he is examining the effects of state and district curriculum policies on course content, teacher attitude, and morale.

Sharon Rushcamp is a doctoral candidate in teacher education at Michigan State University, where she is a research assistant at the Center for the Learning and Teaching of Elementary Subjects.

Lorrie A. Shepard is a Professor of Research and Evaluation Methodology in the School of Education at the University of Colorado at Boulder. Her research focuses on psychometrics and the use of tests in educational settings. Topics of various journal publications include test bias, standard setting, the influence of testing on instruction, teacher testing, identification of mild handicaps, grade retention, and early childhood assessment.

Diane Schilder is a project associate with the State Education Assessment Center at the Council of Chief State School Officers in Washington, D.C.

Marshall S. Smith is Dean of the School of Education and Professor of Education at Stanford University. He directs the CPRE research at Stanford. He has studied and written about several education policy issues including desegregation, school effects, early childhood programs, compensatory education programs, evaluation design, effective schools, the effects of federal policies on state and local practice, and educational indicators. His current work focuses on nationalizing trends in curriculum and systemic education reform.

Regie Stites is a doctoral student at the UCLA Graduate School of Education in the field of Comparative Education. His research interest specializes in Chinese studies. He is presently conducting research on the politics of peripheral literacy, predominantly in rural areas of the People's Republic of China. At the Center for the Study of Evaluation, Stites has designed new types of assessments.

Alexander K. Tyree, Jr. is an assistant professor in the Center for Teaching and Learning at the University of North Dakota. His research concerns school effects on teacher engagement and teaching commitment as well as state curriculum control systems. At CPRE he has studied the content and prescriptiveness of mathematics and social studies curriculum policy systems in four states.

1   The Politics of Curriculum and Testing: introduction and overview

Betty Malen and Susan H. Fuhrman

Throughout the past two decades, state governments have assumed a more expansive, aggressive, and prescriptive role in many domains of education policy (Mitchell 1988). Since the mid 1980s, state governments have become especially active in two domains, curriculum and accountability (Elmore *et al.*1990, McDonnell and Fuhrman 1986). In this fairly brief time period, nearly all states enacted policies to inspire or require more rigor in the academic component of the school program and nearly all states adopted policies to generate and disseminate more detailed assessments of student performance (Blank, this volume).

The signs and seeds of state involvement in aspects of curriculum and accountability have been present for some time (Boyd 1979, Kirst 1988). But this relatively recent, rapid-fire proliferation of policies in these areas signaled a shift in stance. State governments were crossing conventional boundaries of local control, professional discretion, and limited intervention (Fuhrman 1990, Kirst 1988). And, they were embracing a variety of strategies – more stringent graduation requirements, more prescriptive curricular frameworks, more encompassing programmatic regulations, more student performance assessments, and, in some instances, more technical assistance and financial support, more explicit rewards, more severe sanctions – to advance those expressed ends (Goertz 1986, Fuhrman 1990).

This impressive, perhaps unprecedented level of state activity directs attention to and provides the raw materials for a preliminary analysis of the politics of curriculum and testing in the USA. Parallel activism on the part of national governments in other countries underscores the widespread interest in curriculum and testing policies, and broadens the base for considering issues associated with governmental efforts to institute systems of instructional guidance, or, as some might express it, systems of instructional control (e.g., Goodson, this volume).

The 1990 Politics of Education Association Yearbook can be viewed as an anthology of papers that address aspects of a broad, complex, and evolving field of study that seeks to understand such 'core concerns' (Elmore *et al.* 1990) as: (*a*) the development, implementation, and assessment of policies that affect what should be taught in schools and to whom, how instruction should be carried out, and who should decide these matters; (*b*) the forms and effects of governmental action, i.e., the nature of the instruments and symbols government selects or combines to influence individuals and institutions, the manner in which various governmental interventions penetrate practice and operate to promote (or impede) particular policy objectives; (*c*) the ways in which policy processes, designs, and effects interact; and (*d*) the impact of these interactions on broad dimensions of interest, such as the content of schooling, the quality and equity of educational opportunities, and the distribution of power and authority in social systems.

The 1990 Yearbook can also be viewed as a catalyst for identifying prominent patterns

0268–0939/90 $3.00 © 1990 Taylor & Francis Ltd.

that both policy researchers and policy makers may wish to consider. Although the chapters address different aspects of curriculum, testing and accountability policies, employ different analytic perspectives, and develop distinct interpretations, they illustrate more general themes. Thus, this introductory essay provides an overview of the individual chapters and highlights some of the major, crosscutting issues.

Overview of chapters

The chapters in this Yearbook are organized into three sections. The first section catalogues state-level changes in curriculum policy and assesses the initial impacts of select policy changes at different levels of the system. The second section focuses on changes in testing policy and accountability provisions. It explores some of the initial and, in several instances, projected consequences of those changes. The final section addresses systemic reforms of instructional guidance, as they are developing abroad and how they might be developed at the state level in this country.

Curriculum policy

The section on curriculum policy begins with a chapter in which Andrew Porter, Doug Archbald, and Alexander Tyree examine curricular reform in terms of 'a new demanding goal', hard content (i.e., curriculum that focuses on higher order thinking and problem – solving) for *all* students. The authors review obstacles to the achievement of this goal, delineate two prominent strategies that might be used to promote this goal (curriculum control and teacher empowerment), then assess the relative strengths of these strategies for attaining this goal. Using data acquired in four states (Florida, California, New York, and Texas), the authors conclude that 'current practice is nowhere near the goal of hard content for all students'. They argue that each strategy is insufficient, largely because control mechanisms do not address many of the obstacles and empowerment approaches do not explicitly attend the goal. They suggest the two strategies may be interdependent and call for research that sheds light on the connections between policy strategies and policy impacts.

Rolf Blank addresses several control strategies adopted by many state legislatures, namely the modification of course requirements in the areas of math and science, the development of curricular frameworks, and the intensification of state level monitoring and assessment capabilities in these subject areas. The 50-state survey research reported in this chapter demonstrates that increased course requirements are associated with increased enrollments in math and science, but because enrollment increases are often in basic or applied courses, students may be getting more exposure to, not necessarily more rigorous content in these areas. The research reported here also demonstrates that although student testing has become the primary means through which state governments monitor curricular reforms, in the majority of states, tests are not closely aligned with the state's curricular framework. Given these and other findings, the author concludes that existing state data banks provide the basis for developing general indicators of policy impacts but argues that more elaborate, hence more expensive, assessment systems are needed to gauge the extent to which curricular reforms alter the quality of course offerings and foster the development of higher-order skills.

Danise Cantlon, Sharon Rushcamp, and Donald Freeman analyse the interplay between state and district curriculum policies. The authors draw on case studies conducted in Florida, Michigan, and California. They characterize the relationship between state and district policies as a dynamic, purposeful interchange, wherein district policy makers engage in a 'deliberate effort to modify the district's curriculum framework to accommodate changes in state curriculum guidelines'. However, variations in styles of accommodation produce significant differences in the ways state curricular guidelines get implemented in local districts. These variations are capsulized in two models: the district autonomy/compromise model and the district compliance/augmentation model. In the first instance, districts respond to changes in state guidelines through adjustments that preserve the integrity of local curricular frameworks (i.e., marginal modifications that do not fundamentally alter the central components of their curricular frameworks). In the second instance, districts adopt the state curricular frameworks and augment them by designing curriculum guidelines for subject areas not covered by state policy. The authors discuss the implications of these models for understanding how districts will respond to changes in state guidelines and gauging the extent to which these responses will foster the goal of 'teaching for understanding and thinking'.

Janice Patterson explores school-level responses to state-level mandates. The author describes the manner in which schools react to increased graduation requirements and discusses the effect of these actions on at-risk students. The case studies carried out in urban sites indicate that school responses include: (a) the addition of basic or remedial sections of math and science to the school schedule, an adjustment that affects the exposure to but not necessarily the quality of instruction in these areas; (b) the escalation of alternative routes to graduation (e.g., GED training courses, night classes) and the redefinition of existing courses in ways that permit current, often vocational-oriented offerings to become avenues through which academic requirements might be met; (c) the institution of a wide range of drop-out prevention activities that were quite pronounced in schools with a low percentage of at-risk students but less available in schools with high concentrations of at-risk students; and (d) a tendency to place the emphasis, as the author puts it, on graduation rather than education. In terms of general effects on at-risk students, the research reported here indicates that the neither the feared scenario (a push-out effect) nor the desired scenario (a more rigorous, relevant curricula) occurred for at-risk students. In terms of policy recommendations, the author calls for actions that keep children in school to *learn*.

David Cohen examines policy impacts at the classroom level. Through a rich description of a 'revolution in one classroom' in California, the author depicts the complexities embedded in judging innovation and progress, particularly when the desired outcome is as elusive as 'teaching for understanding'. Cohen portrays the tensions apparent in patterns of practice and discusses the paradoxes nested in policies. By demonstrating that a teacher's prior instruction in and experience with a discipline does as much to shape the organization and pedagogy in classrooms as any curricular framework or activity menu, the author illustrates the limits of policy. This single case reveals how difficult it will be for teachers to learn and incorporate new patterns of practice, even when they enthusiastically embrace and conscientiously attempt to follow new policy directives.

Why are the effects of curriculum policies often less than or other than what their framers intended? The section on curriculum policy concludes with a chapter that describes and advocates an approach to the development of 'eductional policy in a situation of uncertainty'. William Clune argues for substantial experimentation with a wide range of policy alternatives (e.g., choice, restructuring, instructional guidance) coupled with systematic examination of the various policy options. Such an approach would enable policy-makers to 'push weak policies in productive directions'. In building the case for this approach, the author defines the 'ideal' policy as one that (a) promotes a practice that holds promise of impacting student achievements; (b) embodies a simple but potent implementation strategy; (c) acquires broad-based enduring political support; and (d) carries modest costs. Using these criteria, Clune offers assessments of current policy alternatives and identifies lines of research that might be used to weigh policy options; develop more ideal policy alternatives, and thereby improve policy effects.

Testing policy and accountability provisions

This section begins with a chapter that traces the development of testing policies and practices in the USA. Eva Baker and Regie Stites argue that testing policies and practices are the result of the 'subtle interplay of social, political, and technical factors' that both reflect and affect the ever-present tensions between equity and quality in American education. This historical analysis provides the basis for an interpretation of the current emphasis on and widespread acceptance of standardized testing practices. It also provides the basis for a series of predictions regarding the role of testing in education reform and a call for assessments that are 'grounded in new conceptions of validity, in social justice and in American values appropriate for our changing student group'.

Lorrie Shephard analyzes testing policies and practices using a particular case in point, kindergarten readiness testing. The author examines how a variety of contextual forces converge to compel local districts to emphasize readiness testing, and how these pressures prompt local districts to take tests designed to inform instructional planning and use them to regulate access and determine placement. The author discusses how these prominent patterns of practice, or 'backdoor policies', contribute to unconsidered and undesirable consequences. The author contends, for example, that 'backdoor policies' are often instituted without explicit or extensive deliberation and that they operate to reinstate tracking, exaggerate age and ability differences, perpetuate ineffective treatments (e.g., retention), deny poor and minority children access to public education or relegate poor and minority children to low ability groupings.

James Cibulka examines the various rationales underlying the accountability movement, identifies three models that capture the alternative rationales, then demonstrates how the design of the policy and the politics of the settlement combine to shape the outcomes of the accountability systems. The state oversight (bureaucratic) model views accountability reporting as a tool for superordinate governments to improve the efficiency of the educational system. The local citizen initiative (responsiveness) model views accountability reporting as a source of political power for and a stimulus for political action by individuals and interest groups. The consumer initiative (market) model views accountability reporting as a means to maximize consumer choice. Through an illustrative case of each model, the author draws several conclusions. First, the state oversight model (South Carolina) produced significant, positive effects (as well as some negative effects) because the accountability system was integrated with other state initiatives and developed through consensual processes that garnered and galvanized the broad-based backing of citizens, civic elites, and school professionals. Second, the local citizen initiative model (Illinois) produced modest impacts because the design was weak. It relied on the power of public disclosure and let the impetus for action reside with local patrons or school officials. In addition the conflicts that surfaced during the enactment process permeated and confounded implementation. Third, the market model (UK) can not be assessed, since implementation has not yet occurred. However, the author argues that although performance assessment has been linked to new market pressures, the settlement necessitated extensive professional involvement at the development stage (an interpretation somewhat different than that offered by Goodson, this volume). This compromise in the settlement, the author projects, may run counter to expanded consumer influence and hence, minimize the impact of this approach.

Systemic approaches to instructional guidance

This section analyzes movements to institute (or reinstitute) system-wide reforms in curriculum and accountability. The first chapter analyzes national curriculum developments in Australia. As R.J.S. MacPherson writes, these developments have 'a chequered history'. The author traces the 'comings and goings' of two national curriculum agencies as well as the fairly recent 'coming' of a third such agency. The cyclical character of federal interest and involvement in curriculum is attributed to a complex set of economic and political forces that prompt a federal government to seek a major role in curriculum despite the absence of constitutional responsibility in this area. A critical factor affecting the most recent movement was the power exercised by a coalition of government officials. The author interprets this dynamic as an indication that a 'dual polity' which seeks to reconcile both 'representative activity and state responses to economic pressures' may be emerging. The author predicts that if economic conditions worsen, 'the governance of curriculum will more and more become a matter of national and Ministerial determination', and, as a result, the curriculum will be increasingly standardized.

The second chapter traces the evolution of a national curriculum in the UK. Ivor Goodson addresses the antecedents of the national curriculum movement, the arguments used to promote the adoption of a national curriculum, the structures created to support it, and the educational assumptions nested in it. Although the national curriculum has been advanced as a measure that would contribute to economic revitalization, the author contends that the underlying rationales go beyond economic justification. The author interprets the national curriculum as a mechanism for the reinstitution of class-biased traditional subject matter, the re-establishment of a national identity, and the reassertion of national control.

The final chapter, by Marshall S. Smith and Jennifer O'Day, argues that what the United States needs is systemic reform that 'can combine the energy and professional involvement of the second wave reforms with a new and challenging state-initiated structure which provides the necessary generalizability of the reforms to all schools within a state'. The authors contend that barriers in the organization and governance of schools – particularly the fragmentation and attendant mediocrity of policies to address curriculum, accountability, professional development, and school working conditions – prevent the development of successful schools and undermine them where they exist. The strategy for systemic reform they recommend combines coherent state-level instructional guidance systems, based on agreement about what students ought to know and characterized by integrated progressive curriculum, assessment, professional development policies, with a restructured governance system that clarifies responsibilities at every level of the system. In some ways a summary chapter for the entire volume, the last chapter illustrates how some of the shortcomings of policies analyzed in the first two sections might be addressed. It also proposes a combination of 'top-down' and 'bottom-up' approaches that might avert the central control dangers identified by analysts from other nations.

Overview of themes and issues

Although chapters in this volume have their own story to tell, they embody common themes and illuminate larger issues. Three are highlighted here. First, whether policies are viewed as the formal actions of government or the dominant patterns of practice, they tend to produce multiple effects, achieve marginal gains, and receive mixed reviews. Second, these marginal gains and mixed reviews reflect the complexity of problems and the limits of policy. Third, the field of curriculum-testing policy, like other branches of policy research, faces challenges that emanate, in large measure, from the nature of the terrain (i.e., dense, changing thickets) and the state of the art (i.e., partial, primitive theories and limited empirical data).

Multiple effects, marginal gains, and mixed reviews

Chapters in this Yearbook consistently illustrate that policies produce many effects. Some of the effects are basically consistent with stated policy aims and others are not.

For example, policies analysed in this Yearbook are associated with a number of consonant effects, such as increased enrollment in math and science courses (e.g., Blank and Schilder); compliance with, at times embellishment of state curriculum guidelines (e.g., Cantlon *et al.*); the expansion of courses and services for at-risk students e.g., Patterson); changes in materials, activities, and teaching techniques used in classrooms (e.g., Cohen); and renewed efforts to develop school improvement plans (e.g., Cibulka). But when the lists of effects are judged in terms of the expressed aims of the policies (e.g., hard content for all students, teaching for understanding), the multiple effects often look more like marginal gains than major breakthroughs. There is little evidence that the proliferation of state curriculum-testing policies has yet precipitated fundamental improvements in the quality of teaching and learning in schools. In part this may be because they did not aim high enough. As Porter *et al.* and Cantlon *et al.* point out, only some states direct curriculum policy at sophisticated notions of teaching and learning; as Smith and O'Day make clear, the recent proliferation of new policies has done little to alter the mediocrity that characterizes the typical American school curriculum, and the fragmentation that characterizes educational policy promotes a focus on the lowest common denominator.

Policies analysed in this Yearbook are also associated with effects that run counter to expressed policy aims. For example, policies can divert energy from school improvement and direct it toward 'damage control' (e.g., Cibulka); they can operate to perpetuate discriminatory practices (e.g., Shephard); and they can operate to put the emphasis on graduation rather than education, on getting through the system, rather than learning in the system (e.g., Patterson).

Such multiple effects, marginal gains, and hence, mixed reviews are familiar themes in policy research (Elmore and McLaughlin 1988, Ingram and Mann 1980, McLaughlin 1987, Lindbloom 1980). They are, nonetheless, important themes. They remind us that policies may be consequential, but not necessarily beneficial. Moreover, as several authors note, Cohen most explicitly, the judgements we make about policy effects are inextricably linked to the lenses we use to look at them and the vantage points and value premises we bring to the interpretation of them. For these and other reasons, (e.g., measurement issues discussed by authors in this volume), a seemingly straightforward task, determining whether a policy produces intended, let alone beneficial effects, poses a very perplexing puzzle.

Complexity of problems – limits of policy

Curriculum and accountability policies have become attached to and cast as solutions for a wide range of problems – the need to develop higher order thinking and problem solving skills, foster economic growth, make education institutions more efficient in their operations and more responsive to their publics – to list a few. As the chapters in this volume point out, these problems are highly complex matters, subject to different definitions of causes and cures, affected by a myriad of factors, and indicative of longstanding value tensions (e.g., Baker and Stites, Cibulka, Porter *et al.*, Smith and O'Day).

While the chapters recognize the complexity of problems, they also reveal the limits of policy in a variety of ways. Several indicate that policies may be based on an incomplete, imprecise understanding of the means–end relationships (e.g., Cibulka, Clune, Porter *et al.*). In some instances it is not clear what approach is the most appropriate response to the problem, however defined, and it is even less clear what combination of policy instruments and strategies might be required to get the more robust remedy in place. As a result, policies seem rooted as much in hunches and hopes as in reason and evidence.

In some instances, relevant knowledge is simply not considered. There is little discussion of rationale or ramification (e.g., Shephard). As a result, policies evolve more by accident than design and operate to create or perpetuate rather than confront and correct problems.

In other cases, policies may not incorporate the full range of available instruments, align them consistently within the domains of education policy or co-ordinate them effectively across other sectors of public policy (e.g., strong reliance on requirements, modest use of capability building illustrated by Cohen; discrepancy between curricular frameworks and performance measures noted by Blank; fragmentation noted by Clune and Smith and O'Day). As a result, opportunities to develop interventions that concentrate and maximize influence are lost and policy seems fragmented, incoherent, and contradictory. Several chapters illustrate that however designed, policy is adjudicated and adjusted at every level of the system (e.g., Cibulka, Cantlon *et al.*, Cohen, Patterson, Smith, and O'Day). Since its essential elements can be embraced or eluded, embellished or diminshed at many junctures, the policy implemented may or may not bear much resemblance to the policy enacted (e.g., Clune). Moreover, however policy gets moderated and mediated as it makes it way to and through the system, it can hit a wall of intricate, inter-related and obstinate factors that numb and nullify intended effects. Since the obstacles to be overcome (e.g., the predispositions and life circumstances of students and teachers) may go well beyond the reach of even the most thoughtfully conceived, carefully crafted education policy, the ability of policy to impact problems is constrained.

The chapters not only unveil a lengthy list of the limits of policy, they begin to explain them by depicting how contextual pressures, conflicting interests, technical advancements (as well as technical gaps) converge and interact to shape policy content and policy impact. In so doing, the chapters remind us that policy serves many purposes and performs many functions, some of which run counter to the development of coherent solutions to compelling problems. For example, since policy operates to recognize and reconcile competing interests, it embraces diverse views of problems and priorities, combines varied, at times contradictory approaches to problems, and becomes a mixture of motives and means that mirrors the relative power of political actors as much as the relative merits of alternative interventions (e.g., Cibulka, Goodson, MacPherson). Since policy operates to stabilize and legitimate systems confronted by environmental presses and triggering events, it represents an immediate reaction to an urgent circumstance at least as much as it constitutes a considered response to a particular problem (e.g., Clune). In these and other ways, the chapters expose the interplay of rational, political, and contextual dimensions of policy making processes, and the manner in which these processes shape policy content. Thus authors unravel the complexities inherent in efforts to develop more coherent, hence more potent policy options (see also Kingdon 1984).

Challenges facing the field of curriculum-testing policy

The chapters in this Yearbook underline some of the challenges facing the field of curriculum–accountability policy. The chapters demonstrate that the terrain we seek to understand is extraordinarily difficult to map. The presence of backdoor policies, the proliferation of governmental actions, the various combinations of instruments embedded in those actions, the revision of policy through formal adjustments or informal modifications all complicate and confound efforts to get a fix on the field. The sheer volume, variety and fluidity of curriculum-testing policy makes classifying interventions, tracking impacts, and assessing effects an exceedingly difficult task. In addition, the chapters demonstrate that the field is guided by orienting frameworks, not overarching theories. We have diverse, at times contradictory, typologies, taxonomies, metaphors, and models. Thus our efforts to understand dense, changing thickets are circumscribed by the partial, primitive nature of our theories. This observation ought not be construed as a condemnation. It is indicative of the newness of our field and it applies to other branches of education and public policy as well. Like other fields of inquiry, we seek to develop a coherent body of knowledge. Given the nature of the phenomenon and the state of the art, we have a good bit of empirical and conceptual work to do. We hope that *The Politics of Curriculum and Testing* expands interest in that ambitious agenda and makes an initial contribution to that evolving venture.

References

BARDACH, E. (1982) *The Implementation Game* (Cambridge: MIT Press).

BOYD, W. L. (1979) 'The changing politics of curriculum policy-making for American schools', in J. Schaffarsick and G. Sykes (eds) *Value Conflicts and Curriculum Issues: Lessons from Research and Experience* (Berkeley: McCutcheon), pp. 73–138.

ELMORE, R. F. and MCLAUGHLIN, M. W. (1988) *Steady Work: Policy, Practice, and the Reform of American Education* (Santa Monica, CA: The Rand Corporation).

ELMORE, R., SYKES, G. and SPILLANE, J. P. (1990) 'Curriculum policy', in P. Jackson (ed.) *Handbook on Research on Curriculum* (New York: Macmillan), in press.

FUHRMAN, S. (1990) *Legislatures and Education Policy.* Paper prepared for the Eagleton Institute of Politics for the Symposium on the Legislature in the Twenty-First Century, 22–29 April.

GOERTZ, M. (1986) *State Educational Standards* (Princeton: Educational Testing Service).

INGRAM, H. M. and MANN, D. (1980) *Why Policies Succeed or Fail* (Beverley Hills: Sage).

KINGDON, J. W. (1984) *Agendas, Alternatives, and Public Policies* (Boston MA: Little, Brown & Co).

KIRST, M. (1988) *Who Should Control Our Schools? Reassessing Current Policies* (Stanford, CA: Center for Educational Research).

LINDBLOOM, C. E. (1980) *The Policy-Making Process, 2nd ed.* (Englewood Cliffs, NJ: Prentice Hall).

MCDONNELL, L. and FUHRMAN, S. (1986) 'The political context of education reform', in V. D. Mueller and M. McKeown (eds) *The Fiscal, Legal, and Political Aspects of State Reform of Elementary and Secondary Education* (Cambridge, MA: Ballinger), pp. 43–64.

McLAUGHLIN, M. W. (1987) 'Learning from experience: lessons from policy implementation', *Educational Evaluation and Policy Analysis*, 9 (2), pp. 171–178.

MITCHELL, D. (1988) 'Educational politics and policy: the state level', in N. J. Boyan (ed.) *Handbook of Research on Educational Administration* (New York: Longman), pp. 453–466.

PART 1. CURRICULUM POLICY

---

2   *Reforming the curriculum: will empowerment policies replace control?*

Andrew C. Porter, Doug A. Archbald, and Alexander K. Tyree, Jr.

Curriculum reform is analyzed from the perspective of hard content for all students. High school mathematics and social studies are used as subject matter examples. Against these expressions of desired ends, current practice is reviewed to illustrate obstacles that reform must overcome. Two approaches to reform are identified, curriculum control and teacher empowerment. Neither of these strategies is new; each has been used in the past in the service of less ambitious curriculum reforms. Drawing on previous experience, we sketch characteristics of control and empowerment and compare their strengths and weaknesses. Four states – Florida, California, New York, and Texas – are used to illustrate where states stand relative to the goal of hard content for all students. Those same states provide illustrations of the two strategies for curriculum reform. Again, high school mathematics and social studies are used to situate the analyses. We observe important differences among states and within states between subjects, both in the extent to which the goal of hard content for all students is approximated and in commitment to the two reform strategies. Generally, state policies are found to be short of what is necessary. Nowhere do we find efforts likely to measure up to the challenge.

For education, the 1980s were a period of great turmoil and unrest. Concerns were framed in terms of economic competitiveness, but lagging student achievement was asserted to be at the root of the problem. Politicians, corporate leaders, and the public agreed that the future of our nation was in the hands of our schools.

A demanding new goal

Neither the sense of urgency nor turning to school for help was something new. The USA has a history of school reform (e.g. Cuban 1990). What distinguished 1980s education reforms from those of earlier years was an emerging consensus around an unprecedented national goal of hard content for all students for the K–12 curriculum. This goal continues into the 1990s.

Hard content means not just the facts and skills of academic work, but understanding concepts and the interrelationships that give meaning and utility to the facts and skills. Fred Newmann and his colleagues define the intended output of hard content as authentic achievement; students need 'to engage in disciplined inquiry, to produce knowledge that has value in their lives beyond simply proving their competence in schools' (Newmann, in press: 4). The emphasis is on students learning to produce knowledge, rather than simply reproduce knowledge. Authentic achievement, then, requires disciplined inquiry: the use of prior knowledge, in-depth understanding, and the integration of ideas and information. This goal of hard content spans the subject matter areas – mathematics, literature, science, social studies, the arts.

0268–0939/90 $3.00 © 1990 Taylor & Francis Ltd.

The 'all students' piece of the goal means exactly that. Hard content is not to be reserved for a privileged few, the academically elite. Hard content is to form a core curriculum that all students experience and that all students 'master'.

Never before has such a challenging goal been set for our schools. Cuban (1990) argues that 'the current passion for all students studying the same academic content' is similar to the goals set by the Committee of Ten in 1893. But there is a difference. In 1893, 'all students' included only a small fraction of the school-age population. Today, over 95% of the children of school age attend school (National Center for Education Statistics 1989: 13). One in four comes from a family living in poverty (National Center for Education Statistics 1989: 25). Clearly, 'all students' means something quite different in the 1990s than it did 100 years earlier.

To understand the ambitious nature of hard content for all students, it is useful to compare it to earlier goals. In the late 1950s and early 1960s, the goal was hard content for the college bound. The Soviet Union had launched Sputnik, and the USA had entered the race to the moon. Then, as in the 1980s, international competitiveness was the goal; schools were the solution. But the race to the moon was seen as being won or lost through the quality of our scientists, mathematicians, and engineers. In that sense, then, the reform goal of the late 1950s and early 1960s was only a fraction as ambitious as the reform goal with which we start the 1990s.

In the late 1960s and early 1970s education reform was stimulated by the Great Society. A concern for educational equity replaced the concern for international competitiveness. Guaranteeing basic skills became the agenda; easy content for all students. This goal, too, is only a fraction as ambitious as what is being asked of schools in the 1990s.

Demanding hard content for all students is an idea that has support from a broad range of advocates and makes sense for a variety of reasons. In the words of the President and the Governors following the historic Charlottesville summit:

> All of our people, not just a few, must be able to think for a living, adapt to changing environments, and to understand the world around them. They must understand and accept the responsibilities and obligations of citizenship. They must continually learn and develop new skills throughout their lives. (National Governors Association 1990: 1)

Recent international comparisons have shown that even the highest achieving students in our schools are not competitive with the very best from other countries. US students do all right on tests involving recall and requiring simple skills, but they are not competitive when called on to solve novel problems and to think analytically (McKnight *et al.* 1987). The apparent explanation for this is straightforward. Instruction in US schools is too little oriented toward understanding and application and too much oriented toward memorization and skills. The problem is even more severe for students from poor families. For them, instruction is limited exclusively to basic skills, with little attention to how such skills might be applied in subsequent study or in the world of work (Oakes 1985). These findings imply that all students could profit from a curriculum that moved in the direction of hard content (i.e. a curriculum focused on higher order thinking and problem-solving).

The demographics of our workforce and the changing nature of the world of work provide economic incentives for the hard content for all students goal. The US workforce must encompass an increasingly large percentage of the work-age population (Grant Foundation 1988); our economy can no longer afford the luxury of writing off 10 to 15% of the population as unfit for employment. Two other factors exacerbate the problem. On the one hand, our workforce must be flexible. No longer can a worker expect to spend his or her entire worklife in a job with unchanging requirements. On the other hand, our workers must be prepared for jobs that involve a much larger percentage of thoughtful work.

> The world of work in the twenty-first century will be less manual but more mental; less mechanical but more electronic; less routine but more verbal; and less static but more varied. (National Research Council 1989: 11)

Academic and economic international competitiveness are not the only rationales for the goal of hard content for all students. Cognitive science research has shown that students learn facts and skills more quickly and retain them longer when the learning of those facts and skills is embedded in a curriculum that emphasizes understanding and application (Schuell 1986). Thus, a curriculum that moves in the direction of emphasizing conceptual understanding and application need not do so at the sacrifice of students' acquiring important facts and skills. Meaningless rote memorization has little lasting value. Students who build their own structures of knowledge retain the facts and concepts that their understanding has organized and made whole. Perhaps not surprisingly, this same cognitive science research has shown that acquisition of facts and skills should not precede instruction on understanding and problem-solving. The two must be learned simultaneously and interactively.

A final rationale for the goal of hard content for all students may be the most telling. Students engaged in a curriculum oriented toward understanding and application are more highly motivated to be active learners than students in a basic skills curriculum, which largely relegates them to a passive role. Students begin school eager to learn and curious about all sorts of things, but their enthusiasm decreases with each passing year of school (National Science Foundation 1980). By middle school, large percentages of students spend large percentages of their time in school bored and inattentive (Powell *et al.* 1985). Obviously, schools cannot be effective unless they find ways to engage their students in learning.

Mathematics

The goal of hard content for all students is not equally represented in all school subjects. Mathematics provides the best example.

In 1989, three reports on mathematics curriculum reform were published:

- *Everybody Counts*, published by the prestigious National Research Council;
- *Science for All Americans*, published by the American Association for the Advancement of Science;
- *Curriculum and Evaluation Standards for School Mathematics*, published by the National Council of Teachers of Mathematics.

This set of reports is extraordinary in a number of respects. Each report reflects the thinking of leading Americans. Classroom teachers, college and university faculty, research mathematicians, scientists and engineers, school administrators, government officials, representatives from business and industry, and parents groups all participated. Given their independence, broad involvement of constituencies, and simultaneous appearance, the reports represent an amazing consensus. Each calls for instruction to provide students with mathematical power: the ability 'to explore, conjecture, and reason logically as well as the ability to use a variety of mathematical methods effectively to solve nonroutine problems' (National Council of Teachers of Mathematics 1989: 5). This concept of mathematical power is wholly consistent with the goal of hard content. Each report also calls for *all* students to develop mathematical power. This concern for equality of educational opportunity is so strong within the mathematics community that it found its way into the title of two of the three reports (i.e. '*All* Americans' and '*Everybody* Counts'). Each is substantial, a separately bound document, professionally produced, and released with much fanfare and coverage by the press. Both the National Council of Teachers of Mathematics and the American Association for the Advancement of Science reports are giving considerable follow-up to furthering their reports' visibility and influence on practice.

Members of the mathematics community recognize that what they want will require much more than minor tinkering with current practice.

> The arithmetic, algebra, geometry, and calculus taught nowadays are mere shadow images of modern mathematics. The mathematical sciences of today blend deep new results from these traditional areas with methods from such applied fields as statistics, operations research, and computer science. (National Research Council 1984: 4)

A call for greater emphasis on developing mathematical power would be challenging enough (e.g. problem-solving, mathematics communication, reasoning), but a substantial shift in the relative emphasis given to topics is also envisioned (e.g. increased attention to statistics, probability, geometry, and discrete mathematics).

Social studies

A strikingly different picture is presented by social studies. The emphasis on conceptual understanding and problem-solving that characterized mathematics is replaced by disagreements among social studies educators about the right topics to be covered. Just as in mathematics, three social studies reports appeared in 1989, but the reforms envisioned by the social studies commissions differ one from another. One report even articulates three separate and different scope and sequence designs.

The Bradley Commission, created by the Educational Excellence Network, was comprised of 17 history educators, including professors and teachers from K–12 schools. Members of the Commission were described in the report as sharing 'only a passion for the study of history and a deep concern about its place in the curriculum' (Gagnon and Bradley 1989: 18). Given the composition of the Commission, it should come as no surprise that they lament 'the erosion of history in favor of a more utilitarian approach' (Gagnon and Bradley 1989: 4). The report requests that 'instruction in the prevalent egocentric expanding horizons curriculum of the early grades, which revolves around the young student's family, neighborhood and community be expanded, if not replaced, by introducing history as well as biography, literature and geography into the social studies framework' (p. 12). History enrichment in the early grades would be followed with substantial history courses in grades 4, 5, and 6. Similar increased attention to history would follow in the secondary school experience.

The Bradley report expresses some concern for taking 'students well beyond formal skills of critical thinking, to help them through their own active learning' (p. 25) and for instruction that finds time for 'discussion of significant thoughtful questions' (p. 41). The real emphasis, however, is on what topics should be covered. This focus on topics is accompanied by a concern for students' knowing facts. Ravitch (1989), writing in follow-up to the Bradley report, cites students' lack of factual knowledge as her primary argument for the need to strengthen history instruction. Similarly, Secretary of Education Bennett (1987), in his James Madison High School sketch of social studies curriculum, featured history and geography and, like Ravitch, cited students' shortcomings in factual knowledge as the reason for increased attention to history. 'Two-thirds of American eleventh graders did not know that the Civil War took place between 1850 and 1900 . . . . Half were unaware that the First World War happened between 1900 and 1950.' He concluded, 'Too many of our students are unfamiliar with the basic facts of their national history and government' (Bennett 1987: 20). Interestingly, Bennett's sketch of a mathematics curriculum put no emphasis upon facts and skills, stressing instead understanding and problem-solving: hard content.

Both the Bradley Report and the James Madison High School curriculum are largely silent on the issue of equal educational opportunity in the social studies. On the one hand, their commitment to the importance of history in the K–12 curriculum implies historical knowledge for all students. On the other hand, the issue of a core curriculum for all students is much less of an issue than was found in mathematics. Perhaps this lack of attention to the 'all students' goal is based on a belief about the organization of social studies instruction in today's school. Grouping and tracking are much less evident in social studies than they are in mathematics. Still, Oakes (1985) found considerable tracking in high school social studies.

The report of the National Commission on Social Studies in the Schools (NCSSS), *Charting a Course: Social Studies for the Twenty-First Century*, also appeared in 1989. The Commission was both larger in number, 33 members, and more diverse than the Bradley Commission (e.g. it included politicians and administrators as well as professors and teachers). While acknowledging merit in the Bradley report, the NCSSS report takes a distinctly more social studies orientation, concluding 'social studies remains a useful term . . . . Widely used in the schools, it has legitimate roots' (p. ix). The social studies orientation of the NCSSS report reflects its composition of the Commission, which included social studies educators and professors from social studies disciplines other than history.

The NCSSS report calls for relatively few major shifts in topics to be covered, but it does call for much greater emphasis on 'hard content' (as defined above):

> Provide opportunities for active engaged participation in civil, cultural and volunteer activities designed to enhance the quality of life. Redundant superficial coverage should be replaced with carefully articulated indepth studies. Content knowledge in the social studies should not be treated merely as received knowledge to be accepted and memorized, but as the means through which open and vital questions may be explored and confronted. (p. 3)

The report draws on cognitive science research as a rationale, citing the importance of students' prior knowledge, cultural differences, and misconceptions, and their need to have opportunities for social construction of knowledge (pp. 23–28).

A third social studies report comes from an ad hoc committee on scope and sequence, created by the Board of Directors of the National Council for the Social Studies ('Feature' 1989). Earlier work had resulted in six alternative scope and sequence designs; the ad hoc committee was charged to 'carefully review existing NCSS statements of scope and sequence and endorse three alternative models' (p. 375). Each of the three endorsed models emphasizes understanding, thinking, reasoning, and problem-solving. Not one makes much out of the issue of whether all students should study the same curriculum. Interestingly, not one of the three takes a narrow history-focused orientation.

The lack of consensus in social studies around the goal of hard content for all students is somewhat paradoxical since, as Jenness (in press) writes: 'Higher order thinking has been a shining goal of the social studies since its conception about 1910 in the schools.' Possibly, consensus around hard content has been derailed by internal disagreements about what topics should receive greatest attention. Should history and geography capture the bulk of the curriculum, or should social studies include other social science diciplines and be more explicitly tied to citizenship education? Unlike the mathematics curriculum, the social studies curriculum must be negotiated among multiple disciplines and a variety of special interest groups concerned with citizenship education.

Obstacles to the goal

If the goal of hard content for all students is to be achieved, a number of obstacles must be overcome. Education in the USA is big business: 2.6 million teachers comprise the bulk of the instructional staff in well over 100,000 public, private, and parochial schools attended by over 45,000,000 students. Recognizing the challenges ahead provides an important backdrop against which to consider alternative reform strategies. Good intentions and faith will not be enough. Nor will heroic efforts of a few individuals suffice.

Current practice

The goal of hard content for all students represents massive change from current practice. Major shifts in the nature of teaching and learning will be necessary in virtually all schools and for virtually all subjects. The size of the required changes are especially great for the very students that schools already find difficult to serve.

In every school subject, and at every level of schooling, teaching and learning are characterized by an emphasis on memorization and skill acquisition. Teacher lectures and drill and practice occupy large percentages of instructional time. A press for coverage has produced a shallow curriculum. The desire for relevance in the 1960s left behind a fragmented curriculum.

This picture of a broad but shallow facts-and-skills-dominated course of study is especially true in schools serving large concentrations of students from low-income families and of ethnic minorities. Even within schools, there are sharp differences in educational opportunity.

There are isolated instances of what Newmann (in press) calls authentic instruction. Occasionally, there are even whole schools that fit the vision, but they are the exceptions not the rule.

The teacher force

Virtually everone agrees that, if there is to be major change in what is taught and learned in schools, the cooperation and expertise of teachers will be essential. Attempts at a teacher-proof curriculum failed. Technology and materials are important, but they are used and interpreted by teachers. This acceptance of the importance of teachers to curriculum reform can be seen in the composition of the commissions cited above. Each included in their membership practicing teachers from K–12 schools, a striking change from most earlier reforms.

Recognizing the centrality of teachers in curriculum reform may, in the long run, produce more effective reform strategies. But, in the short run, it does little to make the task more manageable. Teachers can be change agents, but they can also be the source of substantial resistance.

Hard content for all students will place increasing demands on teacher subject-matter knowledge. If students are to explore topics in depth and to construct their own understandings, then teachers will need in-depth knowledge themselves, not just in a narrow range of a priori defined topical areas, but in a full range of topics that students may pursue. Teachers must not only know their subject matter as other experts might, but they must know their subject matter from a pedagogical perspective as well (Shulman 1986). For example, they must know the common naive conceptions that students bring to the classroom, and they must be flexible in the ways they present ideas and concepts, especially if they are to be effective with all students regardless of aptitude, interest, and cultural background.

Teacher energy is another area for concern. Most past efforts to improve the quality of instruction have asked teachers to do more and to work harder and for longer hours (Porter and Brophy 1988). As a result, these efforts have been rejected by some teachers and have failed to be sustained by others. The goal of hard content for all students suggests a heavy tax on teacher energy. Students are to be active learners, constructing knowledge through conversation, both oral and written. But increases in written and oral conversation will require more teacher time and more teacher attention to individual students.

Teacher beliefs about what students are capable of accomplishing represent yet a third teacher obstacle to realizing hard content for all students. Teachers' conceptions about schooling are, in large part, based on their own experiences. But teachers' school experiences are highly consistent with what is now viewed as inadequate. Since most teachers have neither seen nor experienced schools delivering hard content to all students, many may be unconvinced that it is possible.

If teachers were few in number, these obstacles might not be so problematic. But as has been noted, there are over 2.5 million teachers spread across the country. Even if pre-service teacher education programs were to be revised so that they uniformly produced teachers possessing the necessary subject matter knowledge and beliefs, substantial time would lapse before all techers were replaced. In-service teacher education is a possibility, but it would need to be more substantial than anything yet tried.

Students

If all students came to school healthy, well fed, rested, eager to learn, and convinced of the importance of doing well in school, there might be no need to set a national goal of hard content for all students. This idealized state of student readiness does describe some students, but most students fall short on one or more dimensions. Twenty-five percent of K–12 students come from families living in poverty; and 10% have poorly educated, even illiterate, parents. One in two high school seniors has used illegal drugs, and one in twenty high school seniors drinks alcohol daily. Mobility represents a serious disruption to student learning, too. For example, nearly half of the students in school move to another attendance area at least once during a five-year period. These percentages are even higher for students in low-income inner-city areas (Stern and Williams 1986).

Drug abuse, poverty, and mobility are probably not the greatest obstacles that students present to attaining the goal of hard content for all students. A distressingly large number of students don't see success in school as relevant to their future life changes (Ogbu 1983). Nearly 40% of teachers cite lack of student interest in learning as a major factor limiting their ability to maintain order (National Center for Education Statistics 1989:135). Even those students who do, at least nominally, recognize school success as important are distracted by a variety of out-of-school activities. Increasing numbers of students work significant numbers of hours each school week, leaving them less time and energy for academic work. As Sedlak *et al.* (1986: x) put it, 'There appears to have developed an implicit "bargain" between students and educators in virtually all of our high schools, which results in a de-emphasis on academic learning and student disengagement from learning.' This bargain is struck so that overburdened teachers and distracted students can co-exist in a more comfortable and less troublesome environment. The hard content for all students reform will require breaking the bargain.

Technical problems

There are some technical obstacles, as well. Instructional materials largely match current instructional practice. They present a shallow, broad curriculum with emphasis on coverage of topics. They focus on facts and skills more than understanding and applications. If materials are to be supportive of the new goal, publishers will need to make major revisions to their current products. California's recent experience with mathematics illustrates the problem. Using its NCTM standards-like mathematics framework, California failed to adopt any of the math textbooks reviewed in 1986. Publishers were given a one-year period to revise their textbooks. Some were finally adopted. Still, the revised texts fell far short of the framework ideal. As long as consensus across states is lacking, publishers will be slow to undertake the massive revisions of materials needed. Teachers and students, lacking the support of appropriate materials, will be hard pressed to construct appropriate instructional activities on their own.

Instruments for assessing student achievement present a second technical problem. In a survey of states, Freeman (1989) found that tests were rarely included as a policy instrument for encouraging instruction for understanding and thinking. There is a good reason for this. Tests that validly assess students' ability to apply and use knowledge are not widely available. Enthusiasm for performance-based tests is growing. But these tests have serious difficulties with efficiency and with providing information that is easily aggregated, summarized and transmitted to the public, administrators, and other important audiences. Performance tests can also suffer from selective coverage of what students need to know and know how to do. A great deal of development work is underway, and these efforts may yield the types of tests that are consistent with student outcomes of higher order thinking and problem solving. But until that happens, progress toward the goal of hard content for all students will have to be made in spite of student assessment practices.

School organization and structure present yet a third technical problem. Active learning, in-depth study, authentic conversation, and other characteristics of the desired curriculum don't fit well with schools as they now exist. What few laboratories exist are out of date. Instructional time is highly structured and segmented into 50-minute periods. Close proximity of instructional groups requires quiet and orderly activity. Again changes are needed, but their optimal form is unclear.

Policy strategies for attaining hard content for all students

With each education reform has come increased knowledge about reform strategies (Elmore 1987). Unfortunately, this progress in knowledge has been slow. One reason may be that reforms are the business of practice, not research and theory; the development of reform strategies has been largely theoretical and largely lacking in empirical investigation. In turning its attention to studies of implementation, policy research has begun to correct these deficiencies. But even policy research has rarely moved beyond studies of implementation to address policy effects. A second reason for the slow accumulation of knowledge about reform strategies stems from the failure of most reform efforts. Failures can sometimes clarify strategies that don't work, but they are inefficient data points for identifying what to try next.

At the present time, there are two strategies that receive the bulk of attention (though see McDonnell and Elmore 1987, for an analysis of four policy instruments). One can be labelled control. It is a top-down strategy. In its purest form it begins with a clear statement of what is desired against which all policy instruments, practice, and outcomes are justified. The other strategy has a less agreed-upon label. Here we call it empowerment, but Rowan (1990) has called it commitment. At least on the surface, empowerment is the opposite of control. It is a bottom-up strategy and rarely, if ever, beings with a clear statement of desired outcomes.

In the fragmented world of policy practice, control can be of everything, and empowerment can be for anything. In this chapter, we limit our discussion of control and empowerment to the context of curriculum reform and, more explicitly, to their utility as strategies for achieving hard content for all students. This focus on a particular type of school output adds a unique bottom-up character to our analyses of policy strategies. The result is increased conceptual clarity and stronger implications for practice. Had we selected a different school output (e.g. improved teacher satisfaction, basic skills curriculum), our analyses might well have led to different conclusions about practice and different conclusions about the comparative advantages of the two strategies.

The curriculum control strategy

Our understanding of curriculum control as a policy strategy has been developing at least since the early 1960s. Initially curriculum materials were the primary policy instrument of curriculum control. When materials alone failed to produce the desired results, policy instruments of student assessments (for accountability purposes) and curriculum frameworks were added. Most recently, policy researchers have distinguished control instruments along two dichotomous dimensions: (1) control of outcomes versus control of processess; and (2) requirements of teachers versus requirements of students (Porter 1989). The most complete control system would control both outputs and processes of both teachers and students. Thus, a student assessment program at the state or district level could be used to control student outputs if, for example, high school graduation were dependent on test performance. But the same student assessment program could be used to control outputs of teachers through a merit pay system tied to student performance.

A curriculum control strategy can be more or less prescriptive. Generally, the greater the number and type of outcomes and processes controlled, the more prescriptive the policy. Prescriptiveness is also enhanced through specificity. A mandated textbook is prescriptive of process for teachers and, to some extent, for students. But a mandated textbook with requirements for how the book is to be used and what material must be covered is more prescriptive. A test of minimum basic skills competencies is prescriptive of outcomes; but a test that attempts to assess all that should be taught, not just minimums, is more prescriptive. The more prescriptive the control strategy, the less room for local discretion.

Control strategies can also be characterized by their internal consistency. When all policy instruments in a control strategy prescribe the same outputs and/or processes, the control strategy is internally consistent. But policy formulation is typically piecemeal, occurring incrementally over time, with changing purposes and, often, with little institutional memory. Thus, a basic skills student assessment program can exist in the same control strategy as a curriculum framework calling for hard content for all students. The multiple levels of the school hierarchy also provide opportunities for inconsistency. State policies may be enhanced or contradicted by district policies (Fuhrman and Elmore 1990). Similar consistencies and inconsistencies can occur between district and school policies.

Authority and power are two additional characteristics of control policies. By power is meant the extent to which rewards or sanctions are attached to policy compliance. For example, assessment having important consequences for students, high stakes testing, is a policy instrument with considerable power. Policy authority is, in some ways, the opposite of policy power. Authoritative policies achieve compliance through persuasion; policies with power achieve compliance through demand. According to sociological theory, policies can achieve authority through legal status, consistency with norms, basis in expertise, and charismatic advocacy (Spady and Mitchell 1979).

These four policy characteristics – prescriptiveness, consistency, authority, and power – are hypothesized as characteristics that give curriculum control strategies weight (Porter *et al.* 1988). The more prescriptive, consistent, authoritative, and powerful a control strategy, the more predictive of practice it will be.

Curriculum control strategies can be used either to standardize practice or to shift practice in a desired direction. Sometimes curriculum control strategies are seen as mechanisms for increasing the efficiency of the education system. The idea is that a more rational and accountable system will be a more productive system. Often curriculum control strategies are associated with the goal of basic skills. It was during the 1960s and 1970s, when basic skills were the primary universal goal of schooling, that curriculum control strategies came into prominence. Some believe that curriculum control is antithetical to the goal of hard content for all students (Darling-Hammond 1988). This conjecture has not yet been tested. Neither is it widely held in practice. At the same time that the goal of hard content for all students was acquiring prominence, states and districts were becoming increasingly active in curriculum control.

The empowerment strategy

Thinking about empowerment is, at least from a policy perspective, much less well developed. At the heart of the concept is the belief that qualified and committed teachers, given decision making power, will do the right thing. What is somewhat slippery is that 'the right thing' is rarely, if ever, specified. Linda Darling-Hammond defined and situated the strategy as follows:

> A 'second wave' of American education reform was heralded in 1986 by reports from the Carnegie Forum on Education and the Economy, the National Governors Association, the Education Commission of the States, and the Holmes Group of Education Deans, among others . . . . The group of new reformers is united in its insistence on the need to improve education by improving the status and power of teachers and by 'professionalizing' the occupation of teaching. (1988: 58)

Darling-Hammond is one of the few writing about empowerment who makes a link to the goal of hard content for all students, stating, 'The reformers propose that America's future economic welfare depends on educating most students, rather than only a few, for verbal and technical proficiency and for creative work' (p. 59). All of the advocates of the empowerment strategy talk about teacher competence and teacher commitment as the desired ends to which the strategy is aimed. The assumption is that expert and committed teachers will do what is in the best interest of students. This may or may not be hard content for all students. In reference to the restructuring movement, as one outgrowth of the empowerment strategy, Newmann expresses some doubts. In Newmann's words, 'Most of the talk about school site management, teacher career ladders, or schools of choice, for example, never considers how these mechanisms will teach students to write about literature, to reason about scientific phenomena, or to learn important geographical facts' (in press: 2).

The policy instruments for the empowerment strategy, because of the strategy's newness, are understandably less well developed. Darling-Hammond (1988) listed three. First and foremost is the regulation of teachers. Through improving preparation, both pre-service and in-service, strengthening certification, and being more selective in hiring, the overall quality of the teacher corps is to be improved. Teachers as a profession are to have a significant voice in the formulation and implementation of each policy strategy. The literature on these methods of teacher regulation is extensive. The point of each, however, is to guarantee that K–12 instruction is provided by expert teachers. A second policy instrument is professional control over technical decision making. The rationale for this policy instrument is that expert teachers, if their expertise is to be fully realized, must have control over substantial portions of their work environment. A related argument is that through professional control will come greater teacher commitment. The third policy instrument is provision for ongoing peer review of practice.

Rowan (1990) lists similar policy instruments for the empowerment strategy. He identifies site-based management as a policy instrument in support of teacher decision making power. He identifies efforts to structure the teaching profession (e.g. lead teachers, mentor teachers), team teaching, open space classrooms, and teachers observing each other as specific approaches within the policy instrument of peer review. Rowan is silent on the matter of regulation of teachers, but offers instead three policy instruments that might lead to the development of community in schools: reducing school size, magnet schools, and schools that have control over student entry and exit. Rowan's concern for community in schools may stem from his slightly different starting place. He refers to the strategy as one of commitment, rather than empowerment.

One or another of the many versions of effective schools might also be viewed as fitting within the empowerment strategy. The Holmes Group (1990) calls for professional development schools. Not only do the Holmes Group professional development schools make explicit a commitment to hard content for all students, but the schools are to be learning communities that sustain long-term inquiry by teachers into teaching and learning. Sizer's essential schools are defined along somewhat similar lines. The Coalition of Essential Schools (1989) promotes 'getting students to use their minds well' and 'empowering those (teachers) who were not already articulate and powerful'.

These policy instruments of the empowerment strategy share some common features. First, they lack face validity with the goal of hard content for all students. They are silent on both the nature of the curriculum to be taught and whether or not all students are to have access. Second, the policy instruments are less clearly defined than one might hope. School communities and professional development schools are not easy to create. If a state should adopt either one of these instruments, procedures for implementation would be uncertain. To a lesser extent, the other empowerment policy instruments share the same problem. This may in part be a function of the newness of the empowerment strategy. It may also be inherent to the strategy; how does one mandate grassroots quality and control from above?

A comparison of the two policy strategies

Few comparisons of the curriculum control and empowerment strategies can be found in the literature. What few comparisons do exist are of little value here. All suffer from a failure to make explicit the ends to be served; they address questions along the lines of, Is empowerment a better strategy for improving teacher commitment than curriculum control is a strategy for ensuring basic skills? In addition, some present a one-sided argument, attempting to make the case for one strategy at the expense of the other. Rowan (1990) presents a fairly even-handed account of the information available about curriculum control and empowerment. But his analyses are of the two strategies in general, not their promise for serving the specific end of hard content for all students. Darling-Hammond (1988) is primarily concerned with building a case for empowerment strategies, and in doing so draws on the weaknesses of control strategies.

Efforts at comparisons of control and empowerment are further hampered by a lack of empirical evidence. There is a substantial literature on the implementation of curriculum control policies and an emerging literature on their influences on curriculum practices at the classroom level (e.g. Porter *et al.* 1988). But there is almost no empirical work that traces the influences of curriculum control policies all the way to student achievement. Further, this empirical literature on curriculum control is limited almost exclusively to the goal of basic skills for all students. The goal of hard content for all students is simply too new to have been investigated, though studies are underway (Archbald 1990). Empirical work on empowerment strategies is even more incomplete (Lieberman 1988). There is, of course, a large and productive literature on relationships between teacher expertise and benefits for Students (Whittrock 1986). But the connection between policy instruments for the empowerment strategy and teacher expertise is almost wholly lacking. The strategy is simply too new, especially as a policy strategy, to have been documented and tested.

We compare the two strategies in their ability to deliver on hard content for all students using logical grounds. A later section compares the two strategies on their implementation at the state level.

Face validity: In theory, face validity should be easily achieved in curriculum control policies. When the goal was basic skills, state and district frameworks, testing programs, and mandated materials made clear that basic skills were valued and should be taught and learned. If these same policy instruments are used to promote hard content for all students, they will almost certainly leave little ambiguity about what is desired. Already, some curriculum frameworks, a few instructional materials, and a very few tests illustrate this point. But much work remains to be done.

Teacher empowerment strategies will always suffer from some lack of face validity when judged against the goal of hard content for all students. As has already been stated, empowerment has strengthening the teaching profession as its first and foremost goal. Only secondarily, if at all, is empowerment presented as a mechanism for shifting the curriculum.

Costs: The relative costs of these two strategies can be deceiving. A strong curriculum control strategy would have substantial development costs, much higher than the developmental costs when basic skills were the goal. But the development and implementation costs of a serious effort on teacher empowerment are likely to be even higher. A necessary condition for teacher empowerment is universal teacher expertise in subject matter knowledge and pedagogy. Given the enormous size of the teacher corps, these costs will be high and continuing. Additional resources will be necessary to free teacher time to participate in school management and to provide the student-centered active learning instruction, which is believed to be necessary.

What is misleading about this analysis is that curriculum control policies will almost surely fail if they are put in place without substantially strengthening expertise in the teacher corps. It is one thing to require that hard content be provided to all students; it is quite another for teachers to live up to that requirement. Thus, in our view, the costs of strengthening the teacher corps are common to the two strategies.

Teacher commitment: Regardless of the curriculum goal, teacher commitment to that goal is required if instruction is to be successful. Teacher empowerment strategies recognize this fact and make it their primary focus. They may, of course, be more or less successful. In contrast, teacher control strategies are accused of dampening teacher commitment, though empirical results on this point are mixed (Rowan 1990).

The distinction between curriculum control policies that are authoritative and curriculum control policies that have power may help to explain Rowan's finding of mixed results. If curriculum control policies are developed and communicated in ways that make them authoritative to teachers, then teacher commitment should be enhanced. The argument is that authoritative policies are persuasive; they convince teachers and others that what is being called for is appropriate. Through persuasion, then, policy specifications and teachers' desires become consistent. On the other hand, curriculum control policies that require but do not persuade (i.e. those that gain their strength through power and not authority) may well bring about decreases in teacher commitment. Time may also be an important variable. Persuasion takes time. Newly initiated curriculum control policies, especially those that call for substantial change, cause disruptions, on the one hand, and haven't been in existence long enough to be persuasive, on the other. It is possible that initial drops in teacher commitment immediately following introduction of a curriculum control policy may disappear with time and experience. Unfortunately, no data are yet available on this point.

Can the two reform strategies coexist?

Advocates for empowerment see the empowerment strategy as replacing the control strategy. But policy formulation, in practice, is fragmented and messy. Past experience strongly suggests that policy instruments for empowerment will be added to already existing policy instruments for control. What sounds like the usual hodgepodge of inconsistent education policies might turn out to be a promising approach to achieving the hard content for all students goal. The empowerment strategy suffers from failing to address curriculum questions. Control strategies make clear what is wanted for students, but they fail to address the need for major increases in teacher expertise. If teachers were to be involved in developing control policies, as teachers were seen to be involved in the commissions' specifying curriculum goals for mathematics and social studies, then the resulting curriculum control policies might be authoritative for teachers. With substantial investment in teacher empowerment, such authoritative curriculum control policies might be not only persuasive but effective as well. Some will say we are substituting curriculum leadership for curriculum control. Others may say we are adding curriculum leadership to the list of policy instruments under the empowerment strategy. We would not argue with these interpretations.

A sample of four states

We have studied mathematics and social studies curriculum policies in four states – California, Florida, New York, and Texas. These states were selected because each has undertaken significant curriculum reforms, yet as a group they provide an interesting mix of approaches – key issues in textbook reform, minimum competency testing, and curriculum regulation programs have arisen in these states. Also, these states individually and as a group are important in national politics and education policy. They are large and socially and ethnically diverse. They enroll almost one-third of our nation's public school children.

The goal of hard content for all students is reflected in some ways in both mathematics and social studies in each of the four study states, but there are significant differences among the states, and there are important differences as well between the two subjects that transcend between-state differences.

State goals in mathematics

The California mathematics guide's introduction states, 'the expectations we hold for future graduates must far exceed the historical goal of proficiency in arithmetic . . . . The central concern . . . is developing mathematical power . . . the ability to discern mathematical relationships, reason logically, and use mathematics techniques effectively.' The course content prescriptions for mathematics flow from a coherent rationale on the need for reform, and for the particular problem-solving vision of mathematics articulated in the state's mathematics guide. The guide is filled with numerous definitions of mathematical power, examples of problem-solving, and recommendations for the delivery of instruction.

Mathematics in California's guide is divided into seven strands: number, measurement, geometry, patterns and functions, statistics and probability, logic, and algebra. The guide states *all* students should receive instruction in *each* strand, and 'no student should be limited to the computational aspects of the number strand'.

The guide does not prescribe a single course sequence for all students. In addition to the traditional college-prep mathematics courses, the guide recommends content for several courses, entitled simply Math A, B, and C, that emphasize applications and instruction tailored for students weaker in mathematics. The guide recommends that 'courses should be designed specifically to allow students to shift from one sequence to another' (e.g. Math A – Math B – Geometry; or Algebra 1 – Geometry – Math C).

Florida's mathematics curriculum guide does not have an overarching rationale statement calling for additional emphasis on problem solving and mathematical reasoning. However, the content guidelines for each of the 35 courses described in the state guide *do* frequently mention problem solving in the topics, goals, and objectives prescribed for each course. For instance, the purpose of General Math 1 is to 'strengthen the basic computational skills and to develop problem-solving skills'. The 56 objectives, most of which are computational, include statements like, 'Solve equations of the form $ax = b$, where a, b, and c are whole numbers and a is not 0'.

Florida's content guidelines do not give examples of what the NCTM *Standards* refer to as 'mathematical power', and the guidelines are stated with sufficient generality to leave ample room for teachers to claim (and believe) 'we already do a lot of mathematics problem-solving'.

There is no language in Florida's guidelines about a common curriculum. Florida's guide distinguishes courses by level (e.g. General Math 1, 2, and 3; Informal Geometry, Geometry, and Geometry Honors), with lower level courses containing fewer higher order content objectives.

New York's mathematics guide, like California's, has an extensive rationale. Each 80-page Regents course guide is introduced with a broad set of 'Regents Goals'. These, consistent with the NCTM *Standards* (which are cited), stress goals such as 'the ability to apply mathematical techniques in the solution of real-life problems and to recognize when to apply these techniques'.

Consistent with the NCTM *Standards*, substantial emphasis is placed on problem-solving, on the relatively new topics of statistics and probability, and on using calculators and estimation techniques. Numerous examples are provided.

Students not pursuing the college-prep 'Regents Diploma' in New York generally take General Math, Business Math, and sometimes the first math course in the college-prep sequence. In contrast to the college-prep mathematics course, the non-college-bound mathematics courses have not been the target of reform. The most recent General Mathematics course guide is a 1978 edition, and the Business Mathematics, a 1983 edition. Neither the General Mathematics nor Business Mathematics syllabi have the elaborate rationale, goal, and problem-solving statements found in the college-prep mathematics sequence.

Texas's mathematics guide states, '[this] program deliberately focuses on solving problems and teaching for understanding'. Practicing estimation and using calculators and computers as problem-solving tools are also endorsed. Unlike California and New York guides, it contains no detailed discussion of problem-solving, and no examples are given.

In a format similar to Florida's, Texas's guide contains a page or so of content for each of 22 math courses. The verbs used in writing course objectives include *use* ('use the parallel postulate'), *develop, draw, simplify, factor, define, investigate* ('investigate local, state, and federal tax requirements'), *find* ('find measures of central tendency'), and *solve* ('solve open sentences in one variable').

There is no language in Texas's guidelines about a common curriculum, other than a few sentences implying all students should learn how to problem solve in mathematics ('problem-solving is an underlying approach to the teaching of all mathematics'). Texas's guide distinguishes courses by level (e.g. Fundamental Math, Consumer Math, Pre-Algebra, etc.), with lower level courses containing fewer higher order content objectives.

State goals in social studies

California's curriculum guide places social studies goals in three categories: (1) knowledge and cultural understanding; (2) democratic understanding and civic values; and (3) skills attainment and social participation. 'Critical thinking skills' is one of three major goals in (3) above that, in a one-page discussion, is said to include defining and clarifying problems, judging information related to a problem, and solving problems and drawing conclusions.

Course descriptions are presented in a narrative style, which integrates topic statements, higher order objectives, and examples. For instance, Students should assess the likely causes of the Depression and examine its effects on ordinary people.... They should see the linkage between severe economic distress and social turmoil. Photographs, films, newspaper accounts, interviews with persons who lived in the period, as well as paintings and novels (such as John Steinbeck's *Grapes of Wrath*) will help students understand this critical era. (from 'US History and Geography')

A common thread throughout the content prescriptions is understanding history by knowing the people and events of history (utilizing original materials where possible), by analyzing causal processes, and by examining links between the past and present.

The curriculum guide presupposes that all students should be taught the content prescribed for each social studies course. There is no mention of differential content or instruction for students differing in ability.

Florida's social studies curriculum guide does not have an overarching rationale statment calling for any distinctive approach or set of higher-order thinking goals in social studies. The guidelines for each of the 42 courses described in the state guide consist of statements such as 'understand and appreciate relationships between past and present'; 'utilize . . . reference/study, critical thinking, and decision-making skills'; 'explain the significance of geography on the development of American society'.

There are three levels (introductory, standard, advanced) for each social studies course required for graduation. The introductory level courses' objectives call primarily for identifying people, events, contributions, effects of events (e.g. 'Identify the historical impact of the automobile, television, and computer'). The more advanced courses call for more analysis, explanation, and interpretation (e.g. 'Analyze the impact of fundamental shifts in scientific and technological knowledge').

New York's social studies guide, like California's, begins with a relatively elaborate set of rationale and goal statements, which include many higher order knowledge and skill goals. Lengthy course descriptions (85 pages) are divided into units (e.g. Industrialization), each of which begins with goals and objectives such as 'to understand contrasting economic and social conditions in the South and North after the Civil War'. Each unit has an outline consisting of a sequence of topics, key social science concepts, and model activities (e.g. Give students summaries of *Plessy* v. *Ferguson* (1896) and *Brown* v. *The Board of Education* (1954) and have them hypothesize about reasons for the Supreme Court's reversal of opinion).

The Regents social studies course guides are recommended for use for courses that all students must take. However, only students pursuing a New York Regents diploma must pass the state's Regents exam for each social studies course.

Texas's social studies guide provides a brief (three-page) description of social studies goals, including Developing Skills and Processes (10 skills), such as 'contrasting and comparing', and 'interpreting and synthesizing information from a variety of sources'.

Each of 12 course descriptions begins with a one-paragraph introduction followed by a list of objectives. For instance, in US History

> students study the emergence of the USA as a world power. They learn how geography influences historical developments, analyze economic development and growth, understand the nation's social and cultural developments, and study the political development of the United States from Reconstruction to the present.

Following this introduction are five broad topic areas encompassing 32 objectives, using terms such as *describe*, *identify*, *analyze*, *evaluate*, and *understand*. Use of primary data sources is recommended.

The objectives for the Texas social studies courses are mandated for all students. A section of the guide discusses the need to modify materials and instructional techniques for students differing in ability, English proficiency, or cultural background. The rationale for modification is to ensure all students learn the mandated objectives. No statements call specifically for engaging *all* students in higher order learning.

Comparing the states in mathematics and social studies

Mathematics: California and New York in particular place a heavy emphasis on problem-solving and are in the process of introducing new integrated approaches toward mathematics. The Texas and Florida guides stress problem-solving, but lack a well-defined conception of problem-solving, and the types of problem-solving objectives prescribed in the guides are generally narrower, and more structured, than the conception of mathematical power envisioned in the NCTM Standards. The effectiveness of exhortation ('there must be problem-solving throughout the mathematics curriculum') is doubtless attenuated by the absence of *specific* ideas and examples on how to achieve this.

California is the only state that emphasizes a common core of study. California's guides propose that courses covering the *same* seven 'strands' be set up for *all* students. Mathematics in the other three states is more differentiated by topic and emphasis on mathematical power.

Social studies: Each of the state guides liberally employs the lexicon of 'higher cognitive processes'. California, New York, and Texas rationales and subject goals emphasize higher order skills and processes.

Florida and Texas guides furnish very few specific facts, concepts, and conclusions to be learned in their social studies courses. Instead they use generally stated active-verb outcomes like *analyze, define,* and *evaluate.* The more passive *understand* is used as well. The lack of specificity in defining and giving examples of these processes leaves much room for interpretation in what content should be analyzed (evaluated, compared, etc.), what conclusions should be drawn, and how these processes should be taught.

To varying degrees, each of our states reflects the historical/cultural literacy movement. High school course requirements in history in each of the four states increased in the 1980s reforms – to 2 credits in California, Florida, and Texas; to 3 credits in New York. The California guide is most explicit about and takes the strongest stand on 'historical literacy' and the goal of strengthening students' factual knowledge of history.

The recent campaign to strengthen the role of history in social studies probably has had greater impact at the high school than at the pre-high school level. To increase study of history, states simply mandate more history courses as a requirement for a diploma. At the elementary level, however, while state policies can mandate additional minutes of instruction in history, class time is very difficult to monitor. Further, the (historical) 'expanding horizons' approach at the elementary level is widely accepted and institutionalized and will probably be more resistant to change.

In response to widespread criticism of the mindless race through dates and names in high school history and in pursuit of goals of greater historical literacy *and* higher order thinking, each of the state guides has shortened the scope of history to be studied (particularly US History). Shortened scope enables greater depth of study of particular events and periods of history.

There is only modest variation in how the states reconcile the ideal of a common social studies curriculum with the reality of students differing in ability and academic preparation. Florida's guide distinguishes levels among courses, with fewer higher order objectives for basic than for more advanced courses; California, New York, and Texas do not make these distinctions but discuss the need to tailor instruction to students with different abilities and needs. None of the social studies guides, however, recommends different curriculum *topics* for different students or for different levels of the same course.

Comparison of state curriculum control and empowerment efforts

Throughout the 1970s and 1980s, several states developed systems to control mathematics and social studies curricula. States typically raised high school graduation requirements. States with existing systems of curriculum control built on their strengths. For example, the New York State Education Department (SED) gained Regents' approval for its new 'hard content' NCTM-like mathematics and NCSS-like social studies curricula. With Regents' approval, the New York SED built competency tests into its already developed, powerful, legally and traditionally authoritative Regents' tests. Other curriculum policies in the state tend to build on the established authority and power of Regents' competency or comprehensive tests. Other states, like Texas and Florida, entered the 1970s with minimal or nonexistent curriculum control systems. These states built their systems from scratch through laws and regulations to make schools, teachers, and students accountable to minimum standards of achievement. After years of benign neglect during the Proposition 13 era, California re-established its curriculum control system. California also built on its strength: state subject frameworks based on state and national subject area expertise. Since the early 1980s, California has constructed student tests, instructional materials policies, a school evaluation system, and a staff development program that strongly reflect California curriculum goals. Since local autonomy is required by law, California's State Department of Education (SDE) works to convince teachers and localities of the value of a curriculum that proclaims hard content for all students. As part of the effort to convince teachers and school officials of the validity of their vision of hard content for all, California has relied more on incentives and local empowerment to realize its curriculum objectives.

Intersections of control, empowerment, and hard content for all

The approaches taken to curriculum policy in our four states are difficult to summarize; each state has taken a somewhat different approach. In general, however, there is much greater activity in the control strategy than in the empowerment strategy. Still, when judged against what would be possible in terms of prescriptiveness, consistency, authority, and power, each of the states have left considerable room for increasing their control efforts. Just as each state represents at least some of the aspects of a curriculum control strategy, so also does each state represent examples of the empowerment strategy. Of our four states, California has gone the furthest to employ the empowerment strategy, while New York is the closest example of a state attempting to combine the advantages of control with the advantages of empowerment. While California is also the best example of a state committed to the goal of hard content for all students in both mathematics and social studies, we find no reason to conclude that their curriculum goals require their empowerment approach.

New York curriculum control policies: New York has a strong set of top-down curriculum control policies. New York's graduation requirements, curriculum guidelines, and student tests form a strong web of curriculum control. Underlying that web of policies is a century-old tradition of Regents' testing and Regents' curriculum guides backed by the force of state regulation. The power of this curriculum system lies in the link between student tests required for graduation and the curriculum; the latter are based on the former. Teachers who ignore the curriculum may prevent their students from graduating or from graduating with an advanced diploma (Regents). Partly because of this testing–curriculum link, the New York SED carefully disseminates curriculum guide changes through a lengthy piloting period, followed by a hierarchical statewide in-servicing of teachers (the 'turnkey' system), and distribution of curriculum guides to affected teachers. After developing it for nearly ten years, New York is only now just completing piloting and in-servicing on the new NCTM-like sequential mathematics curriculum for college-bound students.

New York empowerment policies: Such a tightly-linked top-down controlled web of strong curriculum policies is associated with top-down attempts at empowerment. For example, New York has a network of effective schools experts. These experts can help schools diagnose areas of non-effectiveness; help build student, faculty, and administrative collaboration in governance; and plan and implement programs to address particular school problems. But New York uses this empowerment strategy only with schools having the lowest state scores on competency tests. While the process is empowering, the goal is top-down and mandatory: schools must develop plans, implement them, and improve their test scores or face nonaccreditation, more intensive state monitoring, or state take-over. Similarly, state-sponsored in-service aims to inform teachers about the state curriculum, not involve them actively in design or implementation of the curriculum.

New York and hard content: The New York SED curriculum apparatus promotes stratified curriculum in mathematics and social studies. The SED designs hard content for the college-bound and softer content for the non-college-bound. Both the state's general mathematics course guide and the state's competency test in mathematics cover minimum computational skills, the solution of routine problems, and very little content. In social studies, there is only one course guide for required Global Studies and US History. Yet there are two levels of tests: comprehensive for the college-bound, and competency for the non-college-bound. Competency tests in Global Studies and US History require substantially less content knowledge and less proficiency in critical thinking skills than do comprehensive tests. Other New York curriculum policies emphasize the gulf between hard and soft content for different destinations. New York gives two diplomas: one for the college-bound and another for the non-college. The course and test requirements for each differ dramatically in terms of the amount of hard content.

Texas and Florida's curriculum control systems: In a relatively short period, Texas and Florida have developed elaborate systems of curriculum control based on requiring minimum competency instruction and learning. Unlike New York, Texas and Florida only require that all students pass minimum competency tests in mathematics, reading, and writing in order to graduate. The minimum competency test criteria in both states are connected with basic skills curriculum objectives. These together drive highly prescriptive, legally authoritative, and curriculum-matched textbook adoption, school evaluation, and teacher certification policies. Linked together and supported by state law and regulation, these policy instruments form a strong pattern of control over the planning, delivery, and evaluation of minimum competency instruction and learning in each state. Texas may be changing its curriculum focus to more hard content for all. Texas is now implementing a new NCTM-like mathematics curriculum, teacher inservicing, student tests, and textbook adoption standards for all students.

Texas and Florida's empowerment strategies: In Texas and Florida, empowerment occurs in a regulatory form. Neither Florida nor Texas promotes school-level empowerment. For example, Florida requires wholesale school adoption of the state curriculum guidelines, and Texas monitors the extent to which teachers teach the state curriculum. Texas' school evaluation (accreditation) system actually monitors the extent to which teachers follow the state curriculum. In Texas, school evaluators interview teachers to determine how they incorporate the state curriculum (the 'essential elements'), how student grades reflect mastery of the essential elements, and how teachers use required texts to teach the essential elements. School evaluation is largely regulatory, requiring only passive participation of school personnel.

While New York and California rely mainly on teacher college programs to certify teachers, Florida and Texas do more to control directly the teacher certification instrument. Of the four states, only Florida and Texas require teachers to pass one test to enter teaching and another test to gain certification in their field. Florida and Texas have the most elaborate and detailed requirements for certification, including particular courses prospective teachers must pass. Texas requires that secondary teachers pass a test in their certification area that closely mirrors student competency tests in the subject; they must also pass a test in general pedagogy. Texas education officials apparently recommend that prospective teachers study copies of state-adopted student textbooks to pass the test in their subject area (the EXCET test). After gaining certification, teachers must successfully complete an internship in the school that hires them. By regulation and law, school officials are supposed to monitor the interns more intensively than other teachers. Texas further controls the expertise of its teachers through its career ladder system. To advance on the career ladder, teachers must be evaluated by the state-designed system, and they must complete in-service or college courses approved by the state. Salary rises are linked to advancement on the career ladder.

Empowerment in the regulatory states of Texas and Florida is somewhat analogous to state curriculum control efforts. The curriculum control efforts aim to establish minimum standards for student knowledge. Empowerment attempts to raise minimum standards for the teaching occupation.

Texas and Florida's hard content: Since Texas and Florida's curriculum systems were built on ensuring basic skills instruction and learning in all state-funded schools, hard content for all has not become a major goal across the curriculum. Until the late 1980s, both states had built relatively strong regulatory systems in which basic skills instruction and learning in mathematics, reading, and writing formed the hub of major curriculum efforts. While both states required two-and-a-half to three years of social studies with common World History/Geography and US History courses, neither state required that students pass a state test in social studies.

However, Texas has recently modified its mathematics curriculum to model California's mathematics program. How the press for hard mathematics for all students will play out in a state focused on regulating rudimentary learning remains to be seen.

California's curriculum control system: California's curriculum control system has important strengths and weaknesses. Its potential strength depends on the prescriptiveness of its curriculum and the strong consistency between the curriculum frameworks and other state curriculum policies. As in New York, there is a tight fit between the objectives of the curriculum and test items on the state achievement (CAP) test. When the curriculum is revised, the CAP test criteria are revised. The state makes these tests more important by publishing relative test scores of schools in the state, and relative test scores of other schools with similar demographic characteristics. Another important consistency in the California curriculum control system is between the curriculum frameworks and the school evaluation and staff development policy instruments. Both of the latter incorporate the curriculum goals for every subject area, reinforcing the centrality of curriculum goals in the state's educational control efforts.

However, there are other elements in the curriculum control system that suggest weakness. Both the curriculum and the CAP test are less powerful than in the other states.

First, California SDE curriculum guides are only advisory, not required. Second, the CAP test scores are aggregated to the school level; neither teachers nor students are directly affected by student performance on the CAP test. In effect, teachers and students can ignore SDE curriculum since there are no sanctions for failure and no rewards for achievement.

Third, the authority of the social studies curriculum guides is unclear. At the present time there are two social studies curriculum guides, the Model Curriculum Standards (1985) and the Framework (1988). The Model Curriculum Standards were required by state law. In all content areas, the subject area Frameworks are developed every seven years by the California SDE to summarize and renew the overall curriculum. The two guides overlap each other in places but contradict each other in several other places. While the Model Curriculum Standards for social studies reflect the legal authority of the California legislature, the Framework reflects the charismatic authority of the state superintendent and the expert authority of the historians who wrote it. Therefore, despite strong across-policy consistencies, California curriculum control in mathematics and social studies seems to be less powerful and perhaps less authoritative than similar control policies in other states.

California's empowerment strategies: California does more than other states to empower teachers and schools to teach the state-desired curriculum. California has a longer tradition of empowerment, perhaps because empowerment is one of the ways the State Department of Education (SDE) can influence autonomous localities to adopt SDE educational policies. Since 1983, California has required all schools to compare their curriculum to that of the state in all subjects every three years. However, unlike the other states, California does not monitor schools directly. Instead, the state provides incentives to schools to develop their own improvement plans and trains regional and local teachers, administrators, and supervisors in a state-authorized process.

The program uniquely combines the elements of a top-down evaluation process with those of a bottom-up process for which individual schools are ultimately responsible. The state provides a sophisticated, systematic qualitative evaluation process and trains evaluators hierarchically, similar to the turnkey system in New York. Half of the evaluation criteria concern the state curriculum objectives in each subject area, and half concern making the school 'effective'. The state also provides incentives for schools to use the state evaluation system. But schools are free to focus on whatever evaluation goals are most appropriate to their needs: they can identify areas in which they want to develop plans and then have evaluators focus on judging the effectiveness of the implementation of those plans during site visits. In this way, the school improvement program encourages school-site empowerment in the context of broad state curriculum and governance goals.

California also empowers teachers and administrators through state-funded and organized staff development. Prior to 1989, the state provided staff development monies to a number of private and public agencies. The state funded the nationally famous CAL writing project that integrated the teaching of writing across the curriculum. California has also funded leadership academies and numerous other curriculum-related projects designed to enhance the expertise of staff and the effectiveness of schools. Recently, the California legislature allotted at least $20 million a year to a reorganized state staff development system. This system, constructed in part by SDE personnel, builds on the state curriculum frameworks in every subject. Among other things, the system links school improvement plans to regional support and provides money for summer programs to help teachers develop new units for the curriculum.

To encourage teacher enthusiasm for state curriculum goals, California has recently supported a regional development of a unique NCTM-like general mathematics program, Math A. While the curriculum guide for mathematics suggested a course like Math A, it has been up to local teachers to develop the course. When SDE discovered what these teachers had created and found it effective, they encouraged further development. The state has helped teachers reproduce the materials and is now working to export the materials and training to other areas of the state. There are further plans to find a publisher for the program. Thus, California seems serious about empowering teachers and schools to develop local plans that will reflect the state's new curriculum.

California and hard content: Unlike the other states in our study, California explicitly promotes hard content for all students in both mathematics and social studies. Both curriculum guides and state curriculum personnel explicitly promote critical thinking skills, deeper understanding of concepts, and similar understandings associated with hard content. All students take similar CAP tests that assess hard content knowledge and skills in both mathematics and social studies (the twelfth-grade social studies test is under development). At present, curriculum managers in both mathematics and social studies are pressing for tests that measure some of the hard content process objectives. They advocate active demonstration of reasoning, use of problem-solving techniques and decision-making skills, understanding of concepts in depth, and learning to solve non-routine problems.

However, California teachers and students can easily avoid hard content without obvious personal consequences. The twelfth-grade CAP test may measure learning of the hard content curriculum, but how students perform is irrelevant to their own graduation. To graduate, a student could avoid hard mathematics by passing two years of any kind of mathematics course. Similarly, in social studies, a student must only successfully complete one year each of World and US History, and one-half year each of Economics and Government. Student performance on the forthcoming social studies portion of the twelfth-grade test also will not matter for graduation purposes.

State variations in curriculum control and empowerment policies

In the 1980s, each of the four states' curriculum control systems moved toward greater strength. The key policy instruments were graduation requirements, curriculum frameworks, student testing, and instructional materials. Perhaps excepting California, these states have done less to empower staff than they have to control the curriculum. Curriculum control and empowerment systems vary considerably across the four states.

Each of the states' curriculum control systems focuses on some policy instruments or some aspects of policy strength more than others. For example, New York has built its increased graduation requirements, new mathematics and social studies curriculum guides, and matching required student tests onto the traditionally and legally authoritative and powerful Regents' tests. Of all the states, New York's curriculum guides are the most extensive and detailed with regard to actual teacher application. Yet, while highly prescriptive, New York curriculum guidelines seem to lack connection with the state's school evaluation and teacher certification policies, and the state has no policy on curriculum materials.

In a short period of time, Texas and Florida have achieved a remarkable degree of legislatively authorized and powerful cross-policy consistency in their curriculum control system. The focal policy in Florida were the minimum competency and literacy tests, the SSAT-I and SSAT-II, built on minimum standards called 'performance standards'. The focal policy instrument in Texas is the minimum skills curriculum, 'the essential elements';

these are the minimum competency standards in mathematics, reading, and writing (social studies will be added). But the essential elements, at least until the advent of the new mathematics program, lacked the vision of California's hard content for all students. Even with the new version of mathematics, the prescriptiveness of the essential elements does not reach that of New York's unit-level course objectives and model activities.

California's curriculum guidelines reflect the authority of nationally recognized experts and connect consciously and consistently with school evaluation, staff development, student testing, and instructional materials policy instruments. However, the strength of California curriculum policies is constricted by a tradition of local autonomy, the low-stakes nature of student testing, and conflicts in the authority and substance of the two social studies curriculum guidelines.

The four states in our study also vary in the manner in which they attempt to empower or fail to empower staff and schools. In general, states use empowerment as a means to influence and control the teaching and learning of the state curriculum. California uses empowerment strategies to convince teachers and schools to adopt and use the state curriculum frameworks as the basis for education in the school. Since the curriculum is based on hard content for all students, California also uses empowerment to promote positive teacher and school orientations toward hard content learning for all students. New York uses empowerment to enhance Regents' or competency test scores; the SED uses school empowerment strategies to try to force schools with low test scores to score higher, and it uses inservice to disseminate information about changes in the State's top-down curriculum. Texas and Florida use teacher certification, teacher inservice, or teacher career ladders to insure that teachers meet minimum standards of expertise and competence. In short, the states' uses of empowerment reflect their more general purposes of control.

Instead of competing with each other, empowerment and control strategies in individual states seem to be fashioned along the same lines as their control policies. Therefore, increased control may bring increased empowerment; or vice versa. New York's, Florida's, and Texas's empowerment efforts operate from the top down, and do not work to produce local initiative and innovation. Such states' curriculum control efforts may stimulate corresponding efforts to bring schools and teachers into compliance through increased teacher certification, teacher evaluation or state-controlled evaluation and control of instructional delivery. California's empowerment efforts stimulate voluntary adoption of the state curriculum and creative adaptation of the state curriculum to local conditions. California continues to stimulate bottom-up empowerment through staff development and school improvement incentives. At the same time, it also continues to tighten the curriculum guides–testing linkage, and it continues to add more tests of more subjects to the CAP test. In short, empowerment may not replace curriculum control; and control may not replace empowerment. They may proceed together.

Conclusions

Will the goal of hard content for all students be achieved? We believe it will, not in any absolute sense but rather in varying degrees. Already this emerging national goal is reflected in state goals. California is clearly the lead example, at least among our four states. In fact, there is some room for confusion between California and the national level about who is leader and who is follower. For example, the NCTM Standards make reference to the California Mathematics Framework. But, in all four states, both mathematics and social studies goals reflect a concern for hard content.

State reflections of the hard content goal are greatest in mathematics where consensus is greatest at the national level. Social studies, with its disagreements over the extent to which history should dominate the curriculum, provide an important contrast to mathematics. Nevertheless, the call for greater emphasis on history can be found in all four studied states.

Commitment to hard content for all students is less uniformly visible in state goals. Again, California is the lead positive example with the other three states substantially behind. This leads us to predict that, of the two parts of the goal, the 'all students' piece will be the one for which implementation will remain the most variable.

One of the more startling findings from our analyses concerns the nature and timing of national curriculum reports. In 1989, three commissioned reports appeared for mathematics, and three commissioned reports appeared for social studies. We take this as evidence of our claim for emerging consensus around the new goal of hard content for all students. We suspect that the goal is largely in response to *A Nation at Risk* (1983) and subsequent calls for increased standards in education. We also suspect that the increasing visibility of findings from cognitive science research contributed. Our analyses convince us, too, that, at least for this time in our nation's history, the goal of hard content for all students is the right goal.

National reports and state goals are important, but their ultimate utility must be judged in the activity they stimulate and, ultimately, in student achievement. Talk is cheap.

Our analyses of the obstacles to the goal of hard content for all students leave us with a finding and a prediction. The finding is that current practice is nowhere near the goal of hard content for all students. A great deal of change will be necessary in teachers, students, instructional materials, assessments, and school organization and structure. The prediction is that most states and districts will be unwilling to invest what appears to be required. Certainly, we find big differences among states at the present time.

Will empowerment policies replace control? We think not. Policy practices in the four states show that the two strategies coexist, sometimes in purposeful ways but more often because newer empowerment policies have been added to prior control policies. Over time, control policies may fall away, but we predict they will not. First, when judged against the goal of hard content for all students, each policy strategy is incomplete. Empowerment lacks an explicit focus on the goal, and control fails to adequately address many of the obstacles to achieving the goal. By involving teachers and other practicing educators in the formulation and monitoring of curriculum control policies, and through vigorous implementation of empowerment policies, a new curriculum policy strategy may emerge. This seems both desirable and necessary. There is a second and less optimistic reason why we predict control strategies will not fall away. Control strategies have political capital, and they are inexpensive. As new goals for education appear on the national scene, states must respond. One quick response is through formulating control policies. A new state framework and a new student assessment program, each with face validity to the new goal, is a small price to pay. Unfortunately, there is little hope of such control policies having the intended effect without accompanying investments in teacher education, materials development, and the like.

Will there be future shifts in the goals of education? We believe there will be. In the past 30 years, there have been at least three major shifts in what schools are expected to accomplish. First, it was hard content for the academic elite, then it was basic skills for all students, and now it is hard content for all students. We have no prediction as to what the next goal will be; one possibility is a more vocationally-oriented curriculum, another possibility is a curriculum more concerned with moral development of students.

If the goals for education continue to shift over time, it is especially important that policy research increase. Much more needs to be known about the types of policy instruments that can serve the empowerment strategy and about their effects on practice. More needs to be known about the connections between policy and classroom practice – and especially between policy and effects on students. We also need to know more about connections among policies at various levels of the school hierarchy. What are the most effective articulations of state, district, and school level policies? Better answers to these and other questions about policy and practice will go a long way toward increasing the effectiveness of efforts to shift practice in desired directions.

Acknowledgement

The research reported in this paper was supported by the Center for Policy Research in Education, which is funded by a grant from the US Department of Education, Office of Educational Research and Improvement (Grant No. OERI-G-0086-90011), and by the Wisconsin Center for Educational Research, School of Education, University of Wisconsin-Madison. The opinions expressed in this publication are those of the authors and do not necessarily reflect the views of the US Department of Education, Office of Educational Research and Improvement, the institutional partners of the Center for Policy Research in Education, or the Wisconsin Center for Education Research.

References

AMERICAN ASSOCIATION FOR THE ADVANCEMENT OF SCIENCE (1989) *Science for All Americans*. A Project 2061 report on Literacy Goals in Science, Mathematics, and Technology (Washington, DC: AAAS).

ARCHBALD, D. A. (1990) 'Curriculum control and teacher autonomy', paper presented at the annual meeting of the American Educational Research Association, Boston.

BENNETT, W. J. (1987) *James Madison High School: A Curriculum for American Students* (Washington, DC: US Department of Education).

CARNEGIE FORUM ON EDUCATION AND THE ECONOMY (1986) *A Nation Prepared: Teachers for the 21st Century*. Report on the Task Force on Teaching as a Profession (New York: CFEE).

COALITION OF ESSENTIAL SCHOOLS (1989) 'Getting started in an essential school program', *Horace*, 5(3), pp. 1–6.

CUBAN, L. (1990) 'Reforming again, again, and again', *Educational Researcher*, 19(1), pp. 3–13.

DARLING-HAMMOND, L. (1988) 'Policy and professionalism', in A. Lieberman (ed.) *Building a Professional Culture in Schools* (New York: Teachers College Press), pp. 55–77.

ELMORE, R. F. (1987) 'Instruments and strategy in public policy', *Policy Studies Review*, 7(1), 144–186.

ELMORE, R. F. and McLAUGHLIN, M. W. (1988) *Steady Work: Policy, Practice, and the Reform of American Education* (Santa Monica, CA: Rand Corporation).

Alternative scopes and sequences' (1989) Feature section in *Social Education*, 53(6), pp. 375–403.

FREEMAN, D. J. (1989) 'State guidelines promoting teaching for understanding and thinking in elementary schools: a 50-state survey', *Educational Evaluation and Policy Analysis*, 11(4), pp. 417–429.

FUHRMAN, S. and ELMORE, R. F. (1990) 'Understanding local control in the wake of state education reform', *Educational Evaluation and Policy Analysis*, 12(2), pp. 82–96.

GAGNON, P. and the Bradley Commission on History in Schools (eds) (1989) *Historical Literacy: The Case for History in American Education* (New York: Macmillan).

GRANT, WILLIAM T., FOUNDATION COMMISSION ON WORK, FAMILY, AND CITIZENSHIP (1988) *The Forgotten Half: Non-College Youth in America* (Washington, DC: FCWFC).

HOLMES GROUP (1990) *Tomorrow's Schools* (East Lansing, MI: Holmes Group).

JENNESS, D. (in press) *Making Sense of Social Studies* (New York: Macmillan).

LIEBERMAN, A. (1988) *Building a Professional Culture in Schools* (New York: Teachers College Press).

McDONNELL, L. M. and ELMORE, R. (1987) 'Getting the job done: alternative policy instruments', *Educational Evaluation and Policy Analysis*, 9(2), pp. 133–152.

McKNIGHT, C. C., CROSSHITE, F. J., DOSSEY, J. A., KIFER, E., SWAFFORD, J. O., TRAVERS, K. J. and COONEY, T. J. (1987) *The Underachieving Curriculum: Assessing US School Mathematics From an International Perspective*. A national report on the Second International Mathematics Study (Champaign, IL: Stipes Publishing Company).

NATIONAL CENTER FOR EDUCATION STATISTICS (1989) *Digest of Education Statistics* (25th edn) (Washington, DC: US Department of Education).

NATIONAL COMMISSION ON SOCIAL STUDIES IN THE SCHOOLS (1989) *Charting a Course: Social Studies for the 21st Century* (Washington, DC: NCSSS).

NATIONAL COUNCIL OF TEACHERS OF MATHEMATICS (1989) *Curriculum and Evaluation Standards for School Mathematics* (Reston, VA: NCTM).

NATIONAL GOVERNORS ASSOCIATION (1990) *National Education Goals* (Washington, DC: NGA).

NATIONAL RESEARCH COUNCIL (1989) *Everybody Counts: A Report to the Nation on the Future of Mathematics Education* (Washington, DC: National Academy Press).

NATIONAL SCIENCE FOUNDATION (1980) *Science and Engineering Education: Data and Information* (Washington, DC: NSF).

NEWMANN, F. M. (in press) 'Linking restructuring to authentic student achievement', *Phi Delta Kappan*.

OAKES, J. (1985) *Keeping Track: How Schools Structure Inequality* (New Haven, CT: Yale University Press).

OGBU, J. U. (1983) 'Minority status and schooling in plural societies', *Comparative Education Review*, 27(2), pp. 168–190.

PORTER, A. C. (1989) 'External standards and good teaching: The pros and cons of telling teachers what to do', *Educational Evaluation and Policy Analysis*, 27(4), pp. 343–356.

PORTER, A. C. and BROPHY, J. (1988) 'Good teaching: insights from the work of the Institute for Research on Teaching', *Educational Leadership*, 45(8), pp. 75–84.

PORTER, A., FLODEN, R., FREEMAN, D., SCHMIDT, W. and SCHWILLE, J. (1988) 'Content determinants in elementary school mathematics', in D. A. Grouws and T. J. Cooney (eds) *Perspectives on Research on Effective Mathematics Teaching* (Hillsdale, NJ: Erlbaum), pp. 96–113.

POWELL, A. G., FARRAR, E. and COHEN, D. K. (1985) *The Shopping Mall High School* (Boston: Houghton Mifflin).

RAVITCH, D. (1989) 'The plight of history in American schools', in P. Gagnon and the Bradley Commission on History in Schools (eds) *Historical Literacy: The Case for History in American Education* (New York: Macmillan), pp. 51–68.

ROWAN, B. (1990) 'Commitment and control: alternative strategies for the organizational design of schools', in C. B. Cazden (ed.) *Review of Research in Education*, 16 (Washington, DC: American Educational Research Association), pp. 353–389.

SCHUELL, T. J. (1986) 'Cognitive conceptions of learning', *Review of Educational Research*, 56, 411–436.

SEDLAK, M. W., WHEELER, C. W., PULLIN, D. C. and CUSICK, P. A. (1986) *Selling Students Short* (New York: Teachers College Press).

SHULMAN, L. S. (1986) 'Those who understand: knowledge growth in teaching', *Educational Researcher*, 15(2), pp. 4–14.

SPADY, W. G. and MITCHELL, D. E. (1979) 'Authority and management of classroom activities', in D. L. Duke (ed.) *Classroom Management* (78th Yearbook of the National Society for the Study of Education) (Chicago: University of Chicago Press), pp. 75–115.

STERN, J. D. and WILLIAMS, M. F. (eds) (1986) *The Condition of Education*. Statistical Report: Center for Education Statistics (Washington, DC: US Government Printing Office).

WITTROCK, M. C. (ed.) (1986) *Handbook of Research on Teaching* (3rd edn) (New York: Macmillan).

3   *State policies and state role in curriculum*

Rolf K. Blank and Diane Schilder

Many of the education policy initiatives of state legislatures and state boards of education in the 1980s were aimed at improving the quality of elementary and secondary education through upgrading state standards. Researchers are analyzing the effects of the reforms on education in elementary and secondary schools. Many states have expanded their systems for assessing, monitoring, and reporting on schools, teachers, and students. Using data collected from state departments of education, this chapter presents findings from a 50-state comparative analysis of state education policy reforms and curriculum in mathematics and science. Two issues are analyzed: the effects of state policy reforms on curriculum in math and science education, and the strengths and limitations of currently available 50-state indicators of curriculum in math and science. State-by-state data are analyzed on secondary course enrollment in science and mathematics and on the relationship of state curriculum frameworks and statewide assessments of student learning.

State policies and state role in curriculum

Many of the education policy initiatives of state legislatures and state boards of education in the 1980s were aimed at improving the quality of elementary and secondary education through upgrading state standards. The policy initiatives included increasing graduation requirements, revising state curriculum guidelines and frameworks, upgrading teacher certification requirements, and developing and revising student assessment tests. Now, at the end of the 1980s, and the beginning of the 90s, there are several kinds of responses to the state reforms. Researchers are analyzing the effects of the reforms on education in elementary and secondary schools. Many states have expanded their systems for assessing, monitoring, and reporting on schools, teachers, and students. And, additional reforms are being recommended that are aimed at having a more direct impact on the organization of schools and classrooms and the quality of teaching and learning.

One of the key issues in analyzing state policy reforms is the effect of state reforms on curriculum content that students receive. Questions are raised about the reforms' effects on the amount of instruction, the quality of curriculum, and the proportion of students receiving a high quality curriculum. A second issue in analyzing state reforms is how curriculum change should be evaluated. Questions are raised about the levels of the education system at which curriculum should be analyzed, measures that are appropriate for determining change in the curriculum, and how change can be compared among states.

This paper presents findings from a 50-state comparative analysis of state education policy reforms and curriculum in mathematics and science. The analysis is aimed at two research questions:

1. What have been the effects of state policy reforms on curriculum in math and science education?
2. What are the strengths and limitations of currently available 50-state indicators of curriculum in math and science?

0268–0939/90 $3.00 © 1990 Taylor & Francis Ltd.

The research reported in the paper was produced through the State Science/Math Indicators Project of the Council of Chief State School Officers (CCSSO). The Project is supported by the National Science Foundation.

State policies and curriculum in mathematics and science

The curriculum for elementary and secondary education has been a central focus of education reforms in the 1980s. Curriculum content was specifically identified in many national commission reports that focuses on mathematics and science education (National Commission on Excellence in Education 1983, National Science Board Commission on Precollege Mathematics, Science, and Technology Education 1983, Task Force on Education for Economic Growth 1983, Twentieth Century Fund 1983). The poor performance of US students on international assessments in science and mathematics and the relatively low amount of instruction in these subjects for the average US student were frequently cited in the reports as evidence of the fundamental problems in our schools, and as a rationale for proposed education reforms.

In *A Nation at Risk* (1983), the National Commission recommended that three mathematics and three science courses be required for high school graduation. The Commission also recommended making science a 'new basic' in elementary school. The report of the National Science Board, *Educating Americans for the 21st Century* (1983), recommended more time and resources for mathematics and science education, advocated teaching 'science literacy' for all students, and outlined core mathematics and science knowledge and thinking skills that students should learn in school. One of the consistent themes across the various national reports was the need for students to gain scientific literacy and for schools to increase the level of mathematics and science instruction for all students.

Many of the state reforms in the 1980s were aimed at setting higher standards for the amount of mathematics and science instruction in schools. From 1980 to 1987, 43 states increased mathematics course requirements for graduation and 40 states increased science requirements (Education Commission of the States 1985, Blank and Espenshade 1988a). By 1987, 26 states had a state policy giving direction or recommendations to schools on the amount of time to be spent on elementary science and mathematics (Blank and Espenshade 1988a).

A second area of state reforms related to curriculum has been in developing and revising state curriculum guidelines or frameworks. A 1987 survey of state departments of education by CCSSO showed that 38 states had a state curriculum framework which 'establishes goals or standards for instruction' for mathematics and 38 states had a framework for science (Blank and Espenshade 1988b). In some states the curriculum frameworks set a required curriculum for districts, while in others the frameworks are used by districts as goals or instructional objectives for development of local curricula.

Third, state policy initiatives in the 1980s increased the capacity of states to assess student learning through state assessment programs. Accompanying the state-level efforts to reform curriculum provided to students has been expanded state involvement in accountability for education improvement, especially accountability for improved outcomes (Fuhrman 1989). A study of state accountability systems found that state tests of student learning have become the dominant method of accountability (OERI 1988). (The increased state role in education funding is also related to the push of accountability). In 1984, 34 states had state achievement assessment tests in math and 13 states in science

(CCSSO 1984). By 1988, 40 states had achievement assessment tests in mathematics and 27 states in science (CCSSO 1989a).

Research on state curriculum reforms

Several different methods have been used to analyze the effects of state policy reforms on curriculum, and other methods of evaluating reforms have been recommended. One research approach has been to identify and analyze changes in policies related to curriculum. Goertz (1986) conducted a 50-state analysis of state education policy changes and intensively studied the implementation process in four states. The Education Commission of the States (ECS) tracked changes in state graduation requirements (1985) and identified state curriculum reforms in all 50 states related to science, math, and computer science (1987). CCSSO annually reports on state policies in a variety of areas in *State Education Indicators*.

Studies have also examined the content of state curriculum frameworks or guidelines. Freeman (1989) analyzed the integration of approaches to teaching higher order skills in state frameworks and the means by which state education agencies have tried to implement them in schools. An ECS study of the process of implementing new curriculum frameworks for science education in three states identified the steps the states have taken to move curriculum reforms from the intended to the implemented curriculum (Armstrong and Davis 1988). A study conducted for the Southern Regional Education Board by Reilly and Gersh compared the content, goals, and standards for achievement in state curriculum guides (SREB 1989).

Recent research on state reforms has analyzed course offerings and student participation in relation to state policies. Student course enrollment in courses in specific subject areas is one possible indicator of the extent to which science and math curricula are being implemented in schools. Policy Analysis for California Education (PACE), a consortium of university scholars, conducted a study of change in course enrollments related to California policy changes in graduation requirements (Cagampang and Guthrie 1988). The Center for Policy Research in Education (CPRE), supported by the US Department of Education, studied district implementation of curriculum reforms in science and math in six states, and analyzed student course taking in science and mathematics (Clune 1989a).

The number of students taking a given type of course does not give complete information to describe the curriculum content that is taught, but this information provides a useful state-level indicator of the extent to which students receive instruction in a subject area, such as science and mathematics (Murnane and Raizen 1988). It can also provide state-level information to assess the effects of state policies on curriculum trends at the national, state, district, and school levels.

A more in-depth approach to analyzing state curriculum reforms and the implemented curriculum is to measure the curriculum content or topics that are actually taught in schools and classrooms. This approach to analyzing reforms is consistent with the 'second wave' of recommended education reforms in the late 1980s which focused on how change in education can be brought about at the school and classrooms levels. Some of the proposed reforms focused on restructuring schools and increasing teacher professionalism (Carnegie Forum on Education and the Economy 1986), deregulating schools to increase education quality (national Governors' Association 1986), reforming teacher preparation (Holmes Group 1986), and revising curriculum standards in core subject areas (AAAS 1989, NCTM 1989). In science, AAAS has set out goals for science learning for all high school graduates that would change the organization of school science curriculum. In math, the National Council of Teachers of Mathematics has developed curriculum standards for mathematics education at all grade levels which emphasize a more enriched curriculum for all students at earlier grades and a problem-solving approach to instruction (1989).

Many of these 'second-wave' reforms move away from centralized standard-setting, such as state policy reforms, and towards decentralized, school and profession-based reform of curriculum content (Clune 1989b). From this perspective, rates of course-taking are not an adequate measure of change in curriculum. A new study of methods of evaluating state education reforms found that the wide variation in course content among classrooms, schools, and districts results in course enrollment data being an inadequate measure of curriculum content (McDonnell et al. 1990).

One method of measuring curriculum content at the classroom level is through an 'opportunity-to-learn' survey with teachers and students, as used in IEA studies. With data on students' opportunity-to-learn the curriculum topics included in achievement tests, the implemented curriculum can be related to student achievement scores. For example, a detailed analysis of the reasons for low performance of US students on the Second International Mathematics Study (SIMS) showed that a primary factor is the curriculum content students receive (McKnight et al. 1987). Great variability in coverage of curriculum content, repetition of content between grades, concentration on basic skills in arithmetic, and lack of opportunity to study an enriched curriculum were all cited as problems with the typical mathematics curriculum. A long-term study of elementary mathematics content that is implemented by teachers in the classroom showed that content varies widely by teacher and school for students in the same grade. The study confirmed the findings of SIMS that the typical curriculum in US schools has excessive repetition of content and heavy emphasis on skills as opposed to conceptual understanding or application (Porter 1989). Similarly, analysis of students' 'opportunity-to-learn' science curriculum topics tested in the recent international science assessments confirms that many American students do not receive instruction in key areas (LaPointe et al. 1989, Jacobson and Doran 1988). In general, the policy and programmatic relevance of achievement test scores can be enhanced with data on curriculum content. Oakes (1989) has emphasized that the results can be used to pinpoint specific areas of instruction in a subject that students did not receive and areas where instruction needs improvement.

State indicators of curriculum

The Council of Chief State School Officers (CCSSO) has developed a system of state-by-state education indicators. This system of indicators is a result of the state superintendents' collective decision in the mid-1980s to collect and report education data that have high technical quality and that provide useful state-to-state comparisons. CCSSO now publishes an annual report, *State Education Indicators*, which includes state-by-state data on outcomes, policies and programs, and state context.

The National Science Foundation has supported a project of CCSSO to develop state-by-state indicators of the condition of science and mathematics education, as part of the system of indicators. Indicators were selected through a review of recent studies and recommendations on the kinds of indicators that are needed for policy and program analyses and research on science and mathematics education (National Science Board 1983,

Raizen and Jones 1985, Shavelson *et al.* 1987, Murnane and Raizen 1988, Oakes 1986, Blank 1986). Based on the review, CCSSO conducted a survey of state departments of education to determine the availability of state-level data on possible indicators of science and math education (Blank and Espenshade 1988b). In the area of curriculum indicators, relatively few states reported collecting data through direct monitoring of curriculum content in schools and classrooms:

1. Twelve states reviewed school curriculum in science and mathematics, either through accreditation, site visits, or approval of new courses;
2. Four states conducted surveys of teachers, either during the accreditation process, through site visits, or with student assessments;
3. Four states observed classrooms, either during accreditation, with teacher appraisals, or in site visits;
4. Seven states collected data on opportunity to learn in a subject or course, either through one-time studies, student assessments, or site visits.

Two indicators of curriculum that were selected by CCSSO for the state-by-state system were: (a) secondary course enrollment; and (b) the relationship of state tests to curriculum frameworks. The CCSSO survey results showed that over two-thirds of states collect data on student enrollments in secondary courses in science and math. A plan was developed for state reporting of data on course enrollments, and, in the 1988–89 school year, states reported these data to CCSSO for the first time. The survey also provided detailed information on state curriculum frameworks, or guides, for science and mathematics as well as the characteristics of state assessment programs, including subjects, grades, and type of test instrument. With these two kinds of information, an analysis was carried out of the degree of consistency, or 'alignment', between state curriculum frameworks and state assessments. Findings from analysis of these two indicators across states are described in the following two sections of this paper.

Analysis of state course enrollments as indicator of curriculum

National-level data from transcripts of representative samples of high school graduates in 1982 and 1987 show that course enrollments in science and math increased in the 1980s (ETS 1989, Kolstad and Thorne 1989). For example, the percentage of graduates nationally who took physics increased from 14 to 20%, the percentage who took Algebra II increased from 35 to 46%. In this period, the average number of credits earned in math increased from 2.54 to 2.98, and the average number of credits in science increased from 2.19 to 2.63 (ETS 1989), which is an increase of half a credit in each subject. These increases appear to affirm that higher state graduation requirements have produced increased study in science and mathematics, at least in terms of course-taking. This is important since many of the states raised graduation requirements from 1983 to 1985 effective for the class of 1987, 1988 or 1989.

State-level studies show that increases in course enrollments are related to state policies but the increases vary by course level. The PACE study (Cagampang and Guthrie 1988) in California found that increased requirements for graduation produced enrollments increases of 27% in science, 1% in math, and 21% in foreign languages. In math, enrollments increased over 10% in Algebra, and declined in lower level math courses (thus 1% overall increase). In the same period, enrollments in vocational courses and other electives declined. The CPRE study showed that rates of course taking increased following reforms, but the largest increases were in lower-level science and math courses (Clune 1989a).

The state-by-state data reported to CCSSO for 1988–89 allows analysis of policy questions concerning state reforms as well as more general analyses of the condition of science and mathematics education in our secondary schools. Several of the key questions are analyzed in this paper.

1. What level of science and math courses are high school students taking to meet state graduation requirements?

To address this question, the state data are analyzed in two ways. First in tables 1 and 2, data are presented on enrollments in four courses that might be considered benchmarks of student participation in secondary math and science. In tables 3 and 4, the total state enrollments in science and math during one year are presented to show the aggregate enrollments at several course levels.

The four math courses shown in table 1 were selected to show enrollments at various levels and to compare state percentages with results from the 1987 National Transcript Study (Westat 1988, Kolstad and Thorne 1989). The transcript study reported the following percentages for the four math courses:

1. Algebra 1 76%
2. Geometry 62%
3. Trigonometry 19%
4. Calculus (incl. AP) 10%

Table 1 shows that 79% of students in the average (median) state take a 'Formal Math Level 1' course, such as Algebra 1, over their four years of high school.[1] The state percentages vary from 47% in Hawaii to 98% in Louisiana and Montana. An average of 55% of students take Formal Math Level 2 (e.g., Geometry), with state percentages varying from 28% in Wyoming to 86% in Louisiana. The wide variation in percentages of students taking courses at Formal Math Levels 1 and 2 (Algebra 1 and Geometry) can be attributed to a number of factors, including differences in state requirements for graduation and variation by state in proportion of districts and schools offering Formal Math courses as opposed to Review and Informal Math courses. For example, Hawaii has 47% of students taking Algebra 1, but almost all students take a Review or Informal Math course during high school (see table 3). The high percentages taking Formal Math Levels 1 and 2 in Louisiana can be attributed to a state policy requiring that Algebra 1 and Geometry be passed for high school graduation.

State percentages for some courses are affected by the degree of precision in the match between state categories and the CCSSO reporting categories. For example, Louisiana was not able to report 'Basic Geometry' (under Informal Mathematics, Level 2) separately from 'Plane Geometry' under Formal Math Level 2. Thus, the 86% figure includes both levels of Geometry. ('Basic Geometry' was reported by 14 states, varying from 1% in Nevada to 33% in Wisconsin. The National Transcript study did not distinguish between two levels of Geometry).

The percentage of students taking a Formal Math Level 4 (e.g., Trigonometry) course varies from 15% in Arkansas to 39% in North Dakota, and the percentage taking Level 5 (e.g. Calculus) varies from 3% (several states) to 14% in Pennsylvania. The state medians for mathematics are very similar to the national averages from the 1987 Transcript

Table 1. Percentage of high school students taking selected math courses over four years of high school (percentages computed from 1988–89 data).

State	Formal math Level 1 (e.g., algebra) [%]	Formal math Level 2 (e.g., geometry) [%]	Formal math Level 4 (e.g., trigonometry) [%]	Formal math Level 5 (e.g., calculus) [%]
Alabama	57	45	18	5
Arkansas	90	52	15	4
California	76	45	22	9
Delaware	53	43	26	6
Hawaii	47	35	22	3
Idaho	87	50	23	6
Illinois	80	63	24	11
Indiana	59	49	30	7
Iowa	90	73	36	7
Kentucky	68	57	23	6
Louisiana	98	86	31	3
Minnesota	86	67	30	10
Mississippi	74	60	33	3
Missouri	82	55	27	8
Montana	98	68	14	5
Nebraska	95	81	36	10
Nevada	88	47	22	4
New Mexico	89	51	35	10
New York	69	55	28	10
North Carolina	64	55	35	7
North Dakota	90	64	39	3
Ohio	70	57	35	10
Oklahoma	87	48	17	10
Pennsylvania	82	54	n.a.	14
South Carolina	54	50	26	6
Texas	73	68	20	4
Virginia	77	61	34	10
Wisconsin	79	48	23	9
Wyoming	n.a.	28	18	6
Median	79	55	26	7

Notes: For each course, percentage of students in one cohort taking the course over four years is estimated by the one year enrollment for grades 9–12 divided by the total student enrollment for the grade level at which most students take the course.

Illinois data collected 1986–87 school year. Nebraska data include first and second semester enrollment.

Median = median state percentage.

Source: State Departments of Education, Data on Public Schools, Fall 1988.

Study. The state-by-state data confirm the findings from the 1982 and 1987 transcript studies showing the effects of state reforms on increasing enrollments in mathematics.

The state percentages of high school students taking five selected science courses are reported in table 2. The percentages for the corresponding categories from the 1987 Transcript Study are:

1. Earth Science 14%
2. Physical Science 35%
3. Chemistry 45%

Table 2. **Percentage of high school students taking selected science courses over four years of high school (percentages computed from 1988–89 data).**

State	Earth Science 1st year [%]	Physical Science [%]	Chemistry 1st year [%]	Physics 1st year [%]	Biology 2nd year [%]
Alabama	1	61	36	23	15
Arkansas	27	30	34	13	—
California	8	44	31	16	10
Delaware	15	73	45	19	5
Hawaii	12	59	39	20	5
Idaho	58	16	34	15	8
Illinois	20	29	42	21	12
Indiana	26	32	41	19	21
Iowa	26	35	54	26	10
Kentucky	4	38	43	13	26
Louisiana	16	57	51	22	6
Minnesota	15	74	44	22	16
Mississippi	—	—	54	16	66
Missouri	11	58	37	16	36
Montana	46	37	40	21	66
Nebraska	42	43	55	27	30
Nevada	47	7	39	15	17
New Mexico	11	47	36	14	9
New York	54	24	54	29	7
North Carolina	7	87	46	14	14
North Dakota	1	100	48	26	20
Ohio	18	34	47	20	11
Oklahoma	7	31	37	10	35
Pennsylvania	21	23	51	27	13
South Carolina	—	64	48	14	10
Texas	—	80	40	12	6
Virginia	86	4	56	24	14
Wisconsin	21	47	50	23	21
Wyoming	33	20	27	11	15
Median	18	38	43	19	14

Notes: For each course, percentage of students in one cohort taking the course over four years is estimated by the one-year enrollment for grades 9–12 divided by the total student enrollment for the grade level at which most students take the course.

Illinois data collected 1988–87 school year; Nebraska data include first and second semester enrollments.

Median = median state percentages.

Source: State Departments of Education, Data on Public Schools, Fall 1988.

4.   Physics 20%
5.   AP/Honors Biology 35%

Earth Science and Physical Science are generally lower-level high school science courses that are typically taken in 9th grade in order to meet a state or district science requirement. The median state percentages of 18% for Earth Science and 38% for Physical Science are similar to the national average. State enrollments vary widely — for Earth Science from no enrollment to 86% (Virginia) and for Physical Science from no enrollment to 100% (North Dakota). Different state curriculum mandates or guidelines for high school science have a strong effect in determining which of these courses (or General Science) are taught.

For example, Virginia has strongly emphasized teaching of Earth Science and the emphasis is reflected in student enrollments.

The state medians for Chemistry (43%) and Physics (19%) are very close to the national figures. These averages show that state enrollment data confirm the findings of the national transcript study on increases in science enrollments during the 1980s. The range of state percentages for Chemistry is from 27% (Wyoming) to 56% (Virginia), and for Physics the range is from 10% (Oklahoma) to 29% (New York). The Advanced Biology enrollments reported by states (median of 14%) includes more second-year Biology courses than just the Advanced Placement and Honors Biology reported in the Transcript Study (3%). The high enrollments in second-year Biology in states such as Mississippi, Montana, Missouri, and Oklahoma indicate that schools and districts in these states offer students more opportunities for continued study in biology and it is likely that students meet state requirements through concentrating on biology and life science study.

In table 3, state data on math enrollments provide analysis of the relative level at

Table 3.   Proportion of students in grades 9–12 enrolled in math courses in 1988–89 by level.

State	Total students 9–12	Review and Informal [%]	Formal level 1 (Algebra 1) [%]	Formal levels 2–6 (Geom.-Calc.) [%]	Other Math [%]	Total Math [%]
Alabama	203,101	28	16	27	—	72
Arkansas	99,680	n.a.	30	36	—	66
California	1,289,986	21	21	28	5	76
Delaware	27,792	34	15	28	0.1	77
Hawaii	43,858	62	13	22	—	97
Idaho	58,359	19	23	31	2	76
Illinois	500,680	19	21	38	—	78
Indiana	285,367	31	15	32	—	78
Iowa	135,963	17	22	43	8	91
Kentucky	181,861	35	18	34	—	87
Louisiana	201,564	14	30	45	—	88
Minnesota	215,671	11	21	40	—	72
Mississippi	130,119	24	21	37	—	82
Missouri	236,860	21	22	36	3	82
Montana	42,104	19	30	29	—	78
Nebraska	78,132	21	27	49	8	—
Nevada	49,032	28	22	25	—	75
New Mexico	76,688	40	26	33	—	99
New York	743,290	23	19	34	6	81
North Carolina	322,087	31	18	36	—	84
North Dakota	33,627	15	23	41	1	80
Ohio	549,180	28	18	36	1	83
Oklahoma	164,630	22	23	33	2	79
Pennsylvania	500,536	14	21	47	—	82
South Carolina	177,945	46	16	32	2	96
Texas	891,628	34	22	34	—	90
Virginia	283,213	30	21	39	0.4	90
Wisconsin	236,207	34	21	29	—	84
Wyoming	27,285	25	n.a.	19	1	—
Median		25	21	34	2	82

Note: Illinois data collected 1986–87 school year; Nebraska data include first and second semester enrollments.

Source: State Departments of Education, Data on Public Schools, Fall 1988.

which students took Mathematics during the 1988–89 school year. A state percentage in this table represents the proportion of all students in grades 9–12 that took the course during one year. Math course enrollments are aggregated in four course levels: Review and Informal Math (e.g., General and Vocational Math, Pre-Algebra, Basic Geometry), Formal Math Level 1 (Algebra 1), Formal Levels 2–5 (Geometry through Calculus), and Other Math.

Among the 29 reporting states, an average of 82% of students were taking Math courses in October 1988. An average of 25% of students took a Review or Informal Math course, an average of 21% took Formal Math Level 1 (e.g., Algebra 1), and an average of 34% of high school students took a Formal Math course at Levels 2 through 5 (e.g., Geometry, Algebra 2, Trigonometry, Calculus). In Iowa, Louisiana, Minnesota, Nebraska, North Dakota, and Pennsylvania, 40% or more of high school students took a more advanced math course, while less than 30% took an advanced math course in Alabama, California, Delaware, Hawaii, Montana, Nevada, Wisconsin, and Wyoming.

Table 4. Proportion of students in grades 9–12 enrolled in science courses in 1988–89 by level.

State	Total Students 9–12	Earth Science Physical Sci. General Science [%]	Biology 1st year [%]	Bio. 2nd year, Chemistry & Physics 1 & 2 [%]	Other Science [%]	Total Science [%]
Alabama	203,101	23	26	22	1	72
Arkansas	99,680	27	34	15	3	79
California	1,289,986	19	24	15	3	61
Delaware	27,792	27	24	18	0.4	69
Hawaii	43,858	29	23	17	4	73
Idaho	58,359	23	23	15	4	65
Illinois	500,680	20	24	19	0.5	64
Indiana	285,367	22	25	23	1	70
Iowa	135,963	23	28	23	1	75
Kentucky	181,861	11	26	27	0.1	64
Louisiana	201,564	31	25	20	9	84
Minnesota	215,671	22	22	23	2	69
Mississippi	130,119	10	31	34	0.2	75
Missouri	236,860	29	22	26	2	79
Montana	42,104	25	18	33	2	78
Nebraska	78,132	29	34	28	6	96
Nevada	49,032	19	19	22	6	66
New Mexico	76,688	32	33	16	1	82
New York	743,290	27	33	23	5	87
North Carolina	322,087	27	25	15	1	68
North Dakota	33,627	27	27	29	2	85
Ohio	549,180	24	24	19	4	71
Oklahoma	164,630	18	24	21	9	72
Pennsylvania	500,536	19	27	25	—	71
South Carolina	177,948	27	25	18	1	71
Texas	891,628	25	26	14	2	67
Virginia	283,213	25	25	27	0.5	78
Wisconsin	236,207	24	24	20	2	71
Wyoming	27,285	17	18	14	5	52
Median		24	25	20	2	71

Note: Illinois data collected 1986–87 school year; Nebraska data include first and second semester enrollments.

Source: State Departments of Education, Data on Public Schools, Fall 1988.

Table 4 shows the percentage of grade 9–12 students that were taking science courses as of October 1988. The science course enrollments are aggregated in four categories: (a) Earth, Physical, or General Science; (b) first-year Biology; (c) Chemistry, Physics, or second-year Biology; and (d) Other Science. The average percentage of high school students enrolled in a science course was 71%. An average of 25% took a first-year Biology course and 24% took an Earth, Physical, or General Science course. Thus, half of all high school students, and over two-thirds of those taking science, were taking a science course to meet their graduation requirement at the first two course levels. Twenty per cent of students were taking a more advanced science course. In Alabama, Indiana, Kentucky, Minnesota, Mississippi, and Virginia the more advanced science courses (second-year Biology, Chemistry, and Physics) were taken as frequently as either of the categories of lower level courses.

Considering the state-by-state rates of student course-taking in science and math raises a question about the relationship of these rates to state policies.

2. Do states with higher requirements for graduation have more students taking science and math?

Table 5 shows a cross-tabulation of the percentage of students taking math courses by the number of math course credits required for graduation. State math requirements were divided into two categories for purposes of analysis – states requiring three course credits vs. states requiring two credits. Each column shows the total percentage of students taking math and the percent taking Formal Math Levels 2–5 (i.e., Geometry, Algebra II,

Table 5. Proportion of students in grades 9–12 taking mathematics courses by state graduation requirements.

Three courses required			Two courses required		
State	Students taking mathematics [%]	Students taking geom.-calc. [%]	State	Students taking mathematics [%]	Students taking geom.-calc. [%]
Arkansas	91	36	Alabama	72	27
Kentucky	87	34	California	76	28
Louisiana	88	45	Delaware	77	28
New Mexico	99	38	Idaho	76	31
Pennsylvania	82	47	Indiana	78	32
South Carolina	96	32	Mississippi	82	37
Texas	90	34	Missouri	82	36
Virginia	90	39	New York	81	34
			North Carolina	84	36
			North Dakota	80	41
			Ohio	83	36
			Oklahoma	79	33
			Wisconsin	84	29
Median	90	36/38	Median	80	33

Note: Arkansas % students taking math was estimated by adding 66% reported for Formal Math plus 25% median state percentage for Review and Informal math.

Sources: Graduation requirements from CCSSO, 1989a; enrollment data from State Departments of Education, Data on Public Schools, Fall 1988.

Trigonometry, or Calculus courses). The median percentage for all math enrollments among states requiring three credits is 90%, while the median among states requiring two courses is 80%. The median percentage for enrollment in more advanced math courses is 36 to 38% while the median for states with two courses required is 33%. The number of credits that states require appears to have a strong relationship to total math enrollment in a state (average difference of 10%), and a positive, but less strong, relationship to the level of courses that are taken (average difference of 3 to 5% for enrollments in advanced math courses).

In table 6, the percentage of high school students taking science courses is cross-tabulated by state graduation requirements for science. Among the 29 states that reported data, seven require one course or have no state requirement (local policy). The median total percentage taking science among the seven states is 69%, and the median for advanced science courses is 22% of students. Eighteen states require two science courses and two states require three courses. Among these 20 states the median percentage for total science enrollment is 71% and the median for advanced science courses is 20%. These data indicate a weak relationship between number of science credits required for graduation and the rate of students taking secondary science courses. It is possible that the number of states (seven) in the low requirement category is too small for meaningful comparisons of category averages.

In sum, states that increased the graduation requirement in mathematics in the 1980s from two to three courses have higher enrollments in mathematics. Course-taking is also

Table 6. Proportion of students in grades 9–12 taking science courses by state graduation requirements.

Two–three courses required			One course or no state requirement		
State	Students taking science [%]	Students taking adv. science [%]	State	Students taking science [%]	Students taking adv. science [%]
Alabama (2)	72	22	Illinois (1)	64	19
Arkansas	79	15	Iowa (Local)	75	23
California	61	15	Minnesota (Local)	69	23
Delaware	69	18	Montana (1)	78	33
Idaho	65	15	Nevada (1)	66	22
Indiana	70	23	Ohio (1)	71	19
Kentucky	64	27	Wyoming (Local)	52	14
Louisiana (3)	84	20			
Mississippi	75	34			
New Mexico	82	16			
New York	87	23			
North Carolina	68	15			
North Dakota	85	29			
Oklahoma	71	21			
Pennsylvania (3)	71	25			
South Carolina	71	18			
Texas	67	14			
Virginia	78	27			
Wisconsin	71	20			
Median	71	20	Median	69	22

Sources: Graduation requirements from CCSSO, 1989a; enrollment data from State Departments of Education, Data on Public Schools, Fall 1988.

higher for these states in more advanced courses, but the difference from other states is smaller. The data also indicate a two-credit requirement in science does not yield higher science enrollments as compared to those states with a one-credit requirement or no state requirement.

3. Have state reforms increased student enrollments in basic or lower-level science and math courses?

The state-by-state data can provide further evidence related to the findings of the CPRE and PACE studies concerning the effect of higher state course requirements on the types and level of courses students take in science and math to meet the requirements (Cagampang and Guthrie 1988, Clune 1989a). One way of viewing this issue is whether state curriculum reforms have the effect of expanding existing curriculum and instruction in science and math to more students, or have the effect of increasing the proportion of students that take more basic, lower-level courses to meet the requirements. However, another view is that, regardless of the level of difficulty, students are likely to learn more science and mathematics by taking more courses, even if the courses are less rigorous (NASSP 1989, Raizen and Jones 1985). For an analysis of curriculum, trends in student enrollments in basic or applied courses is an important indicator of the effects of state policies even though interpretations of the indicator may differ.

In the analysis of state data on enrollments, it was noted that one-fourth of high school students were taking General Math or Pre-Algebra (i.e., lower-level) math courses in 1988–89, and about one-fourth were taking a lower-level science course in Earth Science, General Science, or Physical Science. It is also possible to more closely examine the level of science courses students were taking in other science fields. The CCSSO course taxonomy and reporting definitions include separate categories for 'applied' vs. 'general' first-year courses in Biology, Chemistry, and Physics. This distinction reflects a strong interest of state science supervisors in the use of the state indicators to track the level of courses students are taking to meet science requirements.

A 'general' first-year course in Biology, Chemistry, and Physics is the traditional first-year course in these fields, typically a broad survey course that introduces the field to students but also is aimed at students planning to pursue further study in science. An 'applied' course is a more basic course emphasizing central principles, concepts, and applications, and typically is aimed at students who are not planning further study in science.

In table 7, state-by-state data are reported on student enrollments in applied and general courses in first-year Biology, Chemistry, and Physics. There is wide variation among states that reported data in each subject. For example, the state percentage of first-year Biology enrollments in applied courses varies from 44% (Delaware) to 1% (North Carolina, Montana), the percentage taking applied Chemistry varies from 39% to .3%, and the percentage taking applied Physics varies from 44% to 1%. These comparative data on enrollments by state provide an initial indicator of the extent to which lower-level, 'applied' courses are being taken by students, and the extent to which schools are offering the courses. However, many states do not include the different course levels in their data collection, and thus state-by-state analyses are limited.

The present data show that in most of the states reporting general vs. applied science categories, there is a substantial portion of students taking applied courses, especially in Biology and Physics. Trend data are needed to determine if enrollments in the applied

Table 7. Enrollments in first-year biology, chemistry, and physics by general vs. applied.

State	Biology–1st year					Chemistry–1st year					Physics–1st year				
	Total	General		Applied		Total	General		Applied		Total	General		Applied	
Alabama	53,806	38,042	71%	15,764	29%	17,315	16,939	98%	376	2%	10,350	6594	64%	3756	36%
California	300,075	201,840	67%	98,235	33%	91,206	*	*	*	*	40,909	*	*	*	*
Delaware	6565	3657	58%	2908	44%	2835	2145	76%	690	24%	1309	1062	81%	247	18%
Hawaii	10,121	6574	65%	3547	35%	4267	2602	61%	1665	39%	1991	1119	56%	872	44%
Idaho	13,224	*	*	*	*	4787	*	*	*	*	2022	1986	98%	36	2%
Illinois +	120,534	*	*	*	*	51,079	50,524	99%	555	1%	25,342	*	*	*	*
Indiana	70,556	55,683	78%	14,873	21%	28,531	28,067	98%	454	2%	13,314	12,816	96%	498	4%
Minnesota	48,195	45,643	95%	2552	6%	23,502	*	*	*	*	13,066	*	*	*	*
Mississippi	39,759	34,956	88%	4803	12%	16,492	*	*	*	*	4573	*	*	*	*
Montana	7578	7543	99.5%	35	0.5%	4061	4067	99.7%	14	.3%	2290	2276	99%	14	1%
Nebraska +	26,219	20,349	78%	5870	22%	10,845	*	*	*	*	5334	5138	96%	196	4%
Nevada	9229	*	*	*	*	4762	*	*	*	*	1805	1611	89%	194	11%
New Mexico	25,289	22,266	88%	3023	12%	6391	*	*	*	*	2434	*	*	*	*
New York	243,630	196,924	81%	48,706**	19%	100,537	*	*	*	*	47,444	*	*	*	*
North Carolina	81,678	81,632	99.9%	46	.1%	34,757	*	*	*	*	10,649	*	*	*	*
North Dakota	9102	8828	97%	274	3%	3943	*	*	*	*	2188	2134	98%	54	2%
Pennsylvania	134,953	11,049	82%	23,904	18%	63,518	*	*	*	*	34,184	*	*	*	*
South Carolina	44,331	*	*	*	*	19,396	*	*	*	*	5686	4741	83%	945	17%
Texas	232,628	177,034	76%	58,594	24%	80,134	32,654	88%	4361	12%	24,228	*	*	*	*
Virginia	70,683	63,323	90%	7360	10%	37,015	*	*	*	*	16,318	16,006	98%	312	2%
Wisconsin	56,566	53,477	94%	3089	6%	28,673	*	*	*	*	13,826	*	*	*	*
Wyoming	4460	4460	100%	*	*	1796	*	*	*	*	725	633	87%	92	13%

Notes   *State does not collect or cannot report for category.

       **Estimated from totals for 7–9.

       + Illinois data collected 1986–87 school year; Nebraska data include first and second semester enrollment.

Source: State Departments of Education, Data on Public Schools, Fall 1988.

courses are actually increasing. As the state science/math indicators continue, CCSSO will be able to collect data from more states and time-series data will become available.

4. How does course taking in science and mathematics differ between girls and boys?

Results from the National Assessment of Educational Progress (NAEP) have shown that boys have higher scores than girls on the earth science, chemistry, and physics portions of the test, but scores for boys and girls are approximately equal on the biology portion of the assessment (ETS 1988). On the NAEP in mathematics, boys consistently perform

Table 8. Enrollments in mathematics by gender.

State	Total	Formal Level 1 (Algebra) Boys [%]	Girls [%]	Total	Formal Level 2 (Geometry) Boys [%]	Girls [%]
California	270,851	50	50	154,025	49	51
Hawaii	5559	46	54	3867	46	54
Illinois +	103,371	50	50	80,422	49	51
Iowa	30,177	50	50	23,607	49	51
South Carolina	28,676	49	51	22,809	47	53
Wisconsin	50,164	50	50	28,198	49	51
Wyoming	1779	54	46	1958	57	43

State	Total	Formal Level 3 (Algebra 2) Boys [%]	Girls [%]	Total	Formal Level 4 (Trigonometry) Boys [%]	Girls [%]
California	130,271	49	51	56,327	53	47
Hawaii	3544	47	53	2166	49	51
Illinois +	69,753	50	50	29,117	54	46
Iowa	19,439	49	51	13,113	54	46
South Carolina	21,667	47	53	10,146	48	52
Wisconsin	20,338	49	51	14,154	54	46
Wyoming	1534	48	52	1209	53	47

State	Total	Formal Level 5 (Calculus) Boys [%]	Girls [%]	Total	Formal Level 5, Adv. Place2 (Calculus) Boys [%]	Girls [%]
California	23,338	56	44	*	*	*
Hawaii	94	41	59	186	54	46
Illinois +	10,524	56	44	2804	59	41
Iowa	2588	55	45	*	*	*
South Carolina	607	62	38	1848	51	49
Wisconsin	5232	55	45	*	*	*
Wyoming	237	54	46	146	68	32

Notes: *State does not collect or cannot report data for category.
+ School year 1986–87.
Source: State Departments of Education, Data on Public Schools, Fall 1988.

Table 9.   Enrollments in biology, chemistry, physics, and earth science by gender.

BIOLOGY

State	1st year			2nd year (AP other advanced)		
	Total	Boys [%]	Girls [%]	Total	Boys [%]	Girls [%]
California	300,075	51	49	34,764	45	55
Hawaii	10,121	48	52	504	34	66
Illinois +	120,534	49	51	14,518	47	53
Iowa	37,534	50	50	31,977	40	60
South Carolina	44,331	50	50	4,530	44	56
Wisconsin	56,566	51	49	12,524	47	53
Wyoming	4460	52	48	1001	48	54

CHEMISTRY

State	1st year			2nd year (AP other advanced)		
	Total	Boys	Girls	Total	Boys	Girls
California	97,206	50	50	6876	58	42
Hawaii	4267	44	56	147	58	42
Illinois +	51,079	49	51	4931	59	41
Iowa	18,321	50	50	*	*	*
South Carolina	19,398	47	53	1409	58	42
Wisconsin	28,673	48	52	5294	54	46
Wyoming	1798	52	48	153	52	48

PHYSICS

State	1st year			2nd year (AP other advanced)		
	Total	Boys	Girls	Total	Boys	Girls
California	40,909	59	41	6976	57	43
Illinois +	25,342	50	40	1329	72	28
Hawaii	1991	55	45	504	34	66
Iowa	9402	59	41	*	*	*
South Carolina	5838	61	39	142	75	25
Wisconsin	13,826	60	40	2642	58	42
Wyoming	725	63	37	24	79	21

EARTH SCIENCE

State	1st year			Advanced		
	Total	Boys	Girls	Total	Boys	Girls
California	29,642	54	46	9030	51	49
Illinois +	25,854	54	46	3108	62	38
Hawaii	1390	56	44	2020	56	44
Iowa	8586	53	47	2020	56	44
South Carolina	*	*	*	177	66	34
Wisconsin	12628	54	56	2305	59	41
Wyoming	2256	55	45	58	64	36

Notes: *State does not collect or cannot report data for category.
    + School year 1986–87.
Source: State Departments of Education, Data on Public Schools, Fall 1988.

better on more complex mathematical procedures than girls (ETS 1988). Given these findings from student achievement tests, it is important for policy analysts to track course enrollments for girls and boys in mathematics and science courses as a possible source of differences in student learning. The Science/Math Indicators Project requested that states report course enrollment data by student gender. For 1988–89, seven states were able to report course enrollments categorized by gender. State data on mathematics reported in table 8 show that as course difficulty increases, the percentage of girls taking the course diminishes. For example, in Algebra I the ratio of girls to boys is evenly distributed. In Trigonometry all states except Hawaii report higher male enrollments than female enrollments. The disparity is larger in Calculus – for example, South Carolina reported that only 38% of the students taking Calculus were girls, and Wyoming reported that only 32% of those taking AP Math were girls.

The data on science in table 9 shows that across the seven states the ratio of girls to boys taking science courses was relatively equal in first-year Biology and Chemistry. For example, California reported first-year Biology had 49% girls, and first-year Chemistry had 50% girls. In Earth Science, Physics and advanced Chemistry courses, more boys were enrolled than girls. For example, in California, first-year Earth Science had 46% girls, first-year Physics had 41% girls, advanced Chemistry had 42% girls, and advanced Physics had 43% girls. The exception is advanced Biology – for example, California had 55% girls in this course. This pattern is consistent across the reporting states.

The results from the state data on course-taking by gender indicate that differences in student achievement scores between boys and girls in Mathematics, Earth Science, Chemistry, and Physics could be a result of significantly higher numbers of boys taking advanced courses. The pattern of state-level findings of enrollments by gender is very similar to findings from the 1987 Transcript Study (Kolstad and Thorne 1989). Trend data at the state level would be important for analyzing gender differences, particularly to determine if some states are able to make more progress in closing the gender gap.

Summary of findings

The results from the state-by-state analysis of course enrollments show that changes in state graduation requirements in the 1980s have affected the science and mathematics curriculum. States with higher requirements in mathematics have more students taking math at all levels, and to a lesser degree more students in advanced math courses. However, in most states a large portion of students are taking basic or lower-level science and math courses to meet requirements. The development of periodic reporting of the course enrollment data will provide trends analysis on specific questions concerning gender effects and changes at different course levels.

Analysis of state curriculum frameworks and state tests

In the 1980s, the number of states with statewide assessment programs rapidly increased. States increased the subjects being tested, such as science and writing, and methods and instruments for testing changed. However, one of the major criticisms of standardized tests that continues, whether the tests are administered nationally, statewide, or by local districts, is that the tests 'drive the curriculum' that is taught in classrooms towards less desirable teaching methods and content (Ferrara and Thornton 1988). An additional

Table 10. State student testing in science and mathematics by grade and type of test.

	Achievement Assessment			Competency-Referenced(c) or Proficiency(p)		
	Science	Math	Source	Science	Math	Source
Alabama	4,8	4,8	Stanford	—	3,6,9(c)11,12(p)	State
Alaska	4,6,8	4,6,8	State/loc.opt.	—		
Arizona	—	1–12	ITBS			
Arkansas	—	4,7,10	MAT	3,6,8	6,8(c)	State
California	8	3,6,8,12	State	—	9–12(p)	State
Colorado	—	—		—	—	
Connecticut	4,8,11	4,8,11	State	—	4,6,8)c)	State
Delaware	11	1–8,11	CTBS	—	8,11(p)	Local option
Dist. of Columbia	1–6	3,6,8,911	CTBS	—	—	
Florida	—	3,7,11	NAEP	—	3,5,8,10(c)	State
Georgia	2,4,7,9	2,4,7,9	ITBS	—	1,3,6,8,(c)10(p)	State
Hawaii	—	3,6,8,10	Stanford	—	3,9–12(p)	State
Idaho	6,8	6,8	ITBS	—	8–12(p)	State
Illinois	3,6,8,11	3,6,8,11	State	—	—	
Indiana	—	—		3,6,8,11	1,2,3,6,8,9,11(c)	State
Iowa	—	—		—		
Kansas	—	—		—	2,4,6,8,10(c)	State
Kentucky	—	—		—	K,1,2,3,5,7,10(c)	State
Louisiana	4,6,9	4,6,9	CAT	11 (p)	3,10(p)	State
Maine	4,8,11	4,8,11	State	—		
Maryland	—	3,5,8	CTBS	—	9(c)	State
Massachusetts	4,8,12	4,8,12	NAEP	—	3,6,9(c)	State
Michigan	5,8,11	4,7,10	State/NAEP	—	—	
Minnesota	4,8,11	3,4,8,11	State/loc.opt	—		
Mississippi	—	—		—	3,5,8,11(c)	State
Missouri	3,6,8,10	3,6,8,10	State	—	9–12(c)	State
Montana	—	6–11	State/loc.opt.	—	—	
Nebraska	—	—		—	—	
Nevada	—	3,6,9	CTBS	—	11–12(p)	State
New Hampshire	4,8,10	4,8,10	CAT	—	—	
New Jersey	3–8,10,11	3–8,10,11	Local option	—	9(p)	State
New Mexico	3,5,8	3,5,8	CTBS	3,5,8,11	3,5,8,11(p)	State/loc.opt.
New York	4,6	3,6,8/9	State	9–12	9–12(p)	State regents
North Carolina	3,6,9	3,6,9	CAT	—	10(p)	State
North Dakota	5,7,9,11	3,5,7,9,11	SRA/ITBS	—	—	
Ohio	—	4,6,8,10	Local opt.	—	4,6,8,10(c)9–12(p)	Loc. opt./state
Oklahoma	3,7,10	3,7,10	MAT	—	—	
Oregon	—	8	State	—	—	
Pennsylvania	4,6,7,9,11	4,6,9,11	State	—	3,5,8(c)	State
Rhode Island	—	3,6,8,10	State	—	—	
South Carolina	4,5,7,9,11	4,5,7,9,11	CTBS	3,6,8	1,2,3,6,8,10(c)9–12(p)	State
South Dakota	4,8,11	4,8,11	Stanford	—	—	
Tennessee	2–8	2–8	State	—	10(p)	State
Texas	—	1,3,5,7,9, 11,12	State	—	—	
Utah	—	5,11	CTBS	—	9–12(p)	Local option
Vermont	—	—		—	—	
Virginia	4,8,11	4,8,11	ITBS	—	1–6(c)9–12(p)	State
Washington	—	4,8,10	MAT	—	—	
West Virginia	—	—		1–8(c)	1–8(c)	State
Wisconsin	—	—		—	3,7,10(c)	State/loc.opt.
Wyoming	—	—		—	—	
Number of States	27	40		7	19(c) 17(p)	

Source: State Departments of Education, reported to CCSSO, 1990.

concern is that 'high-stakes' mandated state assessments have rewards or sanctions associated with student scores, such as grade promotion or high school graduation, which remove decision-making from local districts and schools (Airasian 1988).

Within the scope of this paper, a question about state assessment programs that can be addressed is how, or to what degree, state assessment programs are designed to reflect state curriculum reforms. Knowing that states are trying to influence curriculum as one of the policy reform objectives, it would be useful to know to what extent state tests are designed to be consistent with the direction of state curriculum reforms in science and mathematics. A few states, such as California and Connecticut, have made explicit their intention to align the content of state curriculum frameworks and the content and methods incorporate in state assessments. In these states, the goal is to use student assessments to 'drive' teaching and learning in directions defined by state curriculum objectives. But, what is the pattern across the 50 states?

State assessments can be viewed as a product of state policy-makers' interest in accountability for education outcomes or they can be viewed as a means of assessing curriculum implementation. For either purpose, it is useful to determine the relationship between state curriculum efforts and state assessments of student learning.

State tests by curriculum frameworks

As part of its efforts to develop state education indicators, the CCSSO State Education Assessment Center has identified the characteristics of statewide tests in all 50 states. In table 10 statewide tests in science and mathematics are categorized by type of test (achievement assessment, competency-referenced, proficiency), grades tested in science/math, and source (state-developed test vs. national standardized test). 'Achievement assessments', based on norm-referenced or objective-referenced achievement batteries, are used by 40 states in mathematics, 27 states in science. 'Competency-referenced tests', which usually focus on minimum competences in basic skills, are used by 19 states in math, seven in science. 'Proficiency tests', which are used to certify competence for promotion or graduation, are used in 17 states in math.

Table 11 displays state-by-state information on state curriculum frameworks, or curriculum guides, in science and mathematics. A total of 46 states have a framework or guide in science and mathematics. The 'purposes' of the framework, or guide, were reported by state specialists in science and math: (1) in 17 states a curriculum framework sets out a state curriculum that is required to be implemented by local districts; (2) in 30 states a framework defines curriculum goals within which local curricula shoud be developed; and, (3) in 25 states a framework outlines instructional objectives which may be used in conjunction with a state testing program.

Additionally, two 'uses' of a state curriculum framework, or guide, were reported: (a) a framework is used in 25 states to select or recommend textbooks; and, (b) a framework is used in 21 states to develop or select a state science test and in 29 states to develop or select a state math test.

Cross-tabulation of the information in tables 10 and 11 produces several patterns in the relationship of curriculum frameworks to state tests. Among the 40 states with an achievement assessment test in *mathematics*:

1. 26 state specialists in math (i.e., about two-thirds) reported that a state framework or guide was used to develop or select the assessment instrument;

Table 11. State curriculum frameworks/guides for science and mathematics.

	PURPOSE		USE		
	Required state curriculum	Curriculum goals	Instructional objectives	Select/ recommended textbooks	Develop/ select state tests
Alabama	SM	SM	M	SM	SM
Alaska		SM			
Arizona	SM	SM		SM	M
Arkansas		SM		SM	SM
California		SM		SM	SM
Colorado					M
Connecticut		SM	SM		SM
Delaware		SM			SM
Dist. of Columbia	SM	SM	SM	SM	SM
Florida			SM	SM	SM
Georgia	SM		M	SM	M
Hawaii	SM	SM	SM	SM	
Idaho	S	S	M		
Illinois		SM			
Indiana			S	SM	S
Iowa	SM				
Kansas*					
Kentucky		SM	M	SM	M
Louisana	SM	SM	SM	SM	SM
Maine	No state framework or guide				
Maryland		SM	M		
Massachusetts	No state framework or guide				
Michigan		SM	SM		
Minnesota	Planning a guide				
Mississippi	SM	SM	SM	SM	SM
Missouri		SM	SM		SM
Montana	Planning a guide				
Nebraska	No state framework or guide				
Nevada	SM	SM	SM		M
New Hampshire		SM	M		
New Mexico			SM	SM	SM
New Jersey*					
New York		SM	SM		SM
North Carolina	SM	SM	SM	SM	SM
North Dakota*					
Ohio	No state framework or guide				
Oklahoma		SM	SM	SM	SM
Oregon	SM	SM	SM	SM	SM
Pennsylvania		SM			SM
Rhode Island*					
South Carolina			SM	SM	M
South Dakota		SM		SM	
Tennessee	SM	SM		SM	SM
Texas	SM	SM	M	SM	M
Utah	SM		SM	SM	SM
Vermont*					
Virginia		SM	SM	SM	SM
Washington				SM	
West Virginia	SM	SM		SM	SM
Wisconsin		SM			M
Wyoming	No state framework or guide				

Notes: S = Science, M = Mathematics.
* Framework/guide only for advice and assistance to local districts/schools.
Source: Blank and Espenshade 1988b.

2.   17 state specialists reported that the curriculum framework or guide had the purpose of outlining instructional objectives which could be used with state tests.

Among the 29 states with an achievement assessment in *science*:

1.   19 state science specialists reported that the state science curriculum framework or guide is used to develop or select state tests;
2.   11 reported that the framework or guide had the purpose of outlining instructional objectives which could be used with state tests.

These findings provide a broad picture of the role of state curriculum recommendations in state testing programs. Ideally, the analysis would examine the actual test objectives and content of state tests in relation to a state curriculum framework or guide (Murnane and Raizen 1988). Although this analysis does not focus on content, it does show that in a majority of states with statewide tests the curriculum framework or guide has an indirect relationship (or no relationship) to the tests that are used or developed. A state curriculum framework or guide is used directly to define specific learning objectives for test items in fewer than half the states with statewide science or math tests.

New state models for assessment

The state-by-state list of student tests in science and mathematics does not accurately represent current trends in state testing programs. Since 1988, several states have taken major steps toward developing and implementing alternate types of tests of student learning, such as tests that include techniques of 'performance assessment'. The new types of tests are designed to more closely align state assessments with state curriculum goals and to allow testing of important apsects of learning not emphasized in previous tests. The examples cited here do not represent all of the states that may be moving toward new approaches in student testing, but they do represent important new models among state testing programs.

New York administered a 'science manipulatives test' to all 200,000 fourth grade students, for the first time, in May 1989. The test was one part of a state program evaluation in elementary science. The program evaluation was developed within the state plan for improving elementary science curriculum and instruction. The manipulatives test included five hands-on exercises. Student performance on the exercises was scored by one teacher in each school. The scores are used to produce school-level results, not individual student scores (Blank and Selden 1989).

Connecticut has defined new goals for secondary education called the 'Common Core of Learning'. The Common Core, which was defined by a state committee of policymakers, educators, and citizens, sets out the knowledge and skills in academic subject areas that are expected to be learned by all high school graduates. The state department of education has received a grant from the National Science Foundation to design and implement multiple forms of assessment that will reflect the learning goals for science and mathematics. Performance assessment (hands-on exercises and manipulatives), student portfolios, and open-ended written questions are being considered in the assessment design.

Vermont is developing a method of testing in mathematics and writing that is based on the assumption that the form of testing drives the kinds and quality of teaching. The new assessment will encourage teaching for critical thinking and higher order learning. The assessment will include a unique state standardized test and a system for scoring portfolios of one year of student work. The student and teacher will decide together what three or four pieces of work reflect the students' best work in mathematics and writing, and this set will be submitted to an assessment center of teachers for scoring (CCSSO 1989b).

California is the first state to declare a policy of shifting its testing program to performance assessments. In 1989 the state department of education convened conferences for district administrators and teachers to present current models of performance assessment and to gain their assistance with experiments and field tests for developing new assessments in core subjects. Developing performance assessments is a major recommendation of this year's California 'education summit' (California Department of Education 1990). For two years the California Assessment Program's 12th grade math test has used open-ended items which require students to write an extended answer or to draw a response to a problem.

Maine's state achievement assessments in mathematics and science includes a teacher questionnaire which asks about students' opportunity-to-learn content topics that are being tested. The responses are used for analyses of assessment scores and to examine the relationship of curriculum and teaching strategies to student outcomes.

North Carolina instituted an end-of-course testing program at the high school level in 1985. Currently, the state gives tests in Algebra I and II, Biology, US History, and Chemistry, and tests in Geometry, Physics, and English I are being field-tested. The tests provide information on: (a) each student's performance relative to other North Carolina students; and (b) school and district average scores on the subject are a goals and objectives defined in the state curriculum framework (*Standard Course of Study* and *Teacher Handbook*). Teachers were actively involved in the test development and review process. Test results are used by teachers and administrators (Southern Regional Education Board 1989).

Kentucky's new state legislation to redesign the educational system (which was declared unconstitutional) places emphasis on the state's role in defining goals for learning in academic subjects and in evaluating student outcomes. Performance-based assessments are specifically mandated as the method of evaluating student learning.

These brief descriptions of state efforts to develop innovative, alternative methods of assessing student learning indicate that states may be able to move toward improved alignment of curriculum and instruction goals and the state assessments of curriculum that is learned by students.

Implications of state indicators of curriculum

This paper has presented analyses of state policies and state curriculum in science and mathematics using several different indicators of the effects of policy reforms. The findings from the analysis of state course enrollments show a pattern of wide state variation at each of the course levels in science and math. The state averages confirm findings from national transcript studies that course-taking increased in the 1980s following state policy changes. The analysis of state policies showed that states with a three-credit course requirement for mathematics have higher rates of course-taking in mathematics and slightly higher rates of course enrollment in advanced math courses as compared to states with lower requirements. States with a two-credit requirement in science did not have higher rates of course enrollments than states with lower requirements.

The analysis of the course enrollment indicator also addressed the issue of the level of science and math courses that students are taking to meet state requirements. In science, one-fourth of the high school students in the average state took a first-year Biology course in 1988–89 and one-fourth took a course in Earth Science, Physical Science, or General Science. Twenty per cent of high school students took a course more advanced than first-year Biololgy. Data from some states reveal that enrollments in basic or applied courses comprise up to a third of enrollments in first-year Biology and Physics. In mathematics, one-fourth of high school students in the average state took a math course below the level of Algebra 1 in 1988–89, 21% took an Algebra 1 course, and 34% took a more advanced math course. Thus, even though total enrollments in more advanced math courses increased during the 1980s, a significant portion of students in the average state are taking math courses in high school which are below first-year Algebra, that is, courses offering the content of middle school or junior high school mathematics. The analysis of state course enrollment data on science and math show that these state-collected data can be a useful indicator for analyzing curriculum policies and the implementation of policies and programs in schools. Course data provide a measure of the implemented curriculum in showing the proportion of students receiving various types and levels of science and math curriculum. A state-by-state indicator of course enrollment is useful for making 50-state comparisons and analyses of curriculum trends over a variety of types of courses, but the system offers limited information on course content in any specific course. General findings can be reached about how much and what type of education students are receiving in given curriculum areas, like science and math, but more specific findings on the quality of curriculum provided to students cannot be obtained. This is mainly due to the degree of generalization that is necessary to collect and report data across schools, districts, and states for a feasible cost. For state and local education decision-makers, this kind of general curriculum indicator is useful, it may be less useful to curriculum specialists and teachers.

An advantage of using course data from state departments of education is the efficiency of utilizing data from administrative records. These data provide a broad picture of the range of participation in science and mathematics courses. To analyze differences in content of courses between or within a specific state course category would require other methods of data collection, such as special surveys with teachers or students or teacher logs of content area coverage. The costs of data collection would be higher and the curriculum areas or courses that could be analyzed would be limited. A promising approach for collecting data on implemented curriculum is 'opportunity-to-learn' surveys that can be conducted with student achievement assessments.

The analysis of state curriculum frameworks and state tests provided several findings on state policy effects. States have a much greater role in assessing student learning at the end of the 1980s than they had in the early part of the decade. The developments in state assessment programs supports the view that student testing has become the primary method by which states monitor curriculum and provide state accountability for education. However, the analysis also showed that the effect of policy reforms in many states has been to increase the activity of state departments of education in defining the curriculum content through state mandates or recommendations on curriculum as well as in developing statewide assessment programs. Both of these kinds of state reforms may improve science and mathematics education. The analysis of the linkages between state curriculum frameworks and tests indicates that in a majority of states current statewide test instruments are not closely aligned with the state's recommendations and guidelines for curriculum in science and mathematics. The fact that relatively few states have direclty joined the state role in these two areas indicates that many state tests may not be well designed to assess the achieved curriculum as defined in state curriculum documents.

The summary descriptions of several states' recent efforts to begin implementing new, more 'authentic' methods of student assessment show that state departments of education are confronting the need for greater consistency between state efforts to improve curriculum and instruction and state assessment programs. State assessments that involve hands-on exercises and other forms of performance assessment show strong potential for improving the relationship between state curriculum goals and assessments of learning. These methods of assessment also offer the possibility of more active roles of classroom teachers in the design, implementation, and evaluation steps of the assessment process. Research on state assessments and curriculum that is conducted in the mid-1990s may show a very different pattern than was evident in the 1980s.

Acknowledgement

Data reported in the paper were collected by State Departments of Education on public schools in Fall 1988. This research was supported by a grant from the National Science Foundation, Office of Studies and Program Assessment, Science and Engineering Education.

Note

1. The course enrollment reporting plan divided mathematics courses into three categories — Review, Informal, and Formal Mathematics. Within each category, courses were assigned a level from 1 to 5. This method of categorization allows comparison of mathematics enrollments among states using a standard taxonomy (CCSSO 1988).

References

AMERICAN ASSOCIATION FOR THE ADVANCEMENT OF SCIENCE (1989) *Project 2061, Science for All Americans* (Washington, DC: AAAS).

AIRASIAN, P. W. (1988) 'Symbolic validation: the case of state-mandated, high-stakes testing', *Educational Evaluation and Policy Analysis*, 10(4), pp. 301–314.

ARMSTRONG, J. and DAVIS, A. (1988) *Designing State Curriculum Frameworks and Assessment Programs to Improve Instruction* (Denver, CO: Education Commission of the States).

BLANK, R. (1986) *Science and Mathematics Indicators: Conceptual Framework for a State-Based Network* (Washington, DC: CCSSO, State Education Assessment Center).

BLANK, R. and ESPENSHADE, P. (1988a) '50-state analysis of education policies on science and mathematics', *Educational Evaluation and Policy Analysis*, 10(4), pp. 315–324.

BLANK, R. and ESPENSHADE, P. (1988b) *Survey of States on Availability of Data on Science and Mathematics Education* (Washington, DC: CCSSO, State Education Assessment Center).

BLANK, R. and SELDEN, R. (1989) *Alternative Methods for Assessing Science: Report to the States* (Washington, DC: CCSSO, State Education Assessment Center).

CAGAMPANG, H. H. and GUTHRIE, J. W. (1988) *Math, Science, and Foreign Language Instruction in California: Recent Changes and Prospective Trends* (Berkeley: University of California, Policy Analysis for California Education).

CALIFORNIA STATE DEPARTMENT OF EDUCATION (1990) *Summit: Meeting the Challenge, The Schools Respond, Final Report* (Sacramento, CA: SDE).

CARNEGIE FORUM ON EDUCATION AND THE ECONOMY (1986) *A Nation Prepared: Teachers for the 21st Century*. The Report of the Task Force on Teaching as a Profession (Washington, DC: Carnegie Forum on Education and the Economy).

CLUNE W. H. (1989a) *The Implementation and Effects of High School Graduation Requirements: First Steps Toward Curriculum Reform* (New Brunswick, NJ: Center for Policy Research in Education, Rutgers University).

CLUNE, W. H. (1989b) *Educational Governance and Student Achievement* (Madison, WI: Wisconsin Center for Education Research, University of Wisconsin).

COUNCIL OF CHIEF STATE SCHOOL OFFICERS (1984) *CCSSO Assessment and Evaluation: Notebook* (Washington, DC: CCSSO).

COUNCIL OF CHIEF STATE SCHOOL OFFICERS (1988) *Instructions and Reporting Forms for Data on Science and Mathematics Education in* [each state] (Washington, DC: CCSSO, State Edcuation Assessment Center).

COUNCIL OF CHIEF STATE SCHOOL OFFICERS (1989a) *State Education Policies Related to Science and Mathematics* (Washington, DC: CCSSO, State Education Assessment Center).

COUNCIL OF CHIEF STATE SCHOOL OFFICERS (1989b) *Success for All in a New Century: A Report by the CCSSO on Restructuring Education* (Washington, DC: CCSSO).

EDUCATION COMMISION OF THE STATES (1985) *New Directions for State Teacher Policies* (Denver: Education Commission of the States).

EDUCATIONAL TESTING SERVICE (1988) *The Science Report Card/The Mathematics Report Card* (Princeton, NJ: ETS).

EDUCATIONAL TESTING SERVICE (1989) *What Americans Study* (Princeton, NJ: ETS).

FERRARA, S. F. and THORNTON, S. J. (1988) 'Using NAEP for interstate comparisons: the beginnings of a national achievement test' and 'national curriculum', *Educational Evaluation and Policy Analysis*, 10(3), pp. 200–211.

FREEMAN, D. J. (1989) *State Guidelines for Reshaping Academic Curricula in Elementary Schools: A 50-State Survey* (East Lansing, MI: Michigan State University).

FUHRMAN, S. (1989) *Diversity Amidst Standardization: State Differential Treatment of Districts* (New Brunswick, NJ: Center for Policy Research in Education, Rutgers University).

GOERTZ, M. (1986) *Educational Standards: A 50-State Survey* (Princeton, NJ: Educational Testing Service).

HOLMES GROUP (1986) *Tomorrow's Teachers: A Report of The Holmes Group* (East Lansing, MI: Holmes Group).

JACOBSON, W. and DORAN, R. (1988) *Science Achievement in the United States and Sixteen Countries* (New York: Columbia University).

KOLSTAD, A. and THORNE, J. (1989) 'Changes in high school course work from 1982 to 1987: evidence from two national surveys', paper presented at annual meeting of the American Educational Research Association.

LAPOINTE, A., MEAD, N. and PHILLIPS, G. (1989) *A World of Differences: An International Assessment of Mathematics and Science* (Princeton, NJ: Educational Testing Service).

MCDONNELL, L. M., BURSTEIN, L., ORMSETH, T., CATTERALL, J. S. and MOODY, D. (1990) *Discovering What Schools Really Teach: Designing Improved Coursework Indicators* (Los Angeles: UCLA/Center for Research, Evaluation, Standards, and Student Testing).

MCKNIGHT, C. C., CROSSWHITE, F. J., DOSSEY, J. A., KIFER, E., SWAFFURD, J. O., TRAVERS, K. J. and COONEY, T. J. (1987) *The Underachieving Curriculum: Assessing US School Mathematics from an International Perspective* (Champaign, IL: Stipes Publishing).

MITCHELL, R. (1990) 'Considering standards and assessment, performance assessment: an emphasis on "activity" ', *Education Week*, 24 January.

MURNANE, R. J. and RAIZEN, S. A. (eds) (1988) *Improving Indicators of the Quality of Science and Mathematics Education in Grades K–12*. National Research Council Washington, DC: National Academy Press.

NATIONAL COMMISSION ON EXCELLENCE IN EDUCATION (1983) *A Nation at Risk: The Imperative for Educational Reform* (Washington, DC: US Department of Education).

NATIONAL COUNCIL OF TEACHERS OF MATHEMATICS (1989) *Curriculum and Evaluation Standards for School Mathematics* (Washington, DC: NCTM).

NATIONAL GOVERNORS' ASSOCIATION (1986) *Time for Results: The Governors' 1991 Report on Education* (Washington, DC: National Governors' Association, Center for Policy Research and Analysis).

NATIONAL SCIENCE BOARD COMMISSION ON PRECOLLEGE EDUCATION IN MATHEMATICS, SCIENCE, AND TECHNOLOGY (1983) *Educating Americans for the 21st Century* (Washington, DC: National Science Foundation).

NATIONAL ASSOCIATION OF SECONDARY SCHOOL PRINCIPALS (1989) 'Teaching science in schools: a two-fold task', *Curriculum Report*, 18.

OAKES, J. (1986) *Educational Indicators: A Guide for Policymakers* (New Brunswick, NJ: Center for Policy Research in Education, Rutgers University).

OAKES, J. (1989) 'What educational indicators? The case for assessing the school context', *Educational Evaluation and Policy Analysis*, 11 (2), pp. 181–199.

OFFICE OF EDUCATIONAL RESEARCH AND IMPROVEMENT (1988) *Creating Responsible and Responsive Accountability Systems* (Washington, DC: US Department of Education).

PORTER, A. (1989) 'A curriculum out of balance: the case of elementary school mathematics', *Educational Researcher* 18 (5), pp. 9–15.

RAIZEN, S. A. and JONES, L. V. (eds) (1985) *Indicators of Precollege Education in Science and Mathematics*. Committee on Indicators of Precollege Science and Mathematics Education, National Research Council (Washington, DC: National Academy Press).

SHAVELSON, R., MCDONNELL, L., OAKES, J. and CAREY, N. (1987) *Indicator Systems for Monitoring Mathematics and Science Education* (Santa Monica, CA: Rand Corporation).

SHAVELSON, R., MCDONNELL, L. and OAKES, J. (1989) *Indicators for Monitoring Mathematics and Science Education: A Sourcebook* (Santa Monica, CA: Rand Corporation).

SOUTHERN REGIONAL EDUCATION BOARD (1989) *Assessing the Quality of High School Courses* (Atlanta: SREB).

TASK FORCE ON EDUCATION FOR ECONOMIC GROWTH (1983) *Action for Excellence: A Comprehensive Plan to Improve Our Nation's Schools* (Denver, CO: Education Commission of the States).

TWENTIETH CENTURY FUND TASK FORCE (1983) *A Report of the Twentieth Century Fund Task Force on Federal Elementary and Secondary Education Policy* (New York: The Twentieth Century Fund).

WESTAT, INC. (1988) *Tabulations, A Nation At Risk Update Study as part of the 1987 High School Transcript Study* (Washington, DC: US Department of Education, Center for Education Statistics).

4   *The interplay between state and district guidelines for curriculum reform in elementary schools*

Danise Cantlon, Sharon Rushcamp, and Donald Freeman

Curriculum guidelines are initiated at both state and district levels. This chapter explores the interplay between curriculum policies designed at the local level and those developed at the state level by examining the policy environments in two districts each in Florida, Michigan, and California. The authors suggest that two types of interactive models define the state–district relationship: (*a*) district accommodation/compromise; and (*b*) district compliance/augmentation. Districts that adopt the district accommodation/compromise model have sufficient resources and commitment to design their own independent curriculum guidelines focusing on local needs and priorities. In contrast, districts that use the compliance/augmentation model generally implement state-level policies, yet sometimes go beyond these recommendations with district-devised initiatives.

Local school districts that elect to design their own curriculum guidelines for teachers typically do so within the shadow of state-level policy initiatives. Thus, it is important to understand how district curriculum guidelines are controlled or shaped by state policymakers. Likewise, it is also important to consider how state-level curriculum policies are altered or modified by district policymakers. This study tried to capture these perspectives by casting the central question as, 'What is the interplay between intended curriculum policies designed at the district level and those developed at the state level?'

This study is part of a series of interrelated studies conducted by the Center for Learning and Teaching of Elementary Subjects. There are three limitations on the scope of the study. First, the focus is on curriculum-related initiatives that encourage elementary school teachers to teach for understanding and thinking in five content areas (mathematics, science, social studies, literature, and the arts). A second limitation is the restriction to two districts in each of only three states. If we had examined a broader range of states and districts, it is likely that other patterns would have emerged. A third important caveat to note is that the data base for this paper was limited to descriptions of intended policies and practices; it did not consider the ways in which these policies were actually enacted in local districts and schools. The enacted curriculum is the focus of another on-going study conducted by the Center in selected California classrooms.

We identified three types of policy relationships: inverse, direct, and interactive. Some have argued that in an inverse relationship or zero-sum game, strong state-level curriculum policies will be countered by weak district-level guidelines, and vice versa. Some analysts attribute the dramatic increases in policy activity at the state level during the 1980s to sharp drops in policy activity at the federal level (Astuto and Clark 1986). If a

0268–0939/90 $3.00 © 1990 Taylor & Francis Ltd.

comparable relation holds for the state and district levels, local policymakers will either defer to strong state policy guidelines, or compensate for weak state policies by designing stronger guidelines of their own.

Others have argued that state and local interactions typically bear a direct relationship to one another such that local policy guidelines mirror those at the state level. Several authors have noted that increases in the level of policy activity at the state level have been matched by comparable increases in policy activity at the local level (Cohen 1982, Fuhrman *et al.* 1988). Moreover, Freeman (1983) indicates that district objectives and tests for elementary school mathematics tend to mirror state objectives and tests.

Another position suggests that there are interactive relations between state and local policy guidelines. Based on their analyses of curriculum reform guidelines for high schools, Fuhrman and Elmore (1990) argue that interactions between state and district policy initiatives should be viewed as dynamic interplays in which local policymakers try to satisfy simultaneously both state and local goals: 'Most state and federal policies in the past have engendered a range of local behavior rather than uniform compliance . . . the most typical outcome is some compromise between what high/level policymakers intended and local actors' needs.' Furhman, Clune, and Elmore (1988) further contend that,

> The importance of local context, the extent to which policies coincide with local goals and capacity, has long been appreciated by researchers. However, our findings suggest a much less passive role for districts than past implementation research posits. (p. 254)

Stated in general terms, this study is designed to determine which of the three types of relationships – inverse, direct, or interactive – is the most characteristic of observed relations between state and district policy guidelines within this area of policy activity.

Procedure

Selection of states and districts

In accordance with a design calling for planned sampling of variations in state policy environments, we chose Florida, Michigan, and California for our analyses. According to the results of a survey of curriculum policies in all 50 states (Freeman 1989), these three states have contrasting curriculum policies. Representing one extreme, Florida has strong policies calling for teachers to ensure that students first and foremost master basic skills. At the other extreme, California has strong policies requiring teachers to teach for understanding and thinking rather than to concentrate on basic skills. Finally, Michigan has relatively weak curriculum policies, thereby promoting high levels of district autonomy in the development of such policies (although recently, it has begun to develop policy guidelines that encourage elementary school teachers to teach for understanding and thinking).

Our design for selecting districts within states called for the identification of two districts per state, one a large urban district of 119,000–278,000 students (referred to as either FLA-Large, MI-Large, or CAL-Large) and the other a moderate-sized district of 7500 to 25,000 students (referred to as either FLA-Med, MI-Med, or CAL-Med). The process of selecting the moderate and large districts included: (a) an analysis of socioeconomic status data for individual schools in each district to ensure that the selected districts served diverse student populations; and (b) interviews with curriculum specialists in state departments of education and presidents of state-level professional organizations in an effort to ensure that the selected districts were actively encouraging elementary school teachers to teach for understanding and thinking.

Data base

The data base for this report was derived from two major sources: (*a*) interviews with curriculum specialists in the three state departments of education and six local school district offices; and (*b*) collections of curriculum-related documents identified in these interviews. For example, in describing state curriculum guidelines in California, we drew upon our notes from nine interviews and a collection of more than 50 curriculum-related documents. The derivation of the state-level data base was interviews of curriculum specialists in each state department of education (e.g., mathematics specialist) and state education department personnel who were responsible for major areas of policy activity (e.g., director of the statewide testing program). The interview schedules featured both open-ended questions and more structured questions providing elaboration of specific features of a given initiative.

The interviews served two basic purposes: (*a*) providing an overview of the state's efforts to encourage elementary school teachers to teach for understanding and thinking; and (*b*) helping identify and collect documents depicting these policy initiatives. The process of deriving the data base for analyses of district/level guidelines followed a similar plan. Interviews of curriculum and policy area specialists who played key roles in the development and/or implementation of curriculum guidelines were followed by a collection of all documents cited in each interview. Throughout the subsequent analyses, we tried to ground our inferences in published documents whenever possible rather than relying primarily on the notes from our interviews. As the final step in preparing this report, we asked those we interviewed to confirm the accuracy of our analyses for their state or district. Recommended changes were discussed and some changes were made.

Florida's efforts to counterbalance a strong press for mastery of basic skills

Florida's policies and practices make a clear distinction between those efforts to ensure minimal skills are learned and those which encourage teachers to teach for understanding and thinking. The former are emphasized through the state's *Minimum Student Performance Standards* (Florida Department of Education 1983, 1985, 1986) initially developed prior to 1983 (and updated every five years); the latter are communicated through the *Student Performance Standards of Excellence* (Florida Department of Education 1984), developed after that time. The *Minimum Student Performance Standards* are hierarchically-arranged objectives that students are expected to master by grades 3, 5, 8, and 11 in reading, writing, social studies, mathematics, computer literacy, and science. With the exception of science and computer literacy, they are backed by statewide assessment tests with scores routinely reported in the press. Grade-three promotion and high school graduation are based on students' success in mastering these standards. For students who require extra attention in mastering the minimums, a compensatory program is provided.

In contrast to the *Minimum Standards*, the *Student Performance Standards of Excellence* 'represent a broad spectrum of higher level competencies expected of those who demonstrate progress toward academic excellence in specified fields of study' (Florida

Department of Education 1984: 4). These standards have been established in mathematics, science, social studies, and writing in grades 3, 5, 8, and 12. Unlike the *Minimum Performance Standards*, these standards are not assessed by the state. Instead, districts have been mandated to implement them. This has resulted in a variety of local initiatives. In support of the *Standards of Excellence*, the state department (*a*) sponsors in service activities for district specialists and summer institutes for teachers, (*b*) provides local districts with financial and technical support, (*c*) develops instructional guides to accompany the *Standards of Excellence*, and (*d*) offers an enrichment program called 'Superstars' in mathematics. The latter is an independent program for self-selecting students, and is managed by parent volunteers under a teacher's direction.

Although both the *Minimum Student Performance Standards* and the *Standards of Excellence* are available in mathematics, writing, and science, only the *Minimum Standards* exist in reading and computer literacy. In contrast, social studies has been guided solely by the *Standards of Excellence* until the upcoming implementation of the *Minimum Standards* in the 1989–90 school year.

Florida's policy initiatives to promote teaching for thinking and understanding can be characterized as add-ons to an accountability system dating back to the mid-1970s. While the *Minimum Student Performance Standards* are intended and assessed for all students, the *Standards of Excellence* are directed toward high-achieving students, are not assessed, and are left to districts to implement with locally designed initiatives.

Overview of curriculum guidelines in FL-Med

The most influential teaching policies and practices in this medium-sized district of Florida include district-devised curriculum activities. Some of these initiatives support the state's dual standards. Others overlap with or go beyond state-level initiatives, and still others provide unique initiatives in the absence of state-level directives. FL-Med designed its own curriculum guides and curriculum planning guides for teachers. The curriculum guides in mathematics, social studies, communications (reading and writing), science, computers, health, physical education, music, and the visual arts broadly describe content to be taught and identify for teachers recommended teaching strategies and activities. The curriculum planning guides provide more detail, inform teachers of lesson objectives, demonstrate how the objectives relate to the testing program, and suggest time guidelines to be used in planning.

The district's testing program includes comprehensive achievement tests developed by American Testronics, which are standardized for grades K–8 with national norms. Reading and language, mathematics, and study skills are tested each year for grades K–8, while science and social studies are tested at various grade levels. A special feature of the district testing program is the correlation of district teaching objectives to the testing program. In addition, the district has designed its own Pupil Competency Tests in language arts and math that include items similar to those typically found on the state-mandated minimum assessment. These tests are optional for teacher use, and are generally administered prior to state assessments to inform teachers of students who may require extra attention and to alert students to state-level expectations and testing format.

The textbook adoption policy encourages greater uniformity in the curriculum throughout the district. Textbooks are selected by a district committee whose policies and practices are coordinated with a state-level textbook adoption committee. State law requires that at least 50% of a district's budget for instructional materials must come from a state-approved list that addresses both the *Minimum Standards* and the *Standards of Excellence*.

Staff development programs sponsored by the district for elementary teachers in all subject areas also influence teachers. These programs focus on either the *Minimum Standards* or the *Standards of Excellence*. In-service activities which attract the greatest numbers of teachers are held at local school sites and address topics chosen in response to teacher or district requests. Some in-service programs focus on higher order outcomes, can be generic or subject specific, and are usually conducted so that thinking skills are actively introduced to participating teachers.

Overview of curriculum guides in FL-Large

This large district in Florida also reflects the state's dual standards, both the *Minimum Student Performance Standards* and the *Standards of Excellence*, in district initiatives. Interviews with specialists confirm that the district's instructional objectives and curriculum guides, testing program, textbook adoption policy, and in-service activities all work together to influence how and what teachers teach. District objectives designed to promote a balanced curriculum for grades K–6 are available in social studies, science, language arts and reading, mathematics, health, music, physical education, and art. These include the state-required minimums as well as the *Standards of Excellence*.

FL-Large's district testing program includes district-developed subject area tests which focus on the district's objectives and Stanford Achievement tests in mathematics, reading, and writing for grades K–6. A specialist noted that the district has its own bank of test items for pre- and post-test purposes in all areas of the *Minimum Student Performance Standards*. Teachers can administer items similar to those used in the state-level minimum assessment prior to the state examination. As in FL-Med, this district heavily relies on the state-approved textbook adoption list for selection of texts. Similarly, FL-Large also awards teachers with certification points and college credit for inservice attendance. This district has made a special effort to develop an in-service program for all district teachers that focuses on the teaching of critical thinking.

Interplay between state and local guidelines in Florida

The general style of interaction between state and district policies is similar in both districts; that is, district policymakers comply with state guidelines by restating the *Minimum Student Performance Standards* and *Standards of Excellence* in local initiatives. District and state initiatives often overlap; yet at times, district initiatives expand or go beyond state initiatives. An example of FL-Med's attempts to comply with state directives may be seen in its third-grade math curriculum guide, which correlates for teachers the content to be taught with (*a*) pupil competencies, (*b*) state minimum standards (SSAT), (*c*) the district testing program titled Comprehensive Assessment Program (CAP), and (*d*) the appropriate *Standards of Excellence*. This guide establishes clear ties to 9 of the 10 state-developed *Standards of Excellence* for third-grade mathematics and includes all of the state's *Minimum Student Performance Standards* for this subject and grade. In this way the district accommodates the state's mandate to teach the basics and implement opportunities for higher order outcomes.

Other initiatives in FL-Med and FL-Large call teachers' attention to the state's intended curriculum. For instance, local testing programs provide district-designed minimum assessments in anticipation of the statewide examination. Each district encourages teachers to emphasize content to be covered in the state's minimum competency assessments by citing matches between district and state objectives and by providing activity booklets which address student problem areas. District textbook adoption policies also mirror state-level policies, including references to both sets of standards. Finally, some district initiatives build on or go beyond the state's *Minimum Student Performance Standards* and *Standards of Excellence*. This is best illustrated in some of FL-Med's initiatives. For example, both Florida's *Minimum Standards* and *Standards of Excellence* address writing. This emphasis is reflected in FL-Med's implementation of 'Writing to Read', a computer-based instructional system designed to develop the writing and reading skills of students in kindergarten and first grade. Other district initiatives which elaborate on the implementation of the *Standards of Excellence* can be seen in the inclusion of staff specialists who promote thinking skills activities and workshops, and in thinking skills publications. The specialist in this district typically sponsors generic in-services on higher order outcomes for teachers and works closely with subject-area specialists to integrate thinking skills into subject-specific in-services. This district also publishes a thinking skills continuum, built on Bloom's taxonomy, and a guidebook which lists instructional activities to accompany the continuum.

Finally, this district also has one initiative which has emerged in the absence of either *Minimum Performance Standards* or the *Standards of Excellence*. It has developed a music curriculum guide that links stated music competencies to the district's thinking skills continuum. For example, at the second-grade level, a specific pupil competency such as 'the student will demonstrate the ability to combine long and short sounds into rhythm patterns' will be followed by specific information to the teacher about pupil knowledge (name long and short sounds), comprehension (identify long and short sounds) analysis (arrange long and short sounds to new music), and synthesis (create long and short sounds with rhythm patterns).

Michigan's emerging emphasis on teaching for understanding and thinking

Although Michigan is a local control state, state-level guidance is offered to the districts through (*a*) *Michigan K–12 Program Standards of Quality* (1987c) document, (*b*) *Essential Goals and Objectives* documents (in mathematics [Michigan Department of Education 1988], science [Michigan State Board of Education 1985], social studies [MSBE 1987a], reading [MSBE 1986], writing [MSBE 1985b], and visual arts [MSBE 1990], and (*c*) in-service activities. However, the state-level curriculum initiatives that most influence districts are the Michigan Education Assessment Program (MEAP) tests in reading, mathematics, and science.

The *Michigan K–12 Program Standards of Quality* document provides an overview for school improvement. The intent is for local districts to use this document voluntarily as a guide for self-assessment of instructional programs and for the purposes of achieving a balanced curriculum and effective instruction. The *Essential Goals and Objectives* documents are cited in *The Standards of Quality* document and have recently undergone revision or are currently being revised to include an emphasis on understanding and thinking. These broadly stated guidelines provide a curricular framework for local districts to construct a comprehensive program to meet the instructional needs of their students.

The state-sponsored in-service activities in various subject areas include the teaching of thinking and understanding. For instance, reading workshops focus on the new strategic definition of reading and the new MEAP reading tests. In addition, Hands-on science workshops sponsored by the Department of Education are conducted in 13 regions across Michigan. These statewide regional workshops provide hands-on, easy-to-use instructional materials for teachers that correlate to the *Essential Performance Objectives for Science Education* (MSBE 1985a) document.

The current criterion-referenced MEAP tests are administered annually at the beginning of grades 4, 7, and 10 in the areas of reading and mathematics. The MEAP tests in science are given in grades 5, 8, and 11. All of these MEAP tests currently focus on basic skills that most students should know and be able to do. Schools that have high concentrations of students who fall below a minimum criterion level receive compensatory education funding, which is mandated by 1970 *Public Act 38*. Because students' scores on the MEAP tests are published in the newspapers and are closely scrutinized by the public, the tests receive far more attention from teachers, administrators, and local policymakers than the state's other curriculum/related initiatives. At present, Michigan's intended curriculum is slowly evolving from a strong focus on basic skills to a more comprehensive and coherent framework reflecting both higher order outcomes and basic skills outcomes. The state is attempting to communicate its curriculum guidelines through an alignment of the *Standards of Quality document*, the *Essential Goals and Objectives* documents, and the new MEAP tests in reading, mathematics, and science, which assess curriculum goals. New MEAP tests that stress higher order outcomes in reading, mathematics, and science will follow the revision of the *Essential Goals and Objectives* documents in these three areas. The revised MEAP tests in reading, mathematics, and science are scheduled for implementation during the Fall of 1989, 1991, and 1992, respectively.

Overall, the MEAP tests will focus on cognitive processes rather than on memorized basic skills. For instance, the new MEAP reading tests are based on objectives which view reading as a dynamic and interactive process: 'The new reading objectives are designed to describe the characteristics of a good reader as outlined by reading research' (Michigan State Board of Education 1987b: 4). There are three categories of new objectives: constructing meaning, knowledge about reading, and attitudes and self-perceptions. Thus, new test items measure students' abilities to construct meaning for selected texts, and measure students' knowledge about and attitudes toward reading these texts. In addition, there are topic familiarity items to measure the role of students' background knowledge in their reading comprehension. The topic familiarity items are given prior to the administration of the reading passages.

Moreover, the State Department of Education plans to introduce writing tests in 1991. These tests will stress the process writing approach. In addition, the new MEAP math tests, based on the revised goals and objectives statements, will focus on six process strands (e.g., conceptualization, problem-solving) and eight content strands (e.g., numeration, geometry). These tests may include open-ended items, performance assessments, and the use of calculators, as well as multiple-choice items. Lastly, the upcoming MEAP science tests may also include short-answer essays and performance tasks, as well as multiple-choice items, to assess student understanding.

Overview of curriculum guidelines in MI-Med

Curriculum guidelines in the medium-sized district of Michigan press teachers to ensure that students have mastered basic skills. Until recently this press was closely attuned to the state's intended curriculum. Simply stated, this district follows the state's lead in its design of most curriculum guidelines. The policies and practices which most influence the ways in which teachers teach in this district include (a) district curriculum guides, (b) a district testing program, (c) district-wide textbook adoptions, (d) district-sponsored in-service activities, and (e) time recommendations. Although MI-Med has developed its own curriculum guides in mathematics, science, social studies, reading, music, and art, most of these guides correspond closely to the state's current *Essential Goals and Objectives*. For instance, *The Mathematics Curriculum Guide* (grade 4) lists grade-level objectives, pages in the district-wide adopted textbook, critical objectives, and MEAP-related objectives for each chapter overview. Of 70 grade level objectives, 59 are MEAP-related. In addition, the grade-level objectives in The Elementary Science Guide (grade 6) match the science process objectives in the *Essential Performance Objectives for Science Education* verbatim. Two of the 'inferring' objectives read as follows:

(1)   identify an inference based on an observation;
(2)   identify an inference which utilizes a property of an object discernible by any combination of senses. (Michigan State Board of Education 1985a: 32)

A district testing program has also been implemented that focuses on the district's objectives. Given the close links to the state guidelines, only about 20% of the test items currently focus on student understanding and thinking. Textbooks are chosen by a committee that selects one series to be used district wide. Even though a text's consideration of higher order outcomes is becoming a more important criterion with each new textbook series selected, it is still not of primary importance.

In-services are sponsored by the district for elementary school teachers in mathematics, social studies, science, reading, music, and art. To stay informed about the upcoming changes in the science portion of the MEAP, some teachers in MI-Med attended a three-day state-sponsored workshop. Although there is some emphasis on higher order outcomes, the majority of the in-services do not focus on thinking and understanding. Finally, the district also followed the lead of the state in its recommendations regarding the amount of time elementary school teachers should spend on each subject. However, there is no recommendation on the amount of time devoted to student thinking and understanding.

MI-Med has augmented the state's intended curriculum in the area of fine arts. Examples of MI-Med moving beyond the state curriculum guidelines include the implementation of the Disciplined-Based Art Education method, museum tours, and studio experience for the elementary students. Five out of eight elementary schools (upper grades) have a gallery program in which students participate in visual arts exhibitions. This district has also been working on implementing a comprehensive plan to integrate art with other content areas. In addition, the district's curriculum guide in art encourages teachers to teach for thinking and understanding by having the students express ideas about art, appreciate art, and evaluate art.

Overview of curriculum guidelines in MI-Large

MI-Large's guidelines call for a more balanced curriculum and encourage teachers to teach for thinking and understanding as well as basic skills. In fact, MI-Large led the state in the movement toward higher order outcomes. The district guidelines are backed by consistent support from the deputy superintendent and are advanced across three different policy fronts: curriculum guides, district-level textbook adoptions, and in-service activities. Until recently, these guidelines were also communicated through a district criterion-referenced testing program that focused on the goals and objectives cited in the curriculum guides. However, the district has dropped the testing program due to financial constraints.

The district curriculum guides include strands and objectives focusing on understanding and thinking in social studies, music, art, language arts/English, health, computer technology, math, and science. MI-Large's strands and objectives integrate basic skills with higher order outcomes. Likewise, a central criterion in the selection of district-wide textbooks for the past three years has been the text's treatment of higher order thinking. Finally, many district-level in-services are given which emphasize teaching for thinking and understanding. Some examples include (a) reading workshops on how to teach compatibly with the state's new definition of reading, (b) math workshops on using manipulatives and other topics which encourage teachers to teach for conceptual understanding, and (c) in-services on the cognitive processes (e.g., analyzing, evaluating, problem-solving, decision-making, and inquiry) discussed in *Dimensions of Thinking: A Framework for Curriculum and Instruction* (Marzano *et al.* 1988), a book co-authored by the deputy superintendent. As noted earlier, the district also had a criterion-referenced testing program that aligns with the other initiatives.

Interplay between state and district guidelines in Michigan

Curriculum guidelines in MI-Med have a strong orientation toward basic skills and until recently were closely aligned to the state's intended curriculum. But when the state shifted from a skill-centered curriculum in the area of reading to an approach that promotes strategic reading, the district's guidelines were no longer parallel to the state's intended curriculum. This dissonance created a press for the district to include higher order outcomes in the reading curriculum in order to align with the state and resolve the tension.

The current reading curriculum of MI-Med is based on the state's new definition of reading. For example, MI-Med's *Curriculum Guide in Reading* was revised in 1988, after three years of study, to parallel the state's *Essential Goals and Objectives for Reading Instruction*. Moreover, a new district test modeled after the new MEAP reading tests will be implemented in 1989 and given to students in grades 3–6. Even though this district's reading test is similar in format to the new MEAP reading tests because they both assess the process of reading, it does not duplicate the state test. In-services and staff development programs emphasize the teaching of reading as a strategy. Finally, because the state is planning to assess the process approach to writing, the district is also planning to implement writing as part of its assesment program.

Since the new MEAP mathematics tests will not be in place until 1991 and the current MEAP mathematics tests measure basic skills, MI-Med continues to assess basic skills in mathematics. The district has its own criterion-referenced tests which correlate with the district's objectives and also include MEAP-related objectives. Similarly, since the new MEAP science tests will not be in use until 1992, the district's elementary science program continues to emphasize the development of basic science skills. MEAP objectives related to the science processes are included in the district's science curriculum guides. Although there is still a greater emphasis on basic skills in math and science, the press for thinking and understanding will likely increase as the new MEAP tests are implemented.

The interplay between state and district guidelines in MI-Large is different from that in MI-Med. This is mainly because MI-Large preceded the state in emphasizing teaching for thinking and understanding. According to the deputy superintendent, the state's *Essential Goals and Objectives* documents did not play a prominent role in the development of the district's curriculum strands and objectives. In his view, the district had sound, up-to-date tests and curriculum objectives prior to the state's move toward a more balanced curriculum. The lack of dependence on the state's guidelines is further evidenced by the fact that the district has elected to adopt a single textbook series. In contrast, the state does not have a textbook adoption policy. Another way in which MI-Large's emphasis on teaching for thinking and understanding is distinct from the state's is that many of the district-level in-services and workshops focus on programs designed to teach generic thinking skills, as well as to teach for thinking and understanding in specific subject areas. For example, workshops in math and science sometimes focus on the model lessons in the K-3 curriculum guides, which include higher order outcomes. These model lessons are designed to provide teachers with an idea of how to teach thinking in more concrete ways. Finally, MI-Large has a policy calling for periodic reviews of the curriculum in specific subject areas, whereas the state does not.

Nevertheless, since the state's primary source of influence on districts is through the MEAP tests, it is likely that policymakers in MI-Large will make a deliberate effort to modify their curriculum guidelines to accommodate the upcoming changes in the MEAP tests. For instance, the district has already sponsored in-services focusing on the state's new definition of reading. According to one of the curriculum specialists, attention to student thinking and understanding has increased in the area of reading due to the upcoming MEAP reading tests. In other words, the fact that the state's emphasis on teaching for understanding and thinking will probably differ from that of the district is likely to create at least some minor dissonance between state and local guidelines that district policymakers will seek to resolve.

California's strong press for curriculum reform

According to our recent survey of policy guidelines in all 50 states (Freeman 1989), California's efforts to persuade teachers to teach for understanding and thinking are more comprehensive than those in any other state. These efforts are advanced across six different policy fronts: curriculum frameworks, K-8 curriculum guides, handbooks, statewide tests, state-level textbook adoptions, and in-service activities. Curriculum frameworks cover seven different subject areas: mathematics, science, health, English/language arts, history/social science, foreign languages, and the visual and performing arts, and serve as the cornerstone of policy design. All of the other initiatives are directly tied to ways that the intended curriculum is described in these documents. Framework portrayals of the intended curriculum include narrative descriptions of what should be taught in a given subject area, how the subject should be taught, and to a lesser extent, how student achievement in that area should be assessed. Without exception, recent frameworks press teachers to move away from a skill-centered curriculum and toward a curriculum that promotes student understanding and thinking.

Two sets of documents elaborate on the framework's philosophical descriptions. Model curriculum guides for K-8 translate the frameworks into guidelines for elementary and middle school teachers. This set of documents provides a general sense of desired classroom practice, including specific examples of the kinds of lessons teachers can use to engage pupils in higher order thinking in each subject area. Handbooks provide checklists that local curriculum planners can use as guides in assessing the quality of the instructional programs they provide in each subject.

Textbook adoptions and statewide tests lend authority to the other initiatives. California is the only state that has aggressively negotiated with textbook publishers to develop books or other instructional materials that support the state's call for curriculum reform (i.e., that align with the new frameworks [see Freeman, 1989]). Likewise, California is one of a small number of states that is actively revising its statewide testing program to support the reform movement. For instance, grade 3 and 6 tests will be introduced in 1991 that will (a) align with the new frameworks and (b) include performance tests as well as paper-and-pencil tests in four different subject areas. Finally, California sponsors a number of professional development activities that train teachers and administrators to serve as leaders in implementing the curriculum frameworks in their local districts. Among the many assumptions and features that characterize California's curriculum reform initiatives, five are likely to stand out as particularly salient in the state's curriculum guidelines:

1. The state's emphasis on teaching for thinking and understanding is not compromised by a countervailing emphasis on mastery of basic skills. Nor is it compromised by the assumption that basic skills must be mastered as a precondition for working on higher order outcomes.

2. The press for understanding and thinking is directed toward all students (not just the higher achievers).

3. The design and implementation of curriculum initiatives is guided by a seven-year cycle plan in which one subject area serves as the focus of concern each year. Districts that voluntarily comply with this plan will review their instructional programs in a given subject area during the two-year period following the release of the framework for that area. These reviews will culminate with district adoptions of textbooks from the state approved list.

4. Recent curriculum frameworks describe desired learner outcomes in narrative terms and not as discrete goals and objectives. This action is grounded in the assumption that discrete lists of goals and objectives move teachers away from, rather than toward holistic and integrated approaches to instruction that emphasize higher order outcomes.

5. The state's curriculum initiatives are guidelines, not mandates for local districts. However, most of these initiatives are backed by legislative statutes (i.e., legal authority).

An overview of curriculum guidelines in CA-Med

Curriculum guidelines in this medium-sized district are advanced across four policy fronts: (a) instructional objectives in four different subject areas (mathematics, science, English/language arts, and history/social science); (b) a district testing program; (c) district-wide adoptions of instructional materials; and (d) inservice activities. Two different types of objectives for each grade (K–6) and subject are listed in the K–12 curriculum manual distributed to each teacher: (a) 'essential grade level skills' that portray grade level expectations for all students; and (b) 'extension of skills' that describe activities for more able students. The process of revising objectives in each of the four subject areas parallels the state's seven-year cycle plan. During the three-year period following the release of a new framework, the district (*a*) conducts a self assessment in the subject area represented by the framework (using lists of 'elementary quality criteria' provided by the State Department of Education as guides), (*b*) develops, pilot tests, and implements an updated list of district objectives (using the state's curriculum frameworks, model curriculum standards, and K–8 curriculum guides as resources), and (*c*) selects instructional materials for all schools in the district (from the list of materials approved by the state).

The district testing program includes the Comprehensive Test of Basic Skills (CTBS), a standardized achievement test in grades 1–8, and tests of basic competencies in reading, writing, and mathematics administered in grades 5 and 9. The latter tests are designed by the district and focus squarely on the lists of essential skills. The tests are a product of an earlier state-level accountability initiative calling for districts to develop a system for demonstrating that a given student has mastered essential skills as a precondition for receiving a high school diploma. To assist teachers in identifying areas of program weakness, diagnostic profiles of student performance are prepared annually for each school across all three tests, CAP, CTBS, and basic competency tests.

The district also has a carefully designed procedure for selecting the instructional materials used district-wide. According to the district's curriculum manual, adopted materials must 'foster critical thinking'. The recent adoption of a mathematics text illustrates the selection process. First, members of the district's mathematics committee underwent a year of training (some of which focused on the state framework and curriculum guide) as a precondition for updating the district's mathematics objectives. The objectives then served as criteria for selecting a textbook series from the list of six mathematics series approved by the state. The series ultimately selected was generally recognized as the one that most closely aligned with the state's curriculum framework.

During the year this textbook series was first introduced, almost all of the district's in-service activities centered on helping teachers use the new books successfully. During the preceding year, all teachers were required to participate in a workshop focusing on methods for teaching problem solving. In addition to workshops centering on textbook use, the district's professional development program features a variety of optional activities listed in a *Professional Development Catalog*. Each of these activities centers on teaching critical thinking, either within specific subject areas or as a generic skill. The offerings for a given year typically focus on the subject area in which textbooks are about to be selected or on one of the district's own goals (e.g., writing across the curriculum).

An overview of curriculum guidelines in CA-Large

Approximately 25 of the more than 100 schools in the CA-Large district participate in a special program for racially isolated schools. The Basic Skills Mastery Program (BSMP [a pseudonym]) began in 1980 in response to a court order to improve students' scores on Comprehensive Tests of Basic Skills (CTBS). Centering on basic skills in reading, mathematics, and language arts, BSMP programs are highly structured, focus on stated objectives, and feature a mastery learning model that is backed by district-designed tests and a centralized recordkeeping system. BSMP teachers are supported by extensive in-service activities, a resource teacher in each school, and an abundance of instructional materials.

The district's curriculum guidelines are conditioned, in part, by the perceived needs of BSMP schools and are communicated through four policy initiatives: (*a*) teacher's guides in mathematics, science, social studies, literature, and the arts; (*b*) district-wide textbook adoptions; (c) district-sponsored in-service activities; and (d) a district testing program. The teachers' guides supplement and shape teachers' use of the textbook and other instructional materials in each subject area. For example, in mathematics the teachers' guide mandates that all chapters in the newly adopted textbook series will be covered by the end of the school year. Whereas the instructional objectives presented in the guide are taken verbatim from the textbook, the district has added its own homework assignments and chapter tests. The chapter tests emphasize higher order outcomes to a greater extent than those in the book. Alternative forms of these tests also support teachers' use of the mastery model. As a supplement to the guide, teachers in BSMP schools receive an auxiliary support package that includes extra worksheets and homework assignments as well as scripted lesson plans for troublesome lessons.

The district-wide selection of instructional materials is the only clear link between state and district curriculum guidelines in CA-Large. Stated in simplest terms, the state approves only those materials that align with its curriculum frameworks. The district then takes steps to encourage teachers to follow these materials closely. The textbooks selection process in CA-Large is guided by a detailed master plan and conforms to a modified version of the state's seven-year cycle plan (with the introduction of new textbooks in the four major content areas typically spaced at two-year intervals).

The district also sponsors in-service activities to support teachers' use of state-approved instructional materials. For instance, during the year preceding the introduction of the new mathematics textbooks, four teachers from each school participated in three-day workshops focusing on the new texts. All elementary school principals also participated in a one-day workshop centering on textbook implementation. Those who were trained then taught other teachers in their buildings how to use the new books for the next year. At that time, the district also offered in-services focusing primarily on methodological problems associated with teachers' use of the new books (e.g., use of manipulatives). In recent years, some of the district's in-service programs have also focused directly on the infusion of thinking skills into the curriculum.

The district's testing program includes district-designed, curriculum-embedded tests presented in the teachers' guides (described earlier), and CTBS achievement tests administered in grades 5, 7, 9, and 11. The curriculum-embedded tests align with content covered in the book and play an important role in implementing the mastery model of instruction; the CTBS tests are only moderately aligned with the textbooks' content and are used primarily to identify program strengths and shortcomings. Because both of these tests continue to play a more prominent role in BSMP schools than in the regular schools (CTBS scores must still be reported to the court), BSMP teachers are likely to be more test conscious than their colleagues in other schools.

Interplay between state and district guidelines in California

The interplay between state and district curriculum guidelines is relatively straightforward in CA-Large. Here, policymakers reason that if the state approves only those instructional materials that align with the state's curriculum frameworks, then the district's efforts to encourage teachers to use these materials should move schools toward the state's intended curriculum. In that sense, the teachers' guides, textbook adoptions, and in-service programs all press teachers to implement the state's curriculum guidelines. In mathematics, these guidelines also move BSMP and non-BSMP schools toward a more common instructional program. Yet, these initiatives do not disrupt the integrity of the district's instructional management system in either category of schools. This system focuses primarily on mastery of basic skills and is in many ways at odds with teaching for understanding and thinking as depicted in the state's curriculum framework, particularly in BSMP schools. In other words, the district's curriculum guidelines in mathematics represent a straightforward compromise between state and district goals.

The interplay between state and district guidelines in CA-Med is more complex than in CA-Large. In this setting, the district's curriculum guidelines reflect policymakers' resolution of the tension between the state's recent call for curriculum reform, on the one hand, and the district's perceived need to ensure that all high school graduates can demonstrate mastery of basic skills as outlined in earlier state initiatives on the other. As noted earlier, recent state-level curriculum guidelines were considered throughout the design of the district's curriculum. In two policy arenas these guidelines prevailed: the adoption of a new mathematics series that closely aligns with the state's curriculum framework, and the provision of in-service activities that augment teachers' use of this series. If teachers look to the new textbooks for guidance in deciding 'what' and 'how' to teach (which was the common impression among those we interviewed), these district initiatives should move CA-Med's teachers even closer to the state's intended curriculum.

However, in the other two policy arenas – objectives and tests – the state's call to teach for understanding and thinking in mathematics was counterbalanced by the district's specification of essential skills for high school graduation requirements. Although the clear intent of recent efforts to update the district's mathematics objectives was to revise these statements to more closely align with the state framework and K–8 curriculum guide, these efforts fall short of the mark. For example, two of the district's grade 6 mathematics objectives read as follows:

1.   add, subtract, multiply, or divide fractions or mixed numerals;
2.   use ratios to compare two quantities, find a ratio equal to a given ratio.

The parallel objectives in the state's mathematics framework read:

1.   understand the concept of fractions and their order and, on the basis of this understanding, find their sums, differences, and products;
2.   understand and use ratio and proportion to solve problems. (California State Department of Education 1985: 27)

As these examples suggest, the district's objectives fail to capture the full thrust of the state's call for a meaning-based, rather than a skills-based, mathematics curriculum. This mismatch is further reinforced by the decision to list district objectives in two columns: objectives to be achieved by all students and extension activities 'for students who need an extra challenge'. The state framework takes clear exception to the district's assumption that students should master essential skills as a precondition for working on more challenging tasks.

As noted earlier, the district objectives are backed by the district's testing program. But there are no obvious incentives for teachers to follow their new textbooks closely, nor are there any clear links between the objectives and the texts (e.g., co-ordinated textbook assignments for each objective). In this current form, district guidelines in CA-Med represent a compromise between state and district goals. Two policy initiatives – the district's and tests – focus primarily on the local goal of ensuring that all high school graduates can demonstrate mastery of basic skills, while the other two initiatives – the recent mathematics textbook adoption and district in-service program – move teachers in the direction of the state's intended curriculum.

It is likely that the two California districts will move from a lingering message of basic skills accountability toward an increased emphasis on higher order thinking. This transition will take time for two reasons: (1) the basic skills emphasis has been legitimized by court action and (2) basic skills assessments are currently in place in both districts. This suggests to states and districts trying to encourage teachers to teach for student thinking and understanding that it takes time to dismantle and rebuild curriculum policies.

Discussion

Based on an analysis of the six districts in three states, we conclude that neither the inverse nor the direct model adequately portrays the state–district relationship. The inverse policy relationship posits that strong state-level curriculum policies will be countered by weak district-level guidelines, and vice versa. In our examination of six districts in three states, we did not find local policymakers deferring to strong state policy guidelines, or compensating for weak policies by designing stronger guidelines of their own. Likewise, evidence from our study does not support the direct state–district relationship model which argues that state and local policy guidelines mirror those at the state level.

Rather, the relationship between state and district policies is best described by the interactive model. There was a dynamic and purposeful interplay between state and district curriculum guidelines across each of the six districts and three states in our sample. In each case, district policymakers made a deliberate effort to modify the district's curriculum framework to accommodate changes in state curriculum guidelines but also designed policies according to district needs.

Variations in styles of accommodation resulted in significant differences in the ways that state guidelines were implemented by districts. Moreover, in at least some districts, there was evidence of a compromise between what state policymakers intended and local actor needs (Fuhrman and Elmore 1990). Thus, our analyses provide clear support for the interactive model. Nevertheless, we would make one minor refinement in the portrayal of state and district policy interactions as they apply to curriculum guidelines for elementary schools.

Two models of state and district interaction

Our analyses suggest that districts tend to adopt one of two distinct models of interaction with state curriculum guidelines for elementary schools. We would label these models (a) district accommodation/compromise and (b) district compliance/augmentation.

District accommodation/compromise model: Districts that adopt the district autonomy/compromise model have sufficient resources and commitment to design their own independent curriculum guidelines focusing on local needs and priorities. In this study, these districts included the two California districts and the large district in Michigan.

Backed by a clear sense of autonomy, policymakers in these districts respond to changes in state guidelines in ways that maintain the integrity of the local curriculum framework. For example, when responding to changes in California's state-level curriculum guidelines in mathematics, policymakers in CA-Med made only minor changes in the district's instructional objectives. Similarly, the reading program in MI-Large remained basically intact despite significant change at the state level. And, in both cases, stated goals and objectives were still touted as the core of the district's curriculum guidelines. Nevertheless, changes in the state's guidelines did elicit important accommodations across other areas of policy activity (e.g., textbook adoptions, in-service programs). In CA-Large, district policymakers selected a mathematics textbook series from the list of state-approved materials. But they did not significantly alter the central component of the district's curriculum framework (an instructional management system that supplements and shapes teachers' use of the texts).

District compliance/augmentation model: Districts that adopt the compliance/augmentation model generally implement state-level policies, yet sometimes go beyond these recommendations with locally-devised initiatives. The two districts in Florida and the medium district in Michigan provide the clearest illustration of the district compliance/augmentation model. In Florida virtually all of the state's *Minimum Student Performance Standards* and *Standards of Excellence* were cited in the two districts' curriculum guides. Thus, there were no clear distinctions between state and district curricula in the subject areas that the state guidelines addressed. Moreover, both Florida districts focused teachers' attention on the state's intended curriculum in these subjects through other policy initiatives (e.g., local tests of state objectives).

Yet, these two districts also augmented the state's intended curriculum by designing curriculum guidelines for other subject areas. In FL-Med the district developed its own goals and objectives for the music curriculum and introduced a comprehensive 'Writing to Read' program in kindergarten and first grade, which included the process writing approach. Similarly, FL-Large created its own goals and objectives in music, art, health, social studies, science, mathematics, reading, writing, physical education, literature, and language arts. These actions augmented the state's curriculum in two ways: (*a*) by providing direction for teachers across a broader range of subject areas; and (*b*) by expanding the state's relatively limited efforts to encourage elementary school teachers to teach for understanding and thinking.

Similarly, MI-Med augmented state-level policies in art. MI-Med is using the Discipline-Based Art Education approach which emphasized aesthetics, art criticism, art history, and art production. The Michigan Council for the Arts provides district matching funds for lectures, artist demonstrations, performances, and visual arts exhibitions, which all go beyond the production of art. Over the past two years, this district has been working on a comprehensive plan to integrate art with other subject matter areas. For instance, the role of art could be included in the discussion of civilizations during social studies, in holography during mathematics, and in illustrations during literature.

In our view, the distinction between these two styles of accommodation is important for understanding and predicting the ways in which local districts respond to changes in state policy guidelines. New state initiatives are likely to yield relatively modest changes in local curriculum guidelines in those districts that conform to the district accommodation/compromise model. In contrast, new state initiatives are almost certain to result in major changes in local guidelines in districts that conform to the district compliance/augmentation model.

For other states and districts attempting to focus on higher order thinking, our analysis of interaction in the six districts of three states suggests that complex and idiosyncratic interactions exist between the state and the district. These interactions may impact upon what teachers teach in different ways.

As Porter *et al.*, have indicated (1986), tests influence what is taught in classrooms.

As evidenced in California and Florida, teachers receive conflicting messages about what to teach. In California, the state which has the most coherent state-level initiatives calling for teachers to teach for higher order thinking, districts continue to work with basic skills curricula and testing programs. Florida's state policy continues to require basic skills testing. These basic skills initiatives have been legitimized by court actions. Until these basic skills programs are dismantled, teachers will continue to receive conflicting messages about what to teach.

In addition, as demonstrated in California, the transition to teach for student thinking and understanding takes time. Teaching for higher order thinking may not be within the well-rehearsed knowledge of all teachers, thus signaling the possibility of resistance. There is then, a need for states and districts to persuade teachers to teach for higher order thinking and provide appropriate support and resources.

Finally, for states and districts wishing to move teachers to teach for thinking and understanding, we suggest that the state–district interaction is not restricted to predictable district responses to state initiatives. As our study demonstrates, the role of local curriculum expertise and availability of resources influence what is taught in elementary classrooms. As evidenced in the augmenting districts in this study, a variety of local initiatives are likely to influence and effect the idiosyncratic state–district relationship. There are a number of mitigating factors which press districts to adopt one style of accommodation rather than another. Some of these influences include: the financial resources of the state and district, the subject matter expertise of inservice personnel, or a strong local leader. The acknowledged complexity of interactions between the state and districts is fertile ground for future study.

References

ASTUTO, T. and CLARK, D. (1986) *The Effects of Federal Education Policy changes on policy and program development in state and local education agencies* (Bloomington, IN: Policy Studies Center of the University Council for Educational Administration).

CALIFORNIA STATE DEPARTMENT OF EDUCATION (1985) *Mathematics Framework for California Public Schools* (Sacramento, CA: CAL SDE, Curriculum Framework and Textbook Development Unit).

COHEN, D.K. (1982) 'Policy and organization: the impact of state and federal education on school governance', *Harvard Educational Review*, 52 (4), pp. 474–499.

FLORIDA DEPARTMENT OF EDUCATION (1983) *Minimum Student Performance Standards for Florida Schools, 1984–85 Through 1988–89: Beginning Grades 3, 5, 8, and 11, Mathematics, Science, Social Studies, and Writing* (Tallahassee: FLA DoE).

FLORIDA DEPARTMENT OF EDUCATION (1984) *Student Performance Standards of Excellence for Florida Schools in Mathematics, Sciences, Social Studies, and Writing-:o-grades three, five, eight and twelve* (1984–85 through 1988–89) (Tallahassee: FLA DoE).

FLORIDA DEPARTMENT OF EDUCATION (1985) *Minimum Student Performance Standards for Florida Schools, 1985–86, 1986–87, 1987–88. 1988–89, 1989–90: Beginning Grades 3, 5, 8, and 11, Reading, Writing, and Mathematics* (Tallahassee: FLA DoE).

FLORIDA DEPARTMENT OF EDUCATION (1986) *Minimum Student Performance Standards for Florida Schools, 1986–87, 1987–88, 1988–89, 1989–90: Beginning Grades 3, 5, 8, and 11, computer literacy and science* (Tallahassee: FLA DoE).

FREEMAN, D.J. (1983) *Relations Between State and District Policy: Objectives and Tests* (Montreal, Canada: American Educational Research Association).

FREEMAN, D.J. (1989) *State Guidelines for Reshaping Academic Curricula in Elementary Schools: a 50-State Survey*. Elementary Subjects Center Series No. 10 (East Lansing: Michigan State University, Institute for Research on Teaching, Center for the Learning and Teaching of Elementary Subjects).

FUHRMAN, S., CLUNE, W. and ELMORE, R.F. (1988) 'Research on education reform: Lessons on the implementation of policy', *Teachers College Record*, 90 (2), pp. 237–258.

FUHRMAN, S. and ELMORE, R. F. (1990) 'Understanding local control in the wake of state education reform', *Educational Evaluation and Policy Analysis, 12* (1), pp. 82–96.

MARZANO, R. J., BRANDT, R. S., HUGHES, C. S., JONES, B. F., PRESSEISSEN, B. Z., RANKIN, S. C. and SUHOR, S. (1988) *Dimensions of Thinking: A Framework for Curriculum and Instruction* 1st ed (Alexandria, VA: Association for Supervision and Curriculum Development).

MICHIGAN DEPARTMENT OF EDUCATION (1988) *Michigan Essential Goals and Objectives for Mathematics Education* (Lansing: MI DoE).

MICHIGAN STATE BOARD OF EDUCATION (1985a) *Essential Performance Objectives for Science Education* (Lansing: MI SBE).

MICHIGAN STATE BOARD OF EDUCATION (1985b) *Essential Goals and Objectives for Writing* (Lansing: MS SBE).

MICHIGAN STATE BOARD OF EDUCATION (1986) *Essential Goals and Objectives for Reading Education* (Lansing: MI SBE).

MICHIGAN STATE BOARD OF EDUCATION (1987a) *Essential Goals and Objectives for Social Studies Education in Michigan (K–12)* (Lansing: MI SBE).

MICHIGAN STATE BOARD OF EDUCATION (1987b) *Michigan Educational Assessment Program: Blueprint for New MEAP Reading Tests* (Lansing: MI SBE).

MICHIGAN STATE BOARD OF EDUCATION (1987c) *Michigan K–12 Program Standards of Quality* (Lansing: MI SBE).

MICHIGAN STATE BOARD OF EDUCATION (1990) *Michigan Essential Goals and Objectives for Arts Education (K–12)* (Lansing: MI SBE).

PORTER, A. C., FLODEN, R. E., FREEMAN, D. J., SCHMIDT, W. H. and SCHWILLE, J. R. (1986) *Content Determinants*. Research Series No. 179 (East Lansing: Michigan State University, Institute for Research on Teaching).

5   *Graduation vs. education: reform effect for at-risk youth*

Janice H. Patterson

Because American society equates education with high school graduation, many Americans will judge the success of school reforms that increased graduation requirements by the extent to which high school drop-out rates have increased, decreased, or remained the same. This chapter explores the outcome of school level responses to state mandates that demanded increased graduation requirements, and the effect of these reforms on youth at risk of academic failure. It pays particular attention to one district's use of state monies set aside for drop-out prevention. In addition, the related question of whether graduation or education is the real agenda is discussed. Finally, recommendations are offered for mediating some of the effects of the state requirements and for improving the likelihood of at-risk youth absorbing a curriculum with higher expectations and graduating as competent members of society.

Introduction

Educators and political analysts are familiar with the alarming statistics on high school drop-out rates. Only 60% of Hispanics complete high school (Hodgkinson 1985:10). In New York public schools, one in three students drops out (Carnegie Foundation 1988:xiv). In Boston, 44% of high school students drop-out, and of those who do reach 12th grade, over 40% are functionally illiterate. But it is only in the last decade that the national consciousness has been raised in an attempt to understand the dimensions of the drop-out problem, including its enormous cost to society.

Our economic competitiveness in the world market will suffer as the flow of educated workers is reduced. Analysts predict we will be plagued with lagging productivity, higher training costs of unskilled workers, and traditional areas of high employment, such as clerical and sales, will languish from a lack of employees who have the basic math, reading, and communication skills (Levin 1989:3). Tax revenue will be lost as drop-outs suffer unemployment or an unending trail of low-wage jobs. In addition, the cost of public services will continue to soar as high school drop-outs find themselves on public assistance for survival. Some of those who lack employable skills may turn to illegal activities as an avenue of income and to fill their free time. Pallas *et al.* (1989:19) found that 'the estimated cost to the nation of the 500,000 students per year who leave school prior to graduation is about $50 billion in foregone lifetime earnings alone'. They further suggest that increasing national expenditure on education by 50% would actually be a cost-effective policy.

Since 1983, and the publication of *A Nation at Risk*, school reform has been at the top of the national agenda for education. Yet before 1980 there were few rewards for districts to keep valid, reliable drop-out data. Social issues, particularly in the inner-cities – such as immigration, drugs, crime, alienation, unemployed youth, and early pregnancy – combined with a call for increased emphasis on keeping students in school from the federal and state level, have forced districts to adopt more stringent data collection procedures for tracking students at risk for dropping out. Thus, the fear of rising drop-out rates has

0268–0939/90 $3.00 © 1990 Taylor & Francis Ltd.

stimulated an increased deployment of resources that has improved the chances that low achieving students will meet the requirements established for high school graduation. But let us hope that the commitment of resources goes beyond shepherding students through the requirements for graduation. Let us hope that schools will also take this opportunity to strive to prepare our youth for a lifetime of learning by teaching them the skills of learning, not just preparing them to pass a graduation test.

As of February 1988, 45 states had enacted legislation designed to shore up education in the United States. The reforms have involved strengthening high school graduation requirements, and in 15 states, the successful completion of an 'exit test'. Further, some states have appropriated additional money for counseling and remediation, resources necessary to the success of any attempt to curb the high school drop-out rate.

Because American society equates education with high school graduation, many Americans will judge the success of school reforms that increased graduation requirements by the extent to which high school drop-out rates have increased, decreased, or remained the same (e.g., Committee for Economic Development, Research, and Policy 1987). Early in the reform movement, scholars, practitioners, and policymakers began to worry about the effects of reforms on potential dropouts. There was concern that a restricted core of curriculum requirements might lead to (1) greater academic stratification and less student choice in schools; (2) conflict with other demands on students by families, jobs, and extracurricular activities because of increased time demands; and (3) greater student failure, frustration, and dropping out because of increased academic demands (Hamilton 1984, McDill et al. 1986). Has the increased attention to our education deficit been a boon or a bane to local systems in educating low achievers at risk of dropping out of high school?

This paper explores the outcome of school level responses to state mandates that demanded increased graduation requirements, and the effect of these reforms on youth at risk of academic failure; in addition, the related question of whether graduation or education is the goal is discussed. Two analyses of school responses are discussed. The first examined activity in four states that represented a wide range of policy activity. The second focused on high schools in one urban district two years after the state legislature had authorized and encouraged drop-out prevention programs throughout the state. Finally, recommendations are offered for mediating some of the effects of the state requirements and for improving the likelihood that at-risk youth will absorb a curriculum with higher expectations and graduate as competent members of society. First, definitions of at-risk youth are presented, with information about why youth at risk become drop-outs.

Youth at risk

What is sometimes called the third wave of educational reform has focussed on at-risk youth (Rodriguez et al. 1988:11). There are many definitions of at-risk youth. Levin (1989:1) describes at-risk students as those 'who lack the home and community resources to fully benefit from conventional schooling practices. Such students are especially concentrated among minority groups, immigrants, non-English-speaking families, single-parent families, and poverty populations. Because of poverty, cultural differences, or linguistic differences they tend to have low academic achievement and to experience high secondary school drop-out rates.' He has found that by 6th grade they are two years behind, by 12th grade, four years behind (not including results from those who dropped out and could not be tested). He believes that more than 50% of all 17-year-olds in the school system are at risk (Levin 1986).

Patricia Williams' study (1989:8) of Dade county's drop-out prevention programs (discussed below) includes the following profile of nine characteristics: exceptional education, limited English proficiency, high rate of absence, age above grade level average, low reading scores, more than three schools attended, low GPA, suspensions, and severity (has two or more of the nine characteristics).

The definition that this work leans toward is one noted by Patricia Graham (1987:30): 'My simple definition of a child who is at risk in schools is one who is not achieving academically. Children are at risk in many other domains, through poverty, health, family, or community circumstances. The task of the school is to overcome the school problem ... '

Why do students drop out? One is low academic achievement; data suggest that a pattern of failure often begins in elementary school. Other reasons are a desire to work full time to help support themselves or their families and, for females, pregnancy or marriage.

But the major reason students give for dropping out is a dislike of school, a feeling that it is boring and irrelevant. Thus, the worry that an increase in standards would have an exponential effect on youth at risk who are already having a hard time engaging in academic life – who also have economic concerns and may be dealing with chemical dependancy, pregnancy, and other personal problems – is quite reasonable. In fact, will the new regulations influence those who most need a diploma to improve the quality of their life to simply leave school (Sinclair and Ghory 1987)?

Response to crisis: case I

Through surveys and interviews, these studies examined local school responses or policy activity in four states. Clune *et al.* (1989) and Fuhrman *et al.* (1988) examined data collected from four-states – Arizona, California, Florida, and Pennsylvania – selected to represent a range of policy activity, including increased graduation requirements. (Because the methodology for the larger study has been described in the works cited, it is reported here in a briefer form.) Within each state, districts were selected to represent the same range of policy impact and local capacity inherent in the state level selections. As a result, districts selected included those that would need to initiate more change and those that would need to do very little in response to state level activity, determined in large part by existing requirements and local capacity. Within each district, the school, again, represented a range of policy impact and activity. The four-state sample included 24 districts, 18 elementary schools, nine junior high schools, and 32 high schools. There were 524 interviews conducted at the local level. District respondents included superintendents, assistant superintendents, and specialists within the central administration office. In addition, board members, journalists, union leaders, and representatives of parent/teacher organizations were interviewed. School level respondents included teachers, principals, assistant principals, department heads, and counselors.

Before discussing the major findings on increased graduation requirements that have particular implications for at-risk youth, it is important to consider the following district-developed policies that interact with increased graduation requirements to further raise student standards beyond state minimums. (See Appendix A for state graduation requirements, changes in these requirements, average ranking on student achievement, and the use of high school exit exams).

1. Some districts in the sample reported that students can run out of time to graduate from high school due to repeated failing of required courses. When students have taken the maximum number of allowed credits, they must leave high school whether or not they have attained the grade point average required for graduation.

2. In states and districts where the increase in requirements resulted in the addition of new courses at the local school level, there was considerable variation in the number of periods per school day. In general, the number of periods ranged from five to eight. In some cases, districts' school boards extended the school day to preserve electives, such as vocational education, and allow time for retakes and remediation.

3. In some cases, students must pass high school exit exams before they can receive a diploma irrespective of courses taken or grades achieved. These tests measure basic skill acquisition and generally required about a 6th grade reading level. All districts that instituted competency tests were in states that required exit exams; the districts' tests were developed specifically to prepare students for the state examinations.

4. To assure that all students have exposure to the same content in a school district, some districts instituted subject matter examinations as end-of-course requirements. Some respondents reported that students must pass these exams to get credit for the course.

5. Where a minimum grade point is established as a condition for graduation, students may take the required courses and number of credits and yet never graduate. The consequences of such a policy were reflected in conversations with respondents, particularly high school counselors, and are presented later in this paper.

Major effects of requirements

Overall, the most common change in course offerings was the addition of math and science courses, with 12 of the 13 districts surveyed reported additions in these subjects; 17 of 19 schools in these districts reported additions in math, and 16 of 19 reported additions in science. On average, four sections were added in mathematics and seven in science.[1] Overwhelmingly, additional sections in math and science were at the basic level. Of the 17 schools adding math sections, 15 reported additions of basic, remedial or general math. Of the 16 schools adding science sections, 14 reported additions of basic, remedial, or general science. In most cases, the students in the 'general or basic' courses were those judged by schools to be low achievers in need of basic instruction.

The schools and districts most affected by increased requirements were those most likely to house the greatest proportion of youth at risk of academic failure. As one would expect, districts and schools with little change tended to be affluent, suburban, and white. As reported by Clune *et al.* (1989), college prep students were mostly unaffected by the reforms because they were already taking the minimum required by the state and were guided by college entrance requirements.

On the surface, the changes appear positive for low achievers. If students take science or math courses they would not have taken before the reforms, then exposure to additional content can reasonably be assumed to increase content knowledge. Common sense and research support this contention, i.e., increased time on task results in increased academic learning (Berliner 1979). Thus, it would be reasonable to assume that students who (before the reforms) would have completed a 9th grade general math course as the terminal instruction in mathematics, are now taking algebra. Yet, policy analysts such as McLaughlin (1976, 1987), Marsh (1985), and Purkey and Smith (1983) reported that the implementation process within the school determines the *real* results for students.

Thus we must ask how real are the changes in students' opportunities to learn math and science as a result of increased offerings at the school level. For instance, many respondents reported that higher standards were pushing kids out of school:

> I have no data, but I think the graduation requirements have increased student dropouts. Forty per cent of the students in this district have at least one failure by the time they are seniors. We have a 16% drop-out rate. The requirements make it more likely for someone to be needing requirements who is over age, and that makes the student likely to drop out. Who wants to take an English course when they are 20? (High school principal, Arizona)

> The school has fewer graduates because some students can't make it through general math. Students are coming into that class with only a 4th- or 5th-grade level knowledge of math, even though the state requires that students have a 6th-grade proficiency for graduation from 8th-grade. (High school teacher, Arizona)

> For the college prep kids, the new requirements are fine; for the average students, they just result in a higher drop-out rate. (High school teacher, California)

> Many students feel they can't always meet certain standards. The emphasis is on academic students, and many students' interests lie in the trades. Because of the mandated requirements in academics, there is little time for other things. What happens is they stop attending. There has been an increase in the drop-out rate, no question. (High school teacher, Pennsylvania)

Still, few quoted statistics in support of their beliefs, and other respondents believed the opposite – that drop-out rates were unaffected or that students were graduating in increased numbers:

> No effect on drop-out rate. More drop-out prevention programs were introduced at the same time that the graduation requirements were implemented. To help lower ability students, we lowered class sizes in classes with lower ability to 20, and we raised regular class size to 35 + . (High school counselor, California)

> There is no effect on the drop-out rate, but slower students are taking longer to get through the requirements. (High school principal, California)

Even in cases where respondents had solid knowledge of the drop-out rate, attributing it to an increase in requirements was difficult, if not impossible. Consider what one of the Florida high school principals reported on the issue:

> When kids drop out of school, they don't say they dropped out because of increased requirements. They give responses that just aren't true, but may be acceptable, such as they need to get a job to help support the family. I don't remember anyone ever saying to me that they were dropping out of school because of the RAISE bill that increased graduation requirements.

Ultimately, the connection between higher standards and high school graduation is inconclusive. It is difficult, based on these data, to determine whether drop-outs increased or decreased as a result of increased graduation requirements. (Williams 1987 discusses issues and recommendations related to calculating drop-out figures.) But new quantitative data find higher standards related to lower mean drop-out rates (Bryk and Thum 1989). Graduation rates are improving nationally (Ginsburg *et al*. 1988). Across the states in this study, some reported an improvement and others a decline in graduation rates (see table 1).

Table 1.   Graduation rate in core states.

State	Graduation rate adjusted for migration and unclassified students (Rank among 50 states)	
	1986	*1982*
Arizona	63.0 (47)	63.4 (44t)
California	66.7 (41)	60.1 (49)
Florida	62.0 (50)	60.2 (48)
Pennsylvania	78.5 (14)	76.0 (16)

Note: The adjusted graduation rate was calculated by dividing the number of public high school graduates by public grade enrollment four years earlier. Ninth-grade enrollments included a prorated portion of the secondary school students who were unclassified by grade. Graduation rates were also corrected for interstate population immigration. Information on the number of people of graduating age receiving GEDs is not currently available.

Source: US Department of Education, Office of Planning, Budget and Evaluation, February, 1988.

Interviews with 70 high school teachers in the four states revealed that most believed that increased standards gave low achieving students an increased opportunity to participate in and to gain knowledge in science. In some cases, teachers reported that students who would not have had a third science course were benefiting from taking a course and having exposure to content that they would never have had otherwise.

In spite of positive effects, however, teachers also perceived negatives from the increased graduation requirements. Fifty-three per cent expressed concern about students losing the opportunity to take electives. They pointed out many times in the interviews that low-achieving students, those at greatest risk of dropping out, are those most in need of some engagement in school activity and that, in fact, the electives are often what gets students out of bed in the morning to come to school.

One high school counselor reported that, in spite of the requirement for four years of English, she often delayed the first year of English until the sophomore year to juggle in a 9th-grade elective; she believed that the students having something to look forward to each day was critical.

Other effects of increased requirements

In the districts in this four-state sample, the dedication to keeping students in school did stimulate alternative routes to graduation for those students unable to make it during the regular school day. Popular strategies were GED training, night classes, and redefining courses.

Because students enrolled in special programs are not counted as drop-outs, alternatives to the regular high school curriculum mushroomed. For instance, one Florida school created a GED training class. A 16-year-old student enrolled in the class could take the GED at age 16 instead of 18 and still get a diploma.

Night school was another alternative route. Students who would have been forced to drop out for economic reasons could work during the day and continue school at night. Many day teachers complained that night school courses were not as rigorous as the same courses offered during the day and that they acted to decrease motivation for daytime attendance.[2] However, in a California district, students taking community college courses in the evenings for make-up credit for high school course work received less credit than if the course was taken during the day. One more strategy was for districts and schools to redefine state requirements so that vocational-like courses were acceptable; for instance, to meet state requirements in mathematics – Baking Math and Car Math.

In summary, both positive and negative effects of increased graduation requirements for low-achieving students are evident. Districts, in response to increased graduation requirements, implemented policies and programs that promised to hold greater numbers of students until graduation. These activities were not uniformly productive in terms of improved education, however. There were reports of courses being watered down and of alternative routes to graduation being developed that did not seem to be based on sound educational goals. Thus, at least in some schools, current implementation of increased standards appears to place greater emphasis on graduation than education for youth at risk. The success of the reforms of the 1980s for these students depends on decisions made at the local level to graduate or educate. Improved student achievement will come only if we choose higher standards while providing the educational resources and strategies that enable students to meet them.

Response to crisis: case II

One urban district's response to state level policy is analyzed in this section. The Florida legislature recognized problems and responded to them with a number of reforms, including the RAISE bill and the Drop-out Prevention Act of 1986. This section provides evidence of the early effects of these legislative reform concerns as expressed in interviews with parents and school staff. In 1983, the Florida legislature passed a series of reforms (the RAISE bill) that resulted in the state having the toughest graduation requirements in the country. In 1985, Florida was 48th in retention of high school students (Hodginkson 1985:11), with a 33% drop-out rate (Florida Department of Education 1986). Concern for these students prompted the Florida legislature to pass the Drop-out Prevention Act of 1986, authorizing and defining five prevention programs that school districts were encouraged to offer. Prevention measures focused on providing educational alternatives, disciplinary alternatives, and on education youth services program and on teenage parents and substance abuse.

The legislature also provided for the Center for Drop-out Prevention at the University of Miami. The Center's mission was to provide technical assistance to school districts and community-based groups regarding effective drop-out strategies and to monitor and study results of regulations.

The Center for Drop-out Prevention conducted a study in the spring of 1988 in 22 of

Florida's senior high schools, located in Dade county, to address the issues of whether standards can be raised and drop-out rates lowered at the same time, the impact of these competing forces on actual and potential drop-outs; and the effects on at-risk students of state, district, and school level policies and practices. Patricia Williams' 1989 study, *School Level Response to At-Risk Students*, analyzes the report from the Center and is summarized here.

Dade county is the fourth largest school district in the country (over a quarter of a million students), with a racially, ethnically, and economically mixed population in urban, suburban, and rural locales. Individual drop-out rates for the 20 schools (the two alternative schools were discussed in an appendix) ranged from 1.5 to 12.9, with a mean of 5.8. The smallest school had an enrollment of 1963 and the largest over 3000. Mean percentages for white, black, Hispanic, Asian/Pacific Islanders/American Indians were 29.14, 34.80, 34.74 and 1.31 respectively, reflecting Dade county's large minority population. Percentages of white students in schools ranged from 0.1 to 73.3; black students from 0.6 to 99.3; Hispanic students from 0.5 to 87.4; and Asian/Pacific Islander/American Indians from 0 to 3.2. The largest percentage of students with limited English proficiency was 10.6, the mean 2.62. The mean for students eligible for free or reduced lunch was 10.17.

More effects of requirements

At the beginning of each school year, principals in the districts are provided with a *Drop-out Profile*, to be used as a probability indicator for identifying at-risk students. Students who have two or more of the nine characteristics mentioned earlier in this paper – exceptional educational needs; limited English proficiency; high absence rate; two or more years below grade level average; reading stanine of less than five; attended three, four or more schools; three or more Ds or Fs on GPA; suspensions; and severity – were also targeted for district and, in some cases, school-initiated drop-out prevention efforts. The district's major emphasis was on lower income and minority students.

The areas of greatest concern to school personnel were attendance, academic achievement/credit deficiency, the need for guidance, and the need for job skills or work experience. Nineteen of the 20 regular schools surveyed had programs to address at least one of the first three concerns. Some strategies were district-sponsored or district policy, and others were developed by school personnel on site.

Strategies for improving attendance included contacting parents by mail, telephone, or robot phone (computerized calling system) after five unexcused absences for a semester course and ten from an annual course (although only five schools mentioned complying with this, even though it was district policy); requesting parent conferences after ten unexcused absences (one school); flexible scheduling – a program that permits 60 students to attend school either during the day or at night at hours built around the students' work schedules (two schools); pizza parties for homerooms with the highest attendance, and prizes contributed by local businesses to students with perfect attendance (one school); the Drop-out Prevention Rebate Program – a district-sponsored initiative – which targeted 100 at-risk students for intensive on-site services and included a rebate of $50 per student to the school for each student who remained in school until the end of the year and met the program criteria of attendance, academic achievement, and conduct (eight schools).

The most widely mentioned strategy for boosting academic achievement was various forms of tutoring utilizing teachers and honors students as instructors (11 schools). As well as offering tutoring during, after, and before school and on Saturdays, schools provided language labs for remedial instruction, compensatory education programs for low-level readers, intensive English and math instruction to prepare students for the state assessment test, and tutoring components that were parts of larger programs.

Students who failed to complete course work because of absence and problems coping with a seven-period day, or the number and type of courses required for graduation, were offered optional study halls, make-up schedules, special schedules during summers and night school, flexible scheduling, and adult education programs, as well as share-time programs with vocational technological schools. The introduction of high-interest courses such as drafting and child care into the curriculum was another strategy to improve academic performance and retain students.

The most widely mentioned program initiative in the area of guidance was the district-sponsored Teachers as Advisors Program (14 schools). Teachers selected as advisors assisted individual students in the areas of career development and academic achievement, course selection and planning, credit evaluation, graduation requirements, and post-secondary planning, while maintaining consistent contact with the parents. There were also strategies developed at individual schools, such as a Student Assistance Program, which utilized a counselor, Teacher on Special Assignment, and volunteer teachers.

In addition to these programs, home visits were made by counselors and visiting teachers during the evening. Three schools mentioned using the district-sponsored Students At-risk Program that involved counselors working with at-risk students and their parents in junior high, before the students enter high school.

The use of counselors or other sources of support was emphasized for students with emotional problems. Eight schools participated in group counseling programs, others in the Listener Program, which trains counselors to serve as psychotherapists; and Panthers at Work. Some programs, such as the flexible scheduling program, had guidance components already in place. One school hired a part-time psychologist with discretionary funds.

Nine schools cited the district-sponsored Occupational/Placement Specialist Program, which offered individual and group counseling designed to aid students in the development of career goals. These specialists also conducted exit interviews with students leaving school before graduation to determine their reasons for leaving and to counsel them regarding their educational options. The PIC program, a district and community-based initiative sponsored by the Private Industry Council and South Florida Employment and Training Consortium, was also widely recognized by 11 schools as being a valuable resource. The selection of counselors from the same ethnic and experiential background as students, ethnic support groups that encouraged students to stay in school, and peer counseling programs were also used. Approximately 2900 at-risk students were provided with a multi-year sequence of training and employment opportunities, remedial instruction, counseling, and referrals to social service agencies, where appropriate, as long as they remained in school.

Levels of drop-out prevention activity

One would expect that schools with the largest proportion of at-risk students would have the most drop-out prevention activity. Analyses of the interview and demographic data from the Center's study, however, indicated that personnel from schools with smaller proportions of at-risk students reported more drop-out prevention activity and fewer problems than personnel from schools with large proportions of such students.

The number of activities each school cited as drop-out prevention initiatives, combined with 1986–87 school level demographic data, were used to determine patterns in the sample in levels of drop-out prevention activity. To determine relationships between the characteristics of school populations and the amount of drop-out activity in schools, schools were divided into two categories – those citing six or more activities and those citing fewer than six activities. Although it is not possible to determine from the interview data the effectiveness of prevention activities, the number of students served, or how long the initiatives had been in place, the number of activities does suggest the amount of involvement in drop-out prevention by sample schools.

In table 2, the school population characteristics of the 12 higher activity level schools and the eight lower activity level schools are related to characteristics of the districtwide school population. Half or more of the higher activity schools had a larger percentage of tenth graders passing the SSAT II than was typical across the district; fewer than half the low activity schools demonstrated such achievement. Fewer than half of the higher activity schools had higher percentages of students with other risk characteristics than the district average; more than half of the lower activity schools had a higher percentage of students with those characteristics.

Table 2. School population characteristics districtwide and in higher and lower activity level schools.

Characteristics of school population (district average)	Number of schools above district average	
	Higher activity ($n = 12$)	Lower activity ($n = 8$)
Tenth graders passing communications section of SSAT II (79.3%)	8	1
Tenth graders passing math section of SSAT II (72.35%)	6	3
Students with limited English proficiency (2.62%)	1	5
Students eligible for free or reduced lunch (10.17%)	4	7
Black and/or Hispanic population (69%)	5	6

Source: Williams 1989:18–19.

Why did the schools with lower at-risk populations engage in more drop-out prevention activities than the schools with the higher at-risk populations, where, it would be hoped, a more active drop-out prevention program would have made a significant contribution to reducing drop-out rates? The most successful implementation of programs was dependent on the perception of the drop-out problem and thus the priorities of the school administration, and on the access to specific funding sources. Therefore, the priorities of school personnel, their ability to generate funding, and their strategies for overcoming obstacles to implementation of the programs are indicators of the success of the statewide mandate to encourage the use of these programs. What accounts for the different levels of emphasis on drop-out prevention activities?

Obstacles to effective drop-out prevention strategies

In the case of Dade county, the goals of the legislature were noble, their drop-out prevention program was a bold step in the right direction, and acknowledgement of the at-risk student in a drop-out profile was commendable. But initiatives need to take into account the many obstacles facing schools trying to implement these programs. Some schools are in the same situation as the at-risk student who is struggling to catch up. Perhaps we should designate schools with high proportions of at-risk students and low access to proper facilities, resources, and funding as at-risk schools and create policy that provides the needed support.

Williams' study cited 34 problems school staff perceived as obstacles to higher level activity in the drop-out prevention programs summarized here. It is informative to consider the problems reported here as problems at three levels: state and district, school, and student/community. Across all three levels, reported problems are clustered in table 3 as identified by the letters A–J below.

Table 3. Obstacles reported at state and district, school and student community level.

State and district policies procedures

A.   *Drop-out prevention programs*

1.   Coverage of low-income students was too limited. 'Personnel in one school noted that only 430 students were able to participate out of 2,400 who fit the drop-out profile.' Another program targeted only 100 potential drop-outs, even though some schools had several times that many students who were eligible. In addition, the district was unprepared for the number of schools participating in the project and found it necessary to cut back on funds available to the schools.

2.   Programs were needed to link the school's drop-out activities to developments in the community.

3.   Some students in the schools did not fit the district's at-risk profile. A more expansive profile would include drug and emotional problems, disenfranchisement, and difficult home life.

B.   *Non-academic policies*

4.   Some attendance policies rewarded schools for keeping attendance rates high and encouraged schools to push out students with poor attendance.

5.   Little or no special help was available to students who did not meet legal immigration requirements.

6.   Truancy and child labor laws were not enforced.

7.   The initiative to participate fully in drop-out prevention strategies was left to the discretion of individual schools, which may have had different perceptions of the problem.

C.   *Resources*

8.   Counselor caseloads were extremely heavy, whereas students' needs for more personal attention was high.

9.   There was a shortage of visiting teachers available.

10.   Lack of resources included insufficient funding.

D.   *Academic policies*

11.   Over-age students were already predisposed to not fully participating.

12.   Structurally, the academic year discouraged students from staying or reentering school since students could not earn partial credits when starting over or beginning mid-year.

13.   Even if students fulfilled all their credit requirements, they could not graduate with a regular diploma without passing the SSAT.

14.   Problems meeting increased graduation requirements and standards included an increase in course failures; requiring students lacking only one or two credits to attend school the entire day; limiting summer school to only two credits so students must go into adult education programs; reducing the number of vocational and work programs so that more alternatives were needed to compensate; an increased need for study halls and tutorial programs; and the necessity of 'making up' classes for lower achieving students to meet state requirements.

School level policies/procedures

E.   *Different students' needs unmet*

15.   More flexible and alternative scheduling was needed to integrate students' work schedules into the curriculum.

16.   The needs of students for opportunities for vocational experiences, personal contact with teacher/mentors, and a focus on achievement rather than testing were not met. Apparently, meeting the challenge of the needs of at-risk students does not generate the same enthusiasm as programs geared toward the more academically-oriented. In fact, one school noted that a high level of hostility from the teachers in the school toward efforts to 'save the difficult students at the expense of the more capable' made achieving success difficult.

17.   There was a lack of coordination between vocational centers and schools.

18.   Increased numbers of course levels needed to be added.

19.   Referrals of students in need of counseling were too limited.

F.   *Accounting and disciplinary policies*

20.   School level attendance policies may have had a negative effect on the number of truancies where heavy penalities for tardiness were the policy, or where students who did not report for homeroom were considered absent.

21.   Suspension policies may have created push-outs.

22.   A need for more reliable tracking methods was evident.

G.   *School climate*

23.   Teachers were overloaded with work.

24.   Schools needed a more positive learning climate rather than a 'warehouse' mentality.

Student and community characteristics

H.   Student characteristics

25.   The large number of low-achieving students made it difficult to serve students' needs.

26.   Students' lack of attendance rather than lack of ability contributed to course failures.

27.   Students' poor attitudes toward school impeded their progress toward achievement.

28.   A number of students had serious emotional/personal problems.

I.   *Home lives*

29.   For students with different cultural values from the school, education may not be a high priority, especially due to economic considerations.

30.   Students' home lives created problems for succeeding at school.

31.   More parental involvement was desirable.

32.   Not enough referrals were made to social service agencies.

J.   *Community influences*

33.   The changing demographics of some schools created social class conflicts between students and the school and/or between students in the school.

34.   The effect of community problems – such as substance abuse, crime, poverty, and gangs – was a problem.

In order to explore the question of whether the perception of problems had any relationship to the amount of activity present in individual schools, the 34 problems cited above by personnel were collapsed into 10 subcategories under three categories (see table 3).

Schools followed the district's drop-out profile quite closely in identifying potential drop-outs; for instance, some of the schools with higher activity levels concentrated resources on students who met the district's criteria, although they had many students who were at risk who did not meet the district's criteria. Programs designed to address specific problems, such as attendance, were easier to implement than large scale overhauls of school programs and were more likely to be successful in schools with smaller proportions of students in need. More ambitious programs, such as flexible scheduling incorporated in two higher activity schools, were limited in the number of students who could be served, therefore predisposing them to success. Schools with larger at-risk populations that would have required extreme changes in curriculum scheduling may have seen programs such as these as simply too large and complicated to initiate. Additionally, fewer problems were reported by personnel in most high level activity/low at-risk population schools, except in the area of academic policies.

Schools with all levels of activity reported problems related to student characteristics; the most categories of problems with school/community characteristics were cited in schools with lower activity and high minority populations. Schools with low minority populations reported fewer obstacles due to state or district level policies than did schools with high minority populations.

It is extremely difficult for schools to overcome the many factors that contribute to a student's decision to drop out of school before graduation. The type of change and collaborative efforts that would be most effective require more resources than are presently

Table 4. Categories of problems cited by personnel and 1986–87 drop-out rates for the 20 regular schools grouped by levels of drop-out activity and levels of minority population (school numbers used for identification).

| | PROBLEM CATEGORY | | | | | | | | | | Drop-out Rate |
	State or District[1]		School[2]					Student/community[3]			
*	A	B	C	D	E	F	G	H	I	J	
Hi	02	02	02					02			7.7
	03	03	03	03	03		03	03	03		5.8
		05		05		05		05			5.9
				07				07			7.1
				12	12	12		12		12	5.5
				14	14			14		14	3.0
			15		15		15	15			1.5
HiM			01	01				01			3.4
	04	04	04	04		04		04	04		2.5
		10	10	10	10		10				4.8
	11	11	11	11	11	11	11	11	11		8.4
		19	19		19			19	19		8.1
LM					09			09			5.4
	13		13	13		13		13	13		7.8
	16	16	16	16	16		16	16	16	16	12.9
	17	17	17		17		17	17	17	17	9.0
		18	18	18		18	18	18	18		4.7
	20	20	20	20	20	20	20	20			4.7
L				06	06	06		06			5.0
		08			08	08			08	08	4.4

Note: Due to the unreliability of drop-out rates mentioned earlier, it cannot be inferred that they represent an accurate assessment of percentages of students actually dropping out, or the effectiveness of drop-out prevention activities. Although drop-out rates have not been used for comparison in previous discussions, they serve here, however, as a possible indication of how personnel may perceive the severity of the drop-out problem in their schools.

[1]**State or district level**

A =   Dropout prevention programs
B =   Nonacademic policies
C =   Resources
D =   Academic policies

[3]**Student/community level**

H =   Student characteristics
I =   Home lives
J =   Community influences

[2]**School level**

E =   different student needs unmet
F =   Accounting and disciplinary policies
G =   School climate

***Drop-out Prevention Activity Levels**

Hi =   Higher activity
HiM =   Higher activity, high minority population
LM =   Lower activity, high minority population
L =   Lower activity

available. Unfortunately, this kind of change is most needed in schools with the highest at-risk populations and the least resources to combat obstacles to successful implementation of drop-out prevention strategies.

Recommendations and observations

Equal opportunity means offering the same quality education to all and the support to make it real, if we are to become an educationally classless society. Adler's (1982) Paideia formula requires a concentration on the acquisition of organized knowledge, the development of intellectual skills, and an understanding of ideas and values in order to provide students with a knowledge of nature and culture, the world we live in, social institutions, and ourselves. The issue is the achievement of skills, not graduation. What we teach needs to be the same for all; how we teach needs to be different, according to skill level (Graham 1987).

Americans continue to believe that ability rather than effort determines success; unlike countries such as Japan, which believe that effort is primary (Graham 1987:27). The present approach of providing remedial or compensatory services to improve achievement, may actually contribute to failure by reducing expectations, forcing a slowed-down pace for students who are already terribly behind, drilling on the mechanics of basic without offering opportunities for practical application, operating with a lack of incentives and goals (which simply increases the self-fulfilling cycle of low achievers), and ignoring the potential contributions of the involvement of parents, teachers, and others in the community who could provide mentor role models or share their expertise with students (Levin 1989).

Preventative drop-out measures must, first of all, begin in elementary school, and even pre-school, where at-risk youth can be targeted before they have gotten so far behind. There are several distinguished programs around the country, one of which is the Accelerated School Program at Stanford University. This program centers on accelerating the process of education, instead of slowing it down. Students who are behind to begin with because of at-risk factors, will only fall more behind in remedial classes. The program utilizes high expectations, deadlines, and goals, and uses stimulating materials and methods, including a high use of school and parental and community resources. If we can close the achievement gap by the end of elementary school, at-risk youth may no longer be potential drop-outs in high school (Levin 1989).

A survey of other recommendations (Ascher and Schwartz 1987, Carnegie Foundation 1988, Graham 1987) finds the same themes being advocated over and over:

1. keep public attention on at-risk children;
2. provide more flexibility at the school level to meet the needs of each particular school population – this may include more flexible hiring practices;
3. replace detailed regulations with new models of collaborative evaluation;
4. initiate a bottom-up reorganization of classroom structure, the school day, the school unit; smaller and more personal clusters, e.g., the adoption of a homeroom teacher as a mentor, study groups which would stay together throughout the day; and re-education of teachers and administrators to sensitize them regarding drop-out prevention and alternatives to traditional structures;

5. place a premium on those teachers able to help low achievers excel; reward teachers and administrators for concentrating on the problem;
6. provide more GED and alternative programs;
7. encourage collaboration and linkage with libraries, business, industry, parents, and local and state officials;
8. educators must act politically to ensure reform.

Now we must look into the 1990s. Adults organizing in new ways; schools restructuring education from the bottom up; local, state, and federal agencies paying attention to and providing funds for drop-out prevention programs which include curriculum changes and which take into account the recommendations of policymakers – all of these activities will encourage creativity and risk-taking in ways that will help to keep children in school to learn and earn their diploma.

Acknowledgements

The research reported in this paper was supported by the Center for Policy Research in Education, which is funded by a grant from the US Department of Education, Office of Educational Research and Improvement (Grant No. IERI-G-0086-90011), and by the Wisconsin Center for Education Research, School of Education, University of Wisconsin-Madison. The opinions expressed in this publication are those of the author and do not necessarily reflect the views of the US Department of Education, Office of Educational Research and Improvement, the institutional partners of the Center for Policy Research in Education, or the Wisconsin Center for Education Research.

Notes

1. The higher average number of science sections is influenced by one district adding approximately 17 sections per school due to population growth as well as new science requirements. If we disregard that district's data, the average number of sciences sections added was five.
2. In Florida, a request for a transcript by the adult education program is recorded as evidence of student transfer (not drop-out), even if the student never attends a single adult education class. One Florida principal reported that in an exit interview it is common practice to encourage students to immediately enroll in an adult education class.

Appendix A. High school graduation requirements[a]

Total % of required credits (PRIOR)	Total % of required credits (NEW)	Effective data of new requirements	Change in total % of required credits (CHANGE)	Subject[c]	Prior	New	Change	Rate	Rank[d]	Rank[e,f]	Yes	Year	No
				ARIZONA									
				English	3	4	1						
				Math	1	2	1						
				Science	1	2	1						
				Social Studies	2.5	2.5	0						
18	20	1987	2	CORE	7.5	10.5		63.0	47	t,e 9	X	1976	
				OTHER	10.5	9.5							
				TOTAL	18	20							
				CALIFORNIA									
				English	L.O.	3	3						
				Math		2	2						
				Science		2	2						
				Social Studies		3	3						
L.O.	13	1987	13	CORE		10	10	66.7	41	9[f]	X[1]	1979	
				OTHER		3							
				TOTAL		13							

(Column group headers: "Requirements[b] in core subjects" spans Subject[c], Prior, New, Change; "Graduation rate (1986)" spans Rate, Rank[d]; "Achievement test data (1987)" spans Rank[e,f]; "Exit exam" spans Yes, Year, No.)

FLORIDA

	Local option		
English	4	4	
Math	3	3	
Science	3	3	
Social Studies	3	3	
CORE	13	13	
OTHER	11		
TOTAL	24		

L.O. 24[2] 1987 24 62.0 50 13[f] X 1983 X

PENNSYLVANIA

English	4	3	1
Math	3	1	2
Science	3	1	2
Social Studies	3	2	1
CORE	13	7	6
OTHER	8	6	
TOTAL	21	13	

13[3] 21[3] 1989 8 78.5 14 15[f] X

Notes

a.   Data sources

       Columns 1–8: BELSHES-SIMMONS, G., FLAKUS-MOSQUEDA, P., LINDNER, B. and MAYER, K.
          (1987) 'Recent State Educational Reform: Initial Teacher Certification, Teacher
          Compensation and High School Graduation Requirements'. (Denver, CO: Education
          Commission of the States).
          EDUCATION COMMISSION OF THE STATES (1987) 'Minimum High School
          Graduation Course Requirements' (Denver, CO: ECS).
          GOERTZ, M. E. (1988) 'State Educational Standards: A 50-state Survey (Princeton,
          NJ: Educational Testing Service).
          NATIONAL CENTER FOR EDUCATION STATISTICS (1988) 'The Condition of
          Education: Elementary and Secondary Education' (Washington, DC: US
          Department of Education.
       Columns 9–13: US DEPARTMENT OF EDUCATION. (1988) 'State Education Statistics' Washington,
          DC: DOE, Office of Planning, Budget, and Evaluation.

b.   Requirements are defined as the necessary prerequisites for a standard high school diploma.
c.   Social studies includes courses such as American History, Civics, Economics, state history, etc.
     English includes language arts, communication skills, etc.
d.   Rank includes District of Columbia in 51st place.
e.   Rank and percentile among the 28 states administering the ACT.
f.   Rank and percentile among the 22 states administering the SAT (includes District of Columbia
     in 19th place).
t.   Tied for rank with another state.
N.D. No data given.
L.O. Local option requirements set by local board.

1. Local district sets performance competencies for graduation in California.
2. Florida phased in credit requirements by moving from no state specifications in 1983 to 22 required
   credits in 1985 and 1986 to 24 required in 1989.
3. In 1989, Pennsylvania students must complete 13 credits in the last three years of high school; in
   1989, they must complete 21 credits in four years.

References

ADLER, M. J. (1982) The Paideia Proposal: An Educational Manifesto (New York: Macmillan).
ASCHER, C. and SCHWARTZ, W. (1987) Keeping Track of At-Risk Students. (New York: ERIC
    Clearinghouse on Urban Education, Columbia University).
BERLINER, D. C. (1979) 'Tempus educare', in P. L. Peterson and H. L. Walberg (eds), Research on Teaching:
    Concepts, Findings, and Implications (Berkeley: McCutcheon), pp. 214–229.
BRYK, A. S. and THUM, Y. M. (1989) The Effects of High School Organization on Dropping Out: An Exploratory
    Investigation (New Brunswick, NJ: Rutgers University, Center for Policy Research in Edcuation).
CARNEGIE FOUNDATION FOR THE ADVANCEMENT OF TEACHING (1988) An Imperiled Generation: Saving
    Urban Schools (Lawrenceville, NJ: Princeton University Press).
CLUNE, W. H. (with P. WHITE and J. PATTERSON) (1989) The Implementation and Effects of High School
    Graduation Requirements: First Steps Toward Curricular Reform (New Brunswick, NJ: Rutgers
    University, Center for Policy Research in Education).
COMMITEE FOR ECONOMIC DEVELOPMENT, RESEARCH, AND POLICY (1987) Children in Need: Investment
    Strategies for the Educationally Disadvantage (New York: CEDRP).
FLORIDA DEPARTMENT OF EDUCATION (1986) Summary: The Drop-out Prevention Act of 1986 (Tallahassee,
    FL: FLDoE).
FUHRMAN, S., CLUNE, W. H. and ELMORE, R. F. (1988) 'Research on education reform: Lessons on the
    implementation of policy', Teachers College Record, 90(2), pp. 237–257.
GINSBURG, A. L., NOELL, J. and PLISKO, V. W. (1988) 'Lessons from the wall chart', Educational Evaluation
    and Policy Analysis, 10(1), pp. 1–12.

GRAHAM, P.A. (1987) 'Achievement for at-risk students', paper prepared at Harvard University, Cambridge, MA.

HAMILTON, S. F. (1984) *Raising Standards and Reducing Drop-out Rates: Implications of Research for Recent Secondary School Reform Proposals*. ERIC Document Reproduction Service No. ED 273 570. (Ithaca, NY: Cornell University).

HODGKINSON, H. L. (1985) *All in One System: Demographics of Education, Kindergarten through Graduate School* (Washington, DC: Institute for Educational Leadership).

LEVIN, H. M. (1989) Overcoming the crisis of at-risk students, paper prepared at Stanford University, Standford, CA.

LEVIN, H. M. (1986) *Educational Reform for Disadvantaged Students: An Emerging Crisis* (West Haven, CT: National Education Association).

MARSH, D. (1985) 'The California School Improvement Program Study: implications for the reform of secondary schools', unpublished paper prepared for the Wisconsin Center for Education Research, University of Wisconsin, Madison.

McDILL, E. L., NATRIELLO, G. and PALLAS, A. M. (1986) 'A population at risk: potential consequences of tougher school standards for student drop-outs', *American Journal of Education*, **94**(2), pp. 135–181.

McLAUGHLIN, M. W. (1976) 'Implementation as mutual adaptation: change in classroom organization', *Teachers College Record*, **77**(3), pp. 339–351.

McLAUGHLIN, M. W. (1987) 'Lessons from past implementation research', *Educational Evaluation and Policy Analysis*, **9**(2), pp. 171–178.

PALLAS, A. M., NATRIELLO, G., and McDILL, E. L. (1989) *The Changing Nature of the Disadvantaged Population: Current Dimensions and Future Trends* (Baltimore, MD: Johns Hopkins University, Center for Research on Elementary and Secondary Schools).

PURKEY, S. C. and SMITH, M. S. (1983) 'Effective schools: a review', *Elementary School Journal*, **83**(4), pp. 427–452.

RODRIQUEZ, E., McQUAID, P. and ROSAUER, R. (1988) *Community of Purpose: Promoting Collaboration through State Action* (Denver, CO: Education Commission of the States).

SINCLAIR, R. L. and GHORY, W. J. (1987) *Reaching Marginal Students: A Primary Concern for School Renewal* (Chicago: McCutcheon).

WILLIAMS, P. A. (1987) *Standardizing School Drop-out Measures*. Research report (New Brunswick, NJ: Rutgers University, Center for Policy Research in Education).

WILLIAMS, P. A. (1989) 'School level response to at-risk students', paper prepared for the University of Wisconsin-Madison, Center for Policy Research in Education, Madison, WI.

6   *Revolution in one classroom*

David K. Cohen

This chapter probes the relationship between instructional policy and teaching practice. In the mid-1980s, California State officials launched an ambitious effort to revise mathematics teaching and learning. The aim was to replace mechanical memorization with mathematical understanding. This chapter considers one teacher's response to the new policy. She sees herself as a success for the policy: she believes that she has revolutionized her mathematics teaching. But observation of her classroom reveals that the innovations in her teaching have been filtered through a very traditional approach to instruction. The result is a remarkable *melange* of novel and traditional material. Policy has affected practice in this case, but practice has had an even greater effect on policy.

Introduction

As Mrs Oublier sees it, her classroom is a new world. She reported that when she began work four years ago, her mathematics teaching was thoroughly traditional. She followed the text. Her second graders spent most of their time on worksheets. Learning math meant memorizing facts and procedures. Then Mrs O found a new way to teach math. The summer after her first year of teaching, she took a workshop in which she learned to focus lessons on students' understanding of mathematical ideas. She found ways to relate mathematical concepts to students' knowledge and experience. And she explored methods to engage students in actively understanding mathematics. In her third year of such work, Mrs O is delighted with her students' performance, and with her own accomplishments.

Mrs O's story is engaging, and so is she. She is considerate of her students, eager for them to learn, energetic, and attractive. These qualities would stand out anywhere, but they seem particularly vivid in her school. It is a drab collection of one-story, concrete buildings that sprawl over several acres. Though clean and well managed, her school lacks any of the familiar signs of classy education. It has no legacy of experimentation or progressive pedagogy, or even of heavy spending on education. Only a minority of children come from well-to-do families. Most families have middling or only modest incomes, and many are eligible for Chapter I assistance. A sizeable minority are on welfare. The school district is situated in a dusty corner of southern California, where city migrants rapidly are turning a rural town into a suburb. New condominiums are sprouting all over the community, but one still sees pick-up trucks with rifle racks mounted in their rear windows. Like several of her colleagues, Mrs O works in a covey of tacky, portable, prefab classrooms, trucked into the back of the schoolyard to absorb growing enrollments on the cheap.

Mrs O's story seems even more unlikely when considered against the history of American educational reform. Great plans for educational change are a familiar feature of that history, but so are reports of failed reforms. That is said to have been the fate of the earlier new math, in the 1950s and 1960s. A similar tale was told of efforts to improve science teaching at the time (Welch 1979). Indeed, failed efforts to improve teaching and learning are an old story. John Dewey and others announced a revolution in pedagogy just as our century opened, but apparently it fizzled: classrooms changed only a little, researchers say (Cuban 1984). The story goes on. Since the Sputnik era, many studies of instructional innovation have embroidered these old themes of great ambitions and modest results (Cohen 1988, Gross *et al.* 1971, Rowan and Guthrie 1989).

Some analysts explain these dismal tales with reference to teachers' resistance to change: they argue that entrenched classroom habits defeat reform (Gross *et al.* 1971). Others report that many innovations fail because they are poorly adapted to classrooms: even teachers who avidly desire change can do little with most schemes to improve instruction, because they don't work well in classrooms (Cuban 1984, 1986). Mrs O's revolution looks particularly appealing against this background. She eagerly embraced change, rather than resisting it. She found new ideas and materials that worked in her classroom, rather than working against innovation. Mrs O sees her class as a success for the new California Mathematics Framework. Though her revolution began while the Framework still was being written, it was inspired by many of the same ideas. She reports that her math teaching has wound up where the Framework intends it to be.

But as I watched and listened in Mrs O's classroom, things seemed more complicated. Her teaching does reflect the new Framework in many ways. For instance, she has adopted innovative instructional materials and activities, all designed to help students make sense of mathematics. But Mrs O seemed to treat new mathematical topics as though they were a part of traditional school mathematics. She used the new materials, but used them as though mathematics contained only right and wrong answers. She has revised the curriculum to help students understand math, but she conducts the class in ways that discourage exploration of students' understanding.

From the perspective of the new Mathematics Framework, then, Mrs O's lessons seem quite mixed. They contain some important elements that the Framework embraced, but they contain others that it branded as inadequate. In fact, her classes present an extraordinary *melange* of traditional and novel approaches to math instruction.

Something old and something new . . .

That *melange* is part of the fascination of Mrs O's story. Some observers would agree that she has made a revolution, but others would see only traditional instruction. It is easy to imagine long arguments about which is the real Mrs O but they would be the wrong arguments. Mrs O is both of these teachers. Her classroom deserves attention partly because such mixtures are quite common in instructional innovations – though they have been little noticed. As teachers and students try to find their way from familiar practices to new ones, they cobble new ideas onto familiar practices. The variety of these blends, and teachers' ingenuity in fashioning them are remarkable. But they raise unsettling questions. Can we say that an innovation has made much progress when it is tangled in combination with many traditional practices? Changes that seem large to teachers who are in the midst of struggles to accommodate new ideas often seem modest or invisible to observers who scan practice for evidence that new policies have been implemented. How does one judge innovative progress? Should we consider changes in teachers' work from the perspective of new policies like the Framework? Or should they be considered from the teachers' vantage point?

New materials, old mathematics

From one angle, the curriculum and instructional materials in this class were just what the new Framework ordered. For instance, Mrs O regularly asked her second graders to work on 'number sentences'. In one class that I observed, students had done the problem: $10 + 4 = 14$. Mrs O then asked them to generate additional 'number sentences' about 14. They volunteered various ways to write addition problems about fourteen, i.e. $10 + 1 + 1 + 1 + 1 = 14$, $5 + 5 + 4 = 14$, etc. Some students proposed several ways to write subtraction problems, i.e. $14 - 4 = 10$, $14 - 10 = 4$; etc. Most of the students' proposals were correct. Such work could make mathematical relationships more accessible, by coming at them with ordinary language rather than working only with bare numbers on a page. It also could unpack mathematical relationships, by offering different ways to get the same result. It could illuminate the relations between addition and subtraction, helping children to understand their reversibility. And it could get students to do 'mental math', i.e. to solve problems in their heads and thereby learn to see math as something to puzzle about and figure out, rather than just a bunch of facts and procedures to be memorized.

These are all things that the new Framework invited. The authors exhort teachers to help students cultivate 'an attitude of curiosity and the willingness to probe and explore' (California State Department of Education [CSDE] 1985: 1). The document also calls for classroom work that helps students 'to understand why computational algorithms are constructed in particular forms' (CSDE 1985: 4).

Yet the Framework's mathematical exhortations were general, and offered few specifics about how teachers might respond. The reform manifesto left room for many different responses. Mrs O used the new materials, but conducted the entire exercise in a thoroughly traditional fashion. The class worked as though the lesson were a drill, reciting in response to the teacher's queries. Students' sentences were accepted if correct, and written down on the board. But they were turned down if incorrect, and not written on the board. Right answers were not explained, and wrong answers were treated as unreal. The Framework makes no such distinction. To the contrary, it argues that understanding how to arrive at answers is an essential part of helping students to figure out how mathematics works – perhaps more important than whether the answers are right or wrong. The Framework criticizes the usual memorized, algorithmic approach to mathematics, and the usual search for the right answer. It calls for class discussion of problems and problem-solving as an important part of figuring out mathematical relationships (CSDE 1985: 13–14). But no one in Mrs O's class was asked to explain their proposed number sentences, correct or incorrect. No student was invited to demonstrate how he or she knew whether a sentence was correct or not. The teacher used a new mathematics curriculum, but used it in a way that conveyed a sense of mathematics as a fixed body of right answers, rather than as a field of inquiry in which people figure out quantitative relations. It is easy to see the Framework's ideas in Mrs O's classroom, but it also is easy to see many points of opposition between the new policy and Mrs O's approach (CSDE 1987: 9).

Make no mistake: Mrs O was teaching math for understanding. The work with number sentences certainly was calculated to help students see how addition worked, and to see that addition and subtraction were reversible. That mathematical idea is well worth understanding, and the students seemed to understand it at some level. They were, after all, producing the appropriate sorts of sentences. But it was difficult to understand how or how well they understood it, for the didactic form of the lesson inhibited explanation or exploration of students' ideas. Additionally, mathematical knowledge was treated in a traditional way: correct answers were accepted, and wrong ones simply rejected. No answers were unpacked. There was teaching for mathematical understanding here, but it was blended with other elements of instruction that seemed likely to inhibit understanding.

The mixture of new mathematical ideas and materials with old mathematical knowledge and pedagogy permeated Mrs O's teaching. It also showed up extensively in her work with concrete materials and other physical activities. These materials and activities are a crucial feature of her revolution, for they are intended to represent mathematical concepts in a form that is vivid and accessible to young children. For instance, she opens the math lesson every day with a calendar activity, in which she and the students gather on a rug at one side of the room to count up the days of the school year. She uses this activity for various purposes. During my first visit she was familiarizing students with place value, regrouping, and odd and even numbers. As it happened, my visit began on the fifty-ninth day of the school year, and so the class counted to fifty-nine. They used single claps for most numbers but double claps for ten, twenty, etc. Thus, one physical activity represented the 'tens', and distinguished them from another physical activity that was used to represent the 'ones'. On the next day the class used claps for even numbers and finger snaps for odd numbers in counting off the days. The idea here is that fundamental distinctions among types of numbers can be represented in ways that make immediate and fundamental sense to young children. Representations of this sort, it is thought, will deeply familiarize them with important mathematical ideas, but will do so in a fashion easily accessible to those unfamiliar with abstractions.

Mrs O also used drinking straws in a related activity, to represent place value and regrouping. Every day a 'student helper' is invited to help lead the calendar activity by adding another straw to the total that represent the elapsed days in the school year. The straws accumulate until there are ten, and then are bundled with a rubber band. One notion behind this activity is that students will gain some concrete basis for understanding how numbers are grouped in a base ten system. Another is that they can begin to apprehend, first physically and then intellectually, how number groups can be composed and decomposed.

Mrs O's class abounds with such activities and materials, and they are very different from the bare numbers on worksheets that would be found in a traditional math class. She was still excited, after several years' experience, about the difference that they made for her students' understanding of arithmetic. Mrs O adopts a somewhat cool demeanor in class, but her conviction about the approach was plain as she worked with the students, and her enthusiasm for it bubbled up in our conversations. After three years, she had only disdain for her old way of teaching math.

Her approach seems nicely aligned with the new Framework. For instance, that document argues that 'many activities should involve concrete experiences so that students develop a sense of what numbers mean and how they are related before they are asked to add, subtract, multiply, or divide them' (CSDE 1985: 8). And it adds, a few pages further on, that 'concrete materials provide a way for students to connect their own understandings about real objects and their own experiences to mathematical concepts. They gain direct experience with the underlying principles of each concept' (CSDE 1985: 15).

Mrs O certainly shared the Framework's view in this matter. But it is one thing to embrace a doctrine of instruction, and quite another to weave it into one's practice. For even a rather monotonous practice of teaching comprises many different threads. Hence any new instructional thread must somehow be related to many others already there. Like reweaving fabric, this social and intellectual reweaving can be done in different ways. The new thread can simply be dropped onto the fabric, and everything else left as is. Or new threads may be somehow woven into the fabric. If so, some alteration in the relations among threads will be required. Some of the existing threads might have to be adjusted in some way, or even pulled out and replaced. If one views Mrs O's work from the perspective of the Framework, new threads were introduced, but old threads were not pulled out. The old and new lay side by side, and so the fabric of instruction was different. But there seemed to be little mutual adjustment among new and old threads. Mrs O used the novel concrete materials and physical activities, but used them in a traditional pedagogical surround. Consequently the new material seemed to take on different meaning from its circumstances. Materials and activities intended to teach mathematics for understanding were infused with traditional messages about what mathematics was, and what it meant to understand it.

These mixed qualities were vividly apparent in a lesson that focused on addition and subtraction with regrouping. The lesson occurred early in an eight- or ten-week cycle concerning these topics. Like many of her lessons, it combined a game-like activity with the use of concrete materials. The aim was to capture childrens' interest in math, and to help them understand it. Mrs O introduced this lesson by announcing: 'Boys and girls, today we are going to play a counting game. Inside this paper [holding up a wadded up sheet of paper] is the secret message . . . ' (Observation notes, 5, December 1988). Mrs O unwadded the paper and held it up: '6' was inscribed. The number was important, because it would establish the number base for the lesson: six. In previous lessons they had done the same thing with four and five. So part of the story here was exploring how things work in different number bases, and one reason for that, presumably, was to get some perspective on the base-ten system that we conventionally use. Mrs O told the children that, as in the previous games, they would use a nonsense word in place of the secret number. I was not sure why she did this, at the time. As it turned out, the approach was recommended, but not explained, by the innovative curriculum guide she was using. After a few minutes taken to select the nonsense word, the class settled on 'Cat's eye'. (Observation notes, 5, December 1988. These notes are the source for the remainder of this episode.)

With this groundwork laid, Mrs O had 'place value boards' given to each student. She held her board up [eight by eleven, roughly, one half blue and the other white], and said: 'We call this a place value board. What do you notice about it?'

Cristie Smith, who turned out to be a steady infielder on Mrs O's team, said: 'There's a smiling face at the top.' Mrs O agreed, noting that the smiling face needed to be at the top at all times [that would keep the blue half of the board on everyone's left]. Several kids were holding theirs up for inspection from various angles, and she admonished them to leave the boards flat on their tables at all times.

'What else do we notice?' she inquired. Sam said that one half is blue and the other white. Mrs O agreed, and went on to say that 'the blue side will be the "cat's eye" side. During this game we will add one to the white side, and when we get a cat's eye, we will move it over to the blue side.' With that each student was given a small plastic tub, which contained a handful of dried beans and half a dozen small paper cups, perhaps a third the height of those dispensed in dentist's offices. This was the sum total of pre-lesson framing – no other discussion or description preceded the work.

There was a small flurry of activity as students took their tubs and checked out the contents. Beans present nearly endless mischievous possibilities, and several of the kids seemed on the verge of exploring their properties as guided missiles. Mrs O nipped off these investigations, saying: 'Put your tubs at the top of your desks, and put both hands in the air.' The students all complied, as though in a small stagecoach robbery. 'Please keep them up while I talk.' She opened a spiral-bound book, not the school district's adopted text but *Math Their Way* (Baratta-Lorton 1976). This was the innovative curriculum guide that had helped to spark her revolution. She looked at it from time to time, as the lesson progressed, but seemed to have quite a good grip on the activity.

Mrs O got things off to a brisk start: 'Boys and girls [who still were in the hold-up], when I clap my hands, add a bean to the white side [from the plastic tub].'

She clapped once vigorously, adding that they could put their hands down. 'Now we are going to read what we have: What do we have?' [she led a choral chant of the answer] 'Zero cat's eye and one.' She asked students to repeat that, and everyone did. She clapped again, and students obediently added a second bean to the white portion of the card. 'What do we have now', she inquired. Again she led a choral chant: 'Zero cat's eye and two'. So another part of the story in this lesson was place value: 'Zero cat's eye' denotes what would be the 'tens' place in base-ten numbering, and 'two' is the 'ones' place. Counting individual beans, and beans grouped in 'cat's eye', would give the kids a first-hand, physical sense of how place value worked in this and other number bases.

In these opening chants, as in all subsequent ones, Mrs O performed more like a drill sergeant than a choir director. Rather than establishing a beat and then maintaining it with her team, she led each chant and the class followed at a split-second interval. Any kid who didn't grasp the idea needed only to wait for her cue, or for his table-mates. There were no solos: students were never invited or allowed to count on their own. Thus, while the *leitmotif* in their second chant was 'zero cat's eye and two', there was an audible minor theme of 'zero cat's eye and one'. That several repeated the first chant suggested that they did not get either the routine or its point.

Mrs O moved right on nonetheless, saying that it 'is very important that you read the numbers with your hands'. This was a matter to which she returned many times during the lesson; she kept reminding the children to put their little paws first on the beans on the white square, and then on the cups on the blue square, as they incanted the mathematical chants. It was essential that they manipulate the concrete materials. Whenever she spotted children who were not palpitating beans and cups, she walked over and moved their arms and hands for them.

Mrs O led the bean adding and chants up to five. Then, when the first five beans were down on everyone's card, she asked: 'Now think ahead; when I clap my hands this time, what will you have on the white side?'

Reliable Christie Smith scooped it up and threw smoothly to first: 'Cat's eye.'

Mrs O led off again: 'When you get a cat's eye, put all the beans in a paper cup, and move them over.' She clapped her hands for the cat's eye, and then led the following chant: 'Put the beans in the cup and move them over.'

'Now let's read what we have.' The chant rolled on, 'one cat's eye and zero.' A puzzling undercurrent of 'one cat's eye and one' went unattended. She then led the class though a series of claps and chants, leading up to two cat's eyes. And the claps and chants went on with a methodical monotony, up to five cat's eyes and five. The whole series took about 15 minutes, and throughout the exercise she repeatedly reminded students to 'read' the materials with their hands, to feel the beans and move their arms. By the time they go to five cat's eyes and five, her claps had grown more perfunctory, and many of the kids had gotten the fidgets. But Mrs O gave no ground. She seemed to see this chanting and bean-pawing as the high road to mathematical understanding, and tenaciously drove her team on.

'Now, how many do we have?' 'Five cat's eye's and five beans,' came the chant. 'Now we will take away one bean' [from the 'ones' side of the board]. 'How many do we have?' Again the answering chant, again led by her, a fraction of a second early, 'five cat's eye and four.'

This was a crucial point in the lesson. The class was moving from what might be regarded as a concrete representation of addition with regrouping, to a similar representation of subtraction with regrouping. Yet she did not comment on or explain this reversal of direction. It would have been an obvious moment for some such comment or discussion, at least if one saw the articulation of ideas as part of understanding mathematics. But Mrs O did not teach as though she took that view. Hers seemed to be an activity-based approach: it was as though she thought that all the important ideas were implicit, and better that way.

Thus the class counted down to five cat's eyes and zero. Mrs O then asked, 'What do we do now?' Jane responded: 'Take a dish from the cat's eye side, and move it to the white side.' No explanation was requested or offered, to embroider this response. Mrs O simply approved the answer, clapped her hands, and everyone followed Jane's lead. With this, Mrs O led the class back through each step, with claps, chants, and reminders to 'read' the beans with their hands, down to zero cat's eye and zero beans. The entire effort took 30 or 35 minutes. Everyone was flagging long before it was done, but not a chant was skipped or a movement missed.

Why did Mrs O teach in this fashion? In an interview following the lesson I asked her what she thought the children learned from the exercise. She said that it helped them to understand what goes on in addition and subtraction with regrouping. Manipulating the materials really helps kids to understand math, she said. Mrs O seemed quite convinced that these physical experiences *caused* learning, that mathematical knowledge arose from the activities.

Her immediate inspiration for all this seems to have been *Math Their Way*, a system of primary grade math teaching on which, Mrs O says, she relies heavily. *Math Their Way* announces its purpose this way: 'to develop understanding and insight of the patterns of mathematics through the use of concrete materials' (Baratta-Lorton 1976: xiv). Concrete materials and physical activities are the central features of this primary grade program, because they are believed to provide real experience with mathematics. In this connection the book sharply distinguishes between mathematical symbols and concepts. It criticizes teaching with symbols, arguing that symbols, i.e. numbers –

> are not *the concept* [emphasis in original], they are only a representation of the concept, and as such are abstractions describing something which is not visible to the child. Real materials, on the other hand, can be manipulated to illustrate the concept concretely, and can be experienced visually by the child... The emphasis throughout this book is making concepts, rather than numerical symbols, meaningful (Baratta-Lorton 1976: xiv).

Math Their Way fairly oozes the belief that physical representations are much more real than symbols. This fascinating idea is a recent mathematical mutation of the belief, at least as old as Rousseau, Pestalozzi, and James Fenimore Cooper, that experience is a better teacher than mere books. For experience is vivid, vital, and immediate, while books are all abstract ideas and dead formulations. Mrs O did not mention these sages, but she certainly had a grip on the idea. In this she resembles many primary school teachers, for the view that concrete materials and physical activities are the high road to abstract concepts has become common currency in nursery school and primary grade teaching. Many primary grade teachers have long used physical activities and concrete materials elsewhere in instruction.

In fact, one of the chief claims in *Math Their Way* is that concrete materials are developmentally desirable for young children. Numbers are referred to many times as an 'adult' way of approaching math. And this idea leads to another, still more important: if math is taught properly, it will be easy. Activities with concrete materials, the book insists, are the natural way for kids to learn math: 'if this foundation is firmly laid, dealing with abstract number will be *effortless*' (Baratta-Lorton 1976: 167, emphasis added).

Stated so baldly, that seems a phenomenal claim: simply working with the proper activities and materials assures that math will be understood. Materials and activities are not only necessary for understanding mathematics, but also sufficient. But the idea is quite common. Pestalozzi might have cheered it. Many other pedagogical Romantics, Rousseau and Dewey among them, embraced a version of this view. Piaget is commonly thought to have endorsed a similar idea. So when *Math Their Way* argues that the key to teaching math for understanding is to get children to use the right sorts of activities and materials, it is on one of the main tracks of modern educational thought and practice. The book's claim also helps to explain why it gives no attention to the nature of mathematical knowledge, and so little attention to the explanation of mathematical ideas. For the author seems convinced that such things are superfluous: appropriate materials and activities alone will do the trick.

In fact, the book's appeal owes something to its combination of great promises and easy methods. For it offers teachers a kind of pedagogical special, a two-for-the-price-of-one: students will understand math without any need to open up questions about the nature of mathematical knowledge. The curriculum promises mathematical understanding, but it does not challenge or even discuss the common view of mathematics as a fixed body of material – in which knowledge consists of right answers – that so many teachers have inherited from their own schooling. The manual does occasionally note that teachers might discuss problems and their solutions with students. But this encouragement is quite modestly and intermittently scattered through a curriculum guide that chiefly focuses on the teaching potential of concrete materials and physical activities. The book presents concrete representations and math activities as a kind of explanation sufficient unto themselves. Discussion of mathematical ideas has a parenthetical role, at best.

All of this illuminates Mrs O's indebtedness to *Math Their Way*, and her persistent praise of it. She used the guide to set up and conduct the lessons that I saw, and referred to it repeatedly in our conversations as the inspiration for her revolution. My subsequent comparisons of her classes with the manual suggested that she did draw deeply on it for ideas about materials, activities, and lesson format. More important, her views of how children come to understand mathematics were, by her own account, powerfully influenced by this book.

Math Their Way thus enables Mrs O to wholeheartedly embrace teaching math for understanding, without considering or reconsidering her views of mathematical knowledge. She was very keen that children should understand math, and worked hard at helping them. But she placed nearly the entire weight of this effort on concrete materials and activities. The ways that she used these materials – insisting, for instance, that all the children actually feel them, and perform the same prescribed physical operations with them – suggest that she endowed the materials with enormous, even magical instructional powers. The lack of any other ways of making sense of mathematics in her lessons was no oversight. With *Math Their Way*, she simply saw no need for anything else.

In what sense was Mrs O teaching for understanding? The question opens up a great puzzle. Her classes exuded traditional conceptions of mathematical knowledge, and were organized as though explanation and discussion were irrelevant to mathematics. Yet she had changed her math teaching quite dramatically. She now used a new curriculum specifically designed to promote students' understanding of mathematics. And her students' lessons were very different than they had been. They worked with materials that represented mathematical relationships in the concrete ways that the Framework and many other authorities endorse. Mrs O thought the change had been decisive: she now teaches for understanding. She reported that her students now understood arithmetic, while previously they had simply memorized it.

Is there a solution to this puzzle? It is a nice question. But first consider two other features of her teaching.

New topics and old knowledge

Mrs O taught several topics endorsed by the new Framework, that would not have been covered in many traditional math classes. One such topic was estimation. Mrs O told me that estimation is important because it helps students to make sense of numbers. They have to make educated guesses, and learn to figure out why some guesses are better than others. She reports that she deals with estimation recurrently in her second grade classwork, returning to it many times in the course of the year rather than teaching a single unit. Her reason was that estimation could not be learned by doing it once or twice, and, in any event, is useful in many different problem-solving situations. Her reasoning on this matter seemed quite in accord with the Framework. It calls for 'Guessing and checking the result' as an important element in mathematical problem solving (CSDE 1985: 14). In fact, the Framework devotes a full page to estimation, explaining what it is and why it is important (CSDE, 1985: 4–5).

The teaching that I observed did not realize these ambitions. In one lesson, for instance, the following problem was presented: estimate how many large paper clips would be required to span one edge of the teacher's desk (Observation notes, 6, December 1988). Two students were enlisted to actually hold the clips so that students could see. They stood near the teacher's desk, near enough to visually gauge its width in relation to the clips. But all the other students remained at their tables, scattered around the room. None had any clips, and few could see the edge of the teacher's desk that was in question. For it was a side edge, away from most of the class.

So only two members of the class had real contact with the two key data sources in the problem – visible, palpable clips, and a clear view of the desk edge. As a consequence, only these two members of the class had any solid basis for deciding if their estimates were mathematically reasonable. Even Mrs O was seated too far away to see the edge well, and she had no clips either. The problem itself was sensible, and could have been an opportunity to make and discuss estimates of a real puzzle. But it was set up in a way that emptied it of opportunities for mathematical sense-making.

Mrs O did not seem aware of this. For after she had announced the problem, she went on to engage the whole class in solving it. The two students were told to hold the clips up for everyone to see. Seated at the back, with many of the kids, I could see that they were the large sort of clip, but even then they were barely visible. Mrs O then pointed to the desk edge, at the other end of the room, easily 20 feet from half the class. Then she asked the students to estimate how many clips it would take to cover the edge, and to write down their answers. She took estimates from most of the class, wrote them on the board, and asked class members if the estimates were reasonable.

Not surprisingly, the answers lacked mathematical discrimination. Estimates that were close to three times the actual answer, or one-third of it, were accepted by the class and the teacher as 'reasonable'. Indeed, no answers were rejected as unreasonable, even though quite a few were far off the mark. Nor were some estimates distinguished as more or less reasonable than others. Mrs O asked the class what 'reasonable' meant, and one boy offered an appropriate answer, suggesting that the class had some previous contact with this idea.

There was nothing that I could see or imagine in the classroom that led inexorably to this treatment. Mrs O seemed to have many clips. If eight or ten had been passed around, the kids would have had at least direct access to one element in the estimation problem – i.e. the length of the clip. Additionally, Mrs O could have directed the kids' attention to the edge of the desk that they could see, rather than the far edge that they could not see. I knew that the two edges of the rectangular desk were the same length, and perhaps some of these second graders did as well. But her way or presenting the problem left that as a needless, and mathematically irrelevant barrier to their work. Alternatively, Mrs O could have invited them to estimate the length of their own desk edges, which were all the same, standard-issue models. That, along with passed-around clips, would have given them much more direct contact with the elements of the problem. The students would have had more of the mathematical data required to make sound estimates, and much more of a basis for considering the reasonableness of those estimates.

Why did Mrs O not set the problem up in one of these ways? I could see no organizational or pedagogical reason. In a conversation after the class, when I asked for her comments on that part of the lesson, she did not display even a shred of discomfort, let alone suggest that anything had been wrong. Mrs O seemed to understand the broad purpose of teaching and learning estimation (Interview, 6, December 1988). However, this bit of teaching suggests that she did not have a firm grip on the mathematics in this estimation example. She taught as though she lacked the mathematical and pedagogical infrastructure – the knowledge of mathematics, and of teaching and learning mathematics – that would have helped her to set the problem up so that the crucial mathematical data were available to students.

An additional bit of evidence on this point concerns the way Mrs O presented estimation. She offered it as a topic in its own right, rather than as a part of solving problems that came up in the course of studying mathematics. After ending one part of the lesson, she turned to estimation as though it were an entirely separate matter. When the estimation example was finished, she turned the class to still another topic. Estimation had an inning all its own, rather than being woven into other innings' work. It was almost as though she thought that estimation bore no intimate relation to solving the ordinary run of mathematical problems. But this misses the mathematical point: Estimation is useful and used in that ordinary run, not for its own sake. The Framework touches on this matter, arguing that 'estimation activities should be presented not as separate lessons, but as a step to be used in all computational activities' (CSDE 1985: 4).

When detached from regular problem-solving, estimation may seem strange, and thus isolated may lose some of its force as a way of making sense in mathematics. I wondered what the students might have learned from this session. They all appeared to accept the lesson as reasonable. No students decried the lack of comprehensible data on the problem, which they might have done if they were used to such data, and if this lesson were an aberration. No one said that they had done it differently some other time, and that this didn't make sense. That could mean that the other lessons on estimation conveyed a similar impression. Or it may mean that students were simply dutiful, doing what they had been told because they had so often been told to do so. Or it may mean only that students took nothing from the lesson. Certainly school is full of mystifying or inexplicable experiences, that children simply accept. Perhaps this struck them only as another such mystification. It is possible, though, that they did learn something, and that it was related to Mrs O's teaching. If so, perhaps they learned that estimation was worth doing, even if they didn't learn much about how to do it. Or perhaps they acquired an inappropriate idea of what estimation was, and what 'reasonable' meant.

Was this teaching math for understanding? From one angle, it plainly was. Mrs O did teach a novel and important topic, specifically intended to promote students' sense-making in arithmetic. It may well have done that. Yet the estimation problem was framed so that students had no way to bring mathematical evidence to bear on the problem, and little basis for making reasonable estimates. It therefore also is possible that students found this puzzling, confusing, or simply mysterious. These alternatives are not mutually exclusive. This bit of teaching for understanding could have promoted more understanding of mathematics, along with more misunderstanding.

New organization and old discourse

Mrs O's class was organized to promote 'co-operative learning'. The students' desks and tables were gathered in groups of four and five, so that they could easily work together. Each group had a leader, to help with various logistical chores. And the location and distribution of instructional materials often were managed by groups rather than individually. The new Framework endorses this way of organizing classroom work. It puts the rationale this way: 'To internalize concepts and apply them to new situations, students must interact with materials, express their thoughts, and discuss alternative approaches and explanations. Often, these activities can be accomplished well in groups of four students' (CSDE 1985: 16).

The Framework thus envisions co-operative learning groups as the vehicle for a new sort of instructional discourse, in which students would do much more of the teaching. In consequence, each of them would learn from their own efforts to articulate and explain ideas – much more than they could learn from a teacher's explanations to them. And they would teach each other as well, learning from their mates' ideas and explanations, and from others' responses. The Framework explains: 'Students have more chances to speak in a small group than in a class discussion; and in that setting some students are more comfortable speculating, questioning, and explaining concepts in order to clarify their thinking' (CSDE 1985: 16-17).

Mrs O's class was spatially and socially organized for such co-operative learning, but the instructional discourse that she established cut across the grain of this organization: the class was conducted in a highly structured and classically teacher-centered fashion. The chief instructional group was the whole class. The discourse that I observed consisted either of dyadic exchanges between the teacher and one student, or of whole-group activities, many of which involved choral responses to teacher questions. No student ever spoke to another about mathematical ideas as part of the public discourse. Nor was such conversation ever encouraged by the teacher. Indeed, Mrs O specifically discouraged students from speaking with each other, in her efforts to keep the class orderly and quiet.

The small groups were not ignored. They were used for instructional purposes, but they were used in a distinctive way. In one class that I observed, for instance, Mrs O announced a 'graphing activity' about mid-way through the math period. She wrote across the chalk board, at the front of the room 'Letter to Santa?' Underneath she wrote two column headings: 'Yes' and 'No'. Then she told the children that she would call on them by groups, to answer the question.

If she had been following the Framework's injunctions about small groups, Mrs O might have asked each group to tally its answers to the question. She might then have asked each group to figure out whether it had more 'yes' than 'no' answers, or the reverse. She might then have asked each group to figure out how many more. And she might have had each group contribute its totals to the chart at the front of the room. This would not have been the most challenging group activity, but it would have meaningfully used the small groups as agents for working on this bit of mathematics.

Mrs O proceeded differently. She used the groups to call on individual children. Moving from her right to left across the room, she asked individuals from each group, *seriatim*, to come to the front and put their entry under the 'Yes' or 'No' column, exhausting one group before going on the next. The groups were used in a socially meaningful way, but there was no mathematical discourse within them.

Mrs O used the small groups in this fashion several times during my visits. The children seemed quite familiar with the procedures, and worked easily in this organization. In addition, she used the groups to distribute and collect instructional materials, which was a regular and important feature of her teaching. Finally, she regularly used the groups to dismiss the class for lunch and recess: she would let the quietest and tidiest group go first, and so on through the class.

Small groups thus were a regular feature of instruction in Mrs O's class. I asked her about co-operative grouping in one of our conversations: did she always use the groups in the ways that I had observed? She thought she did. I asked if she ever used them for more co-operative activity, that is, discussions and that sort of thing. She said that she occasionally did so, but mostly she worked in the ways I had observed.

In what sense was this teaching for understanding? Here again, there was a remarkable combination of old and new math instruction. Mrs O used a new form of classroom organization that was designed to promote collaborative work and broader discourse about academic work. She treated this organization with some seriousness. She referred to her classwork as 'co-operative learning', and used the organization for some regular features of classroom work. When I mentally compared her class with others I had observed, in which students sat in traditional rows, and in which there was only whole-group or individual work, her class seemed really different. Though Mrs O runs a tight ship, her class was more relaxed than those others I remembered, and organized in a more humane way. My view on this is not simply idiosyncratic. If Larry Cuban had used this class in the research for *How Teachers Taught* (1984), he probably would have judged it to be innovative as well. For that book relies on classrooms' social organization as an important indicator of innovation.

Mrs O also judged her classroom to be innovative. She noted that it was now organized quite differently than during her first year of teaching, and she emphatically preferred the innovation. The kids were more comfortable, and the class much more flexible, she said. But she filled the new social organization with old discourse processes. The new organization opened up lots of new opportunities for small group work, but she organized the discourse in ways that effectively blocked realization of those opportunities.

Reprise

I have emphasized certain tensions within Mrs O's classes, but these came into view partly because I crouched there with one eye on the Framework. The tensions I have discussed were not illusory, but my angle of vision brought them into focus. Another observer, with other matters in mind, might not have noticed these tensions. Mrs O certainly didn't notice them, and things went quite smoothly in her lessons. There was nothing rough or ungainly in the way she and her students managed. They were all used to each other, and to the class routines. They moved around easily within their math lessons. The various contrary elements of instruction that troubled my mental waters did not disturb the surface of the class. On the contrary, students and teacher acted as though the threads of these lessons were nicely woven together. Aspects of instruction that seemed at odds analytically appeared to nicely co-exist in practice.

What accounts for this smoothness? Can it be squared with the tensions that I have described within these classes?

Part of the answer lies in the classroom discourse. Mrs O never invited or permitted broad participation in mathematical discussion or explanation. She held most exchanges within a traditional recitation format. She initiated nearly every interaction, whether with the entire class or one student. The students' assigned role was to respond, not initiate. They complied, often eagerly. Mrs O is an attractive person, and was eager for her students to learn; in return, most of her students seemed eager to please. And eager or not, compliance is easier than initiation, especially when so much of the instruction is so predictable. Much of the discourse was very familiar to members of the class; often they gave the answers before Mrs O asked the questions. So even though most of the class usually was participating in the discourse, they participated on a narrow track, in which she maintained control of direction, content, and pace.

The Framework explicitly rejects this sort of teaching. It argues that children need to express and discuss their ideas, in order to deeply understand the material on which they are working (CSDE 1985: 14, 16). Yet the discourse in Mrs O's class tended to discourage students from reflecting on mathematical ideas, or from sharing their puzzles with the class. There were few opportunities for students to initiate discussion, explore ideas, or even ask questions. Their attention was focused instead on successfully managing a prescribed, highly structured set of activities. This almost surely restricted the questions and ideas that could occur to students, for thought is created, not merely expressed, in social interactions. Even if the students' minds were nonetheless still privately full of bright ideas and puzzling mathematical problems, the discourse organization effectively barred them from the public arena of the class. Mrs O employed curriculum that sought to teach math for understanding, but she kept evidence about what students' understood from entering the classroom discourse. One reason that Mrs O's class was so smooth was that so many possible sources of roughness were choked off at the source.

Another reason has to do with Mrs O's knowledge of mathematics. Though she plainly wanted her students to understand this subject, her grasp of mathematics seemed to restrict her notion of mathematical understanding, and of what it took to produce it. She had taken one or two courses in college, and reported that she had liked them; but she had not pursued the subject further. Lacking deep knowledge, Mrs O seemed unaware of much mathematical content and many ramifications of the material she taught. Many paths to understanding were not taken in her lessons – as for instance, in the Santa's letter example – but she seemed entirely unaware of them. Many understandings or inventive ideas that her students might have had would have made no sense to Mrs O, because her grip on mathematics was so modest. In these ways and many others, her relatively superficial knowledge of this subject insulated her from even a glimpse of many things she might have done to deepen students' understanding. Elements in her teaching that seemed contradictory to an observer therefore seemed entirely consistent to her, and could be handled with little trouble.

Additionally, however much mathematics she knew, Mrs O knew it as a fixed body of truths, rather than as a particular way of framing and solving problems. Questioning, argument, and explanation seemed quite foreign to her knowledge of this subject. Her assignment, she seemed to think, was to somehow make the fixed truths accessible to her students. Explaining them herself in words and pictures would have been one alternative, but she employed a curriculum that promised an easier way – i.e. to embody mathematical ideas and operations in concrete materials and physical activities. Mrs O did not see mathematics as a source of puzzles, as a terrain for argument, or as a subject in which questioning and explanation were essential to learning and knowing – all ideas that are plainly featured in the Framework (CSDE 1985: 13-14). *Math Their Way* did nothing to disturb her view on this matter. Lacking a sense of the importance of explanation, justification, and argument in mathematics, she simply slipped over many opportunities to elicit them, unaware that they existed.

So the many things that Mrs O did not know about mathematics protected her from many uncertainties about teaching and learning math. Her relative ignorance made it difficult for her to learn from her very serious efforts to teach for understanding. Like many students, what she didn't know kept her from seeing how much more she could understand about mathematics. Her ignorance kept her from imagining many different ways in which she might teach mathematics. These limitations on her knowledge meant that Mrs O could teach for understanding, with little sense of how much remained to be understood, how much she might incompletely or naively understand, and how much might still remain to be taught. She is a thoughtful and committed teacher, but working as she did near the surface of this subject, many elements of understanding and many pedagogical possibilities remained invisible. Mathematically, she was on thin ice. But she did not seem to know it, and so skated smoothly on with great confidence.

In a sense, then, the tensions that I observed were not there. They were real enough in my view, but they did not enter the public arena of the class. They lay beneath the surface of the class's work; indeed, they were kept there by the nature of that work. Mrs O's modest grasp of mathematics, and her limited conception of mathematical understanding simply obliterated many potential sources of roughness in her lessons. And those constraints of the mind were given added social force in her close management of classroom discourse. Had Mrs O known more math, and tried to construct a somewhat more open discourse, her class would not have run so smoothly. Some of the tensions that I noticed would have become audible and visible to the class. More confusion and misunderstanding would have surfaced. Things would have been rougher, potentially more fruitful, and vastly more difficult.

Practice and progress

Is Mrs O's mathematical revolution a story of progress, or of confusion? Does it signal an advance for the new Math Framework, or a setback?

These are important questions, inevitable in ventures of this sort. But it may be unwise to sharply distinguish progress from confusion, at least when considering such broad and deep changes in instruction. After all, the teachers and students who try to carry out such change are historical beings. They cannot simply shed their old ideas and practices like a shabby coat, and slip on something new. Their inherited ideas and practices are what teachers and students know, even as they begin to know something else. Indeed, taken together those ideas and practices summarize them as practitioners. As they reach out to embrace or invent a new instruction, they reach with their old professional selves, including all the ideas and practices comprised therein. The past is their path to the future. Some sorts of mixed practice, and many confusions, therefore seem inevitable.

The point seems fundamental, yet it often goes unnoticed by those who promote change in teaching, as well as by many who study it. Larry Cuban's *How Teacher Taught* is a happy exception (1984). Cuban explained that 'many teachers constructed hybrids of particular Progressive practices grafted onto what they ordinarily did in classrooms' (personal communication), Cuban dubbed this approach to the adoption of innovations 'conservative progressivism' (Cuban 1984).

But these mixed practices affect the judgements that teachers and observers make about change in teaching. For instance, the changes in Mrs O's teaching that seemed paradoxical to me seemed immense to her. Remember that when she began teaching four years ago, her math lessons were quite traditional. She ignored the mathematical knowledge and intuitions that children brought to school. She focused most work on computational arithmetic, and required much classroom drill. Mrs O now sees her early teaching as unfortunately traditional, mechanical, and maladapted to children's learning. Indeed, her early math teaching was exactly the sort of thing that the Framework criticized.

Mrs O described the changes she has made as a revolution; I do not think that she was deluded. She was convinced that her classes had greatly improved. She contended that her students now understood and learned much more math than their predecessors had, a few years ago. She even asserts that this has been reflected in their achievement test scores. I have no direct evidence on these claims. But when I compared this class with others that I have seen, in which instruction consisted only of rote exercises in manipulating numbers, her claims seemed plausible. Many traditional teachers certainly would view her teaching as revolutionary.

Still, all revolutions preserve large elements of the old order as they invent new ones. One such element, noted above, was a conception of mathematics as a fixed body of knowledge. Another was a view of learning mathematics in which the aim was getting the right answers. I infer this partly from the teaching that I observed, and partly from several of her comments in our conversations. She said, for example, that math had not been a favorite subject in school. She had only learned to do well in math at college, and was still pleased with herself on this score, when reporting it to me years later. I asked her how she had learned to do and like math at such a late date, and she explained: 'I found that if I just didn't ask so many whys about things that it all started fitting into place' (interview, 6, December 1988). This suggests a rather traditional approach to learning mathematics. More important, it suggests that Mrs O learned to do well at math by avoiding exactly the sort of questions that the Framework associates with understanding mathematics. She said in another connection that her view of math has not changed since college. I concluded that whatever she has learned from workshops, new materials, and new policies, it did not include a new view of mathematics.

Another persistent element in her practice was 'clinical teaching', that is, the California version of Hunter's Instructional Theory Into Practice (ITIP). Hunter and her followers advocate clearly structured lessons: teachers are urged to be explicit about lesson objectives themselves, and to announce them clearly to students. They also are urged to pace and control lessons so that the intended content is covered, and to check that students are doing the work and getting the point, along the way. Though these ideas could be used in virtually any pedagogy, they have been almost entirely associated with a rigid, sonata-form of instruction, that is marked by close teacher control, brisk pacing, and highly structured recitations. The ITIP appears to have played an important part in Mrs O's own education as a teacher, for on her account she learned about it while an undergraduate, and used it when she began teaching. However, she also has been encouraged to persist: both her Principal and Assistant Principal were devotees of Hunter's method, and have vigorously promoted it among teachers in the school. This is not unusual, for ITIP has swept California schools in the past decade. Many principals now use it as a framework for evaluating teachers, and as a means of school improvement. Mrs O's Principal and Assistant Principal praised her warmly, saying that she was a fine teacher with whom they saw eye to eye in matters of instruction.

I asked all three whether clinical teaching worked well with the Framework. None saw any inconsistency. Indeed, all emphatically said that the two innovations were 'complementary'. Though that might be true in principle, it was not true in practice. As ITIP was realized in Mrs O's class among many others, it cut across the grain of the Framework. Like many other teachers, her enactment of clinical teaching rigidly limited discourse, closely controlled social interaction, focused the classroom on herself, and helped to hold instruction to relatively simple objectives.

As Mrs O revolutionized her math teaching, then, she worked with quite conventional materials: A teacher-centered conception of instructional discourse; a rigid approach to classroom management; and a traditional conception of mathematical knowledge. Yet she found a way to make what seemed a profound change in her math teaching. One reason is that the vehicle for change did not directly collide with her inherited ideas and practices. *Math Their Way* focused on materials and activities, not on mathematical knowledge and explanation of ideas. It allowed Mrs O to change her math teaching in what seemed a radical fashion while building on those old practices. This teacher's past was present, even as she struggled to renounce and surpass it.

Mrs O's past also affected her view of her accomplishments, as it does for all of us. I asked, in the Spring of 1989, where her math teaching stood. She thought that her revolution was over. Her teaching had changed definitively. She had arrived at the other shore. In response to further queries, Mrs O evinced no sense that there were areas in her math teaching that needed improvement. Nor did she seem to want guidance about how well she was doing, or how far she had come.

There is an arresting contrast here. From an observer's perspective, especially one who had the new Framework in mind, Mrs O looks as though she may be near the beginning of growth toward a new practice of math teaching. She sees the matter quite differently: she has made the transition, and mastered a new practice.

Which angle is most appropriate – Mrs O's or the observer's? This is a terrific puzzle. One wants to honor this teacher, who has made a serious and sincere effort to change, and who has changed. But one also wants to honor a policy that supports greater intelligence and humanity in mathematics instruction.

It is worth noticing that Mrs O had only one perspective available. No one had asked how she saw her math teaching in light of the Framework. She had been offered no opportunities to raise this query, let alone assistance in answering it. No one offered her another perspective on her teaching. If no other educators or officials in California had seen fit to put the question to her, and to help her to figure out answers, should we expect her to have asked and answered this difficult question all alone?

That seems unrealistic. If math teaching in California is as deficient as the Framework and other critiques suggest, then most teachers would not be knowledgeable enough to raise many fruitful questions about their work in math by themselves, let alone answer them. We can see some evidence for this in Mrs O's lessons. Their very smoothness quite effectively protected her from experiences that might have provoked uncertainty, conflict, and therefore deep questions. But even if such questions were somehow raised for Mrs O and other teachers, the deficiencies in their practice, noted in many recent reports, would virtually guarantee that most of these teachers would not know enough to respond appropriately, on their own. How could teachers be expected to assess, unassisted, their own progress in inventing a new sort of instruction, if their math teaching is in the dismal state pictured in the policy statements demanding that new instruction?

Additionally, if teachers build on past practices as they change, then their view of how much they have accomplished will depend on where they start. Teachers who begin with very traditional practices would be likely to see modest changes as immense. What reformers might see as trivial, such teachers would estimate as a grand revolution – especially as they were just beginning to change. From a perspective still rooted mostly in a traditional practice, such initial changes would seem – and be – immense. That seemed to be Mrs O's situation. She made what some observers might see as tiny and perhaps even misguided changes in her teaching. But like other teachers who were taking a few first small steps away from conventional practice, for her they were giant steps. She would have to take many more steps, and make many more fundamental changes before she might see those early changes as modest.

So, if California teachers have only their subjective yardsticks with which to assess their progress, then it seems unreasonable to judge their work as though they had access to much more and better information. For it is teachers who must change in order to realize new instructional policies. Hence their judgement about what they have done, and what they still may have to do, ought to be given special weight. We might expect more from some teachers than others. Those who had a good deal of help in cultivating such judgement – that is, who were part of some active conversation about their work, in which a variety of questions about their practice were asked and answered, from a variety of perspectives – would have more resources for change than those who had been left alone to figure things out for themselves.

The same notion might be applied to policies like the new Framework, that seek to change instruction. We might expect only a little from those policies that try to improve instruction without improving teachers' capacity to judge the improvements and adjust their teaching accordingly, for such policies do little to augment teachers' resources for change. In Mrs O's case, at least, the Framework has been this sort of policy. We might expect more from policies that help teachers to cultivate the capacity to judge their work from new perspectives, and that add to teachers' resources for change in other ways as well. The new instructional policy of which the Framework is part has not done much of this for Mrs O.

What would it take to make additional, helpful, and usable guidance available to teachers? What would it take to help teachers pay constructive attention to it? Neither query has been given much attention so far, either in efforts to change instruction or in efforts to understand such change. Yet without good answers to these questions, it is difficult to imagine how Mrs O and most other teachers could make the changes that the Framework seems to invite.

Policy and practice

Mrs O's math classes suggest a paradox. This California policy seeks fundamental changes in learning and teaching. State policy-makers have illuminated deficiencies in instruction and set out an ambitious program for improvement. Policy thus seems a chief agency for changing practice. But teachers are the chief agents for implementing any new instructional policy: students will not learn a new mathematics unless teachers know it and teach it. The new policy seeks great change in knowledge, learning and teaching, yet these are intimately held human constructions. They cannot be changed unless the people who teach and learn want to change, take an active part in changing, and have the resources to change. It is, after all, their conceptions of knowledge, and their approaches to learning and teaching that must be revamped.

Hence teachers are the most important agents of instructional policy (Lipsky 1980, Cohen 1988). But the state's new policy also asserts that teachers are the problem. It is, after all, their knowledge and skills that are deficient. If the new mathematics Framework is correct, most California teachers know far too little mathematics, or hold their knowledge improperly, or both. Additionally, most do not know how to teach mathematics so that students can understand it. This suggests that teachers will be severely limited as agents of this policy: how much can practice improve if the chief agents of change are also the problem to be corrected?

This paradox would be trivial if fundamental changes in learning and teaching were easy to make. Yet even the new Framework recognizes that the new mathematics it proposes will be 'difficult to teach' (CSDE 1985: 13). Researchers who have studied efforts to teach as the Framework intends also report that it is difficult, often uncommonly so. Students cannot simply absorb a new 'body' of knowledge. In order to 'understand' these subjects, learners must acquire a new way of thinking about a body of knowledge, and must construct a new practice of acquiring it (Lampert 1988). They must cultivate strategies of problem solving that seem relatively unusual and perhaps counter-intuitive (DiSessa 1983). They must learn to treat academic knowledge as something they construct, test, and explore, rather than as something they accept and accumulate (Cohen 1988). Additionally, and in order to do all of the above, students must un-learn acquired knowledge of math or physics, whether they are second graders or college sophomores. Their extant knowledge may be naive, but it often works.

A few students can learn such things easily. Some even can pick them up more or less on their own. However, many able students have great difficulty in efforts to 'understand' mathematics, or other academic subjects. They find the traditional and mechanical instruction that the Framework rejects easier and more familiar than the innovative and challenging instruction that it proposes.

If such learning is difficult for students, should it be any less so for teachers? After all, in order to teach math as the new Framework intends, most teachers would have to learn an entirely new version of the subject. To do so they also would have to overcome all of the difficulties sketched just above. For, as the Framework says of students, teachers could not be expected to simply absorb a new 'body' of knowledge. They would have to acquire a new way of thinking about mathematics, and a new approach to learning it. They would have to additionally cultivate strategies of problem solving that seem to be quite unusual. They would have to learn to treat mathematical knowledge as something that is constructed, tested, and explored, rather than as something they broadcast, and that students accept and accumulate. Finally, they would have to un-learn the mathematics they have known. Though mechanical and often naive, that knowledge is well settled, and has worked in their classes, sometimes for decades.

These are formidable tasks, even more so for teachers than students. For teachers would have a much larger job of unlearning: after all, they know more of the old math, and their knowledge is much more established. Teachers also would have to learn a new practice of mathematics teaching, while learning the new mathematics and un-learning the old. That is a very tall order. Additionally, it is difficult to learn even rather simple things – like making an omelette – without making mistakes. But mistakes are a particular problem for teachers. For one thing teachers are in charge of their classes, and they hold authority partly in virtue of their superior knowledge. Could they learn a new mathematics and practice of mathematics teaching, with all the trial and error that would entail, while continuing to hold authority with students, parents, and others interested in education? For another, teachers are responsible for their students' learning. How can they exercise that responsibility if they are just learning the mathematics they are supposed to teach, and just learning how to teach it? American education does not have ready answers for these questions. However, there was no evidence that the Framework authors, or educators in Mrs O's vicinity had even asked them. It is relatively easy for policy-makers to propose dramatic changes in teaching and learning, but teachers must enact those changes. They must maintain their sense of responsibility for students' accomplishments, and the confidence of student's parents, and members of the community. Unfortunately, most schools offer teachers little room for learning, and little help in managing the problems that learning would provoke.

The new mathematics Framework seemed to recognize some problems that students would have in learning a new mathematics. But the state has not acted as though it recognized the problems of teachers' learning. Mrs O certainly was not taught about the new mathematics in a way that took these difficulties into account. Instead, the CSED taught her about the new math in a way that closely resembled the very pedagogy that it criticized in the old math. She was told to do something, like students in many traditional math classrooms. She was told that it was important. Brief explanations were offered, and a synopsis of what she was to learn was provided in a text. In effect, California education officials offered Mrs O a standard dose of 'knowledge telling'. The state acted as though it assumed that fundamental instructional reform would occur if teachers were told to do it. New goals were articulated, and exhortations to pursue them were issued. Some new materials were provided. Although the state exhorted teachers to devise a new pedagogy for their classes, it did so with an old pedagogy.

If, as the Framework argues, it is implausible to expect students to understand math simply by being told, why is it any less implausbile to expect teachers to learn a new math simply by being told? if students need a new instruction to learn to understand mathematics, would not teachers need a new instruction to learn to teach a new mathematics? Viewed in this light, it seems remarkable that Mrs O made any progress at all.

What more might have been done, to support Mrs O's efforts to change? What would have helped her to make more progress toward the sort of practice that the Framework proposed? It is no answer to the question, but I note that no-one in Mrs O's vicinity seemed to be asking that question, let alone taking action based on some answers.

This new policy aspires to enormous changes in teaching and learning. It offers a bold and ambitious vision of mathematics instruction, a vision that took imagination to devise and courage to pursue. Yet this admirable policy does little to augment teachers' capacities to realize the new vision. For example, it offers rather modest incentives for change. I could detect few rewards for Mrs O to push her teaching in the Framework's direction –

certainly no rewards that the state offered. The only apparent rewards were those that she might create for herself, or that her students might offer. Nor could I detect any penalties for non-improvement, offered either by the state or her school or district.

Similar weaknesses can be observed in the supports and guidance for change. The new Framework was barely announced in Mrs O's school. She knew that it existed, but wasn't sure if she had ever read it. She did know that the principal had a copy. The new Framework did bring a new text series, and Mrs O knew about that. She knew that the text was supposed to be 'aligned' with the Framework. She had attended a publisher's workshop on the book, and said it had been informative. She had read the book, and the teachers' guide. But she used the new book only a little, preferring *Math Their Way*. The school and district leadership seem to have thought *Math Their Way* was at least as well aligned with the Framework as the new text series, and permitted its substitution in the primary grades.

Hence the changes in Mrs O's practice were partly stimulated by the new policy, but they were weakly guided and supported by it, or by the state agencies that devised it. There was a little more guidance and support from her school and district: she was sent to a few summer workshops, and she secured some additional materials. However, when I observed Mrs O's teaching there seemed to be little chance that she would be engaged in a continuing conversation about mathematics, and teaching and learning mathematics. Her district had identified a few 'mentor teachers' on whom she could call for a bit of advice if she chose. There was no person or agency to help her to learn more mathematics, or to comment on her teaching in light of the Framework, or to suggest and demonstrate possible changes in instruction, or to help her try them out. The new mathematics Framework greatly expanded Mrs O's obligations in mathematics teaching without much increasing her resources for improving instruction. Given the vast changes that the state has proposed, this is a crippling problem.

Mrs O's classroom reveals many ambiguities, and, to my eye, certain deep confusions about teaching mathematics for understanding. But she has been more successful in helping her students to learn a more complex mathematics than California has been in helping her to teach a more complex mathematics. From one angle this situation seems admirable: Mrs O has had considerable discretion to change her teaching, and she had done so in ways that seem well-adapted to her school. Though I may call attention to the mixed quality of her teaching, her superiors celebrate her work. But from another angle it seems problematic. If we take the Framework's arguments seriously, then Mrs O should be helped to struggle through to a more complex knowledge of mathematics, and a more complex practice of teaching mathematics. For if she cannot be helped to struggle through, how can she better help her students to do so? Some researchers and other commentators on education have begun to appreciate how difficult it is for many students to achieve deep understanding of a subject, an appreciation that is at least occasionally evident in the Framework. There is less appreciation of how difficult it will be for teachers to learn a new practice of mathematics instruction.

Acknowledgement

This work is sponsored in part by the National Center for Research on Teacher Education and the Center for the Learning and Teaching of Elementary Subjects, College of Education, Michigan State University. It is funded by the Office of Educational Research and Improvement, Grant No. R117 P8000 4, US Department of Education. The opinions expressed in this paper do no necessarily represent the position, policy, or endorsement of the Office or the Department. The essay was improved by comments from my colleagues in the study: Deborah Ball, Ruth Heaton, Penelope Peterson, Dick Prawat, Ralph Putnam, Janine Remillard, Nancy Wiemers, and Suzanne Wilson. Comments from Magdalene Lampert and Larry Cuban were most helpful. This paper also appears in *Educational Evaluation and Policy Analysis* 12(3) and is reprinted with permission. Copyright 1990, by the American Educational Research Association.

References

BARATTA-LORTON, M. (1976) *Math Their Way* (Boston: Addison-Wesley).

CALIFORNIA STATE DEPARTMENT OF EDUCATION (1987) *Mathematics: Model Curriculum Guide* (Sacramento: SDE).

CALIFORNIA STATE DEPARTMENT OF EDUCATION (1985) *Mathematics Framework For California Public Schools, Kindergarten Through Grade Twelve* (Sacremento: SDE).

CUBAN, L. (1984) *How Teachers Taught* (New York: Longman).

CUBAN, L. (1986) *Teachers and Machines* (New York: Teachers College).

CUBAN, L. Personal communication, 28 April 1990.

COHEN, D.K. (1988) 'Teaching practice: plus ça change...', in P.W. Jackson (ed.), *Contributing to Educational Change: Perspectives on Research and Practice* (Berkeley, CA: McCutchan), pp. 27–84; also published in the *National Center for Research on Teacher Education*, Michigan: Michigan State University, 88–3, September 1988.

DISESSA, A. (1983) 'Phenomenology and the evolution of intuition', in D. Gentner and A.L. Stevens (eds) *Mental models* (Hillsdale, NJ: Erlbaum), pp. 267–298.

GROSS, N., GIAQUINTA, J. and BERNSTEIN, M. (1971) *Implementing Educational Innovations* (New York: Basic).

LAMPERT, M. (1988) *Teachers' Thinking About Students' Thinking About Geometry: The Effects of New Teaching Tools* (Cambridge, MA: Educational Technology Center).

LIPSKY, M. (1980) *Street Corner Bureaucracy* (New York: Sage).

ROWAN, B. and GUTHRIE, L.F. (1989) 'The quality of Chapter 1 instruction: results from a study of 24 schools', in R. Slavin, N.L. Karweit and N.A. Madden (eds) *Effective Programs For Students At Risk* (Boston: Allyn & Bacon), pp. 195–219.

WELSH, W.W. (1979) 'Twenty years of science curriculum development: a look back', *Review of Research in Education*, 7, pp. 282–306.

7   *Educational policy in a situation of uncertainty; or, how to put eggs in different baskets*

William H. Clune

This chapter is about how to approach educational policy in a situation of uncertainty about policy effectiveness. It argues that, rather than putting all of our eggs in one basket, like choice, we should experiment with various approaches, such as both curriculum controls and choice. The chapter thus rejects recent claims of choice as a 'panacea' (Chubb and Moe 1990b), not because they are necessarily untrue, but rather because they are untested.

Maintaining a diversified strategy is especially important because of the potential value of combinations of policies (e.g., enlightened instructional guidance enhancing the impact of decentralized policies of both choice and school restructuring; school restructuring providing models for the supply side in choice systems).

Progress for all of the policies depends upon strengthening the system of educational indicators, student assessments, and sophisticated data bases, as does the possibility for a major breakthrough in basic educational technology (such as greater precision of learning goals).

The thesis in this paper is that the main policy instruments (or approaches) being adopted and experimented with in education today represent rational responses to weak measurement and technology ('measurement and technology' as used in the analysis of 'government failure' in public finance, [Wolf 1988]). Policy experimentation in an environment of great uncertainty is likely to yield two apparently inconsistent results. On the one hand, one would not predict significant success across the board, such as substantial gains in student achievement. On the other hand, since each policy approach may be at the threshold of significant gains in productivity, research and policy should concentrate on bringing potentially major gains to light.

Five general approaches to educational policy are reviewed in this paper: school finance, educational indicators, instructional guidance, school restructuring, and choice. Instructional guidance refers to a set of policies aimed at changing curriculum and pedagogy: curriculum frameworks, instructional materials, student tests, and teacher training. Because of its importance, instructional guidance will receive extra discussion in this paper.

Student achievement as the central goal of policy

Part of the problem with educational policy is the adoption of the praiseworthy, but challenging goal, of substantially raising student achievement. Education not only can but actually does have a score of objectives and purposes in the broad context of society and politics (e.g., child care, certification, recreation, social control). For central policy to have a strong goal, however, there must be some degree of political consensus around a limited set of objectives. That purpose today is significant gains in economic productivity through so-called basic (as opposed to job specific) skills (Bishop 1988, McDonnell 1988, National Center on Education and the Economy 1990, National Commission on Excellence in Education 1983, Resnick and Resnick 1985). The importance of economic productivity can be seen not simply in the scores of reform proposals emphasizing that factor, but also in the important political role played by American business in school reform (see Firestone *et al.* 1989).

Political consensus about the goals of schooling also affects almost every aspect of educational policy, as will become obvious in the unfolding discussion of this paper. For example, the great importance of questions about the viability of systems of instructional guidance is directly linked with the importance of centrally defined goals. Without such goals, a 'low' level of achievement might have quite different meaning (for example, a minimum degree of literacy); and we could readily accept the great diversity of educational goals which might result from highly decentralized educational systems, such as unregulated choice.

In other words, it is the political consensus around ambitious goals which prevents us from solving all our policy problems by simply lowering expectations.

Four generic problems besetting the policy goal of increased student achievement

Uncertainty about our ability to meet the goal of substantially raising student achievement is the result of four general problems:

Poor understanding of effective practice (weak technology): the current push for gains in student achievement, is unfortunately, not well matched by knowledge about how to produce such gains. Economic research has largely failed to discover an 'education production function' (which educational inputs produce gains in educational outcomes [Hanushek 1989]). Most 'obvious' policies and interventions do not improve learning (for example, increases in average funding, reductions in class size, hiring teachers with more advanced degrees [Coleman *et al.* 1966, Jencks *et al.* 1972, 1979]). Research on specific pedagogies shows high variability and transience of outcomes (Rivlin and Timpane 1975). While student outcomes vary substantially across teachers and classrooms (suggesting, for example, the existence of more and less effective teachers and teaching techniques), research has not learned much about the source of this variation (Hanushek 1990).

Serious problems of policy implementation: education policy also has serious problems of changing educational practice from centers of influence, that is, of policy implementation. Ultimately, educational achievement in the USA depends on the capacities and motivation of literally millions of teachers and learners in many thousands of schools. The relevant behaviors to be influenced are almost the worst possible candidates for central control: decentralized, diffuse, discretionary, responsive to local context, influenced by embedded culture, both educational and social, and heavily impacted by race and socioeconomic class. Efforts to provide strong central direction encounter a characteristic set of problems: variation in local capacity, formal compliance, cooptation by local practice, negligible impacts, unanticipated effects, and so forth (see generally Clune 1983, 1985, Elmore and McLaughlin, 1988, McLaughlin 1987).

Serious problems of political organization and policy formation: most social policy in the USA is plagued by problems of political organization. To be effective, educational policy must be carefully designed and highly co-ordinated. Yet many characteristics of the political system militate against these qualities: extreme decentralization (coupled, ironically, with heavy bureaucratization at least in the case of large cities), extreme political pluralism (a multitude of education interest groups whose strength is reinforced by special, and fragmentary, educational programs), and extreme politicization (e.g., activist legislatures producing short-run, partial programs [Cohen in press, Fuhrman 1990]). The extent of the flaws in the political process is paradoxically confirmed by the number and intensity of efforts currently under way to correct these flaws (e.g., statewide comprehensive school reform projects, backed by business groups; integrated planning efforts centered in state chief state school officers and departments of education; the emergence of national achievement goals and educational measurements; and a surge in popularity for consumer choice in education based partially on the hope of simplified governance).

Significant cost constraints: The prospect for major, across the board increases in educational funding seem very limited, indeed. The USA has not experienced a significant growth in real income for a generation (Bowles *et al.* 1983, Edsall 1984). Recently educational funding has recovered some earlier losses, and in some places, made modest gains (Odden 1990). Substantial increases in student achievement might be achievable by massive infusions of new money (for example, cutting class sizes by 75%), but, under current conditions, wholesale fiscal force feeding is out of the question. Cost constraints also are related to the weak state of knowledge about educational productivity. On the one hand, there is little point in making new resources available until we can reduce the inefficiencies of the way we employ all resources, existing and new. The difficulty of getting anything valuable out of new resources is one main frustrations of contemporary results-oriented school finance litigation (see, for example, Liebman 1990). Conversely, as knowledge about productivity improves, it should be possible to raise achievement by reallocation of resources.

Consequently, there is strong pressure and determination behind the option of using existing funds more efficiently. Education (in developed countries) commands enormous resources (e.g., millions of hours of instruction by a fairly highly trained work force). Reallocation of this large stock of existing resources toward more efficient uses theoretically could produce major gains in achievement.

Contemporary approaches to educational policy as rational responses to the four difficulties, with a special focus on instructional upgrading (as the grand strategy of educational reform)

This section of the paper argues that a variety of contemporary educational policy approaches can be seen as rational responses to the four challenges of educational policy outlined above. 'Rational' does not mean fully effective in meeting the challenges. On the contrary, the distinctive configuration of each type of policy represents a kind of 'mini-max' solution to the challenges, attacking a subset of problems in a potentially productive way, while slighting, or ignoring, other problems. Thus, both the strengths and weaknesses of each policy discussed can be analyzed in a framework of the four problems.

To simplify and clarify analysis, let us say that an ideal policy would satisfy all four criteria by offering the following four attributes:

1. promotion of a practice with a probable substantial impact on student achievement;
2. a simple, powerful implementation strategy;
3. powerful, coherent, and sustained political support;
4. moderate cost.

No policy possesses all four attributes, and the object of discussion here is to describe strengths and weaknesses of various policies measured against these ideals.

Educational indicators and student assessments (1) facilitate an impact on student achievement by providing critical information for research and policy formation; (2) may serve to motivate educational practitioners (when published in such documents as 'school report cards'), are relatively simple to implement (almost by definition, since the objective is to produce summary data); (3) are supported by a powerful political movement toward educational accountability; and (4) are quite inexpensive relative to operating costs.

On the other hand, (2) indicators become most problematic when used to change behavior (Richards 1988), while (4) their helpful simplicity and clarity becomes the target of political protest.

School finance reform historically has been aimed at equalization and rationalization of inputs to schooling, especially financial resources (Coons *et al.* 1970). Equalization of inputs (1) is a logical response to a weak knowledge base (reflecting the almost complete failure to establish an educational production function); (2) is simple to implement (involving redirection of financial aid); (3) is supported by a long standing political movement toward equity and centralization in school finance and (4) is, in principle, after costs of transition, no more expensive than disequalizing systems.

On the other hand, (1) redistribution of resources is unlikely, by itself, to increase student achievement; and (3) political resistance accompanies both redistribution and extra resources as solutions to the (4) cost problem (sometimes requiring court intervention which, however, creates its own resistance [Clune 1984].

School restructuring (Elmore 1990) (1) aims at experimentation and innovation (both logical responses to a weak knowledge base); (2) depends on a decentralized unit in the chain of implementation (the school); (4) relies primarily on existing stocks of financial and human resources; and (3) is supported political movements toward school site autonomy and the efficiency of decentralized organization.

On the other hand, (1) the connection between school site management and student achievement is far from clear (Malen *et al.* in press); (2) state governments find it quite difficult to stimulate local innovations (Fuhrman in press); school level innovations seem generally difficult to sustain and generalize (Clune in press); and (4) cost savings may be dependent on extra work by teachers which is not sustainable in the long run (Carnoy and MacDonell 1989).

Family choice in education is based on a coherent theory of enhanced educational effects (competition, community, engagement, specialization, de-bureaucratization) [Chubb and Moe 1986, 1990a], is implemented through decentralized decision-making, relies on existing levels of funding, and is supported by the powerful ideology and politics of consumer choice.

On the other hand, (1) observed effects on student ahievement are quite small (Blank in press, Levin in press, Witte 1990) and fundamentally problematic given alternative political purposes (e.g., economic stratification, see Moore [in press] and Orfield [in press]; (2) the simplicity of decentralized implementation is substantially undermined by the probability of complex regulation aimed at both equity and efficiency outcomes (for example, a strong system of instructional guidance, discussed below [see Levin in press]); (3) the effort to 'remove politics through politics' is quite problematic both in terms of the probability of initial adoption and the possible complexities of regulation; and (4) the small gains available from choice systems may be especially questionable given surprisingly substantial extra costs (for example, of extensive systems of transportation, small numbers of pupils [Orfield in press]).

The policy effectiveness of instructional guidance

This section of the paper will analyze the strengths and weaknesses of the most powerful and popular strategy of educational reform, instructional guidance aimed at instructional upgrading. Most of the reforms of the 1980s fell in this category (graduation requirements, new student tests, curriculum controls, etc.); and the topic has been given fresh significance by choice advocates who claim every system of bureaucratic control of education and thus the entire 1980s reform movement – is bound to fail (Chubb and Moe 1990b). The perspective of this paper is that choice, along with other popular polices, is not a panacea, but is characterized by its own distinctive set of strengths, weaknesses and uncertainties.

Instructional guidance is an effort to raise achievement by involving students in more challenging educational content. Policy instruments used to achieve the goal can be classified generally as 'instructional guidance systems' and include specific policies such as curriculum alignment aimed at higher order thinking (alignment of curriculum guides, instructional materials, and student testing); limitations on course selection (required curriculum); acceleration of students through the curriculum (e.g., abolishing retention in grade); and teacher training and professionalization (both in service and preservice, through both formal policy and professional networks).

Both the strength and weaknesses of academic upgrading can be analyzed according to the four criteria of policy effectiveness. Let us begin with the strengths.

Strengths of instructional guidance

Probable substantial impact on student achievement: A broad array of research supports the proposition that students learn more in more difficult courses. Students tend to learn what they are taught (the so-called 'opportunity to learn' body of research), even when controlling for initial achievement and social class (Coleman *et al.* 1966, 1982, Gamoran 1987, Raizen 1988, Raizen and Jones 1985, Wiley and Harnischfeger 1974). Curriculum content is the strongest determinant of high school achievement and the main reason for differences in achievement between public and private schools (Bryk *et al.* in press).

Furthermore, curriculum in the USA is far from the most rigorous or efficient possible. Recent gains in mechanical skills among US students, and declines in problem-solving, probably are due to an emphasis on mechanics in the curriculum (Smith and O'Day in press). Studies of curriculum content indicate an astonishing lack of new material added each year and a disproportionate emphasis on drill and practice, especially for low income and minority students (Porter 1989). Repetition of material through retention in grade, affecting a large number of students, is ineffective and costly (O'Day and Smith 1990, Shepard and Smith 1989).

A simple, powerful implementation strategy: academic upgrading has much to recommend it from an implementation point of view. Schools have the capacity to offer more advanced courses. Rather than asking schools and teachers to take on a new responsibility for which they are ill-equipped, academic upgrading simply asks that an existing organizational routine be expanded. In a simplified version, upgrading asks schools to teach existing material earlier and perhaps add something new at the top of the sequence. In a more sophisticated version, such as new national standards in mathematics (National Council of Teachers of Mathematics 1989), the material is upgraded and better sequenced at every level. Furthermore, schools generally respond to policies requiring them to change course requirements and content. Significant shifts in course content followed changes in state high school graduation requirements and university entrance requirements. If state law requires a course in World Geography, high schools will offer that course in place of the current offerings, even when teachers vehemently disagree with the idea. Far from being an exotic activity, offering basic academic courses and counting credits is the essence of the normal organizational routine of schooling (Clune 1989).

Powerful, coherent, and sustained political support: The level of political support for academic upgrading is remarkable. Academic upgrading was the central focus of educational reform in the 1980s and promises to maintain its centrality at least until the end of the century (McDonnell 1988, National Commission on Excellence in Education 1983, Resnick and Resnick 1985). This support appears to rest on a convergence of two political ideals: economic productivity and educational tradition. Traditional academic training does seem to improve productivity, especially the more demanding courses (like Algebra, as opposed to General Math [Meyer 1988]). At least many researchers and business leaders accept the link between academic training and productivity, providing a kind of social consensus. And academic training has powerful social support within the educational and political establishments, for example, it reflects the way almost all teachers were taught, it is reinforced by the system of higher education, and it is congruent with popular social and political culture (the 3Rs, the basics, mainstream social studies, etc.).

Moderate cost: Potential moderate cost is a major attraction of academic upgrading. The essential insight is the huge stock of instructional resources already in place (kids in school for 12 years, millions of teachers) and the large amount of waste which exists in this instructional system both in terms of repetitiveness of instruction and low levels of time on task. Slack already in the system, so the argument goes, greatly exceed the magnitude of any possible new resources.

Weaknesses of instructional guidance

Problem with effects on achievement: Although it seems that almost all students could benefit from a more challenging level and faster pace of instruction, the precise instructional content which is most desirable is very poorly understood. For example, high schools teach Algebra, requiring significant prerequisites to do so, and insist on about a 70% level of mastery for a passing grade. From the point of view of a goal like economic productivity, each one of these practices is extremely problematic. Is Algebra, some other mathematical skill, or some other skill entirely, a better choice for economic productivity (debates over minimum competency testing and vocational education show the viability of this question)? Do students really need mastery of prior skills before taking Algebra, or could anyone take the subject without prior preparation? Assuming Algebra is a desirable subject, what is the return in economic productivity to different levels of coverage and mastery (for example, what about 30% mastery of the simplest operations)? In fact, current pedagogical practices in academic subjects, like Algebra, probably are more the product of custom, and perhaps linkages with higher education in the same and related subjects, than any coherent theory of student outcomes.

As a result of the poor understanding of basic learning goals, there has been an almost total failure of detailed design of how to deal with student heterogeneity, both at the individual and group level. At the individual level, the problem is basically how fast to go with students of different abilities and prior achievements; this decomposes into problems of what mixture of skills (problem solving, mechanics) and what level of mastery. With groups, the problem is, even assuming a model of ideal speed for different kinds of students, how to organize instruction in groups of students with different abilities. (Which one of these problems is more serious – upgrading for the individual or group – is an interesting question. The tracking problem usually is described as a response to heterogeneity of groups but would be much easier to resolve if we understood how fast to move with individuals.)

Problems with implementation: The first problem with implementation is a great irony: while policy has a poor model of precise learning goals and how to deal with student heterogeneity, practically every school and every teacher has a fully articulated model, though drastically different ones from teacher to teacher and school to school. These models, or approaches, have proven exceptionally difficult to modify. Thus, the ingrained culture of schools and teachers resists upgrading precisely because a theory of appropriate content and pacing is already embedded in the culture itself (see Cohen, this volume).

A second set of problems concerns the policy instrument of instructional guidance itself. Problems with instructional guidance include: poor choice of educational content (e.g., the minimum competency movement [Jaeger and Title 1980, Linn *et al.* 1982]); excessive prescriptiveness of guidance (to some extent an outgrowth of mastery learning [McNeil 1986, Rosenholtz 1987]); inadequate attention to the training of teachers, both new and experienced; inadequate understanding of how to obtain the active and enthusiastic cooperation of teachers (see Porter *et al.* 1990, this volume; insufficient attention to school wide planning; and insufficient attention to diversity of school problems and objectives (see the school level adaptations described in Levin [1988]; on the intrinsic advantages of school level action, see Clune [in press]).

Problems with political support: Political support for instructional guidance is stronger in principle than in specifics and, thus, is difficult to move off status quo. Popular consensus on the issue is fairly thin beneath the surface and riddled with contradictions, for example, higher order thinking and problem solving v. mechanics and factual memorization, social orthodoxy v. analysis in social studies, vocational v. academic education.

As a result, the nature of the new direction in upgrading which will be supported by politics is currently unclear. Traditional academics still enjoy major strength, for example, improvements in math, science, and writing. But there is at least one major alternative. A major critique of traditional academics is building within both the business and educational establishments based on need for relevance and engagement (National Center on Education and the Economy 1990) (and terminating, perhaps, in the kind of two-tier educational system existing in Europe and Japan).

The fragmentation and incoherence of US policymaking in education strongly affects instructional guidance systems, which depend heavily on a number of carefully designed components coordinated with each other and sustained over time. Because of the multitude of parties with access to educational policy, instructional guidance tends to come in disjointed bursts and waves – different kinds of tests, different kinds of curriculum guidance, teacher training governed by different assumptions than instructional guidance, and so forth (Cohen in press).

Problems with moderate cost: The argument made earlier about inefficiency in the large stock of existing resources seems basically sound. Lots of room exists for making our existing resources do a better job. A potential problem in the area of costs is the distribution, rather than the level, of resources in a newly designed system, for example, the need for higher levels of per pupil funding in urban and rural areas. Even this, however, would not seem that serious a difficulty if people can be persuaded about the probability of major gains in achievement.

Strategic policy and research: pushing weak policies in productive directions

The preceding review of major policy options in education supports the assertion made at the outset about the paradox, or incongruity, of pursuing strong educational goals (substantial gains in student achievement) through weak policy instruments. All of the policies have not just minor flaws but glaring weaknesses in one or more of ideal elements of effective policy.

This section of the paper will take the analysis one step further and suggest what kinds of policy and research might be undertaken to push the policies toward some kind of a frontier of productivity. In its present form, each policy is unlikely to produce substantial gains in achievement, yet, as a distinctive response to the problems of educational policy, each also has significant potential. How might such potential be maximized? My thoughts here are preliminary and offered as much as examples of an important style of thinking as serious proposals for action.

Educational indicators and student assessment: This is probably the area of greatest technical sophistication and political maturity. The focus on how to measure student learning in the National Assessment, the development of national goals, and interest in performance assessment (Archbald and Newmann 1988), all testify to significant policy momentum. The major stumbling block seems to be the development of state student assessments which are technically defensible (e.g., providing meaningful measures of student gain) and related to state curriculum goals (Blank 1990, this volume).

Thus, research should focus on the development of high quality assessments (Smith 1990, Smith and O'Day 1990, this volume); while policy concentrates on the adoption of high quality assessments at the state level.

School finance reform: The great opportunity currently is the emergence, once again, of new political motivation and significant new resources primarily through court decisions (for example, New Jersey, Kentucky, Texas [Thro 1990]). From the point of view of student achievement, the problem is, simply, whether the new spending can improve on the 'shot in the dark' strategy of fiscal equalization. The most rational response to the problem would seem to be combining fiscal equalization with some vigorous experimentation in the other policy areas described in this paper.

School restructuring: School restructuring probably is the most technically obscure and politically immature of all the policies. Little is understood either about the forms and effects of restructuring at the school level or how to combine central policy guidance with vigorous local initiative. It is especially important not to cut off experimentation before we understand more about the range of local options and the kinds of state policies which can support them. Accordingly, both research and policy should maintain an experimental posture and focus on extending the range of, and gathering relevant information about, available policy options (David *et al.* 1990, Elmore 1990).

Family choice: I sense that choice is at a critical crossroads in its development as a policy instrument. Strong political momentum about the general concept is unfortunately combined with uncertainty and hesitation about specific policy directions. The critical problem seems to be designing systems which offer the chance of significant improvements in achievement, especially for disadvantaged students. The best mechanism for achieving this purpose appears to be the encouragement of highly motivated 'niche' players, such as alternative schools run by community activists. The critical challenge to this type of niche player is the adoption of burdensome regulations of choice plans which raise entry costs by requiring comprehensive educational services for all types of students. In other words, my sense is that choice is entering a period of critical policy debate, in which the virtues of a market system for meeting a variety of needs through a variety of responses will compete against the ideal of the single school meeting all needs through comprehensive regulation. This will not be an easy debate, raising such questions as how best to serve handicapped students in a highly differentiated system and how the traditional special interest politics of education will respond to the potential of diversity and choice (Chubb and Moe 1990a, 1990b). Thus, much of the key work in research and policy will concern the design and politics of progressive choice systems, including the redesign of legislation normally considered outside the purview of choice (e.g., special education).

Instructional guidance and upgrading: Research and policy on instructional guidance and upgrading is relatively mature and has considerable political momentum (especially in the policies of national lead states such as Connecticut, New York, and California). The agenda for research and policy is fairly clear and should proceed by trying to achieve three important objectives: the construction of coherent systems of instructional guidance which have a strong impact at the school and classroom level (for example, by delivering instructional materials and teacher training), the gradual introduction of higher order thinking and problem solving into curriculum content, and the design of systems which maximize participation, enthusiasm, and responsibility on the part of teachers.

Perhaps the most important research question about instructional guidance is precisely the one raised by Chubb and Moe, whether it can be done well, especially in the fragmented political system of the United States (Chubb and Moe 1990a,b); see Cohen (in press) for an elegant description of the incoherence of US instructional guidance as it actually impacts on instruction. This major issue involves two sub-issues. The first is getting a fix on the seriousness of the conflicts between central control and decentralized action within even the best designed system of instructional guidance. Can central policy really deliver high quality instruction to the classroom (Darling-Hammond in press)? How serious are the conflicts between central and local control and autonomy (for example, suppression of valuable local goal formation and teacher motivation)? Research on the best designed systems of instructional guidance in other countries may help answer these questions. The second sub-issue is whether a minimally effective instructional guidance system is possible in the fragmented, politicized system of educational policy in the US. Research on the better US systems (e.g., Connecticut, New York) and fundamental aspects of the policy process in the USA (e.g., Fuhrman 1990) may help answer these questions. As Chubb and Moe (1990a) suggest, the credibility of instructional guidance in the USA may be the crucial factor in whether politics switches emphasis to decentralized alternatives, like choice.

Conclusion

This paper has advocated, essentially, the strategy of capitalizing on both the strengths and weaknesses of current policy options in education by pushing each policy as strongly as possible toward the nearest available frontier of productivity. Maintaining a diversified strategy (pushing forward with all policies rather than putting all our eggs in one basket) also is important because of the potential value of combinations of policies. Enlightened instructional guidance might enhance the impact of decentralized systems like choice and restructuring. Experiments in school restructuring might provide models for supply side innovation in choice systems. Comprehensive school finance reform might yield important insights about effective policies and practices.

Given the strong emphasis on both research and development characterizing this strategy, policymakers should take special note of the importance of adequate data and analysis. The preceding 25 years have been characterized by gains in education research at the expense of confidence in education policy (as one intervention after another was proven ineffective). It is as if (as I said at a conference commemorating educational research) research was moving forward and policy was moving backward (Wisconsin Center for Education Research 1989). Against this historical background, neither researchers nor policymakers will be prepared to accept strong claims without adequate data and analysis. In a milieu of experimentation, educational indicators and sophisticated data bases take on added importance as the necessary infrastructure for policy development.

Policy analysts also should keep in mind the possibility of major advances in educational technology (in the broad sense of precise objectives and powerful teaching strategies). Suppose we could define the skills of economic productivity, and teach these skills, with something of the same precision that we can define and teach the skills of flying an airplane (a complex skill which, however, could be mastered at an acceptable level by a large percent of the total population in a fairly short period of time and assessed with a high degree of reliability and validity). Enormous gains in efficiency and effectiveness probably would result: learning in a shorter time, individualized instruction, perhaps aided by computers, and so on. This kind of precision and power has been the dream of the minimum competency testing and mastery learning, movements which apparently floundered on a misconception and underestimation of desirable instructional content and goals. Marshall Smith and Jennifer O'Day's paper (this volume) on the gains in basic skills during a period of reduced financial resources seems to show the potential power of greater precision in educational technology.

Where a breakthrough in basic technology might occur is hard to say. The contemporary ferment over a new kind of education for the average student (hands-on, vocationally relevant, replacing traditional college prep but maintaining a high level of cognitive content) may have such a potential (National Center on Education and the Economy 1988, Shanker 1989, Wehlage et al. 1989). In the meantime, the mere possibility of such a breakthrough is yet another reason for continued development and debate over student assessments. Assessments are, among other things, the main focus of sustained research, development, and social deliberation about precise definition of the desirable ends of schooling, as seen, for example, in the debate over so-called performance assessment (e.g., portfolios of writing rather than multiple choice exams) [Archbald and Newmann 1988].

Lacking such a breakthrough, because of the complexity and uncertainty of its subject matter, educational policy analysis requires a difficult blend scientific rigor and informed judgment, social skepticism and advocacy. Striking the right balance between negativism and advocacy, undue pessimism and optimism, seems almost impossible to do. Either one, pessimism or optimism, no solutions or false solutions, timid claims of inflated claims, can prevent progress. Educational reforms of the past frequently have become educational policy problems of the present (according to various critics, a partial list would include: retention in grade, mastery learning, drill and practice, direct instruction, minimum competency achievement testing, career education, vocational education, school desegregation, categorical grants, the large comprehensive high school, and the entire bureaucratic organization of schooling). With regard to the contemporary enthusiasm for choice, are the optimists at fault for making excessive claims, or the pessimists for not recognizing the possibility of a substantial marginal improvement? Even with good data and analysis, only a process of informed judgment can reduce to a tolerable level the subjective element of answers to such questions. Contemporary political pressure to increase student achievement makes progress possible but also increases the probability of serious mistakes.

Perhaps the most important point about the atmosphere of uncertainty is the danger of reducing support for research and development exactly when that support is most needed. Identifying the most productive research may be difficult, but continued research is essential to reduce the zone of uncertainty.

Acknowledgement

Aspects of this paper were presented in seminars to staff of the World Bank at Stanford University on 1989 and 1990. The research reported in this paper was supported by the Center for Policy Research in Education, which is funded by a grant from the US Department of Education, Office of Educational Research and Improvement (Grant No. OERI-G-0086-90011), and by the Wisconsin Center for Education Research, School of Education, University of Wisconsin Madison. The opinions expressed in this publication are those of the author and do not necessarily reflect the views of institutional sponsors including the US Department of Education, Office of Educational Research and Improvement, the institutional partners of the Center for Policy Research in Education, or the Wisconsin Center for Education Research.

References

ARCHBALD, D. A. and NEWMANN, F. M. (1988) *Beyond Standardized Testing: Assessing Authentic Academic Achievement in the Secondary School* (Reston, VA: National Association of Secondary School Principals).

BLANK, R. K. (1990, this volume) 'State policies and state role in curriculum', in S. H. Fuhrman and B. Malen (eds) *The Politics of Curriculum and Testings* 1990 Yearbook of the Politics of Educational Association (Philadelphia: Falmer Press).

BLANK, R. K. (in press) 'Educational effects of magnet high schools', in W. H. Clune and J. F. Witte (eds) *Choice and Control in American Education*, volume 2 (Philadelphia: Falmer Press).

BISHOP, J. (1988) 'The productivity consequences of what is learned in high school', discussion paper prepared for the Center for Advanced Human Resource Studies, Cornell University.

BOWLES, S., GORDON, D. M. and WEISSKOPF, T. E. (1983) *Beyond the Wasteland: A Democratic Alternative to Economic Decline* (Garden City, NY: Anchor Press/Doubleday).

BRYK, T., LEE, V. and SMITH, J. (in press) 'High school organization and its effects on teachers and students: an interpretive summary of the research', in W. H. Clune and J. F. Witte (eds) *Choice and Control in American Education*, volume 1 (Philadelphia: Falmer Press).

CARNOY, M. and MACDONELL, J. (1989) *School District Restructuring in Sante Fe, New Mexico*. Research Report Series RR-017 (New Brunswick, NJ: Rutgers University, Center for Policy Research in Education).

CHUBB, J. E. and MOE, T. M. (1986) 'No school is an island: politics, markets and education', *The Brookings Review*, 4(4), pp. 21–36.

CHUBB, J. E. and MOE, T. M. (1990a) 'Choice *Is* a panacea', *The Brookings Review*, 8.

CHUBB, J. E. and MOE, T. M. (1990b) *Politics, Markets, and America's Schools* (Washington, DC: The Brookings Institution).

CLUNE, W. H. (1983) 'A political model of implementation and implications of the models for public policy, research, and the changing roles of law and lawyers', *Iowa Law Review*, 69(1), pp. 47–125.

CLUNE, W. H. (1984) 'Courts and legislatures as arbitrators of social change. Review of 'Educational policymaking and the courts: An empirical study of judicial activism', *Yale Law Journal*, 93(4), p. 763.

CLUNE, W. H. (with M. VAN PELT) (1985) 'A political method of evaluating the Education for All Handicapped Children Act and the several gaps of gap analysis', *Law and Contemporary Problems*. 48(1), pp. 7–62.

CLUNE, W. H. (with P. White and J. Patterson) (1989) *The Implementation and Effects of High School Graduation Requirements: First Steps Towards Curriculum Reform* (New Brunswick, NJ: Rutgers University, Center for Policy Research in Education).

CLUNE, W. H. (in press) 'Educational governance and student achievement', in W. H. Clune and J.F. Witte (eds) *Choice and Control in American Education*, volume 2 (Philadelphia: Falmer Press).

COHEN, D. K. (1990, this volume) 'Revolution in one classroom', in S. H. Fuhrman and B. Malen (eds) *The Politics of Curriculum and Testing*, 1990 Yearbook of the Politics of Education Association (Philadelphia: Falmer Press).

COHEN, D. K. (in press) 'Governance and instruction: the promise of decentralization and choice', in W. H. Clune and J. F. Witte (eds) *Choice and Control in American Education*, volume 1 (Philadelphia: Falmer Press).

COLEMAN, J. S. *et al.* (1966) *Equality of Educational Opportunity* (Washington, DC: Government Printing Office).

COLEMAN, J. S., HOFFER, T. and KILGORE, S. (1982) *High School Achievement: Public Catholic and Private Schools Compared* (New York: Basic Books).

COONS, J. E., CLUNE, W. H. and SUGARMAN, S. D. (1970) *Private Wealth and Public Education* (Cambridge, MA: Harvard University Press).

DARLING-HAMMOND, L. (in press) 'Instructional policy into practice: the power of the bottom over the top', *Educational Evaluation and Policy Analysis*.

DAVID, J. L., COHEN, M., HONETSCHLAGER, D. and TRAIMAN, S. (1990) *State Actions to Restructure Schools: First Steps* (Washington, DC: National Governors' Association).

EDSALL, T. B. (1984) *The New Politics of Inequality* (New York: W. W. Norton and Co).

ELMORE, R. F. (ed.) (1990) *Restructuring Schools: The Next Generation of Educational Reform* (San Francisco: Jossey-Bass).

ELMORE, R. F. and MCLAUGHLIN, M. W. (1988) *Steady Work: Policy, Practice, and the Reform of American Education*. R-3574-NIE/RC) (Santa Monica, CA: The Rand Corporation).

FIRESTONE, W. A., FUHRMAN, S. H. and KIRST, M. W. (1989) *The Progress of Reform: An Appraisal of State Education Initiatives* (New Brunswick, NJ: Rutgers University, Center for Policy Research in Education).

FIRESTONE, W. A., FUHRMAN, S. H. and KIRST, M. W. (1990) 'Implementation, effects of state education reform in the '80s', *NASSP Bulletin*, pp. 75–83.

FUHRMAN, S. H. (1990) 'Legislatures and education policy', paper presented at the Eagleton Institute of Politics Symposium on the Legislature in the Twenty-First Century, 27–29 April, Williamsburg, VA.

FUHRMAN, S. H. (with P. Fry) (in press) 'Diversity amidst standardization: State differential treatment of districts', in W. H. Clune and J. F. Witte (eds.) *Choice and Control in American Education*, volume 2 (Philadelphia: Falmer Press).

GAMORAN, A. (1987) 'The stratification of high school learning opportunities', *Sociology of Education*, 60, pp. 135–155.

HANUSHEK, E. (1989) 'The impact of differential expenditures on school performance', *Educational Researcher*, 18(4), pp. 45–51.

HANUSHEK, E. A. (1990) 'The impact of differential expenditures on school performance', *Issue Analysis*, March (Washington, DC: American Legislative Exchange Council).

JAEGER, R. M. and TITLE, C. K. (eds) (1980) *Minimum Competency Achievement Testing: Motives, Models, Measures, and Consequences* (Berkeley, CA: McCutchan).

JENCKS, C. S., SMITH, M., ACLAND, H., BANE, M. J., COHEN, D., GINTIS, H., HEYNS, B. and MICHELSON, S. (1972) *Inequality: A reassessment of the Effect of Family and Schooling in America* (New York: Basic Books).

JENCKS, C., BARLETT, S., CORCORAN, M., CROUSE, J., EAGLESFIELD, D., JACKSON, G., McCLELLAND, K., MUESER, P., OLNECK, M., SCHWARTZ, J., WARD, S. and WILLIAMS, J. (1979) *Who gets Ahead? The Determinants of Economic Success in America* (New York: Basic Books).

LEVIN, H. M. (1988) *Accelerated Schools for At-Risk Students*. CPRE Research Report Series RR-010 (New Brunswick, NJ: Rutgers University, Center for Policy Research in Education).

LEVIN, H. (in press) 'The theory of choice applied to education', in W. H. Clune and J. F. Witte (eds) *Choice and Control in American Education*, volume 1 (Philadelphia: Falmer Press).

LIEBMAN, J. A. (1990) 'Implementing *Brown* in the nineties: political reconstruction, liberal recollection, and litigatively enforced reform', *Virginia Law Review*, 76(3), pp. 349–435.

LINN, R. L., MADAUS, G. F. and PEDULLA, J. J. (1982) 'Minimum competency testing: cautions on the state of the art', *American Journal of Education*, pp. 1–47.

MALEN, B., OGAWA, R. and KRANZ, J. (in press) 'What do we know about school based management: a case study of the literature', in W. H. Clune and J. F. Witte (eds) *Choice and Control in American Education*, volume 2 (Philadelphia: Falmer Press).

McDONNELL, L. M. (1988) 'Coursework policy in five states and its implications for indicator development', working paper prepared for The Rand Corporation, Santa Monica, Ca.

McLAUGHLIN, M. W. (1987) 'Lessons from past implementation research', *Educational Evaluation and Policy Analysis*, 9(2), pp. 171–178.

McNEIL, L. M. (1986) *Contradictions of Control: School Structure and School Knowledge* (New York: Routledge & Kegan Paul).

MEYER, R. H. (1988) 'Applied versus traditional mathematics, new econometric models of the contribution of high school courses to mathematics proficiency', (paper prepared for the National Assessment of Vocational Education, Washington, DC).

MOORE, D. (in press) 'Voice and choice in Chicago', in W. H. Clune and J. F. Witte (eds) *Choice and Control in American Education*, volume 2 (Philadelphia: Falmer Press).

NATIONAL CENTER ON EDUCATION AND THE ECONOMY (1990) *America's Choice: High Skills or Low Wages!* (New York: NCEE).

NATIONAL COMMISSION ON EXCELLENCE IN EDUCATION (1983) *A Nation at Risk: The Imperative for Educational Reform* (Washington, DC: US Government Printing Office).

NATIONAL COUNCIL OF TEACHER OF MATHEMATICS (1989) *Curriculum and Evaluation Standards for School Mathematics* (Reston, VA. NCTM).

O'DAY, J., SMITH, M. S. (1990) 'Retention policies in US schools', paper prepared for the Center for Policy Research in Education, Rutgers University, New Brunswick, NJ.

ODDEN, A. (1990) 'Education funding changes during the 1980s', *Educational Policy*, 4(1), pp. 33–47.

ORFIELD, G. A. (in press). 'Do we know anything worth knowing about educational effects of magnet schools', in W. H. Clune and J. F. Witte (eds) *Choice and Control in American Education*, volume 2 (Philadelphia: Falmer Press).

PORTER, A. C. (1989) 'A curriculum out of balance: the case of elementary school mathematics', *Educational Researcher*, 18(5), pp. 9–15.

PORTER, A. C., ARCHBALD, D. A. and TYREE, A. K. (1990, this volume) 'Reforming the curriculum: will empowerment policies replace control?', in S. H. Fuhrman and B. Malen, (eds) *The Politics of Curriculum and Testing*, 1990 Yearbook of the Politics of Educational Association (Philadelphia: Falmer Press), pp. 11–36.

RAIZEN, S. A. (1988) *Increasing Educational Productivity through Improving the Science Curriculum.* CPRE Research Report Series RR-006 (New Brunswick, NJ: Rutgers University, Center for Policy Research in Education).

RAIZEN, S. A. and JONES,, L. V. (eds) (1985) *Indicators of Pre-College Education in Science and Mathematics: A Preliminary Review* (Washington, DC; National Academy Press).

RESNICK, D. P. and RESNICK, L. B. (1985) 'Standards, curriculum and performance: a historical and comparative perspective', *Educational Researcher*, 14(4), pp. 5–20.

RICHARDS, C. E. (1988) 'A typology of educational monitoring systems', *Educational Evaluation and Policy Analysis*, 10(2), pp. 106–116.

RIVLIN, A. and TIMPANE, M. (1975) *Planned Variation in Education: Should We Give Up or Try Harder?* (Washington, DC: The Brookings Institution).

ROSENHOLTZ, S. J. (1987) 'Education reform strategies: will they increase teacher commitment?' *American Journal of Education*, 95(4), pp. 534–562.

SHANKER, A. (1989) 'The revolution that is overdue', keynote speech delivered at the Conference on Choice and Control in American Education, University of Wisconsin-Madison, 17–19 May, 1989.

SHEPARD, L. A. and SMITH, M. L. (1989) *Flunking Grades: Research and Policies on Retention* (New York: Falmer Press).

SMITH, M. S. (1990) 'Policy coherence: a model for states, schools, and districts' (paper prepared for the annual meeting of the Association for Public Policy Analysis and Management, 18–20 October, San Francisco, CA).

SMITH, M. S. and O'DAY, J. (1990, this volume) 'Systemic school reform', in S. H. Fuhrman and B. Malen (eds) *The Politics of Curriculum and Testing*, 1990 Yearbook of the Politics of Educational Association (Philadelphia: Falmer Press).

SMITH, M. S. and O'DAY, J. (in press) 'Educational equality: 1966 and now', in D. Verstegen (ed.) *Spheres of Justice in American schools*, 1990 Yearbook of the American Education Finance Association (New York: Harper & Row).

THRO, W. D. (1990) 'The third wave: the impact of the Montana, Kentucky, and Texas decisions on the future of public school finance reform litigation', *Journal of Law and Education*, 19(2), pp. 219–251.

WEHLAGE, G. G., RUTTER, R. A., SMITH, G. A., LESKO, N. and FERNANDEZ, R. R. (1989) *Reducing the Risk: Schools as Communities of Support* (Philadelphia: Falmer Press).

WILEY, D. E. and HARNISCHFEGER, A. (1974) 'Explosion of a myth: quality of schooling and exposure to instruction, major education vehicles', *Educational Researcher*, 3(4), pp. 7–12.

WISCONSIN CENTER FOR EDUCATION RESEARCH (1989) *Highlights of Educational Research.* A conference to celebrate the 25th anniversary of the Wisconsin Center for Education Research, University of Wisconsin-Madison, WI.

WITTE, J. F. (1990) 'Choice in American education' paper prepared for the Policy and Planning Center, Appalachia Educational Laboratory, Charleston, WV.

WOLF, C., Jr. (1988) *Markets or Governments? Choosing between Imperfect Alternatives* (Cambridge: MIT Press).

8   *Trends in testing in the USA*

Eva L. Baker and Regie Stites

This chapter traces the development of testing policies in the USA and focuses on the use of academic tests of aptitude and achievement. The thesis of the chapter is that testing policy is a result of a subtle interplay of social, political, and technical factors. Thus, the nature of the development of testing in the USA is linked fundamentally to its democratic principles, the emergence of scientific ideas, and the social and economic reality of an immigrant and heterogeneous society. Conflicts among these factors have shaped the day to day reality of testing and its use in the US system. The chapter is organized into sections chronologically. Each attempts to provide an integrated discussion of social and political contexts and explicit motives for US test development as well as, where appropriate, technical summaries of the major features of the assessment themselves. This approach is structured to illuminate the recurring themes that have influenced or are likely to influence future US testing practices. The chapter closes with a discussion of critical issues in the design of assessments for the future.

Historical origins

Where did formal tests come from? The first large-scale standardized examinations were born out of the struggle for control of the state between bureaucratic and aristocratic power bases in late Imperial China more than 1000 years ago. The Chinese civil service examinations were an outgrowth of a Confucian ideology of education and statecraft which asserted that men with sufficient talent and moral character to maintain order in the state must be sought out in the population at large. The measure of such talent was knowledge of the classics; the assumption was that given sufficient and appropriate schooling such talent could be discovered and nurtured in men from all ranks of society (Ho 1962, Kracke 1981, Chaffee 1985, Needham 1970, Franke 1960).

In the West, large-scale examinations emerged much later and in a very different ideological climate. The Enlightenment infused Western conceptions of merit with liberal, egalitarian ideals largely absent from Eastern thought. While the Confucian tradition viewed merit as a quality that was earned through the successful assimilation of a corpus of orthodox wisdom, in the post-Enlightenment era in the West, value has gradually come to be associated with innate qualities and capacities of individuals. Evolution, the *grande ideé* of the late nineteenth and early twentieth centuries, was both a reflection of this ideological shift and, by focusing attention on individual variation within human populations, the catalyst for developments in the technology of mental testing.

Technical development of testing in the USA: the early years of mental testing

The mental testing movement which dominated the field of psychology in the first half of the twentieth century is commonly thought to have grown out of attempts to extend the theory of natural selection introduced with the publication of Darwin's *The Origin of*

0268–0939/90 $3.00 © 1990 Taylor & Francis Ltd.

Species in 1859. One important aspect of Darwin's theory, summed up by the phrase, 'survival of the fittest', was the link between 'fitness' and adaptation to a particular environment. Seeing evolution as a process by which a species perfects itself by perpetuating the traits of its most able members led many to seek ways to measure individual differences in the key trait of intelligence while ignoring the importance of environmental factors in the development of this trait (Cronbach and Suppes 1969). This perspective led to the development of differential psychology and the dominance of the study of individual differences.

Two of the most influential early workers in the field of mental measurement were Francis Galton in the United Kingdom and Wilhelm Wundt in Germany. Galton's major contribution was his systematic empirical approach to the problem of finding ways to measure levels of inherited intellect. Like his contemporaries in the late nineteenth century, Galton posited a concept of 'unified intelligence' which could be correlated with measures of such elemental processes as reaction time and the ability to discriminate between weights (Cronbach and Suppes 1969). Working in his laboratory in Leipzig, Wundt laid the foundations for the field of experimental psychology. Two Americans who studied with Wundt, G. Stanley Hall and James M. Cattell, were to become very influential in the American development and application of psychological testing.

Models of mental testing

Galton's work also laid the foundations of statistical technique required for the development of large-scale standardized testing. The formulation of the normal distribution provided a scientific basis for interpreting measured differences in natural phenomena, such as heights of trees, weights of newborns, and by extension, particular components of human abilities. A significant breakthrough in the field of mental testing came from the work of the French psychologist Alfred Binet and his collaborators. In the 1890s, Binet had made progress in the field of mental testing by focusing on the study of complex processes such as attention, reasoning, and judgment. In 1904, he was commissioned by the Paris schools to design a test that could be used to determine which of their nonlearners were mentally defective. The result was the 1905 Binet scale, which brought together a wide range of short tasks including a number of diverse reasoning skills such as ordering, naming, and comparing. The major innovation in Binet's scale was its pragmatic solution to the problem of linking test results to predictions of school performance. To do this Binet ignored the specifics of the reasoning process and selected problems on which childrens' performance corresponded to teachers' identification of them as average or feeble-minded. Binet did not imply that a given score defined anything innate or permanent, nor did he mean that the score measured 'intelligence' (Hale 1982). It was on this basis that the first applications of psychological measurement to educational decisionmaking were made (Haney 1984). Note that the primary index of validity was rooted in teachers' decisions about the classification of individuals, in comparison to one another, a concept subsequently lost for more than a half century. Another related development was the reporting metric which integrated a developmental, age-linked basis for describing a child's status. 'Mental age' was the concept derived from this process. Test tasks were classified in terms of difficulty by looking at the average age of students who were successful at the task. In 1912, the concept of intelligence quotient or IQ developed; IQ was found by dividing the mental age of the child by his/her chronological age.

Roots of large-scale assessment

Even before the Binet scale was developed, testing was used in US society, particularly in the employment realm. In 1814, for example, the Army used formal examinations to test surgeons. Both Army and Navy military academies screened prospective candidates with tests (Zeidner and Drucker 1988). The US Congress passed the Civil Service Act in 1883 following the assassination of President Garfield by a disgruntled office seeker. This act created the civil service examination system, and by the turn of the century, half of all federal jobs were awarded on the basis of competitive examinations (Zeidner and Drucker 1988). The goal of such a system was to identify the best candidates and to assure that the decision-making process was equitable.

Before the First World War, testing programs were also developed by large US corporations in an effort to use scientific selection procedures to ameliorate perceived labor problems such as turnover, accidents, and strikes (Link 1919). Psychologists, notably Scott and Thorndike, developed tests for industry. Hollingsworth developed and tried out tests for 20 types of work (Hollingsworth 1915).

The USA provided fertile ground for the spread of standardized testing since in the public view tests seemed to offer a 'truly democratic device for the identification of talent' (Cronbach and Suppes 1969:77). One of the first uses of standardized testing as a means of evaluating the performance of schools in America was the efforts of Joseph Mayer Rice. In 1891, Rice, a pediatrician with a strong interest in German pedagogy, was commissioned by *Forum Magazine* to write an appraisal of American education. To do this, Rice devised a spelling test that he had administered to 16,000 students between the years 1895 and 1897. Through fairly sophisticated statistical analysis of the results Rice was able to show that the levels of pupils' attainment on his test bore no relation to the minutes a week they had spent in spelling drills. Following Rice's example, scales were devised for the assessment of achievement in other subjects, including handwriting, arithmetic, and drawing (Cronbach and Suppes 1969). It is significant that Rice's original purpose was to assess American educational quality, using tests for programs rather than for the selection of individuals. Nonetheless, because of the availability of normative statistical models and the need to choose from among the many for jobs and other opportunities, selection and classification testing continued to dominate testing practice. A third obvious reason was the relative scarcity of education as an available commodity and the concurrent general respect for those in the teaching profession.

From the First World War to 1950: the growth of standardized testing

Two developments caused a tremendous amount of attention in America to be focused on the field of mental testing in the first quarter of the twentieth century. The first was the development of the Stanford–Binet Scale by Lewis Terman at Stanford University in 1916, and the second was the development and use of the Army's Alpha and Beta tests during the First World War.

Lewis Terman studied under G. Stanley Hall in the influential psychology department founded by Hall at Clark University. Like his mentor and his mentor's mentors, Galton and Wundt, Terman assumed that intelligence was a unified and general ability (Cronbach and Suppes 1969). Another assumption that Terman shared with these men was a strong belief in the hereditary basis of intellect. Apparently Binet did not share this hereditarian bias, and felt that the testing of reasoning should be the basis for diagnosing underdeveloped abilities and a guide for remedial instruction (Wolf 1973, Gould 1981).

Selection tests

The major impetus for the subsequent adoption of mental testing in American schools in
the early twentieth century was the development and use of mental tests as a means of
screening Army recruits during the First World War. When the USA declared war on
Germany in 1917, Robert Yerkes called a meeting of the American Psychological
Association to discuss the possible contributions of psychology to the war effort. This
meeting brought together the leading intellectual lights in the field of psychometrics, and
was sponsored by the National Research Council and the American Psychological
Association. The meeting resulted in steps to construct two tests of reasoning, the Army
Alpha test for literates and the Army Beta test for illiterates. Over the next two years, the
Army Alpha test was administered to nearly 2 million recruits, with the result that almost
8000 men were discharged as mentally unfit. The Army tests had several significant
repercussions. First, the publication of the results of the testing focused a great deal of
public attention on the uses of mental testing, particularly the ability to test great numbers
of individuals efficiently. More nefarious consequences occurred. For example, data were
reported that described mental age of whites, European immigrants based on their country
of origin, and blacks. These analyses were thought to demonstrate that darker people
(from Southern Europe, for instance) were less intelligent than fairer people of Western
and Northern Europe, views supporting economic prejudices of the period. The data from
the Army tests were used widely for various purposes. One of the most ignoble of these
was the Immigration Act of 1924 which placed restrictions on immigration from countries
that the Alpha test showed to be sources of inferior mental stock (Haney 1984); indeed,
those data may provide a lingering rationale for racism in current day America.

Soon after the Army Psychological Division was dismantled, Robert Yerkes and
Lewis Terman received a grant from the Rockefeller Foundation to develop a standardized
intelligence test to be used in America's schools. The National Intelligence Tests published
by the World Book Company were the result. During the 1920s these and other tests of
intelligence were widely applied to classify students into ability groups for the purposes of
instruction. This period was characterized by the emergence of commercial test publishing
as big business and the flaring up of heated public debates over the uses of standardized
testing. As we shall see, both trends have continued to the present day.

Expansion and experimentation

The 1930s were years of rapid growth in the educational testing enterprise. Oscar Buros
began to chronicle this growth with the publication of annual inventories of psychological
tests in the early thirties. Haney (1984) notes that the Buros *Educational, Psychological, and
Personality Tests of 1933 and 1934* was only 44 pages long, while the 1938 edition of what
was to become the *Mental Measurements Yearbook* had expanded to more than 400 pages
and listed over 4000 tests. For example, the present edition, *The Tenth Mental
Measurements Yearbook* (Conoley and Kramer 1989), includes more than 1000 pages.

Another landmark of the educational research was the *Eight Year Study* begun by
Ralph Tyler in 1933 in an effort to assess the impact of education over an extended period.
The purpose of this effort was not to develop testing programs, but to gather information
in order to reform high school curricula. What was notable about Tyler's efforts was that
he returned to the dual legacies of Rice and Binet in his research, grounding his testing
and assessment efforts in school tasks and interpreting his findings in terms of the

evaluation of programs rather than the classification of individuals. It was probably no accident that the leaders of the next generation in educational psychology and testing, Benjamin Bloom, Lee J. Cronbach, and Chester Harris, to name a few, were young researchers assisting in the *Eight Year Study*.

One of most significant developments in educational uses of standardized testing in the second quarter of the twentieth century was in the area of college admissions. The College Entrance Examination Board had been founded at the turn of the century as the result of a need to bring some uniformity to the college admissions process. Up until the 1920s, the only form of examinations they administered were essay tests in the classics and other subjects. In 1925, the Board appointed a committee of experts, including Carl Brigham and Robert Yerkes, who were given the task of constructing a test suitable for large-scale administration. They chose a multiple-choice format examination. This test was first administered to 8000 candidates in June 1926. At first, only one score was given, but by 1930 the presence of two factors had been detected and from that time on mathematical and verbal scores have been reported separately. The essay component remained in place until the coming of the Second World War, when it was abandoned as an expedient; it has not returned as of 1990. The failure to resume the essay examination after the war was a result of the discovery that the multiple-choice examination was an equally accurate predictor of first year college performance (Conoley and Kramer 1989).

Preoccupation with the mobilization for the Second World War provided another impetus for testing research. In 1939, the Personnel Testing Section of the Adjutant General's Office of the US Army was formed with a principal occupation to conduct research on testing military personnel. One result was the Army General Classification Test (AGCT), developed in 1940, which was to measure the learning ability of recruits. Interestingly, in 1941 two Spanish language versions of the test also were developed. The test consisted of 140 to 150 multiple choice items on vocabulary, block counting, and arithmetic. Scores from these tests were converted to scales not dissimilar from those used in previous measures – with an average score of 100 and a standard deviation of 20. It is most important to note the difference in concept of the Army Alpha/Beta tests and the AGCT used in the Second World War. The first was conceived as a measure of native ability; the second as a measure of trainability. A point noted in a publication of the Army Personnel Research Section is critical here: ' . . . intelligence tests do not measure native mental capacity. They measure actual performance on test questions. A test is a fairly valid measure of the native capacities . . . when everyone tested has had equal opportunity and equal incentive to develop the abilities measured' (Zeidner and Drucker 1988:35).

Testing from 1950–1970: tensions in equity and quality in US education

The two decades following the end of the Second World War were a period of renewed public and professional attention to the methods and uses of standardized testing. One reason for this interest was the great expansion of higher education in this period. A second even greater source of impact was attention of the federal government on the quality and equity of US education during this period. These socio-political factors, aided by developments in testing technology, led to a great expansion in the scale and uses of standardized testing.

Following the Second World War, the GI Bill of Rights made post-secondary oppor-tunity available to millions of veterans who otherwise would have had neither aspirations nor resources to pursue study at colleges and universities. To accommodate this large pool of potential admittees, large-scale testing techniques needed to be available. According to Robert Thorndike (1971), the development of optical scanners and nascent computer technology in the post-Second World War period had several important effects on educational testing. First, it assisted the expansion of testing programs to keep pace with expanding high school and college enrollments by making testing feasible on a much larger scale than previously possible. The growth in the number of candidates taking the SAT over this period reflects this change. In 1948 the SAT was administered to about 20,000 applicants. By the 1963–64 academic year that number had increased to over a million, and by 1967 the number was nearly 2 million (Thorndike 1971). Not only did the number of takers of the SAT greatly increase over this period, but the American College Testing Program (ACT) was created and grew to a significant fraction of the size of its competitor, the SAT. Second, it legitimated in another context the multiple choice test model. Our best and brightest, and their influential parents, accepted the validity of such tests for college admissions. Thus, the experience of being tested successfully themselves bred not contempt but reaffirmation of the accuracy of the measure for use by others.

Testing in the fifties and sixties: the federal role in education

Perhaps the major impetus to the future of standardized testing was the expanding role of the federal government, as it became more directly involved in American education. What stimulated the attention of the Federal Government in regard to education? One major concern was international competitiveness, a theme that recurs periodically in US history. In the Cold War atmosphere of the 1950s, education became an important front in the competition with the Soviet Union, whose acquisition in the early 1950s of nuclear capability startled US leaders. In 1955, the National Merit Scholarship Corporation was founded and took on the task of identifying and supporting the further education of our most promising students. These students were needed for US science and technology to keep pace with the Soviets. The Societ Union's launching of the Sputnik satellite in 1957 exacerbated beliefs in the weakness of the American educational system. One of the first responses by the US Congress to the shock of Sputnik was 1958 passage of the National Defense Education Act (NDEA), which included among its provisions funding for training of experts in science, in mathematics, and in educational testing. An additional consequence of the NDEA was the stimulation of curriculum revision for elementary and secondary education. Some of the fruits of that curriculum effort were to be more modern views of testing.

Equity

Educational practice was also shaped by growing concerns over the equity of the American educational system. The Supreme Court's 1954 decision in Brown v. Board of Education focused public attention on the problem of equal educational opportunity for the nation's low-income and minority students. Civil rights became a major concern of the society. In 1965, as part of Lyndon Johnson's Great Society program, the Elementary and Secondary Education Act (ESEA) was passed in an effort to remedy inequities in the American educational system. Title I of this act provided local school districts with funds to be used for compensatory education programs. Title I also required periodic program evaluation.

This program evaluation was meant to provide accountability at the local level and also to provide Congress with information on how well Title I was performing for the nation as a whole. These two aims led to some difficulties in designing appropriate methods of evaluation, a concern which was central in creating the subspeciality in education of program evaluation. Title I required that resources be provided to students with achievement disadvantages. On the one hand, designing a national evaluation of Title I would require standard criteria, measures, and design to ensure that local data could be combined in a meaningful way. On the other hand, this sort of standardization worked against the aim of local accountability (Echternacht 1980). At first, Congressional dissatisfaction with the low quality of evaluations which resulted from trying to serve these two conflicting aims led to gradual centralization of Title I evaluations and a great deal of attention to the forms and methods of testing and test reporting at the local and state levels.

Another educational research effort, derived from equity issues, indirectly influenced the debate over testing practices. The Coleman Report of 1966 was a direct response to public concerns about the equality of educational opportunity available to minority students in the American educational system. Based on the results of a standardized test of verbal ability, James Coleman and his University of Chicago colleagues concluded that 'schools bring little influence to bear on a child's achievement that is independent of his background and general social context' (Coleman 1966). This report synthesized growing disenchantment with the efficacy of the US educational system, and pushed the enterprise most dramatically in its downward slide in public repute. For the field of achievement testing, the Coleman Report generated debates about the adequacy of its view of school effectiveness. The Coleman Report formally reduced the question of how well schools serve low-income and minority students to a single criterion, student performance on multiple-choice tests of basic skills (Madaus 1989).

Nature–nuture, once again

Concern over the equity of American education and the fairness of standardized testing as a measure of achievement of low-income and minority students were increased in the late 1960s by a re-emergence of the debate over the relative contributions of heredity and environment to intelligence. The Coleman Report's pessimistic view of schools' effectiveness in raising minority achievement levels, and the persistence of a gap between white and black performance on the SAT gave renewed vigor to hereditarian explanations of intellectual differences of the early part of the century. Debate on this issue was fueled by Arthur Jensen's 1969 article in the *Harvard Educational Review* titled 'How can we boost IQ and scholastic achievement?' In this highly controversial piece, Jensen argued that differences in white and black intellectual abilities as measured by standardized tests were predominantly attributable to group rather than to individual differences. Jensen's article created a furor, charges of racism, picketing and catcalling at professional meetings, and political reactions from minority interest groups. Jensen's actual interpretations are much more cautious than reported in the press, but the specter of hereditarian explanations of intellect at a time when civil rights and equity issues were principal banners of the populace put to rest any scrap of the intellectual acceptability of such analyses (Ogbu 1982).

Criterion-referenced testing in the sixties

Research in psychology and education was consumed by social issues during this period. An exception was a line of psychological research that was to have great impact in the area of testing; this research grew from the military and industrial training experiences in the 1940s. Developed and expanded during this period were performance-oriented training programs, based in part on analyses of B. F. Skinner and his colleagues. Skinner took the perspective that complex tasks could be subdivided and effectively learned by anyone with minimal entry skills. By conducting careful analyses of tasks, sequencing material in small steps, and providing reinforcement, learning could be 'controlled'. Although a flurry of applications followed, including mechanical teaching machines and early computer programs, precursors to many of today's drill and practice courseware, Skinner's work had major impact on the area of testing. This impact occurred in two ways. First, influential approaches to teacher training were developed that drew in large measure from Skinner's work (Popham and Baker 1970). These approaches depended upon the explicit statement of desired objectives of teaching – behavioural objectives. The critical criterion for such an objective was that it could be operationally stated in measurable terms. 'To understand a concept' was inappropriately vague formulation; 'to be able to compose an essay' or 'to answer 80% of a set of multiple choice questions' were deemed sufficiently rigorous, although in retrospect they use statements of test format as masquerades for real control of learning. According to the analyses of the time, complex tasks, such as solving science problems, were first to be transformed into behavioral objectives, and then further subdivided into components. This routine resulted in the generation of many, many sub-objectives, each of which was to be measured (to assure learning had occurred). This process had been imported from job analysis practices undertaken by psychologists for military and industrial tasks. At the time, and to this day, the majority of such tasks from the military and industry are procedural in nature and emphasize routine behaviours.

Not surprisingly, members of the measurement community recognized that tests of such objectives differed from conventional formulations of ability measurement in a number of ways. Glaser (1963) summed up the differences between tests where performance is interpreted in terms of achieving a criterion (or objective) and tests where interpretation depends upon the relative position of the individual in a distribution, such as norm-referenced achievement tests (and mental tests as well). Glaser used the term criterion to mean the 'continuum of knowledge acquisition, ranging from no proficiency at all, to perfect performance', and his aim was to develop assessment instruments that would permit identification of the specific behaviours that a learner has acquired (Glaser 1963). Glaser and others at the time applied this criterion-referenced testing to school learning, and the programmed instruction period blossomed, in profusion. One must recall that the focus on real school tasks for assessment began with Binet and was supported by Ralph Tyler's *Eight Year Study* and his influential writings.

Criterion-referenced tests began a wave of activity lasting until the present time. Their popularity can be attributed both to two attributes:

1.   They redefined what was tested (and therefore the basis of merit judgments) into components that could be inspected, i.e., the sub-objectives they represented. This window on assessment contrasted with more black-box views of assessment as constructs, abilities or capacities that were measured by the particular items. Since these items were often barely described, there was no easy way to confirm their accuracy, appropriateness or fairness.

2.   Criterion-referenced testing also was consistent with the societal view toward equity and the notion that performance should be measured in terms of goal achievement and not relative standing.

There were in fact a number of attempts to integrate the idea of criterion-referenced measurement in a school task context during this period. The most notable was the introduction in 1965 by Tyler of the National Assessment of Educational Progress (NAEP), a set of exercises intended to be administered periodically on a sampling basis to give a picture of American students' achievement. A sample task might be solving some arithmetic problem. The role of NAEP was to provide information about student performance levels, general inferences about the total system's quality, and models for innovative test practices.

Persistent issues

The expansion of the testing enterprise in the 1950s and 1960s raised a number of social and political issues. Thorndike (1971) divided these issues into four categories. In the first category, he grouped issues related to the impact of testing on education. During this period the US public voiced concerns over what they saw as over reliance on testing in the schools. Public concerns about the negative effects on the learning process which ensued from the overuse of objective tests and the resulting habit of 'teaching to the test' were also common in this period. A second category of concerns were related to the specter of massive infringements on the public's right to privacy raised by the development and use of large-scale testing technology. A third area of concern was related to doubts about the fairness of standardized tests when used with minority groups in the USA. Finally, the issue of maintaining uniform standards of quality in testing in the face of major expansion was also an important area of concern in this period.

Standards for testing in the fifties and sixties

The increasing size of the testing enterprise and the high level of public attention on testing in the post-Second World War period led to concerns over testing standards within the psychological community. In 1953, the American Psychological Association (APA) issued a set of *Ethical Standards of Psychologists* which included 19 principles concerning the sale and distribution of tests. The next year, 1954, the APA collaborated with the American Educational Research Association (AERA) and the National Council on Measurements Used in Education (NCMUE, later NCME) in compiling *Technical Recommendations for Psychological Tests and Diagnostic Techniques*. This was followed in 1955 by the AERA and NCME's *Technical Recommendations for Achievement Tests*. The publications of these standards reflected a high degree of concern about uniformity and quality in testing among professionals and their need to stave off criticisms arising from growing public concerns over the fairness and legitimacy of standardized tests. Publications of this sort have been reworked and reissued in subsequent decades. The most recent effort is *The Code of Fair Testing Practice in Education* (American Psychological Association 1988).

Assessment in the seventies: equity and quality revisited

Just before and during the 1970s, testing issues were eclipsed largely by social concerns, including a general rebellion against authoritarian means – part of the reactions of the populace to the war in Viet Nam and the Nixon presidency. Public demands for changes in the forms and uses of commercialized standardized testing, engendered by equity concerns, became common. In 1968 the National Association of Black Psychologists reacted to public perceptions of the lack of fairness of testing for minorities by calling for the reform of standardized test forms and applications. The National Education Association voted for a moratorium on standardized testing in the schools for the 1972–3 academic year. In 1972 and again in 1974 the National Association for the Advancement of Colored People (NAACP) called for a cessation of standardized tests whenever these tests had not been corrected for cultural bias. In 1975 the National Association of Elementary School Principals joined in the attack on standardized testing and published many critical articles in their group's journal. In 1980, Ralph Nader's consumer advocate group put together a scathing critique of the Educational Testing Service, resulting in part in a Truth in Testing law in New York which requires the publication of actual test items used in the SAT.

Minimum competency testing

One outgrowth of these concerns about the validity of tests was the decision by state governments to administer their own versions of tests to assure the quality of educational services for all students. Although such legislation had the dual purpose of equity and quality, its consequences show the dangers of predicting the utility of any public policy. Beginning in the 1970s and persisting on the books today, state after state developed minimum requirements for graduation, requirements which included performance on a criterion-referenced competency test. A minimum competency test was further distinguished by a 'cut score', or the dividing score between acceptable and failing performance. The sanction for poor performance was denial of the high school diploma to the student. Statewide minimum competency testing spread rapidly, by 1987, more than 40 states had minimum competency testing programs. Some states, and sometimes local districts, imposed such tests for promotion from grade to grade or automatic assignment to remedial classes. Because these tests also were administered to large populations of students, they tended to consist of multiple-choice items not dissimilar to those given on commercially-available standardized tests. In fact, some of the same commercial companies contracted with states to develop such tests and prepared tests that raised some of the same issues of equity that have clouded the commercial testing enterprise. The first applications of these tests generated highly publicized legal cases, most notably the Debra P. case in Florida in 1978, charging that the schools had provided neither adequate notice nor preparation for the test and that the test disproportionately denied rights to minority students. Decisions in this and other cases, including the assignment and labeling of students as educationally handicapped, resulted in the reduction of the standards set on tests to truly minimum levels and vitiated the intent of the minimum competency movement. While in flower, however, such tests did manage to have certain demonstrable effects on schools. They demonstrated that schools would focus instruction on tested outcomes (although since the standards were so low, the tests actually resulted in reducing the quality of the curriculum for many students). They also demonstrated to states that they could require a heretofore locally-controlled entity (a local public school district) to participate in an accountability context.

Towards new assessment models

On the intellectual front, however, the 1970s provided a foundation for optimism for testing into the twenty-first century. First, in the field of cognitive psychology, researchers attempted to dig deeper than ever before, beyond behavioral analyses of student learning. Hypotheses dealing with cognitive processes by Rumelhart (1977), Wittrock (1975), Norman (1975), and Bransford (1973) led the way for reformulating teaching and learning (Stevens and Collins 1980). These more complex formulations also provided an intellectual basis, supplementing social concerns, for the critical review of the nature of testing. The full implication of this work was not clear in the seventies, particularly with regard to testing. But in combination with the remnants of competency-based testing, such formulations stimulated new approaches to the measurement of school skills, with specific emphasis on complex cognitions and higher order thinking skills.

One early manifestation of cognitive views was the change in practices of writing assessment. Early in the twentieth century, there had been mechanisms for the measurement of essay performance. During subsequent decades, writing performance was all but eradicated in any large-scale assessment model, because of feasibility constraints, including the cost of scoring and the unchallenged acceptance of multiple choice technology. One line of research at UCLA's Center for the Study of Evaluation (CSE) attempted to reinsert writing into the measurement options available to policymakers. The approach used a type of criterion-referenced measurement model, where writing was judged in terms of the student's attainment of particular criteria rather than in normative terms; that is, in comparison to other students. Standards of objectivity, reliability, and economic feasibility were also important. The critical issues confronted in writing assessment, including the problem of developing task specifications that match the cognitive complexity desired from students and the training of raters to provide valid but speeded responses, will have great influence on attempts in the future to reform testing. As a consequence of this research, states attempting to employ writing assessment in their state-wide assessments have used approaches pioneered by CSE. Writing assessment approaches fell within a broader line of inquiry developed during this period: the exploration of domain-referenced achievement testing. Domain-referenced testing (Baker 1974, Hively et al. 1968) is a variant of criterion-referenced measurement, and serves as a bridge between that approach and more complex cognitive measures. In setting the specifications for the domain, the test designer is mindful of the cognitive tasks required of the learner and the structure of the tasks that must be explicated to assure validity (Baker and Herman 1983). A critical feature of domain-referenced testing is the clear description of the class, attributes, or dimensions of the subject matter of interest, the processes students are expected to demonstrate, and the scoring criteria. What encourages this strategy as a powerful option is the explicit linkage of subject matter dimensions to the design of test items.

A fourth, more technical and yet still significant contribution during this period was related to uses of tests for estimating program or system effects rather than individual effects. Multiple-matrix sampling (Sirotnik 1970) permits the concurrent sampling of students and items to reduce testing time and increase reliability of performance estimates. This is important if testing time is regarded as intrusive and if individual student decisions are not required. A fifth contribution notable from the research literature was the increasing attention to qualitative approaches for assessing performance. Such approaches, derived from linguistic and anthropological methods, were not applied in formal testing situations, but rather were used to explore research hypotheses. An excellent summary by K.A. Ericsson (1987) describes procedures for collecting samples of real behavior and subjecting them to protocol analysis. A final line of inquiry, with older roots and significant implications, developed from Lord's (1980) formulations of item response theory as an approach in contrast to the prevailing models developed by earlier psychometricians.

The eighties: the reform agenda and testing

The focus of education in the 1980s was educational reform. This section will consider the impetus for such reform, particularly the role of assessment in these reforms, the impact of such reforms, and the legacy of reform for assessment.

The impetus for reform

The 1980s began in the USA with education's retreat from equity issues. This perspective was strengthened by the publication of *A Nation At Risk* in 1983 (National Commission on Excellence in Education) and raised one more time the alarm that US students were not succeeding at desired levels. What made this cry compelling, however, were two interlocking factors. First, international comparisons revealed that US students were performing significantly poorer than many of our trading partners, in particular the Japanese, Koreans, and Western Europeans; and second that the trade balance suggested that US products were not holding their own in the competitive arena, partly because of failures of the system to train adequately immigrants and others outside of the economic mainstream (Johnson and Packer 1987).

States responded to *A Nation at Risk* with a variety of reform efforts (Pipho 1985), many of which involved assessment. Darling-Hammond and Berry (1988) characterized these reforms as first (1983–85) or second (1986 or later) wave reforms. Strengthening assessment for students and teachers and raising standards for curriculum requirements were first wave reforms focused on productivity. Second wave reforms focused on decentralization and professionalization of teaching (McDonnell and Pascal 1988), a set of topics to be treated shortly. Critics have noted that the educational system implemented such top-down reforms on a symbolic level (Ellwein and Glass 1986) that permitted the appearance but not the reality of higher standards to be in place. This charge may be especially true of student testing, where passing scores were often adjusted to assure reasonable proportions of attaining students. Such findings are not particularly surprising in view of the rather consistent findings about over two decades of the impact of top-down reform (McLaughlin 1987, Elmore and McLaughlin 1988). But in the early days, the rhetoric of assessment counted for more than the reality. Consequently, the testing business cranked up again, this time with states leading the way, for assessments at the system level, for individual student reporting, and for school report cards, with expanded testing in subject matters beyond the usual reading, writing, and arithmetic. Teachers were tested, and school district superintendents' jobs were at risk if test scores did not move in the appropriate direction – up. Baker (1989) points out that the role of assessment radically changes when it is conceived simultaneously to be the reform itself and the metric to evaluate the impact of reform. As the reform, its purposes have been variously described as to communicate and clarify goals, to motivate students and teachers, and to focus instruction. Such functions, particularly when linked to sanctions for students, teachers, or school districts, raise the consequences of failure for all participants. Prominent educators (Bracey 1987, Popham 1987, Shepard 1987) have debated the utility of test-driven instruction. Negative effects of such instruction-focused assessment include the undue focus on test-taking skills (Bain and Stites 1989) as opposed to learning subject matter skills in an integrated way. The task of education is perceived as to raise test scores rather than to educate children. The strategy of molecular decomposition for teaching, used earlier in the design of programmed instruction, has been renewed today in the way many percieve the schools' goals. A parallel response has been to entrench, even further, programs where students are provided separately tracked, unequal, and opportunity-limiting curricula (Oakes 1985).

Impact of testing and reform

What has been the impact of all of this reform? A series of questions has been raised, and all impinge on assessment practices. On the negative side, there have been increased allegations of cheating and collusion of school officials in attempts to make test performance appear on the upswing (Cannell 1988, 1989, Linn *et al.* 1990). While these concerns are undoubtedly overstated, they do feed the public's disbelief about the quality of education in this country. For example, on the topic of test preparation, there are concerns that certain practices are inappropriate. Popham (1990) describes inappropriate practices where students practice the exact form of the test, or practice earlier versions of the test. Other approaches to test preparation may be legitimate, such as the practice of test taking skills in general or the practice of skills in multiple formats such as essay, oral, multiple choice, and short answer, which demonstrate the transfer of skill across modalities in a single subject matter. While Popham's analysis is at odds with some propositions from cognitive psychologists, it nonetheless illustrates the level of public concern on this issue.

When assessments are conceived as dependent measures for reform, do they show positive impact? One would expect with all the practice and attention, impact would be easily demonstrated. To date, looking at quoted statements by the Secretaries of Education for the last three years, and corroborating comments related to assessments in the several states, the answer is a fuzzy 'no'. No effects show up on national measures of student performance, either from reports by the National Assessment of Educational Progress (NAEP), school completion rates, or any other accepted measure, even including somewhat inappropriate measures like the Scholastic Aptitude Test (SAT). Such findings raise issues about the quality of the reforms themselves, the declining quality of social and economic environments for students, and, most obviously, of the sensitivity of the measures themselves to educational reform efforts.

The quality of measures

Educational reform has recently confronted a fundamental issue in the evaluation of impact: that the tests that have been proliferating may neither be the types most appropriate to assess student learning nor most likely to help improve instruction. Critics such as Resnick (1990), Resnick and Resnick (in press), Madaus (1989) and others have or are now in the process of publishing extended treatises on this issue. State departments of education, in New York, Connecticut, Vermont, California, Illinois and Michigan, to name just a few, have embarked on strategies designed to improve the legitimate integration of assessment and instructional practice. Additional indicators of the effects of reform, focused more on instructional process than exclusively on student outcomes, have been created to determine the immediate impact reform has in the schools (McDonnell *et al.* 1990). Glaser *et al.* (1987) summarize the implications for testing of cognitive research, and innovative designs have been tried in subject matter assessments of science and history (Shavelson *et al.* 1990; Baker *et al.* in press). In one of its last acts of the eighties, the National Assessment Governing Board, in charge of NAEP direction, authorized a panel to propose steps to alter NAEP's approach to testing. These changes would move a significant portion of the assessment exercises to a performance assessment model that provides longer time, cognitively more complex and more integrated tasks for students (Baker 1989).

The impact of assessment reform in the eighties also interacted with second wave reforms. As Darling-Hammond and Berry (1988:9) pointedly noted, the second wave reformers claimed the schools of the 1980s were: ' . . . too rigid, too passive, and too rote-oriented to produce learners who can think critically, synthesize and transform, experiment and create'. The authors note that these arguments are 'identical to those . . . at the turn of the century, and again in the 1960s. Indeed, with the addition of a few computers, the Carnegie Report's scenario for a twenty-first century school is virtually identical to John Dewey's account of the twentieth century ideal.'

Their remedies included decentralization, and the new litany of buzzwords – teacher empowerment, school site management, and educational restructuring. Will these bottom-up strategies square with top-down quality control? The educational pendulum swings, but rarely with such neck-cracking speed. Accommodations will be necessary to avoid further conflict, dysfunctional symbolism, and deterioration of the educational enterprise.

Towards the turn of the century: prospects for assessment

This section will be noticeably speculative in its consideration of the future of tests. It will discuss the policy context from the vantage point of 1990 and make some guesses about its impact on assessment. Secondly, it will consider the likely impact of technical advances during the next ten years.

Policies and assessment

The statement of educational goals articulated by President George Bush in his state of the Union address in 1990 presages a continued focus on achievement and accountability at all levels. One inference is that the USA is moving inexorably toward a national test and a national curriculum. Congressional interest in the validity of NAEP data and the development of indicators of educational quality further signals the continuing importance of formal assessment systems. But as usual in policy matters, counterbalances are also quickly generated. For instance, even the discussion of a federal bill to provide $100 million to improve the utility of assessment for Chapter I teachers and children is a significant act, whatever its legislative chances of success. If the political changes in Europe permit the sustained reduction in defense spending, the rhetoric is in place for an expansion of educational spending in the next few years. It is both a demand of our trading partners and a national moral exigency. Such expansion can only be accomplished when measures and accountability devices are authorized.

A second impetus to policymaking will follow from the experimentation in performance assessments and other alternatives to traditional multiple choice standardized tests. First, we can safely predict that students' scores will initially look even worse on newer, more complex, tougher measures than they do on existing standardized tests. Unfortunately, we predict minority students will continue at a disadvantage on many such tests for a period. This disadvantage may disenchant many present proponents of new forms of testing. Minority interest groups may raise particular concerns, especially because such tests are susceptible to biases in scoring students' observed performance. Another issue will be the linkage between measures rooted in the idiosyncrasies of classroom and teacher and those necessary for comparison and accountability. Yet in time, if hypotheses about the importance of linking cognitive processes, instruction, and assessment are correct, and if safeguards about the biases of raters against students of different cultural heritage can be overcome, then the achievement of all students should show dramatic growth.

Technical developments

A second impact will be renewed research effort to develop an appropriate set of psychometric principles to deal with performance assessment options, including strategies for characterizing and sampling content, for efficiently scoring responses, for characterizing the consequences of such assessments, and for developing reporting schemes useful to school personnel and public alike (Messick 1989, Baker and Linn 1990). Such new psychometrics will require radically rethinking or even giving up construct models derived from differential psychology, a set of principles influential throughout most of this century. Particularly of interest are issues of transfer, knowledge representation, and problem solving in subject matters, in integrated tasks, over time, and in groups.

In addition, renewed interest in assessment of the affective realm, looking at conative or volitional aspects of performance (Snow 1989) will grow. Students will need to demonstrate their commitment to tasks over time, their workforce readiness, their social competence in team or group performance contexts. Motivation for school and for performance on tests of achievement should be recognized as a significant problem. For example, we have little data to suggest that US students' poor performance is not simply due to their lack of seriousness about the testing enterprise, particularly compared to students in other cultures. One option is to explore the development of measures and instructional strategies that will link achievement and motivation in the minds of these students. Each of these areas will require new infusions of research, experimentation, and development.

Advances in the use of technology in testing will permit more efficient administration, scoring and reporting of student performance, and will also open new opportunities to assess student learning processes presently unobtainable without technology (Baker *et al.* 1990).

Formal testing

The formal testing process, even in response to the National Educational Goals, is unlikely to become an exclusively federal enterprise. State and local agencies will continue to follow up local control mandates with measures of their own design. The commercial testing industry, which experienced continuous growth in the last twenty years, will continue to expand, despite the reduced numbers of students predicted for schools in the period. The industry's growth will be achieved particularly in the employment sector. There, because of changes in mandatory retirement ages, new demands for recertification, or a new form of exit testing, will dominate.

Conclusion

Daniel Resnick has suggested that popular acceptance of standardized testing in the USA is a function of three long-standing features of American Society: first, a compelling business interest in making the most efficient use of human resources; second, an egalitarian tradition which is reflected in a desire to reward talent at all levels of society; and finally, an acceptance of the need for national standards to moderate and limit the autonomy of local interests (Resnick 1981). We would add that testing will have a legitimate place in US education when it can connect these features of US society with the recognition of new standards for quality assessments. It is time, perhaps a happy convergence, to change the reality and image of tests and assessments. They must be grounded in new conceptions of validity, in social justice and in American values appropriate for our changing student group. Tests must be fair, must represent significant cognitive tasks with meaning for test takers, and must be seen as only a part of a national educational information system that fully measures educational quality. The rosy future for testing will probably not occur, however, without dialectic, dissent, conflict, and retrogression. Reviewing the historical background of assessment convinces us that we will see in the future significant amounts of what we have experienced in the past. Most important, we must remember the child. As Emerson wrote: 'I believe that our own experience instructs us that the secret of education lies in respecting the pupil.' The quality of our assessments are a public way of adhering to his advice.

Acknowledgement

This work was supported by the Center for the Study of Learning, Nichinoken Institute in Japan, and by a grant from the Office of Educational Research and Improvement, pursuant to grant number G0086-0003. However, the opinions expressed do not necessarily reflect the position or policy of these agencies and no official endorsement by these agencies should be inferred.

References

AMERICAN PSYCHOLOGICAL ASSOCIATION (1988) *The Code of Fair Testing Practice in Education* (Washington, DC: APA).

BAIN, J. and STITES, R. (1989) *Parents' Reaction to Standardized Tests* (Los Angeles: UCLA Center for the Study of Evaluation).

BAKER, E.L. (1974) 'Beyond objectives: domain-referenced tests for evaluation and instructional improvement', *Educational Technology*, 14 (6), pp. 10–16.

BAKER, E.L. (1989) 'Performance assessment in large-scale settings', presentation to the National Assessment Governing Board, Austin.

BAKER, E.L. and HERMAN, J.L. (1983) 'Beyond linkage', *Journal of Educational Measurement*, 20 (2), pp. 149–164.

BAKER, E.L. and LINN, R. (1990) *Advancing Educational Quality Through Learning-Based Assessment, Evaluation, and Testing*, Institutional Grant Proposal for OERI Center on Assessment, Evaluation, and Testing, pp. 1–22.

BAKER, E.L., NEIMI, D., HERMAN, J. and GEARHAR, M. (1990) 'Validating a hypermedia measure of knowledge representation', paper presented at the American Educational Research Association Annual Meeting, Boston.

BAKER, E.L., FREEMAN, M. and CLAYTON, S. (in press) 'Cognitive assessment of history for large scale testing', in M.C. Wittrock and E.L. Baker (eds) *Testing and Cognition* (Englewood Cliffs, NJ: Prentice Hall).

BRACEY, G.W. (1987) 'Measurement-driven instruction: catchy phrase, dangerous practice', *Phi Delta Kappan*, 68, (9) pp. 683–686.

BRANSFORD, J.D. and JOHNSON, M.K. (1973) 'Consideration of some problems of comprehension', in W. Chase (ed.) *Visual Information Processing* (New York: Academic Press) pp. 382–438.

CANNELL, J.J. (1988) 'Nationally normed elementary achievement testing in America's public schools: how all 50 states are above the national average', *Educational Measurement: Issues and Practice*. 7 (2), pp. 5–9.

CANNELL, J.J. (1989) *How Public Educators Cheat on Standardized Achievement Test* (Albuquerque, NM: Friends of Education).

CHAFFEE, J. (1985) *The Thorny Gates of Learning in Sung China* (Cambridge: Cambridge University Press).

COLEMAN, J.S., CAMPBELL, E. Q., HOBSON, C. J., McPARTLAND, J., MOOD, A. M., WEINFELD, S. D. and YORK, R. L. (1966) *Equality of Educational Opportunity* (Washington, DC: Office of Education, Department of Health, Education, and Welfare).

CONOLEY, J.C. and KRAMER, J.J. (1989) *The Tenth Mental Measurements Yearbook* (Lincoln, NB: University of Nebraska Press)

CRONBACH, L.J. and SUPPES, P. (eds) (1969) *Disciplined Inquiry* (New York: Macmillan).

DARLING-HAMMOND, L. and WISE, A.E. (1988) *The Evolution of Teacher Policy* (Santa Monica, CA: The RAND Corporation).

ECHTERNACHT, G. (1980) 'Title I evaluation and reporting system: development of evaluation models', in G. Echternacht (ed.) *Measurement Aspects of Title I Evaluation* (New York: Jossey-Bass), pp. 1–16.

ELMORE, R.F. and McLAUGHLIN, M.W. (1988) *Steady Work: Policy, Practice, and the Reform of American Education* (Santa Monica, CA: The RAND Corporation).

ELLWEIN, M.C. and GLASS, G.V. (1986) *Standards of Competence: A Multi-Site Case Study of School Reform*, CSE Technical Report 263 (Los Angeles: UCLA Center for the Study of Evaluation).

ERICSSON, K.A. (1987) 'Theoretical implications from protocal analysis on testing and measurement', in R.R. Ronning, J.A. Glover, J.C. Conoley and J.C. Witt (eds.) *The Influence of Cognitive Psychology on Testing* (Hillsdale, NJ: Lawrence Erlbaum), pp. 191–228.

FRANKE, W. (1960) *The Reform and Abolition of the Traditional Chinese Examination System* (Cambridge: Harvard East Asian Monograph).

GLASER, R. (1963) 'Instructional technology and the measurement of learning outcomes: some questions', *American Psychologist*, 18 (8), pp. 519–521.

GLASER, R., LESGOLD, A. and LAJOIE, S. (1987) 'Toward a cognitive theory for the measurement of achievement', in R.R. Ronning, J. Glover, J.C. Conoley and J.C. Witt (eds) *The Influence of Cognitive Psychology on Testing and Measurement* (Hillsdale, NJ: Lawrence Erlbaum), pp. 41–85.

GOULD, J. (1981) *The Mismeasure of Man* (New York: W.W. Norton).

HALE, M. (1982) 'History of employment testing', in A.K. Wigdor and W.R. Garner (eds) *Ability Testing: Uses, Consequences and Controversies, Part II: Documentation Section* (Washington, DC: National Academy Press), pp. 3–14.

HANEY, W. (1984) 'Testing reasoning and reasoning about testing', *Review of Educational Research*, 54 (4), p. 601.

HIVELY, W., PATTERSON, H. and PAGE, S. (1968) 'A universe of defined system of arithmetic achievement test', *Journal of Educational Measurement*, 5 (4), pp. 275–290.

HO, P.-T. (1962) *The Ladder of Success in Imperial China* (New York: Columbia University Press).

HOLLINGSWORTH, H.L. (1915) 'Specialized vocational tests and methods', *School and Society*, 1.

ICHISADA, M. (1981) *China's Examination Hell* (New Haven: Yale University Press).

JOHNSTON, W.B. and PACKER, A.H. (1987) *Workforce 2000: Work and Workers for the Twenty-First Century* (Indianapolis, IN: Hudson Institute).

KRACKE, E.A. (1968) *Civil Service in Early Sung China* (Cambridge: Harvard-Yenching Institute).

LINK, H.C. (1919) *Employment Psychology: The Application of Scientific Methods to the Selection, Training and Grading of Employees* (New York: Macmillan).

LINN, R.L., GRAUE, M.E. and SANDERS, N.M. (1990) *Comparing State and District Test Results to National Norms: Interpretations of Scoring 'Above the National Average'*. CSE Technical Report 308, Grant Number OERI-G-86-003. Los Angeles: UCLA Center for Research on Evaluation Standards, and Student Testing.

LORD, F.M. (1980) *Applications of Item Response Theory to Practical Testing Problems* (Hillsdale, NJ: Lawrence Erlbaum).

MADAUS, G.F. (1989) 'Test scores as administrative mechanisms in educational policy', *Phi Delta Kappan*, 66 (9), pp. 611–617.

MCDONNELL, L.M., BURSTEIN, L., ORMSETH, T., CATTERALL, J.S. and MOODY, D. (1990) *Discovering What Schools Really Teach: Designing Improved Coursework Indicators* (Santa Monica, CA: The RAND Corporation).

MCDONNELL, L.M. and PASCAL, A (1988) *Teacher Unions and Eductional Reform* (Santa Monica, CA: The RAND Corporation).

MCLAUGHLIN, M.W. (1987) 'Learning from experience: lessons from policy implementation', *Educational Evaluation and Policy Analysis*, 9 (2), pp. 171–178.

MESSICK, S. (1989) 'Validity', in R.L. Linn (ed.) *Educational Measurement*, 3rd edn (New York: Macmillan), pp. 13–104.

NATIONAL COMMISSION ON EXCELLENCE IN EDUCATION (1983) *A Nation at Risk: The Imperative for Educational Reform* (Washington, DC: NCEE).

NEEDHAM, J. (1970) 'China and the origins of qualifying examinations in medicine', in J. Needham (ed.) *Clerks and Craftsmen in China and the West* (Cambridge: Cambridge University Press), pp. 379–95.

NORMAN, D.A., RUMELHART, D.E. and the LNR RESEARCH GROUP (1975) *Explorations in Cognition* (San Francisco: Freeman).

OAKES, J. (1985) *Keeping Track: How Schools Structure Inequality* (New Haven, CT: Yale University Press).

OGBU, J. (1978) *Minority Education and Caste* (Orlando, FL: Academic Press).

PIPHO, C. (1985) 'Tracking the reforms, part 5: testing can it measure the success of the reform movement?' *Education Week*, 22, p. 19.

POPHAM, W.J. (1987) 'The merits of measurement-driven instruction', *Phi Delta Kappan*, 68 (9), pp. 679–682.

POPHAM, W.J. (1990) 'Appropriateness of teachers' test-preparation practices', paper presented at a Forum for Dialogues Between Educational Policy-makers and Educational Researchers, UCLA.

POPHAM, J. and BAKER, E.L. (1970) *Systematic Instruction* (Englewood Cliffs, NJ: Prentice Hall).

RESNICK, D.P. (1981) 'Testing in America: a supportive environment', *Phi Delta Kappan*, May, 62 (9) pp. 625–628.

RESNICK, L. (1990) 'Assessment and educational standards', presentation to the Promise and Poll of Alternative Assessment conference, Washington, DC.

RESNICK, L.B. and RESNICK, D.P. (in press) 'Assessing the thinking curriculum: New Tools for educational reform', in B.R. Gifford and M.C. O'Connor (eds) *Future Assessments: Changing Views of Aptitude, Achievement, and Instruction* (Boston: Kluwer Academic Publishers).

RUMELHART, D.E. and ORTONY, A. (1977) 'The representation of knowledge in memory', in R.C. Anderson, R.J. Spiro and W.E. Montague (eds) *Schooling and the Acquisition of Knowledge* (Hillsdale, NJ: Lawrence Erlbaum) pp. 99–135.

SHAVELSON, R., PINE, J., GOLDMAN, S., BAXTER, G. and HINE, M.S. (1990) 'Alternative technologies for assessing science achievement', paper presented at the American Educational Research Association Annual Meeting, Boston.

SHEPARD, L.A. (1987) 'The harm of measurement driven instruction', paper presented at the American Educational Research Association Annual Meeting, Washington, DC.

SIROTNIK, K. (1970) 'An investigation of the context effect in matrix sampling', *Journal of Educational measurement*, 7 (3), pp. 199–207.

SNOW, R.E. (1989) 'Toward assessment of cognitive and conative structures in learning', *Educational Researcher*, 18 (9), pp. 8–14.

STEVENS, A.L. and COLLINS, A. (1980) 'Multiple conceptual models of a complex system', in R. Snow, P. Federico and W. Montague (eds) *Aptitude, Learning, and Instruction: Cognitive Process Analysis of Learning and Problem Solving* (Hillsdale, NJ: Lawrence Erlbaum) pp. 177–197.

THORNDIKE, R. (1981) 'Eductional Measurement for the seventies', in R. Thorndike (ed.) *Educational measurement*, 2nd edn (Washington, DC: American Council of Education) pp. 3–14.

WITTROCK, M.C., MARS, C. and DOCTOROW, M. (1975) 'Reading as a generative process', *Journal of Educational Psychology*, 67 (4), pp. 484–489.

WOLF, T. (1973) *Alfred Binet* (Chicago: University of Chicago Press).

ZEIDNER, J. and DRUCKER, A.J. (1988) *Behavioral Science in the Army: A Corporate History of the Army Research Institute* (Alexandria, VA: Army Research Institute).

9   *Readiness testing in local school districts: an analysis of backdoor policies*

Lorrie A. Shepard

This policy analysis of readiness testing in local school districts has three parts: (1) a summary of research on issues comprising the policy context; (2) a review of readiness test uses and validity; and (3) an analysis of policy consequences. The apparent need for districts to judge children ready or unready for school is a phenomenon of the 1980s and follows from a constellation of interconnected changes: major (and inappropriate) shifts in the kindergarten curriculum, dramatic increases in kindergarten retention, a middle-class trend to redshirt children so that as six-year-olds they will have an advantage in kindergarten, and the promulgation of readiness checklists in the popular press. Readiness tests and developmental screening measures can be distinguished both as to content and purpose, but in practice they are often used interchangeably. The content of academic readiness tests is questionable given recent research in emergent literacy and cognitive psychology. Developmental tests are not appreciably different from IQ measures yet one set of measures is politically acceptable and the other is not. None of the available measures is sufficiently accurate to support special placement decisions for individual children such as two-year kindergarten programs or delayed school entry. Many of the policies associated with readiness testing have evolved without considered debate, hence the reference to 'backdoor' policies. Unconsidered policy consequences include: assignment of children to ineffective special programs like transition rooms, reinstitution of tracking, exaggerated age and ability differences, further escalation of curriculum, and teaching to the test. Several major national reports have suggested curricular changes that would improve learning for all children and make it unnecessary to screen any children out of school.

Many have lamented the change in contemporary kindergartens from a children's garden to an academic bootcamp. A concomitant change, much less publicly debated, is the growing expectation that it is necessary to decide when a child is ready to go to school. Whereas before children naturally went to kindergarten when they were 5 years old or to first grade when they were 6, today parents and schools are under increasing pressure to judge whether normal children are ready for kindergarten. Widespread use of readiness tests in the 1980s is part of this trend. Although academic readiness tests have existed since the 1930s, they tended to be used by researchers or by classroom teachers to plan reading instruction. The use of such measures to determine whether children should stay home or go to a special grade, like pre-kindergarten or transitional-first, is a relatively recent phenomenon.

    The middle part of this chapter is addressed to readiness testing – the prevalence of readiness testing, the purposes of various kinds of tests such as developmental screening measures vs. academic readiness tests, and the validity of these instruments for their intended purposes. However, the focus of the chapter is not primarily on measurement or technical issues. Although it is worth knowing that these tests are inaccurate for many of the uses to which they are put, tests per se are not the cause of the current state of affairs. Greater insight is likely to be gained by asking (*a*) why so many school districts have begun administering readiness tests; and (*b*) what the intended and unintended consequences of their use might be.

0268–0939/90 $3.00 © 1990 Taylor & Francis Ltd.

In answer to the first question, the first section of the chapter is a summary of the policy context of readiness testing. To understand why many school districts feel compelled to try to assess readiness, or why in some cases they have unwittingly turned developmental screening measures into readiness gates that control entry to school, one must understand something about a constellation of interconnected changes: major shifts in the nature of kindergarten curriculum, dramatic increases in kindergarten retention rates, new practices of sending children home after three months of kindergarten or keeping them out until they are 6, and articles in the popular press implying that children should delay school entrance if they cannot cut with scissors or perform other skills. The tests themselves can then be discussed in light of the impetus to judge children ready or unready for school. The last section of the chapter is devoted to the largely unconsidered policy consequences of readiness testing, including the reinstitution of tracking and further escalation of age-inappropriate curriculum.

Thus the chapter is intended to provide a policy analysis of readiness testing in local school districts. A theme which recurs throughout the chapter is that many of these policies are implicit or unconsidered, hence the reference in the chapter title to backdoor policies. The focus is on school district policies because the lion's share of testing of young children in the USA occurs under the auspices of local districts. The analysis is equally applicable to state-mandated programs aimed at testing individual children before they enter kindergarten or first grade. The same issues would not necessarily pertain in the case of large-scale national sampling surveys akin to the National Assessment, although elsewhere (Shepard 1987) I have described how a national effort to collect early childhood assessment data should avoid the connotation of encouraging the kinds of inappropriate local practices described here.

The policy context of readiness testing

Escalating curriculum

The kindergarten curriculum today is oriented toward academic skills, becoming more and more like the first grade of 20 years ago. Although early-childhood specialists are undoubtedly tired of hearing the chorus of similar analyses on this topic, it is essential to repeat the widely agreed upon arguments as background to the present analysis.

The changes in expectations about what is to be taught in kindergarten are the result of subtle and reciprocal influences rather than considered policy change. As more and more children attend preschool (now more than 50% nationally), and watch *Sesame Street*, kindergarten teachers have gradually raised their expectations about what their pupils should already know when they enter school, things like letter names that once were taught in kindergarten – and have borrowed replacement content from first grade. We have referred to these shifts in kindergarten and first grade curricula as the 'escalation of curriculum' (Shepard and Smith 1988); Cunningham (1988) called it 'academic trickle-down'.

Perhaps one of the strongest influences on kindergarten has been the recent attainment of nearly universal participation, which has allowed first-grade teachers to demand as prerequisites the pre-reading skills that used to be taught in first grade. By the very fact of universal participation, kindergarten has become a part of real school. As a result it has lost its special status as a place for children's social development and transition to school. Without conscious debate about the pre-school character of kindergarten,

kindergarten goals are now likely to be developed by primary grades curriculum committees following a subject-matter organization that is the downward extension of later-grades curriculum.

To some policymakers an accelerated pace for learning and pressure to master the next-grade's content may seem to imply a tremendous victory for educational excellence. It sounds as if today's kindergartners are learning more. However, the escalation of academic demand is seen to be detrimental by almost all experts in both early childhood education and subject-matter specialties because too often the escalation is focused narrowly on isolated pre-reading and numeracy skills without opportunities for more integrated, conceptual learning, and because it fosters teaching methods that are incompatible with how young children learn. For example, in her study of a sample of kindergartens in Illinois, Durkin (1987) found that phonics instruction was a daily occurrence in kindergarten, but was only rarely taught in the context of using phonics to understand what words 'say'.

In today's kindergarten children are made to sit for long periods of time filling out worksheets rather than listening to stories, counting with real objects, or drawing their own pictures. Because there are implicit efficiency demands created by the need to cover more material, teachers often resort to teaching by rote. Despite their knowledge of child development research, which says that 5-year-olds learn from concrete, hands-on experiences, teachers do not provide opportunities for children to learn about measuring at the water table or about addition in the context of playing store because these activities take too much time (or worse still, because public constituencies see 'playing' as a waste of instructional time). In her commentary on the new paper-and-pencil kindergarten, Martin (1985) noted the irony of expecting to develop children's language skills if the kindergarten 'consigns the children to their chairs to work in silent isolation' (p. 318). In the concluding section of the chapter, I refer to numerous position statements by professional organizations calling for more developmentally appropriate curriculum.

Previously we have noted that there are two groups of children who are the victims of this narrow, drill-for-first-grade kindergarten curriculum: those who fail by its age-inappropriate demands who under other circumstances would have done quite fine, and those who appear to succeed. Those who compete successfully are harmed because by-rote instruction does not facilitate insightful learning (Shepard and Smith 1988). Hatch and Freeman (1988), in their studies of Ohio kindergartens, have suggested that teachers are also victims. Although teachers have been significant participants in the curriculum shifts, many are under considerable stress because of the dissonance between what they feel they must teach and their own knowledge of developmentally appropriate instructional practices. Similarly, in our own work (Shepard and Smith 1988, Smith and Shepard 1988), we found that teachers in some schools felt forced to teach kindergarten as they do because of the demands of first-grade teachers, pressures from parents (especially to accelerate reading instruction), and accountability pressures in the later grades.

Increased flunking in kindergarten

Sharply increased rates of kindergarten retentions during the 1980s can be attributed to the new curricular demands against which many children are judged to be inadequate. Current retention practices are also engendered by a set of beliefs widely shared among educators and parents: (1) that repeating in kindergarten is an entirely benign intervention; (2) that both cognitive readiness and maturity are biological traits which should not be hurried; and (3) that the gift of an extra year will allow children to excel without being pushed (Smith and Shepard 1988). Kindergarten retention and other extra-year programs like pre-K and pre-first are seen as ways to provide more appropriate curriculum (unavailable in the regular grades) and to protect unready children from the aversive experience of a high-pressure first grade.

Kindergarten retention is another example of a policy implemented at the grassroots level on a broad scale without there having been policy-level discussions about its rationale or possible ramifications. The desirability of kindergarten retention as a corrective for unreadiness had been promulgated teacher to teacher and via workshops conducted by private groups such as the Gesell Institute of Human Development. The benefits claimed for allowing children an extra year to grow are largely based on testimonials. Parents are often told, for example, that their child will become a leader if he or she is given the 'gift of time'. To the extent that research has been cited in support of these claims, advocates have relied on what is termed the 'youngness research'. Because there is research showing that the youngest first graders have lower achievement on average than the oldest first graders (see Shepard and Smith 1986), it has been assumed that kindergarten retention would create for retainees the advantage of being oldest. However, as noted in the Shepard and Smith review, the simple age advantage in these studies is small (only about 7 or 8 percentile points) and disappears on average by third grade.

Rather than assuming that an extra year will benefit children by making them more ready for first grade, empirical evidence is needed. In fact, controlled studies contradict the claim that unready children do better in first grade if they wait a year. Controlled studies typically compare groups at the end of first grade who were matched on sex, age, and assessed unreadiness at the time they first entered kindergarten. There are now 16 such studies available (see Shepard 1989); one study had very positive results, i.e., favoring the retained group at the end of first grade (Turley 1979); another study had very negative results showing that the extra-year children were significantly worse off on both achievement and social emotional measures, when followed from grade 1 through grade 6, than the developmentally immature children whose parents had refused the extra year placement (Mossburg 1987). The preponderance of studies showed essentially no difference academically between retained children and 'unready' children who went directly on to first grade. Given that kindergarten retention is often encouraged for the emotional well-being of the child rather than for academic gain, it is odd that most of these studies did not include self-concept or school attitude measures; those that did found either no difference or negative effects for retention (Shepard 1989). Because many advocates believe that kindergarten retention is effective only when children are selected for immaturity rather than for learning problems, it is worth noting that conclusions from the 16 controlled studies do not look any different if we isolate only those studies where children were selected for immaturity and provided a special transitional program rather than simply repeating kindergarten. In Mossburg's study, for example, children were placed in transition room because of developmental immaturity.

Holding children out of kindergarten until age 6

Yet another trend that follows from, but also contributes to, the escalation of curriculum is the fad for 'academic redshirting'. Borrowed from athletic redshirting which allows college athletes to mature physically while protecting their years of eligibility, the idea is for 5-year-olds to sit out a year so that as 6-year-olds they will be more mature (and more competitive) in kindergarten. The arguments for staying home a year (or, more likely, spending another year in preschool) parallel the arguments for retention, i.e., the practice is intended to protect unready children from struggling in an environment that is too demanding for their level of maturity. The Gesell Institute (1982) recommends staying home a year, or one of the various two-year kindergarten placements, for the 33% of potential kindergartners they estimate to be developmentally too young. From their reading of the youngness research described above, Uphoff and Gilmore (1986) recommend almost categorically that 'EVERY child under the age of five years, six months should wait a year before starting kindergarten' (p. 6). In our experience, the practice of holding children out of school is sometimes initiated by the school, with a principal, for example, warning all of the parents at the March 'kindergarten round-up' to keep their summer-birthday boys at home (interview data 1984). In other cases, it appears to be initiated by parents based on what they have read in the popular press or heard from other parents.

At a 1989 Wingspread Conference on Kindergarten attended by 27 state-level early childhood coordinators, many of the state representatives reported that delayed entry to kindergarten was a significant phenomenon in their states leading to the 'graying' or ageing of the kindergarten population. In their discussions of the holding-out phenomenon, these early childhood specialists also gave the practice an importantly different connotation. They characterized it as middle-class advantage-seeking. Rather than its being used to protect children seriously at risk because of their immaturity, specialists see it being used as one more strategy in the 'get-your-kid-to-Harvard' arsenal of affluent parents.

In a preliminary study aimed at assessing the magnitude of the holding-out phenomenon and its relation to socio-economic status, Shepard et al. (1989) gathered basic demographic information for kindergartners from 19 Colorado school districts (accounting for two-thirds of the state's kindergartners). Data for 12 of the 19 districts reflected the holding-out pattern. In these districts substantial numbers of children were missing (as many as 50% of the expected frequency) in the youngest three to four months of the kindergarten age distribution. In addition, redshirted children from the previous year could be seen in the four months immediately above the normal age range for kindergartners. The holding-out pattern was especially pronounced for boys. The 12 districts where holding-out was observed were all suburban districts, consistent with the claim that redshirting is a middle-class phenomenon. In contrast, six metropolitan and urban districts serving relatively lower socio-economic communities did not show signs of holding out. As one research director from this latter group of districts commented, 'Our parents have just gotten the idea that it is good to get their kid into school as soon as possible.' (Why would they want to delay school entry?) At the individual level, socio-economic data were available in only one district; there the correlation between parental education and the decision to hold young boys out of kindergarten was 0.37.

In the final section of the chapter, I take up the policy implications of redshirting. To the extent that 6-year-olds help to define kindergarten norms, meeting their needs moves the kindergarten curriculum further away from instruction attuned to the needs of children who have just turned 5. Redshirting obviously increases the age heterogeneity of kindergarten classrooms. And to the extent that the middle-class hypothesis is true, it increases the 'disadvantage' of normal 5-year-olds from poor families who come to school at age 5 years 0 months and are asked to compete with children who are 6 years 3 months old, come from affluent homes, and have had three years of Montessori preschool experience.

Diagnosis of unreadiness by magazines and local newspapers

Clearly the various aspects of the readiness context interact with one another. Curriculum shifts lead to retention and redshirting which feed the cycle, causing more age-inappropriate academic demands. A key agent fostering these trends is the popular press. Although we do not have systematic data to assign relative weights to the influence of preschool teachers, kindergarten teachers, other parents, or published articles about readiness, it is fair to say on the basis of numerous examples that articles in newspapers and magazines are a contributing factor in parents' decisions to redshirt their kindergartners. Furthermore, feature stories about school readiness have been especially important in creating the current climate of opinion whereby the decision to enter school is now a dilemma rather than the normal course of events.

The following is a typical lead-in to a back-to-school news story:

> Ben Kapnik turned 5 on 14 July but he won't be entering kindergarten this Fall, even though the cutoff date for the school he will eventually attend is 15 September. Instead Ben will take a third year of private Montessori preschool. Ben isn't small for his age, nor is his development abnormally slow in any area. He is anything but culturally deprived; his parents have been reading aloud to him since he was 3-weeks-old. But, after considerable research, Ben's parents decided that it would be best to retain him, so he will start kindergarten at 6 rather than 5. (Simons 1988: 1)

And later the parents continue in their own words:

> 'We just kept hearing positive things about waiting, and no negatives', Kapnik said, 'It's just that we thought he might get a boost from being one of the older ones. Why not help your child be a star, if you can?' (Simons 1988: 2)

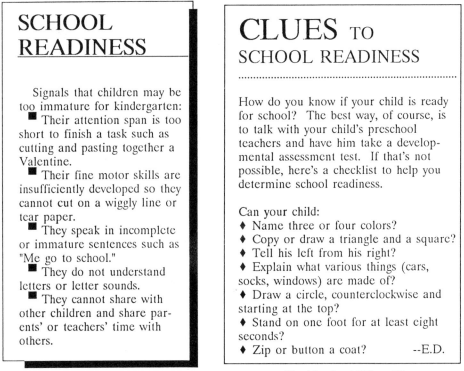

SCHOOL READINESS

Signals that children may be too immature for kindergarten:
■ Their attention span is too short to finish a task such as cutting and pasting together a Valentine.
■ Their fine motor skills are insufficiently developed so they cannot cut on a wiggly line or tear paper.
■ They speak in incomplete or immature sentences such as "Me go to school."
■ They do not understand letters or letter sounds.
■ They cannot share with other children and share parents' or teachers' time with others.

(Blackman, 1988, p. 8-B)

CLUES TO SCHOOL READINESS

How do you know if your child is ready for school? The best way, of course, is to talk with your child's preschool teachers and have him take a developmental assessment test. If that's not possible, here's a checklist to help you determine school readiness.

Can your child:
♦ Name three or four colors?
♦ Copy or draw a triangle and a square?
♦ Tell his left from his right?
♦ Explain what various things (cars, socks, windows) are made of?
♦ Draw a circle, counterclockwise and starting at the top?
♦ Stand on one foot for at least eight seconds?
♦ Zip or button a coat?   --E.D.

(Davidowitz, 1988, p. 80)

Figure 1: Two examples of readiness checklists from the popular press.

The article goes on to present the other side of the story with quotations from educators and researchers concerned about the trend to send 6-year-olds to kindergarten.

Although we have not yet collected a representative sample of newspaper and magazine articles nor conducted a systematic content analysis, we do have 50 examples of such articles and a preliminary typology for scoring the likely message to the reader. I have also formed an impression as to the major themes or ideas conveyed by these articles. First, as previously mentioned, they suggest that school entrance poses a dilemma for parents, captured in headlines such as, 'Parents wonder when to send kids to kindergarten' (Blackman 1988: 8-B). Second, news articles tend to reify the categories of 'ready' and 'unready' children even when they later quote from early childhood experts who say that this is a meaningless dichotomy. Thirdly, articles imply that there are scientific or expert ways of knowing when a child is 'ready' by offering checklists for parents to evaluate their children. Two sample checklists, one from *Working Mother* and one from *The Denver Post*, are shown in figure 1. Finally, the popular press encourages redshirting by implicitly congratulating parents who have been shrewd enough to use this strategy. For example, a 13 November 1989 story in *Time* was entitled, 'The redshirt solution: for some children, delaying kindergarten is the right choice' (Elson 1989).The article endorsed redshirting as the appropriate response to overly-academic kindergartens, provided yet another checklist to determine if delaying kindergarten is warranted, and contained virtually no criticism of the practice.

Purposes, extent, and validity of readiness testing

Readiness testing in local school districts is an integral part of the cycle of escalating curriculum and an ageing kindergarten and first-grade population. For the most part, the need to measure and remove children who are not capable of keeping pace can be seen as a response to increasing instructional demands. But readiness testing also fuels the cycle by raising the standards as to what it takes to be qualified for kindergarten. In the current climate, even 'readiness' tests that are not used to make decisions about school entry contribute to the public perception that not all age-eligible children are ready for school.

In this section, I outline the different types of decisions that are made on the basis of readiness tests and developmental screening instruments. Data collected in a recent survey for the National Forum on the Future of Children and Families are used to document the extent of each practice. Then I discuss the validity issues associated with each testing purpose.

Purposes for testing

Measurement specialists will always tell you that test validity depends on test use. A test may be valid for one purpose and not for another; it may even have adequate reliability for some use but be too inaccurate to support other more critical decisions. Therefore, to judge the technical adequacy of readiness tests, it is essential to know their purpose. Before considering the specific uses of readiness tests or developmental assessments in local school districts, it is helpful to recognize key dimensions that distinguish generally among types of test use. The first distinction is between individual and group uses of test results. Is the test score used to assess the performance of individual children, or is it used to evaluate groups, as in school or district accountability reports? If tests are only used for groups and not to make decisions about individuals, they do not have to meet such stringent standards of accuracy, because group means are more stable than individual scores. The second dimension has to do with the consequences or importance of the test results. For example, individual consequences of tests vary in importance from a low score on a weekly quiz to failing the bar exam. The consequences of group test results vary from research contexts where groups are anonymous and unaffected by test results to accountability situations where there may be serious ramifications if schools score poorly.

There are two principal, overarching uses of tests for pre-kindergarten and kindergarten children in local school districts: developmental screening and readiness testing. Both types involve decisions about individual children. Developmental screening can be thought of as a preliminary step in the identification of children as handicapped. If the initial, brief screening suggests that children may have serious learning or developmental problems, they are referred for a more in-depth developmental assessment. Because there is potential harm in either mislabeling a child as handicapped or in failing to detect a handicap that might be remediable, the accuracy of screening measures is relatively important; however, screening tests are only preliminary to more thorough assessments and, therefore, do not have to meet the more stringent criteria of the developmental assessments themselves. Readiness tests are the focus of this chapter, and are much more difficult to characterize both as to content and purpose. Meisels (1987) defined readiness tests as measures of 'curriculum-related skills a child has already acquired-skills that are typically prerequisite for specific instructional programs' (p. 4). In fact, this characterizes only one, albeit the most prevalent, mode of readiness testing. A more generic description of readiness tests would be to say that they are intended to inform instructional decisions, but that the meaning of the concept of readiness depends on one's theoretical views about learning. More will be said about competing conceptions of readiness in the later discussion of validity.

Theroretical viewpoints also shape the particular kinds of decisions that are made on the basis of readiness tests. The Gesell School Readiness Test is based on the maturationist developmental theories of the 1920s and 1930s. It does not satisfy Meisels definition of a readiness test because it includes content more like developmental screening measures rather than curriculum-related material. It is used extensively, however, to make decisions about whether children are ready for regular kindergarten or first grade. (Therefore, I treat the Gesell Test in a category of its own, distinct from developmental screening measures and academic readiness measures.) Because Gesell's theory stressed that readiness was biological and could not be hurried – children are either ready or they are not – Gesell's followers want to assign children to different places according to their assessed readiness stage. The Gesell Tests are used to place children in two-year kindergarten programs, or to send them home to wait a year. Because these decisions result in significant diversions from the normal course of a child's progress in school, tests used for this purpose must meet the highest standards of accuracy for individual decisions, analogous to tests used for Special Education placements.

Readiness tests like those described by Meisels, composed of prerequisite academic skills, derive from the behaviorist tradition which requires that learning be broken down into constituent elements. Behaviorism also allowed that learning was highly amenable to instructional intervention. Therefore, construed from this perspective readiness is seen as a continuum of skill acquisition. And tests like the Metropolitan Readiness Test are intended for use by teachers to plan instruction in the regular classroom rather than to place children in a separate program. Because classroom instructional decisions are much less momentous in the lives of individual children, these measures can be more informal and do not have to satisfy so stern a standard of psychometric accuracy.

Although these three types of tests (developmental screening measures, the Gesell, and academic readiness measures) are often used in practice in ways consistent with their distinctively different purposes and rationales, there is also in practice a great deal of confusion and cross-over among these types. For example, developmental screening measures and academinc readiness tests, both of which come from intellectual traditions of instructional intervention, are nonetheless used by many school districts to make wait-a-year decisions, i.e., kindergarten retentions or placements in transitional grades (Gnezda and Bolig 1988, Meisels 1987). To note the confusion is not to say, however, that the tests would necessarily be more accurate if they were each remanded to their intended purposes. The statistical correlation with first-grade achievement might be about the same from one category of test to the next. Instead the indiscrimate misapplication of these measures is mentioned as an indication of how little thought appears to have been given to underlying measurement (and educational) issues when these tests are adopted. Consistent with this observation, in Gnezda and Bolig's (1988) survey of 50 state-level early childhood specialists, the perception of respondents was that local districts select readiness instruments for one of three major reasons: familiarity (e.g., neighboring districts use it); intensity and success of marketing strategies by test publishers (especially cited regarding the Gesell); and the ease and cost of test administration. Similarly, policymakers seem to adopt wholly either biological or background explanations as to why unready children should be kept out of first grade without recognizing arguments in these terms and without confronting their inherent contradictions.

Very recently yet another use has emerged for screening/readiness measures which is to identify 'at-risk' children for placement in extended-day kindergartens. In many locales the resources are not available for full-day programs for all children, therefore those with the greatest need are selected. Here the justification for the use of the tests seems to be strictly actuarial. In other words, there are not specific definitions of 'at risk' put forth, e.g., 'immature' in the case of the Gesell, 'disordered development' in the case of screening measures, or 'does not know his letter sounds' in the case of academic readiness tests; instead, measures in either of the last two categories are used because they are correlated with success in first grade and because in either case, low scores warrant extra instructional help. Gesell Tests are not as likely to be used for this purpose because Gesell proponents tend to maintain better control over the philosophical rationale associated with their tests; and they would strongly disapprove of giving extra help to low scoring (i.e., developmentally young) children because they do not believe that readiness can be helped by intervention.

In a few instances states and local school districts use readiness tests like the *Metropolitan Readiness Test* for group purposes, i.e., the average readiness score of all the kindergartners in the school or district is reported for accountability purposes. This use of readiness tests is relatively infrequent and is, therefore, not considered further in this chapter. Suffice it to say that group reporting of readiness scores is technically appropriate so long as the results at the end of the kindergarten year are not interpreted as evidence of the quality of teaching in kindergarten. How a child performs on these measures at the end of kindergarten is a reflection of opportunities to learn in all of the previous five years of the child's life. Therefore these tests cannot be used as outcome measures to evaluate programs without adequate controls of prior experiences. They are more likely to be useful as status measures (i.e., for needs assessment) or as input measures, e.g., to help interpret more accurately the meaning of first grade outcomes.

Empirical data on the extent of readiness testing

To have some sense of the policy importance of readiness testing issues, it would be helpful to know how many children are affected. Given the various purposes for giving tests to pre-kindergarten and kindergarten children, how prevalent is each type of testing? The Gesell Institute has estimated, for example, that their tests are used in 18% of school districts nationally. A nationally representative survey of school districts is absent; the best data available are provided by a recent survey of the 50 states conducted by Gnezda and Bolig (1988) for the National Forum on the Future of Children and Their Families sponsored by the National Research Council. According to their report, developmental and health screenings are mandated in 19 states and occur to some extent at the local level in an additional 20 states. In all 39 of these states, screening occurs prior to kindergarten, with a few states providing screening again before first grade. Readiness testing before kindergarten is mandated in four states and occurs locally in an additional 26 states; readiness testing before first grade is mandated in six states and occurs locally in 37 states. Considering the two readiness policies jointly only three states did not report the occurrence of either pre-kindergarten or pre-first-grade readiness testing.

One of the major findings of the Gnezda and Bolig (1988) study was that readiness testing is predominantly a local phenomenon with almost no scrutiny or control exerted by state agencies. Their findings, therefore, relied on the perceptions of the state-level early childhood specialists whom they interviewed. Nevertheless, their results summarized below help to elaborate on the categories of test use described in the preceding section.

1. Screening is generally meant to identify individual needs for special attention in the classroom, further specific diagnosis, or additional services. However, many of the people interviewed suggested that screening data are often used as one factor in influencing parents' decisions to delay enrolling their children for a year, denial of kindergarten entry, and placement in special programs, such as junior or developmental kindergarten. (p. 3)
2. Kindergarten readiness was perceived to serve similar purposes as screening. In most cases, respondents suggested that readiness test results were used with other indicators for placement, denial of entry into kindergarten, identification of special needs, and as a guide to teachers for curriculum planning. (p. 3)
3. By far the most common use of (first-grade readiness test) results is for placement in either regular or special first-grade programs, and retention. Eight states also mandate testing to determine program impact and accountability. (p. 3)

Thus respondents tended to see a connection between testing practices and concomitant trends nationally to delay school entry, to retain children in kindergarten, or to make special placements in two-year kindergarten programs. In states where these practices were cited, respondents estimated that between 10 and 50% of each age cohort was not reaching first grade on time.

The Gnezda and Bolig survey also provides some insight as to the political impetus for such extensive interest in readiness testing. In the 23 states with mandated screening or readiness testing, most of the mandates were enacted in the mid-to-late 1980s and were attributed by the respondents to 'educational reform efforts, concern over the accountability of schools and of teachers, greater interest in identifying and serving children "at risk" of school failure, and a downward extension of academics' (p.4).

Content validity and predictive accuracy

This is the only technical section of the chapter, but is not a long-winded account of the reliability and validity coefficients (if known) associated with each of the widely used readiness tests or screening measures used as school readiness tests. In my view there are only a few technical and conceptual issues concerning these tests that need to be understood from a policy perspective. First, I consider what the tests measure, particularly concerns about the content of academic readiness measures, the Gesell, and other developmental measures. Then, I address the predictive accuracy of these measures. How good are the best predictors at foretelling who will fail in first grade?

Content validity: Academic readiness tests measure things like letter recognition, vocabulary (by picture identification), letter–sound correspondence, language concepts, and counting. Although these tests now throw in a few number-oriented items, readiness measures are still highly similar to the reading-readiness tests of previous decades. As noted earlier, pre-reading tests were created beginning in the 1930s according to the principles of behaviorist psychology which attempts to break learning down into prerequisite subskills. At the time, a conception of instruction that allowed for remedial intervention was an improvement over previous fixed-ability theories. However, given the discoveries of cognitive psychology from the past 20 years and the research on emergent literacy over the same period, we can clearly say that the learning theory underlying current readiness tests is outmoded and seriously flawed.

Stallman and Pearson (1990) have provided a history of reading readiness research and a thorough analysis of the content of current measures. Their explanation of the fallacious assumptions underlying readiness tests parallels closely the larger arguments being heard today about the conceptual limitations of standardized achievement tests (Resnick and Resnick 1990) which foster by-rote instruction in the early grades. These tests rely on the outmoded assumptions of decomposability and decontextualization, whereby complex skills are broken down into component skills, practiced in isolation, and then are expected to be assembled at some later time like a piece of machinery. Unfortunately, as current research has shown, the old theory did not provide for conceptual organization of interrelated ideas, nor did it provide for the development of thinking and reasoning skills. With respect to early reading in particular, the old theory could lead to practice with shape recognition rather than listening comprehension and other activities designed to help children understand that the purpose of reading is to get meaning from text. Thus, most reading researchers dispute the use of readiness tests because the tests perpetuate allegiance to a model of beginning reading instruction that is no longer valid. From their exhaustive review, Stallman and Pearson concluded that readiness tests look very much like those designed in the 1930s, very much like each other, and nearly identical to the tests accompanying the readiness level of basal reading programs. What follows is the picture they paint of the substance of these measures:

> In terms of the ways children are tested on formal measures of early literacy, most are, to say the least, disconcerting. Children are tested on isolated skills in decontextualized settings rather than on reading tasks in situations in which they are asked to behave like readers. This conclusion is supported by several pieces of data. First, the examples presented to illustrate skills tested portray a picture of isolated, not integrated, reading skills. Second, recognition, not production or even identification, dominates as the primary mode of cognitive processing. One wonders what happened to the theory of reading as a constructive process. Third, when they recognize things, children are usually asked to respond to either a picture or something the teacher says. At the very least, real reading involves identification of words in sentences. Finally, what dominates the whole enterprise when children actually take the test is test-taking behavior filling-in bubbles, moving the marker, making sure everyone is in the right place. These activities may be related to test taking, but they have nothing to do with reading. (Stallman and Pearson 1990: 38)

The *Gesell School Readiness Test* is a broader measure of cognitive and social development and of perceptual–motor abilities than are academic readiness tests. It appears to be remarkably similar to IQ tests for the same age children. In fact, there is no greater substantive difference between the tasks on the Gesell and the Stanford–Binet for 5-year-olds than between the Stanford–Binet and the Wechsler Preschool and Primary Scale of Intelligence. In the only empirical study available, the Gesell Test was not shown to have discriminant validity from IQ, i.e., the Gesell correlated as highly with an IQ test as with a Piagetian measure of development (Kaufman 1971).

To say that the Gesell Test resembles IQ measures is not automatically a criticism. If one wanted to make accurate predictions about 'success' in first grade, (a complex criterion with academic, social, and behavioral dimensions), one would reasonably include measures of cognitive abilities, language development, social awareness, and perceptual-motor abilities – as do the Stanford–Binet and most developmental screening measures. To assess whether a particular child may be developmentally handicapped, deficient screening test results are followed up by more thorough evaluation including an individually administered IQ test. What is worrisome about the Gesell, and in fact about unconsidered uses of developmental screening measures as school-entry gates, is that their similarity to IQ measures is not recognized. Practitioners and policymakers rightly eschew the use of IQ tests to decide who can go to school because – after 20 years of controversy – there is some shared public understanding that performance on IQ measures is influenced by past opportunities to learn (albeit a reasonably accurate indicator of current functioning in the school setting). The same thing can be said about readiness tests and various developmental measures including the Gesell. But under the guise of measuring school readiness rather than intelligence these tests are publicly acceptable. The willingness of school districts to use tests with a readiness or developmental label but not to use IQ measures is particularly curious given the increasingly actuarial tone of testing purposes, i.e., the use of tests is justified because they are thought to predict school success.

Predictive validity: Just how accurate are these tests for their current uses? To answer this question properly would require an entire chapter in and of itself. No wonder educators without measurement training are confused. I have had 20 years experience as a psychometrician and I find making sense of the technical underpinnings of many of these tests a hopeless muddle. Some of the widely used instruments cited by Gnezda and Bolig (1988) do not have reliability and validity data. For others, the authors throw numbers around from a single study or an odd sample of subjects, or show the correlation with the old version of the same test rather than the needed predictive validity evidence. Reviews in *The Ninth Mental Measurements Yearbook* (1985) are intended to help the uninitiated reader through this maze, but are not uniformly helpful because in some cases the reviewers say it is perfectly alright not to have validity data because the test is a criterion-referenced test. This assertion is simply not true when tests are used for predictive purposes rather than for instruction. Often reviewers do not explain that a test may be acceptable for one purpose and not for another. In contrast, an example of a good review is Boehm's (1985) review of the *Brigance K and 1 Screen for Kindergarten and First Grade*, which she says is useful in making curriculum decisions. Boehm warns, however, against using the Brigance for 'readiness and placement decisions' (p. 225), given that it has no norms, and no reliability and validity data.

My sense of the relative statistical quality of these measures can be summarized as follows. Academic readiness tests like the Metropolitan tend to have the highest predictive correlations with first grade achievement measures on the order of 0.6 to 0.7. (One should be a little wary of these very high relationships, since they have the advantage of paper-and-pencil tests used for both predictor and criterion and they often have the least time elapsed from time 1 to time 2.) In general, academic readiness measures accompanying the major standardized test batteries are in the same ballpark as IQ tests in terms of their ability to predict first-grade success. The various developmental screening measures, if they have data, tend not to be quite such potent predictors. The Gesell has been severely criticized by numerous reviewers in the past for not having reliability and validity data. In recent studies of the Gesell, correlations with later school measures have ranged from 0.23 (Graue and Shepard 1989) to 0.5 (Walker 1989).

On technical grounds readiness tests are perfectly adequate for making instructional decisions about which skills a child has mastered and which need more practice. Crossing over and using developmental screening measures for instructional purposes is also defensible statistically although in both cases educators should be asking whether the content of these tests makes sense as a curricular framework. Developmental screening measures tend not to have very impressive correlations with first grade outcomes but they may be perfectly adequate for their original purpose as a preliminary screen. Even with relatively modest correlations such measures are reasonably good at identifying the more serious cases of developmental delay and are intended to be follwed up with more in-depth assessment. Developmental measures are not up to the task, however, of making decisions like two-year kindergarten placements or delayed entry to school. Nor are the academic readiness measures. None of the currently available measures, by whatever name, is accurate enough to support special placement decisions. As we have discussed previously (Shepard and Smith 1986), the Metropolitan was never intended by its authors to sort children into ready and unready groups. We picked it for demonstration purposes because it had the highest correlation we could find with first-grade outcomes and still it would lead to a one-third error rate in making special placements, i.e., one-third of those said to be unready would actually be successful on the outcome measure. The Gesell has a corresponding error rate of one-half. To understand this calculation, suppose that a school principal calls a meeting of the parents of 30 children who are scheduled for transition room next year because of their developmentally young performance on the Gesell; she should be prepared to tell the group that because of the error in the test, 15 of the 30 children were falsely identified as unready (and that she doesn't know which ones).

Summary: Changes in the kindergarten and first-grade curriculum and worries about children being too young to cope have created a climate nationally such that there is great pressure to make judgments as to who is ready for school and who is not. Readiness tests and developmental screening measures misused as readiness tests have been widely adopted by local school districts and in some cases are mandated by states to address these issues. Unfortunately none of the available measures is sufficiently accurate to support special placement decisions for individual children such as two-year kindergarten programs or delayed school entry. In addition, the content of academic readiness tests is questionable given recent research in emergent literacy and cognitive psychology. Developmental tests, including the *Gesell School Readiness Test*, are not appreciably different from IQ measures, yet one set of measures is politically acceptable and the other is not.

Unconsidered policy consequences

Throughout the chapter I have attempted to convey the extent to which changes in kindergarten and first-grade curriculum have evolved without conscious debate and evaluation (although a great deal of criticism has arisen now after the fact). Some policy changes have been conscious decisions, however, such as the decisions to institute readiness testing or two-year kindergarten programs. As noted by Gnezda and Bolig (1988) these policies may have been adopted by individual classroom teachers, school principals, local boards of education, or the state legislature (in the case of testing). Although these decisions were consciously made, it is still accurate to say that they were made without full knowledge of their consequences. An understanding of the wisdom of these practices has tended to be one-sided. For example, teachers fear the effects of sending low-skilled or immature children into an aversive first-grade, so they are willing to retain them in kindergarten believing that an extra year will have only beneficial effects. Legislators hear that unready children do poorly in school and conclude that a test should be given to detect their unreadiness and fix it before allowing them to go on to first grade. Legislators make this decision without knowledge of the quality of the tests or the effects of an extra year on first-grade performance. Furthermore, in addition to not knowing how individual children will be affected, decision-makers fail to consider the collective effect of their policies on the larger system. For example, what does readiness testing do to the access of poor and minority children to public education? What does redshirting advice do to the age and ability range in kindergarten?

In the discussion that follows I outline briefly the unconsidered policy consequences of readiness testing, extra grades before first grade, and delayed school entry. I conclude with a summary of recent national early childhood reports that offer an alternative policy perspective.

Fallible tests followed by ineffective treatments

In the course of studying the phenomena of readiness testing and kindergarten retention, we have often been struck by the observation that the burden seems to be on proving that a child is normal and thus entitled to normal progress in school. The mind-set to find unready children for their own good is so strong that many educators are willing to use highly fallible tests because some information is presumed to be better than no information. Beliefs about first-grade readiness are sometimes so strong that teachers operate on the principle 'When in Doubt, Retain'. This is not the first time in public education that a treatment, presumed to be unambiguously a benefit, has been imposed on individual children using fallible tests. The rush to create pre-kindergarten and transition programs in recent years parallels the over-filling of self-contained classrooms for the mildly retarded during the 1950s and 1960s. Because Special Education was believed to be an unmitigated help the abiding policy was 'When in Doubt, Place'. Only after extensive research demonstrating the stigma of special placement and greater learning gains for mildly handicapped learners in the regular classroom was the policy of 'least restrictive environment' adopted.

If the intended treatment may not be effective, or may even be harmful, why isn't the presumption to treat children normally unless proven otherwise? I raise this issue because there are ways to address the problem of fallible measurement: if that were the only problem, simply gather more data. If one wants to insist on retention and parents complain about holding children back because of a test, make the decision based on the test plus teacher judgment, or so the strategy goes. In fact, this remedy has been adopted in situations like Georgia's, where the use of a kindergarten test for admission to first grade was hotly contested. The real issue is not how to make the test more accurate, however, if the intended treatment is ineffective. From a policy perspective, the most important findings are not about the inaccuracy of readiness tests but the research evidence of the ineffectiveness of two-year kindergarten programs discussed in the first section. Contrary to the Georgia legislator's beliefs, children who are less skilled or developmentally younger than their peers do not do better in first grade after an extra year of kindergarten than if they had gone directly to first grade. And even children as young as 5 and 6 do understand that there is something wrong with them if they are not competent enough to go to first grade with their classmates (Shepard and Smith 1989).

Reinstitution of tracking

Tracking by ability is still widely practiced in US schools. (I use the term 'tracking' to refer to the practice of assigning children to separate classrooms on the basis of academic ability as opposed to the practice of 'grouping' by instructional level within classrooms.) Despite its continued practice, tracking in the elementary grades is much less prevalent than it once was; and there are some common, research-based understandings among educators that tracking is detrimental for children consigned to the low track. Nonetheless, tracking by any other name continues to re-emerge as a popular remedy to the problem of teaching heterogeneous groups of children.

Readiness testing is associated with the backdoor reinstitution of tracking which we have observed in several different forms.

1. Two-year placements for at-risk children: When readiness tests or developmental tests are used to place 'at-risk' children in two-year kindergarten programs, the result is a group of children who are lower in cognitive ability (as currently assessed), on-average younger, and disproportionately from poor and minority backgrounds. (See Ellwein and Eads [1990], for example, for data on the correlations between test performance and socio-economic background and ethnic group membership on several well-known readiness measures.) In some cases children in developmental kindergartens or transition first grades receive a highly desirable curriculum, akin to what early childhood experts say should be the developmentally appropriate curriculum in regular kindergarten and first grade; however, they have had to suffer the special placement, segregation from their peers, and the extra year to get it. Worse still, in other cases children judged to be unready do not receive a very desirable curriculum but rather one that is characterized by regimentation and drill on prerequisite skills (Smith and Shepard 1988).

2. Separate classrooms for at-risk children: Likewise, when tests are used to assign at-risk children to extended-day kindergarten, the result is to create relatively homogeneous groups of low-skilled children who are segregated from their normal peers. In some cases the effects of tracking in an extra-year program or an at-risk kindergarten are even carried forward to first grade by placing all of these children in the same first grade class because of their common instructional needs. Apparently educators are not thinking of these decisions as tracking decisions or they might have considered alternatives such as spending limited extended day monies for an extra aide in the regular kindergarten or for a special afternoon program following heterogeneous placements in the regular morning program. Instead they think of special placements, which disproportionately affect boys and children from lower socio-economic backgrounds, as unambiguous benefits for the unready children thus assigned.

3. Two-year placements based on the Gesell: Characterizing the use of the Gesell Test to make extra-year placements is somewhat more problematic because its advocates insist that it is not intended to select low-ability children. Given the cognitive demands of the test, however, if the test alone is used to make selections it will produce a relatively low-ability group; we have observed this to be the case in some applications. In other cases, however, summer birthdates and being a boy are considered in addition to the test, and consistent with the Gesell philosophy low-scoring children with 'learning problems' are sent directly on to first grade because retention is believed to work only with immature children rather than for those with low intelligence (Scott and Ames 1969). In these situations some participants in transition programs may be quite able cognitively. Nonetheless, they are tracked and given instruction adjusted down to their presumed level of readiness which as described above may or may not be a very desirable curriculum depending on the local instructional program. Even when the mode of instruction in extra-year programs is developmentally appropriate, one has to ask why these very normal children could not have received appropriate instruction in the regular program and without the extra year. The Gesell perspective assumes implicitly that developmentally immature children are cognitively as well as behaviorally behind their peers; therefore, it is held to steadfastly that they 'never catch up' and hence are never allowed to rejoin their age-mates even after a time when maturity should no longer be a factor.

Exaggerated age and ability differences

Although intended to make groups of children more alike in terms of their readiness for school, in fact practices of readiness testing, two-year kindergarten placements, and redshirting are making the groups of children attending kindergarten and first grade more heterogeneous and therefore more difficult to teach than before these policies began. The policies assumed that there was a well-understood continuum of ability (or two states called ready and unready). The idea was to lop off the bottom end, and move it to be in line with the top end by virtue of the extra-year placement, thus reducing the heterogeneity of the group. It stands to reason, however, that if the tests are inaccurate and the treatment is ineffective that the range of abilities will stay approximately the same, except that we now must add the heterogeneity created by age. Some kindergartners are just barely 5 and some are $6\frac{1}{2}$. Because of extensive retention practices and redshirting a significant number of children begin first grade as 7-year-olds.

Furthermore, to the extent that redshirting is a middle-class phenomenon, socio-economic difference are now added to age differences. In Graue's (1990) ethnographic study of conceptions of readiness in three kindergarten settings, there was indeed a close association between parents' social class and holding 5-year-olds out of school. More importantly there was no indication in Graue's data that middle-class parents were holding out children who might be inept or poorly qualified for kindergarten at the normal time. Rather their children knew their letters and numbers as 5-year-olds, but waited to enter kindergarten as 6-year-olds when they were already readers. In this context, it appears to be very difficult for teachers to remember that kindergarten is for 5-year-olds. There is a tendency to let the older half of the class which now includes several well-schooled 6-year-olds set the standard against which normal 5-year-olds from poor families and without preschool experience are judged to be incompetent.

Further escalation of curriculum

Delayed school entry and extra-year programs increase both the age range and the average age of children in kindergarten and first grade. Thus, while it can be said that these various policies began as a response to a curriculum in first grade that had become too demanding and aversive for normal 6-year-olds, there is a clear tendency for each of the responses to feed the escalation. The 'youngness research' cited earlier shows a small but nonetheless reliable achievement difference between the oldest and youngest children in first grade. Removing the youngest 5-year-olds from a kindergarten class and replacing them with a half-dozen 6-year-olds can be expected to shift the class average upward by only 2 or 3 percentile points at most. However, as we have described previously the effect of more older children is appreciable if teachers attend to the $5\frac{1}{2}$-year-olds and 6-year-olds as the normative group (Shepard and Smith 1988).

Remember that many of the children in the older group of kindergartners are there because their parents sent them to an extra year of preschool or because they are repeating kindergarten. They have longer attention spans and know the rules for conducting business in the classroom. Consistent with the trends that led to the escalation in the first place, teachers eliminate from their whole group instruction normal kindergarten things that now only a few children don't know (see Graue 1990). Middle-class parents who may have held their children out nominally to avoid too much pressure nonetheless apply pressure the next year to ensure that their 6-year-old kindergartners are adequately challenged: 'My child was reading when he came to school. What have you done for him?' (Graue 1990, Shepard and Smith 1988).

The continued escalation of instructional demands in kindergarten and first grade because of readiness testing, retention, and redshirting is perhaps the most serious example of unconsidered policy consequences. Not only do these practices exacerbate the problem they were intended to solve but now the cycle of escalation has a life of its own. If schools attempt to respond to the policy recommendations of national early childhood organizations and curriculum specialists discussed in the last section, they can create more developmentally appropriate curricula and discontinue readiness testing and retention practices. But redshirting is now firmly established in the minds of many parents and preschool teachers. Therefore in the examples I know of, change is more difficult because of the continued demands of 6-year-olds coming into kindergarten. However, the teachers in these settings at least have the perspective not to treat normal children, 5 years and 0 months old, as if they were the aberrant cases.

Readiness tests as curriculum

Thus far the discussion has focused on the effects that readiness testing has on individual children and indirectly on the curriculum by fostering the trend to send older children to kindergarten. Might readiness tests also have a direct effect on curriculum? Are kindergarten teachers influenced to teach the content of readiness tests in ways analogous to the undue influence of high-stakes standardized tests on instruction in later grades (Resnick and Resnick 1990)?

Here my comments must necessarily be more speculative because systematic data on the extent of these influences are not available. Specific examples can be cited on either side of the issue. During the first year of kindergarten testing in Georgia, for example, news accounts had it that 'CAT academies' had sprung up and that children were drilled on skills in kindergarten classrooms in preparation for the spring test. In contrast, in one school district that we studied extensively, schools with high kindergarten retention rates had very regimented, skills-oriented curricula, but these emphases could not be attributed to a readiness test (Smith and Shepard 1988). In other examples, however, especially where 'at-risk' children are involved, the remedial kindergarten program comes to resemble the local screening-skills checklist (Graue 1990, Karweit 1989). These occurrences are especially worrisome because it means that children who are perceived to be behind are consigned to a by-rote drill-oriented curriculum and denied more important early literacy and language development experiences. Stallman and Pearson's (1990) negative analysis of the content of readiness tests caused them to fear what inappropriate messages about reading young children might acquire from the short-term experience of taking the test. Consider how much more serious their concerns are when test-like tasks became the standard fare for everyday instruction. Again, we have no way of knowing how frequently these practices occur – but we have seen them. As Stallman and Pearson explain, the isolated-skills model that dominates readiness tests is mirrored in basal text materials. Therefore, in many cases where this type of instruction persists, it is not the fault of the tests. We are particularly troubled, however, over instances where a readiness test is used to decide who is at risk and then drill on the readiness tasks becomes the course of instruction.

Conclusion

Readiness testing by local school districts is a procedural response to a much more complicated set of issues than is typically understood at the time that tests are adopted. The kindergarten and first-grade curricula have become too demanding, focusing narrowly on rote learning of skills, which cannot be recommended even for the 'fast' kids who appear to be keeping up. Instead of changing the curriculum, the implicit 'backdoor' policy has been to find ways to remove unready children by encouraging young 5s to stay home, retaining children in kindergarten, and giving readiness tests to deny entry to kindergarten or first grade.

What policymakers have not known, be they classroom teachers or state legislators, is that readiness tests are not technically accurate enough to support their use in making crucial decisions that alter a child's normal progress in school. They have not known that controlled studies show no academic gains and sometimes emotional harm from extra-year kindergarten programs. Furthermore, decision-makers have not considered the systemic effects of their policies. Poor and minority children are over-represented in the group of children failing readiness tests, and are thus denied access to public education or are assigned to the low-ability group in a backdoor form of tracking. As middle-class parents catch on to the fad of 'redshirting' (sending 6-year-old readers to kindergarten), differences between rich and poor children are further exaggerated. Various policies that produce an older population of kindergarten and first grade children unwittingly feed the cycle of escalation they were intended to cure.

What can be done to short-circuit this cycle of events? The alternative policy perspective, suggested by several national reports, is one that denies any validity to the concept of 'readiness' as popularly construed. All children are ready to learn something at every age. There is not a biological or psychological threshold that makes some children ready for school learning and others not. Instead of readiness as the dominant concern, these national position statements are characterized by two important themes:

'developmentally-appropriate curriculum' and making school ready for the child rather than the other way around.

The National Association for the Education of Young Children has described at length the kinds of integrated and experienced-based activities that are appropriate for the learning needs of 5- and 6-year-olds (Bredekamp 1987). They have particularly emphasized that a developmentally-appropriate curriculum recognizes both the average developmental level of children in a classroom and the large range of abilities that is also a normal aspect of development. For example, they note that early childhood programs should 'provide for a wider range of developmental interests and abilities than the chronological age range of the group would suggest'. Furthermore, adults should be 'prepared to meet the needs of children who exhibit unusual interests and skills outside the normal developmental range' (p. 4). Thus the NAEYC proposes a school entrance and early grades promotion model with no rejects.

Concerns about the harms of the current curriculum in kindergarten and first grade were addressed in a joint statement by the Association for Childhood Education International, the Association for Supervision and Curriculum Development, the International Reading Association, the NAEYC, the National Association of Elementary School Principals, and the National Council of Teachers of English. They cited the following concerns of particular import to this chapter:

> 1. Many pre-first grade children are subjected to rigid, formal pre-reading programs with inappropriate expectations and experiences for their levels of development.
> 2. Little attention is given to individual development or individual learning styles.
> 3. The pressures of accelerated programs do not allow children to be risk-takers as they experiment with language and internalize concepts about how language operates . . .
> 4. The pressure to achieve high scores on standardized tests that frequently are not appropriate for the kindergarten child has resulted in changes in the content of programs. Program content often does not attend to the child's social, emotional and intellectual development. Consequently, inappropriate activities that deny curiosity, critical thinking, and creative expression occur all too frequently. (International Reading Association 1986).

Perhaps the report which best captures the idea of an alternative to judging readiness is the report of the California School Readiness Task Force (1988) which took as its title, 'Here They Come, Ready or Not', in keeping with their conclusion that 'schools should be changed to fit the needs of students rather than to continue to try to fit the children into programs that are inappropriate' (p. ix). Like the NAEYC, they recommended that classroom organization and teaching methods be responsive to the heterogeneous skills and abilities of children in the early grades. Oddly, as has been shown here, if schools can return to a policy of admitting all 5-year-olds to kindergarten and all 6-year-olds to first grade, they will encounter less heterogeneity among students than they currently face as a result of ineffective policies intended to make children uniformly ready.

References

BLACKMAN, J. H. (1988) 'Parents face kindergarten dilemma: where and when to send their child?', *The Denver Post*, 3 April, 1-B, B-8.

BOEHM, A. E. (1985) 'Review of Brigance K and 1 Screen for Kindergarten and First Grade', in J. V. Mitchell (ed.), *The Ninth Mental Measurements Yearbook*, Vols I and II. (Lincoln, NB: The Buros Institute of Mental Measurements of the University of Nebraska-Lincoln.), pp. 223–225.

BREDEKAMP, S. (ed.) (1987) *Developmentally Appropriate Practice in Early Childhood Programs Serving Children from Birth through Age 8* (Washington, DC; National Association for the Education of Young Children).

CALIFORNIA STATE DEPARTMENT of EDUCATION (1988) *Here They Come, Ready or Not: A Report of the School Readiness Task Force* (Sacramento, CA: Cal SDE).

CUNNINGHAM, A. E. (1989) 'Eeny, meeny, miny, moe: testing policy and practice in early childhood', paper prepared for the National Commission on Testing and Public Policy, University of California, Berkeley.

DAVIDOWITZ, E. (1988) 'Is your child ready for kindergarten?' *Working Mother*, 11 (6), pp. 79–83.

DURKIN, D. (1987) 'A classroom-observation study of reading instruction in kindergarten', *Early Chidhood Research Quarterly*, 2 (3), pp. 275–300.

ELLWEIN, M. C. and EADS, G. M. (1990), 'How well do readiness tests predict future school performance?', paper presented at the annual meeting of the American Educational Research Association, Boston.

ELSON, J. (1989) 'The redshirt solution: for some children, delaying kindergarten is the right choice', *Time*, 13 November, p. 102.

GESELL INSTITUTE OF HUMAN DEVELOPMENT (1982) *A Gift of Time: A Developmental Point of View* (New Haven, CT: GIHD).

GNEZDA, M. T. and BOLIG, R. (1988) *A National Survey of Public School Testing of Pre-kindergarten and Kindergarten Children* (Washington, DC: National Forum on the Future of Children and Families, National Research Council).

GRAUE, M. E. (1990) 'Socially constructed readiness for kindergarten in three communities', unpublished doctoral dissertation, University of Colorado at Boulder.

GRAUE, M. E. and SHEPARD, L. A. (1989) 'Predictive validity of the Gesell School Readiness Tests', *Early Childhood Research Quarterly*, 4 (3) pp. 303–315.

HATCH, J. A. and FREEMAN, E. B. (1988) 'Who's pushing whom? Stress and kindergarten', *Phi Delta Kappan*, 70, pp. 145–147.

INTERNATIONAL READING ASSOCIATION (1986) 'Literacy development and pre-first grade: a joint statement of concerns about present practices in pre-first grade reading instruction and recommendations for improvement', *Childhood Education*, 63 (2), pp. 110–111.

KARWEIT, N. (1989) 'Effective kindergarten programs and practices for students at risk', in R. Slavin, N. Karweit, and N. Madden (eds) *Effective Programs for Students at Risk* (Boston: Allyn & Bacon), pp. 103–142.

KAUFMAN, A. S. (1971) 'Piaget and Gesell: a psychometric analysis of tests built from their tasks', *Child Development*, 42 (5), pp. 1341–1360.

MARTIN, A. (1985) 'Back to kindergarten basics', *Harvard Educational Review*, 55 (3), pp. 318–320

MEISELS, S. J. (1987) 'Uses and abuses of developmental screening and school readiness testing', *Young Children*, 42 (2), pp. 4–6, pp. 68–73.

MITCHELL, J. V. (ed.) (1985) *The Ninth Mental Measurements Yearbook, Vols I and II*. (Lincoln, NB: The Buros Institute of Mental Measurements of the University of Nebraska-Lincoln).

MOSSBURG, J. W. (1987) 'The effects of transition room placement on selected achievement variables and readiness for middle school', unpublished doctoral dissertation, Ball State University.

RESNICK, L. B. and RESNICK, D. P. (1990) 'Tests as standards of achievement in schools', in *The Uses of Standardized Tests in American Education: Proceedings of the 1989 ETS Invitational Conference* (Princeton, NJ: Educational Testing Service.)

SCOTT, B. A. and AMES, L. B. (1969) 'Improved academic, personal, and social adjustment in selected primary-school repeaters', *The Elementary School Journal*, 69 (8), pp. 431–439.

SHEPARD, L. A. (1987) 'The assessment of readiness for school: Psychometric and other considerations', in G. H. Brown and E. M. Faupel (eds), *The Assessment of Readiness for School: Implications for a Statistical Program* (Washington, DC: Center for Education Statistics).

SHEPARD, L. A. (1989) 'A review of research on kindergarten retention', in L. A. Shepard and M. L. Smith (eds), *Flunking Grades: Research and Policies on Retention* (London: Falmer Press), pp. 64–78.

SHEPARD, L. A., GRAUE, M. E. and CATTO, S. F. (1989) 'Delayed entry into kindergarten and escalation of academic demands', paper presented at the annual meeting of the American Educational Research Association, San Francisco.

SHEPARD, L. A. and SMITH, M. L. (1986) 'Synthesis of research on school readiness and kindergarten retention', *Educational Leadership*, 44 (3), pp. 78–86.

SHEPARD, L. A. and SMITH, M. L. (1988) 'Escalating academic demand in kindergarten: counterproductive policies', *The Elementary School Journal*, 89 (2), pp.135–145.

SHEPARD, L. A. and SMITH, M. L. (1989) 'Academic and emotional effects of kindergarten retention in one school district', in L. A. Shepard and M. L. Smith (eds), *Flunking Grades: Research and Policies on Retention* (London: Falmer Press), pp. 79–107.

SIMONS, J. (1988) 'When to start summer's children in school', *Denver Parent*, 2 (12), pp. 1–2.

SMITH, M. L. and SHEPARD, L. A. (1988) 'Kindergarten readiness and retention: a qualitative study of teachers' beliefs and practices', *American Educational Research Journal*, 25 (3), pp. 307–333.

STALLMAN, A. C. and PEARSON, P. D. (1990) 'Formal measures of early literary', in L. M. Morrow and J. K. Smith (eds), *Assessment for Instruction in Early Literacy*. (Englewood Cliffs, NJ: Prentice Hall), pp. 7–44.

TURLEY, C. C. (1979) 'A study of elementary school children for whom a second year of kindergarten was recommended', unpublished doctoral dissertation, University of San Francisco.

UPHOFF, J. K. and GILMORE, J. E. (1986) *Summer Children: Ready or Not for School?* (Middletown, OH: J & J Publishing).

WALKER, R. N. (1989) 'The Gesell Developmental Asessment: psychometric properties', unpublished manuscript, Gesell Institute of Human Development, New Haven, CT.

10   *Educational accountability reforms:*
performance information and political power

James G. Cibulka

The movement toward accountability reporting for elementary and secondary schools has been widespread, in the USA as well as in some other countries. This development involves use of performance information, particularly assessment of pupil achievement, to make comparisons among schools and other units. Despite its popularity, the rationale for accountability reporting is unclear. For example, it is not resolved whether performance information is to prompt action by citizens and interest groups acting politically, through oversight by superordinate governments applying mandates, rewards and sanctions, or by individual consumers through market decisions. Several accountability reporting systems, operating in South Carolina, Illinois, and the UK, are reviewed. Each system is built principally around one of the three alternative rationales. The analysis demonstrates how the policy design and policy settlement operating in each case are key to understanding the outcomes which may be expected to flow from the accountability reporting system. South Carolina's policy design integrates performance reporting with a variety of other state initiatives, and the policy settlement has built widespread commitment to the reforms by the citizenry, civic elites, and school professionals. This has created a performance accountability system with strong impact. In Illinois, by contrast, the impact has been marginal due to the policy design, which left initiative in using the report card to local citizens and officials rather than state officials, and by a conflictual policy settlement. In the UK, the Thatcher Government has linked performance assessment to new market pressures on poorly performing schools. Implementation has yet to occur, but the complex assessment system has required extensive professional involvement at the development stage, which may conflict with expanded consumer influence.

Introduction

For many decades, states in the USA have been expanding student testing programs, but since the 1960s, well prior to the current educational reform movement, the rationale for this expansion has shifted.[1] This trend has been referred to as 'high-stakes' (rather than 'low-stakes') testing (Corbett and Wilson 1988). The growing sophistication of testing technology has led to comparisons of various test results across schools and school districts. These test data have been supplemented by a broad range of other performance 'indicators' (attendance rates, drop-out rates, expenditures, tax rates, etc.) designed to increase public information about educational performance. Government officials either have published performance data themselves or required their development and public release by local school officials. Performance accountability systems were operative in all but five states by 1987 (Orland and Stevenson 1990).

In this chapter I examine several alternative ways that this development toward performance accountability in public education has been evolving. Three specific cases are used to illustrate these alternatives, including both the USA and UK.[2]

My primary focus in this chapter is on the *political* uses of accountability reporting. The comparative reporting of test results and other 'performance' information can be viewed as part of the long-standing struggle for control of educational policy between lay

0268–0939/90 $3.00 © 1990 Taylor & Francis Ltd.

and professional interests and between local and central (state or national) interests. The actual political effects of accountability reporting, as we shall see, appear to depend on many factors such as how the performance reporting is embedded in a larger policy design and how much latitude at the implementation stage is left for professionals (rather than laypersons) or local interests (rather than state officials) to interpret and manage the reporting process and its outcomes.

Rationales for accountability reporting

As a starting point, there is little disagreement in principle with the idea that accountability reporting is desirable. In the USA, with its tradition of popular sovereignty, the idea that 'the public has a right to know' is nearly unassailable. To resist it sounds undemocratic, elitist. In recent years, this argument on the basis of principle has been joined by another convincing instrumental argument; international economic competition requires better information and improved performance. Even in the UK, whose lack of a written constitution and monarchial tradition has made it somewhat easier for government to insulate itself from public scrutiny, the Thatcher Government successfully defended the need for performance information on schools, and educational reform generally, as a matter of economic necessity.

Yet when one moves beyond these generalities, there is great controversy about what performance information is to be reported and how it is to be done. At root, these are arguments over the goals of schooling, on which there is notoriously little public consensus, and over whose political interests shall prevail. Some of the major issues follow.

The indicators to be reported

There are a variety of measures which can be employed, including 'outcomes' such as achievement test scores, drop-out rates, and attendance rates; 'input' quality indicators such as class size, staff characteristics, and expenditures (also viewed as an efficiency indicator); as well as community context measures.

The reporting of outcome measures is especially controversial to educators. Some critics charge that comparisons are unfair because of unequal student endowments and resources among districts and schools. Another criticism is that some measures, such as standardized tests, do not accurately or completely measure what schools are attempting to do. This leads to arguments about how to structure the comparisons among potential reporting units (classrooms, schools, districts, states).

What is a meaningful comparison?

How performance information is aggregated is a critical decision. One issue is whether to permit comparisons of performance results down to the classroom level. Critics charge that this leads to unfair comparisons among teachers, who are not responsible for the endowments they inherit from earlier school performance, only the 'value' they add to the child's endowment. Proponents generally see this kind of information as a prerequisite to linking monetary compensation to improved teacher evaluation, through such devices as merit pay.

Whether to release information permitting school comparisons seems less controversial, because it is widely acknowledged that district comparisons mask great variation among schools within a district both in resources, educational tasks, and student performance.

It is also debated whether to report simply a mean for the classroom, school, or district or to report proportions of pupils falling into various points on the distribution (e.g., lowest quartile or highest decile). Again, means can conceal a great deal. Perhaps more widely debated is whether to report raw performance data or to adjust the data by placing units such as schools in comparable 'performance bands' so as to place their performance next to a similar peer group. The argument for adjusting scores is that it allows for fair comparisons and competition; under such circumstances, school officials are more likely to set meaningful goals because their comparison frame is with other schools facing similar constraints (resources, community support, student characteristics, and other variables which predict variation in student achievement). The downside of this approach, say critics, is that it obscures who the low performers really are and offers them an excuse for not improving.

How performance information will be used

It is far from clear for whose use performance information is intended. Performance information can induce improvements in educational outcomes by one of several means: state regulatory actions, whether rewards or sanctions (bureaucratic efficiency); self-initiated local citizen initiative and resulting corrective actions of local school officials (political responsiveness); or direct consumer pressure or control (market efficiency). The choices among these alternative approaches involve broad philosophical arguments about which values government should promote through accountability reporting and which of these values is most likely to improve educational outcomes.

If central governments are the impetus for reform, using the performance data to induce change by local school officials, then the logic is one of *bureaucratic efficiency*. The view that accountability reporting should serve as a tool for state action to improve the efficiency of the education system builds on the idea that government policy in a federal system rests on a chain of authority from superordinate units to subordinate ones.

By contrast, plans which emphasize *responsiveness* as paramount rather than the efficiency of state action are built on a different conception of political authority. In its purest application, the responsiveness rationale uses public disclosure of information as the key element which drives government to improve. The idea that government is a public business and that the public has a right to know how correctly or how efficiently its tax dollars are being spent springs both from populist suspicions of government and the idea of popular sovereignty. The assumption is that increased comparative information on school performance is itself a source of political power and that it will mobilize local action where required.

The logic of responsiveness is quite in keeping with the idealistic assumptions about democratic processes one frequently finds in high school civic texts; the vision of political life offered here is one of rational, concerned citizens carefully weighing all the available facts and communicating their concerns to attentive and responsive public officials. It is political imagery favored by political progressives over a half-century ago and was remarkably effective in shaping the ideology of school administration in America.[3]

Citizen participation models: The broader literature on political participation alerts us to the role which educational attainment, time, and related political resources play in voting, group activity, volunteering, contacting government officials, and other forms of political participation. This literature indicates a strongly upper-middle-class bias (Verba and Nie 1972). The literature on citizen participation in education extends this finding (Zeigler, Jennings, and Peak 1974, Tucker and Zeigler 1980). We can expect this same bias to appear when the government makes new information available to citizens. Highly educated persons may be more inclined to avail themselves of the new information as a source of power. Building on this literature, one might be led to hypothesize that performance reporting will have variable effects across school neighborhoods and even communities when socioeconomic status is taken into account, other factors being equal.

Interest group theory: The debate over whether US public school systems are excessively autonomous reform institutions or whether they are responsive to public pressures never has been resolved. For example, electoral processes rarely are issue oriented or result in involuntary turnover of board members (Zeigler *et al.* 1974). Yet much empirical research in interest group theory establishes that group mobilization increases governmental responsiveness (Dahl 1961, Truman 1951). Interest group theory views public policy as a product of partisan mobilization. This mobilization may occur even where individual citizen participation is minimal, and the priorities of interest groups may or may not parallel those of the general public, or even the general membership of these interest groups. Thus, performance reporting can improve the responsiveness of the political system to public demands either through mobilization of individual citizens or through interest groups, or some combination of these.

To recap, so far we have reviewed both the logic of bureaucratic efficiency and political responsiveness as approaches to accountability reporting. A third view is one of *market efficiency*. The idea that performance information can lead to local action without government regulation is quite compatible with a view of government which prefers minimum government and market processes involving direct consumer choice rather than majority rule.

According to public choice theorists, the political process is a much less efficient mechanism than economic markets for allocating consumer preferences (Niskanen 1971). Structuring service delivery in order to maximize consumer choice overcomes disadvantages of majoritarian decision making – it is quicker, cheaper (requiring less government machinery to enforce it) and optimally more efficient because it more closely matches the preferences of a larger number of individuals than majoritarian solutions forcing everyone to consume the same services. It avoids displacement of the public's rights by government officials because they become accountable for clear goals (Michaelsen 1981).

This brief review of several different rationales underlying different approaches to accountability reporting demonstrates that as public policy, accountability reporting does not have a clear political rationale.[4] Under these circumstances, it is not surprising that different kinds of accountability reporting have evolved. A useful classification system has been provided by the Office of Educational Resarch and Improvement (1988) at the US Department of Education. It is pointed out that responsibility for the development of the accountability system can be located at the state level, local level or shared between both. Also, the accountability system can have direct policy links, such as a state requirement that school districts and schools within them develop school improvement plans if performance indicators fall below a certain standard. This leads OERI to suggest a three-by-two typology with six possible performance accountability systems: state systems with policy links; state systems without them; local systems with policy links; local systems without them; mixed systems with policy links; and mixed systems without policy links.

One important dimension left unaddressed by the OERI typology is how tightly or loosely coupled the performance accountability system is with other policies of the state or local district. Perhaps the key feature is whether student performance assessments are tied to a uniform curriculum. Unlike policy linkages which require some action after the publication of performance indicators – what we might call back-end coupling, the features cited here are examples of 'front-end coupling' because they integrate the indicator system closely with other state policies. The premise of both kinds of coupling is that if a reporting system is part of a broader delivery system, these linkages increase the likelihood that indicators will receive attention by school boards, teachers, administrators, and parents.

What consequences flow from performance reporting

Depending on whether one is a champion or critic of accountability reporting, quite different scenarios are conjured up concerning its alleged effects.

The principal arguments critics wage against accountability reporting are largely the same that have plagued the controversies over IQ and achievement testing for nearly a century (Cronbach 1975). One line of analysis concentrates on the equity effects of accountability reporting, arguing that increasing reliance on a common set of performance indicators, particularly standardized tests, inadvertently hurts the children, schools, and districts most in need of help. Allegedly the measures cast them as failures and isolate them politically from resources and other support they desperately need.

The second objection focuses on the goal displacement resulting from accountability reporting. Allegedly it narrows teaching 'to the test', stifles innovation, and weakens local control in favor of state priorities.

Despite these criticisms, the fact that large numbers of states now have accountability reporting systems indicates that proponents of accountability reporting have garnered more political support than its critics have.[5]

Public policies: a framework for resolving ambiguities

It is through the passage of laws and the implementation process which follows their adoption that these ambiguities in problem definition and resolution must be resolved.

A law is both a *policy design* reflecting 'rational' problem solving and a *policy settlement* among contending powerful interests. A law is a policy design because, as Allison (1971), Peterson (1976), and others have pointed out, government policy can be understood as instrumentally rational action. One need not take the view that policies meet all the criteria of a rational planning model (clear goals, delineation of alternatives, reasoned selection from among available means, etc.) to see policy as problem-solving. Decision-makers begin from some statement of a problem, however inchoate, and strive for a solution, however proximate. Their actions are guided by 'best available thinking' subject to many constraints on rational problem solving in organizational contexts (Lindblom 1968, Wildavsky 1979). There is no consensus among students of public policy as to what mix of rationality and politics does shape policy adoption and implementation.

At the same time, a law reflects the balance of power among contending interests, each of whom normally wishes to shape the law favoring its economic, social, or political interests. In this sense, laws are policy settlements among these contending interests and typically reflect a ruling coalition's conception of the interests of the coalition (Greenstone and Peterson 1973). The political bargaining which leads to this policy settlement may be consensual and pluralist or conflictual and ideological. (Peterson 1976).

Often the policy which emerges is a blend of rational problem-solving and power considerations. Different approaches to policy design may reflect the array of interests backing that design. On the other hand, arguments over policy design rarely can be reduced to calculations of interests alone. Matters of what 'ought' to be and the proper means of reaching those ends often play a dominant role in the shaping of a policy design. In the last decade and a half considerable attention has been given to the implementation of government policies and the problems which result at this post-adoption stage (e.g., Berman and McLaughlin 1975, Pressman and Wildavsky 1973). In reality, though, many implementation problems have their origins at the point of policy adoption. Perhaps the best known defense of the need for greater rationality in law-making is Lowi (1969), who argues that implementation breakdowns result from ambiguities and contradictions in the laws themselves.

Political processes at the implementation stage can reflect *flaws in policy design* or *realities of the policy settlement*. Once a policy is adopted and becomes law, its implementation tends to be characterized by low visibility. Under such conditions it is relatively easier for the original policy settlement represented in a statute to be undermined by compromises in a series of 'implementation games' (Bardach 1977). The processes by which this watering down occurs include promulgation of rules, strategies of enforcement, and standards of evaluation. Regulatory politics often are cited as the most flagrant examples of how the undermining of original legislative and executive intent can occur, as regulators and the regulated bargain to reshape the policy (Meier 1985).

How can these implementation politics reflect the policy design of a law? Some of the implementation politics may simply continue unresolved arguments over what purpose accountability reporting should serve. At the same time, later implementation problems may also be shaped by aspects of the policy settlement; one example is the amount of relative power conferred on producers and consumers to influence implementation processes and outcomes through the statute's design. In the case of accountability reporting, governments are distributing information about school performance, and information is potentially as valuable a political commodity as money, labor, or other perquisites. The control of this information – how and when it is released, to whom, and with what consequences – is a political question as much as a technical one. What is at stake is a potential shift in authority between parents and school officials and between state and local officials, which is an example of what McDonnell and Elmore (1987) refer to as 'system-changing' policies.

Thus, it is both an intellectual puzzle and a political problem how best to use performance information to improve educational policy.[6] Intellectually, there are various choices available about how to organize and release the information, and what, if anything to do with it once released. At the same time, these decisions affect the potential distribution of power among various actors. In the next section it shall be demonstrated that the way the policy design and policy settlement address these issues sets the stage for implementation politics and for the outcomes of the policy.

Three cases of accountability reporting

We shall examine several examples of government policies designed to provide performance information on schools. Two of the cases are from US states, Illinois and South Carolina. The third case is Great Britain.[7] The three cases illustrate quite different approaches to accountability reporting. For the sake of simplicity, these three approaches shall be characterized as 'state oversight', 'local citizen initiative', and 'consumer initiative'. (The labels indicate the dominant emphasis in the accountability system, even though the reforms may accommodate other emphases as well.) Thus, the cases illustrate the basic ambiguity at the heart of performance reporting as a concept, as well as the different issues of policy design and implementation which these alternatives raise.

State oversight in South Carolina

The origin of the major education reform legislation in South Carolina was the Education Improvement Act (EIA) of 1984, one of the most comprehensive laws passed in the country. It created programs for early childhood education; remedial and compensatory basic skills programs; higher standards; tougher attendance policies; incentive programs; intervention programs; improved salaries and training for teachers and principals; efforts to improve business and community support; expanded programs for gifted and advanced students; funding improvements; and greater accountability for results. Reform was funded with a significant sales tax increase approved by the voters. The reforms were designed to be fully implemented by 1989–90.

Performance reporting was not part of the 1984 legislation, but evolved from an initial concern for collecting data on schools deemed to be deficient. In South Carolina the school performance report initially is prepared by the schools and districts, sent to the state, and then returned, after additions are made, to the local districts. The actual performance report is used as an internal document by boards and staff, in consultation with state-mandated School (and District) Improvement Councils, in effect since 1977 but strengthened in EIA.

An annual report is released by the districts and each school, providing a summary of the test data as well as other information from the performance report. Through percentile ranking the school performance report provides comparisons of a school's achievement, student attendance rate, teacher attendance rate and student dropout rate with other South Carolina schools. Three-year trends are utilized. Assessment instruments include criterion-referenced basic skills tests (the Basic Skills Assessment Program) in reading, math, and writing at sixth, eighth, and tenth grades; the norm-referenced California Test of Basic Skills in five grades; and beginning in 1989–90 the Stanford Test. It is important to note that South Carolina had strong state testing programs prior to the inception of performance reporting, dating back to 1978 and even earlier. Initially there was no linkage between these tests and a state curriculum, but BSAP created momentum for this to occur in an effort to align what is taught and what is assessed more closely.

For reporting purposes schools also are grouped into one of five categories with other comparable schools, based on regression techniques, following an approach pioneered in California, and test results are reported for one's comparison group. Performance in relation to state basic skills minima are reported as well as information on whether the district meets minimum standards for each of the accreditation criteria (e.g., teacher certification, instructional time, attendance, etc.).

In addition to the requirement for the performance report to be linked to local planning, there are several other ways performance reporting is linked to policy consequences at the state level. First, performance results are released to the public at the same time as a state performance report is released by a special Select Committee of the state legislature, which includes business, civic, and educational leaders. The law mandates monitoring of EIA by two blue-ribbon committees, with much of the on-going work conducted by a third group, the Joint Business Education Subcommittee. These oversight committees are intended to maximize public attention and encourage comparisons between local schools, districts, and the state.

Second, the law created a special Division of Public Accountability within the state department of education, answerable directly to the state legislature, which releases its own annual report, *What Is the Penny Buying for South Carolina?*, evaluating the progress of the reforms.

Third, according to provisions in the 1984 Act, schools and districts can be declared 'educationally impaired' for failure to meet one or more accreditation standards. In the early years of the law over 30 schools and school districts were so identified. Despite the unpopularity of these designations with local officials in the 'educationally impaired' schools, they received extensive state assistance.

Fourth, under the provisions of the School Incentive Program, schools which show exceptional gains in basic skills automatically receive incentive award money distributed on a per pupil basis, and principals and teachers (individually or as a group) are eligible for incentive funds for superior performance, partly based on accountability criteria.

Therefore, the performance report and annual report are part of a complex, interdependent set of policy measures designed to reform South Carolina's public schools. The reporting process in South Carolina is 'integrated' closely with other state policies designed to enhance local performance. This policy design did not emerge all at once, but has taken shape over a number of years.

Performance reporting in South Carolina, then, has had significant policy impacts. Most of the superintendents and principals with whom we spoke described performance reporting, and the broad package of reforms to which this particular policy is linked, in a very positive light. Virtually every superintendent was able to cite some positive change in policy and practice which ensued due to the accountability reporting process. By contrast, one recent analysis by Ginsberg and Berry (1990; see also Ginsberg *et al.* 1990), argues that the reforms have had a debilitating effect on teachers and principals. Yet their survey data also indicate that these same personnel have many positive things to say about the improvements wrought by EIA.

Two types of positive reaction turned up in our analysis. One group of superintendents described themselves, and were so described by state officials, as being internally motivated to respond to the state reforms. In these districts the superintendent readily embraced the state objective of improving performance and saw the reporting process as one element in that strategy. The legislation could be linked to a widely shared state objective, the development of South Carolina's economy. Further, the long history of testing in South Carolina has meant that performance reporting is seen by many school officials as merely an extension of that development. Many school officials spoke of initiatives that they and their staffs had begun, using the reporting data to diagnose what needed changing. Important modifications to curriculum were cited, particularly augmentation of the high school curriculum for the college-bound, and also basic skills areas. Recently, many initiatives have been made in the early elementary years.

Other superintendents responded in anticipation of the widespread public concern over improving the quality of South Carolina's public schools. This behavioral pattern has been described by political scientists as 'anticipatory responsiveness'. The specific psychological dynamics vary – avoidance of conflict, fear of reprisal, a generalized orientation toward doing what will please one's key referent groups. Quite a number of South Carolina superintendents express some reservations about accountability reporting, particularly the excessive paperwork and regulation it entails. Yet they also describe the intense public pressure on many fronts, making it politically impossible to take a negative posture toward the reforms. Moreover, they could not ignore the reporting process even if they wished to, since it is so closely linked to other aspects of the state reform strategy such as accreditation, school incentive rewards, teacher and principal incentive programs, and the process by which some schools might be designated 'educationally impaired'. Responsiveness to one's local board cannot be separated from responsiveness to state mandates, given the sanctions that can attend ignoring state reform goals.

While some aspects of the reforms have proven controversial, they rather than the reporting system itself became the object of concern, such as the criteria by which some schools and districts have been declared impaired. A new policy which deregulates high performing districts is not directed at eliminating the reporting system, but rather using it to qualify for the 'reward' of deregulation. Moreover, the School Incentive Program, and to a lesser degree the Teacher and Principal Incentive Programs, have given large numbers of schools a reason to accept accountability reporting. The aggregation of schools into comparable reporting bands, while not perfect, tends to legitimate competition, since one is paired with like schools. Up to 25% in each group can be winners, based on gain scores, a methodology which eliminates the excuse that 'we can't win because of the type of pupil we have'. This approach also gives wealthy lighthouse districts an incentive to win from performance reporting, and removes the probability of winning owing to endowed factors outside one's control. It seems worth noting that despite the presence of educationally impaired criteria, far more individuals, schools, and districts have been winners than losers. Some of the losers later have become winners in the School Incentive Program.

The key to the political success of this policy design is that it represents a favorable policy settlement. Former Governor Richard Riley pulled together a diverse coalition of supporters by launching an ambitious public relations campaign to gain passage of an education reform bill. It became the centerpiece issue of his administration. Riley began with inadequate votes in either house of the legislature and even in his own Democratic Party, which controlled one house of the legislature, but eventually Riley managed to build a winning bipartisan coalition. According to one key aide, education reform was less a Republican–Democratic split than a split between the 'Old South' legacy and those who wished for South Carolina to join the 'New South'. Thus, the key to Riley's support was the wide backing he received from business leaders representing this growth perspective. It is not surprising that the educational establishment was largely in a defensive posture in this campaign. Yet its reluctance was mitigated by the fact that Riley was making education a priority and committed his administration to vastly increasing financial support for the long poorly-funded public school system of the state. Further, despite strong state initiative, the new legislation left considerable room for local initiative in some areas (Ginsberg and Berry 1990).

Perhaps the best evidence of the strength of the policy settlement is that EIA has the support of Riley's successor, Governor Carroll Campbell, a Republican. Despite EIA's funding shortfalls due to state financial problems, in 1989 the legislature recommitted itself to education reform when EIA's five year goals had been evaluated. A new reform package 'Target 2000: School Reform for the Next Decade' was passed in the 1989 legislative session. Among the provisions of this new legislation are policies which strengthen the accountability provisions at the school, district, and state levels; school productivity criteria now include drop-out rates and higher-order thinking skills.

It is important to underscore that accountability reporting in South Carolina was not *simply* a matter of state oversight. Citizen support and initiatives helped to propel the process of reforming the state's public schools. Reform has emphasized some mix between state accountability and local autonomy. Whereas some commentators have interpreted this as a balance (Timar and Kirp 1989), we believe that state policy oversight continues to be the key feature which drives educational reform in South Carolina.

Local citizen initiative in Illinois

The Better Schools Accountability Act (1984) of the State of Illinois (later included in the education reform Public Act 85-1422) requires all school districts to disseminate a report card to the public by 31 October each year, beginning in 1986. The report card is a 12-page booklet, prepared by the Illinois State Board of Education. State officials list its aim as an 'effort to provide a better informed public' and to improve support for 'good education'. The report card is released to local school boards (at a regular board meeting), taxpayers, parents, and a newspaper 'of general circulation' by 31 October. The report card must be sent home to the parents, in a manner determined by the school but consistent across the district and consistent with other reporting mechanisms in place. After the state prepares the report card, it may be modified in limited ways by the district and may contain supplementary information. The Illinois State Board of Education has prepared 'A Parent's Guide' to understanding the school report card.

The report contains statistics, narrative information, and graphs. Information is provided at the school, district, state, and, where possible, national levels, in most cases permitting comparisons among these levels on a year-only basis. The categories exemplify an input–process–output model. The following categories are reported, drawing on data provided to the state by local district and school personnel:

> *Student characteristics*: enrollment, low-income; limited-English proficiency; student attendance rate (using state comparisons for comparable schools); students' mobility; and chronic truancy.
>
> *Academic performance of students*: percentile rankings by quartile on the Iowa Test of Basic Skills (reading comprehension and vocabulary) for grades 3, 6, 8, and 10 on a phase-in basis, again compared by school, district, and state performance. ACT scores are reported, as well as percent of students not promoted to the next grade and the high school graduation rate.
>
> *The instructional setting*: length of school year; average class size; enrollment in high school courses; average minutes of instruction; percent of senior class who are college preparatory, general education and vocational education; average minutes per day of instruction; pupil–teacher/administrator experience, education, and race/ethnicity (both counts and ratios). The above are aggregated at different levels, depending on the measure.
>
> *Financial information*: expenditures by fund (amount and percentage), salaries; operating expenditures per pupil; and per capita tuition. The latter are compared to the state average, to districts of similar type and size (by absolute amount and percentile ranks).

No policy consequences are attached to the performance reporting process, either rewards or sanctions from the state. Thus, the policy design places much less emphasis on state oversight than on citizen initiative for interpreting and acting on the school report card.

Only a few of the dozen Illinois school superintendents could cite any changes triggered by the state report card. All but one of the superintendents did give qualified endorsement to the report card process. The shortcomings they observe in the report card, e.g., the lack of meaningful comparisons among school districts with different educational tasks owing to their student populations and their unequal fiscal support, contribute to their lack of initiative in using the report card to make concrete improvements.

This lack of initative on their part to use the data for school improvement and a tendency toward only limited external pressure for change resulted in inaction, i.e., largely token responses to the mandate. Most superintendents in Illinois with whom we spoke saw the reforms as a mandate imposed by the state legislature and enforced by the state board. School officials in wealthier districts generally sided with the point of view that the report card gave them an unfair advantage and argued that the report card was not necessary for them because their districts had been performing well on comparative measures already, and had actively sought to improve a sound educational program prior to the report card being distributed. Those in wealthier districts emphasized the unfairness of test comparisons in which no effort was made to adjust for the students coming to the school, parental support, or the fiscal resources available. These superintendents felt the need to speak on behalf of the poorer districts, arguing they could not politically raise this themselves.

School officials in poor districts agreed that their districts were disadvantaged by overall state comparisons, and they have not been at the forefront of the consistent opposition to the report card. For the poor districts, the principal political task has been 'damage control', requiring them to 'explain away' the low performance of their student populations on standardized tests. Supplementary information added to the report card by the local district and school served this end. Further, the failure to establish meaningful comparison cohorts permitted many of these school districts to fall back on timeworn excuses and to dismiss the findings not as a critical policy finding but rather as the product of flawed methodology. Thus, an unintended consequence of the report card was to reinforce strong preconceptions about the good performance of more well-educated, affluent districts, and poor performance of school districts with impoverished, uneducated citizens.

Occasionally school administrators have used the report card to push their own pet proposals (Crowson and Morris 1987, Pancrazio 1990), but this pattern of internal organizational response to the report cards appears to be the exception. The only changes attributable to the report card reported by school officials were that some administrators now encourage teachers to cover particular topics in the curriculum earlier in the year prior to the date on which the test is administered, and test-taking is emphasized for students in some districts. Yet the use of the reporting process to diagnose what could be done to improve curriculum and instruction is not the norm.

Despite the fact that 'citizen action' appears to be the implicit reform vehicle contemplated by the release of performance information, there is little evidence that this has occurred. There was remarkably little direct pressure on school officials from parents concerning the report card. Principals and superintendents were more likely to report a modest number of inquiries from parents in communities with better educated populations. Parents always have expressed concern about their children's school in these communities, and performance reporting does not seem to have altered the degree of interest.

If individual citizen action has not been widespread, it is also the case that interest group activity has not been typical either. In the Chicago area, some real estate agents used the information to steer clients toward particular school districts, and this has generated pressure in a few places. Occasionally, civic leaders expressed an interest in report card results and placed pressure on the superintendent and board. Pressure from business leaders due to the report card was almost nonexistent. One notable exception of public pressure generated by the report card was the use of test score data from the October 1987 report card by Secretary of Education William Bennett, who cited evidence that 35 of Chicago's 64 high schools had scored in the lowest percentiles, giving support to his charge that Chicago's public schools were the 'worst in the nation' (Hess 1990).

The print and electronic media have been the most active 'constituency' for the report cards. In major metropolitan areas, particularly Chicago, it is common for the metropolitan dailies to publish test comparisons without giving school officials an opportunity to put their own interpretation on the results. In some communities this has led to great pressure on the board, or led the board on its own, to demand improvements. Among local community papers and in small cities media interest varies, but even where interest is quite keen, superintendents frequently enjoy access to reporters and publishers and are able to put their own gloss on results which might prove unflattering.

There are other constraints on the role of the media as educational reformers. Without sustained public interest in the report card, media pressure on school officials tends to be short lived. Performance results remain an issue only to the extent that parents or other interest groups mobilize, and this has not occurred.

Of course, these limited consequences of the Illinois report card may not persist. For example, pressure is mounting in Illinois for a challenge to the state educational financing system, and report card data would be a valuable tool in demonstrating inequities among districts.

These thus-far meager results of performance reporting in Illinois reflect both the policy design and policy settlement. A policy design relying so heavily on public disclosure and local citizen initiative rather than state oversight could be expected to generate disappointing results. Yet no other option was considered seriously in Illinois, where the tradition of strong local control made a report card itself a radical idea. Indeed, the historically rather weak role of the state board of education was reflected in absence of a tradition of state testing, the absence of efforts toward a state curriculum or toward performance based accreditation, and little state intervention in local school districts where corrective action might be warranted, except those placed on 'Financial Watch' or 'Certification of Financial Difficulty'. Thus, performance reporting was not part of an interlocking set of state policies designed to reinforce one another.

The policy settlement surrounding performance reporting in Illinois was conflictual, and this led to later implementation difficulties. In February 1985, Republican Governor James R. Thompson had announced an Illinois Better Schools Program in his State-of-the-State address, including a report card among his proposals. In the ensuing months of the legislative session, Democrats opposed this provision, while Republicans favored it. Late in the legislative session, Republicans held the reform act up until Democrats agreed to a report card.

Given this partisanship over the design of the education reforms, it is not surprising that implementation difficulties followed. An advisory task force created by the State Superintendent to spearhead smooth implementation of the report card became bogged down in controversy. Representatives of the educational establishment, with the notable exception of the State Board of Education who supported performance reporting, lobbied hard against school-by-school comparisons and fought efforts of citizen advocacy groups to broaden reporting criteria to include performance measures not specifically required by the law, such as attainment data by race, gender, and handicap categories (Pancrazio 1990). To bolster support, the State Superintendent Ted Sanders augmented the task force membership with more supporters of the report card concept, such as the Illinois League of Women Voters. Administrator groups in particular actively opposed the report card; for example, they refused to use a state-developed video on the report cards for its purpose as an informational tool for parents, instead using it to 'inform' and mobilize administrators.

Ironically, an objective observer can find many guarantees for local control which emerged out of the policy settlement discussions. It was left to local discretion how to make the report available to parents, whether to supplement the report card with locally-developed information, how to define a college-preparatory program (which influences reporting on the percent of seniors completing a college-preparatory program), and so on.

While these compromises were being hammered out in the task force in 1986, the school boards association and administrator groups, aided to some degree by both teachers unions, attempted to change the law so that only districts and not individual schools would report their performance. Such changes were resisted successfully by school advocacy groups, taxpayer and business groups, and the State Board of Education. Subsequent efforts to water down the bill in the legislature and a media campaign directed at the Governor have failed. In time, efforts to change the bill began to focus on improvements to the law rather than its outright repeal.

Thus, while the Illinois report card may survive, this does not mean that it is seen as legitimate by school officials or important by the public-at-large. Many educators accuse the state, and Governor Jim Thompson, of playing by a double standard, demanding improvements in Illinois public schools but not funding the improvements as originally promised. Thompson eventually succeeded in raising additional income-tax revenues for Illinois' public schools. (However, he was twice elected on a platform of fiscal austerity, followed by revelations of serious state revenue problems, a fact which greatly polarized the state legislature and added an air of partisanship to his advocacy.) His failure to raise additional money for public schools for a long period sent an ambivalent message from the state to the public. School officials, both those who supported reform and those who opposed it, argued that they lacked money to implement state-mandated reforms.

This failure has especially hurt financially poor school districts. The designation by the state of 181 school districts on the state superintendent's financial watch list (nearly a fifth of the state's school districts) is an implicit acknowledgement of the state's failure to carry its end of the bargain, resulting in a widening gap between rich and poor in Illinois school district financing. A decade ago Illinois provided over 48% of state and local expenditures. This dropped to 39% in 1983, a year before the reforms, increased modestly to 43% thereafter, and has declined to approximately 40% recently.

When this fact is combined with the perception that the Illinois performance reporting establishes unfair bases of comparison and that the process creates many losers, it is not surprising that this policy instrument has had little success.

Consumer action in the UK

The third case of accountability reporting, as was suggested at the start, proceeds on a very different set of premises than those which animate the policies of South Carolina and

Illinois. The recent education reforms in the UK are largely the product of Prime Minister Margaret Thatcher's enthusiasm for market solutions in the area of domestic policy rather than the tradition of strong government provision and regulation favored by earlier Labour governments. The Education Reform Act of 1988 passed by Parliament reflected a policy design which largely embraced the provisions favored by Mrs Thatcher and her advisors, with few concessions to critics, either those from the Labour Party or discontented Tories either. It has been interpreted widely as the most important piece of education legislation since the passage of the Butler Act in 1944.

Very briefly stated, the act calls for reforms in curriculum, assessment, governance and funding, whose total operation is intended to be mutually reinforcing.

The national curriculum, which is meant to take up no more than approximately three-quarters of total instruction, will include three core subjects (English, mathematics, and science), seven other foundation subjects, and religious education. Attainment targets, which are descriptions of knowledge and activities to be attained, are required for each core and foundation subject for 7-, 11-, 14-, and 16-year-olds. This will be linked to an assessment system at those ages, about which more will be said presently.

Governance reforms shift considerable authority away from local education authorities (LEAs) – the equivalent of school districts and school boards in the USA – to newly elected governing boards at the school level (previously appointed by the LEA). Designated seats on these boards for parents have been expanded. These boards have considerably expanded powers over budgets, while LEA budget authority over funding allocations to schools has been reduced and been made subject to central government approval. School budgets are now heavily enrollment driven, which is an effort by the Government to limit the ability of LEAs to set artificial enrollment caps which in the past have protected unpopular schools and allegedly promoted underutilization of space.

Parents who are unhappy with the performance of a school can now 'opt out' of the LEA's control and operate with central government support. This can be done based on a simple majority vote of the parents, with central government approval.

Therefore, one important purpose of the new assessment system is to provide parents with performance information about their child's school. The national assessment is to serve several purposes – formative data on individual pupils; diagnostic information to offer appropriate remedial help and guidance as they progress through school; summative data on pupils at age 16; and evaluative data on pupils aggregated at the classroom, school, district, and national levels (Task Group on Assessment and Teaching [TGAT] 1987). Under these provisions, teachers are to share such performance information ('profiles of attainment') with parents at ages 7, 11 and 14.

This ambitious approach to assessment attempts to be both teacher-centered and provide comparative information for accountability purposes. Because of the large number of attainment targets within each subject, profile components and subject aggregate distributions will be used to prepare reports on individual pupils to parents, whose performance will be compared to classroom peers, school peers, and national standards.

Each child's performance will be reported on a scale of 1–10 for each subject. Thus, what is contemplated is a system of criterion-referenced hierarchical levels which is not age-related, although it is expected that an average student will cover one level every two years.

Because the system is quantitative, numbers allow student performance to be reported in a simplified manner for national comparisons. Yet because the system allows for differentiation, variation, and progression, it is intended to encourage better teaching to students at their levels and possibly new classroom organization.

The assessment process attempts to combine traditional standardized tests with other forms of assessment (standardized assessment tasks) administered by the teacher, e.g., practical oral and written tasks. Accordingly, there is a need to assure comparable administration and marking by teachers. This comparability can be achieved by two methods. 'Moderation' involves group discussion of individual teacher assessments and appropriate adjustment of individual scores to match the national standards and test results. Alternatively, where this time-consuming process is impractical, local variations from national standards can be made statistically by the central government.

These ambiguities led one prominent academic to label the TGAT report a 'trick or treat' proposition (Gipps 1988). In the instance before us, it is not clear whether the assessment scheme will truly provide for teacher control over a meaningful assessment system, or whether it will provide a cover for a nationally defined set of standards to which local variations must be adjusted. The heart of the matter is whether performance information can serve both the educative needs of individual pupils and national standard setting simultaneously, and how these can be combined through a reporting process that is meaningful to parents as well as a wider public audience. Further, like many educators, Gipps worries that the new system will increase competition among pupils, in line with the Government's view that the UK's economic problems are due to a lack of competitiveness and that educational competition at various levels will contribute to economic recovery. And many experts worry about possible racial and ethnic bias in the new assessment system, despite TGAT's efforts to address this issue as well as the possible narrowing of teaching due to assessment and even laundering of results (Nuttall 1989).

After considerable debate, TGAT decided against reporting school results in adjusted scores which take account of socio-economic differences in the school's pupil 'intake'. This had been done for many years by the Inner London Education Authority (ILEA), but TGAT's authors reasoned that such adjustments would lead to complacency. This view comported well with the highly critical view of ILEA taken by the Thatcher Government, such that ILEA was abolished in the 1988 Reform Act and educational services returned to control by the London boroughs in the same manner as education is controlled in outer London.

The policy settlement which has emerged on performance reporting, and assessment more broadly, is rather different than the overall policy design of the Education Act of 1988 passed by Parliament and sponsored by the Thatcher Government. Much criticism was waged at the rapidity with which the 1988 Act moved through Parliament (Haviland 1988, Simon 1988). Yet efforts to design an assessment system were already on a parallel implementation track, which reflected a different political process of extensive involvement by professional groups. The outline for a national system of assessment had come out of discussions of a national curriculum, specifically a National Curriculum Consultative Document released in 1987 by the Department of Education and Science (DES), the national cabinet-level ministry of education in the UK. The Secretary of State for Education and Science thereupon created the Task Force on Assessment and Testing (TGAT) for advice on how to structure such a system. The fact that TGAT was advised to take into account, among other things, limits on costs, once again underscored that the Government wished to place heavy (although not exclusive) reliance on standardized tests for a performance reporting system. Of the ten members on TGAT, a majority were educationalists, either practitioners or academicians. At the same time the DES had convened a National Curriculum Council with Subject Working Groups developing attainment targets and programs of study for the national curriculum.

Recommendations for a national curriculum had been occurring since at least 1977 and enjoyed support from various political parties. What remained contentious was how much of the total educational content a national curriculum might consist of, and this issue was not resolved until after the 1988 Education Act had been passed and long after the outlines of the national curriculum and assessment system had been developed independently.

Thus, the development of performance reporting was a product of extensive involvement by the affected professional interests, quite unlike other elements of the policy design in the Education Reform Act itself, reflecting as that did the Thatcher political agenda.

Even if the Government might have preferred otherwise, it is hard to imagine that any other strategy than professional consultation would have been possible. The design of curriculum, to be sure, might be done by university experts as had been tried in the USA after Sputnik (a strategy with disastrous consequences for educational reform, it might be pointed out), but in the UK at least, university experts were unlikely to be more politically supportive of Thatcher's education agenda than educationists themselves, particularly since Thatcher was waging war of sorts on higher education at the same time.

Further, on the matter of assessment, the technical expertise of educationists was even more essential to the Government's plans than in the area of curriculum. The fact is that in matters so technical the Thatcher Government could hardly hope to do an 'end run' on the educational establishment. So they were stuck, as it proved to be, with what the latter came up with. At various points in the deliberations the Secretary of State at the time Kenneth Baker, as well as the Prime Minister herself, expressed their disquiet at the emerging recommendations, along with prominent members of the New Right in the Tory Party. For example, in accepting the TGAT report in 1988, the Secretary of State described the proposed model for moderating teacher judgements with national standards (my word) to be costly and complicated.

The Secretary's reaction illustrates that TGAT represented a potentially problematic development for other aspects of the Government's policy design. Open enrollment, and the performance information to the public which will feed the process of competition among schools, is intended to save money by leading to the closing of large numbers of underutilized schools. This will be to little avail if the assessment system proves too costly and if it weighs in too heavily on the diagnostic rather than evaluative side of the ledger.

The implementation process of teacher assessment only began in September 1989, and the standardized assessment tasks will not need to be in place until 1991. Thus, it is too early to tell how implementation of assessment will evolve, and whether it will serve to foster the market competition Thatcher's Government aims for. In a country otherwise characterized by strong political partisanship in the governance of education, the issues surrounding assessment have become incredibly technical and muddled and not easily susceptible to public discussion and oversight.

Thus, while it is possible to envision a national debate on assessment and a clear choice being rendered as to its purpose and direction, such a path seems unlikely. More likely, in the manner characterisitc of low-visibility implementation politics operating within the province of bureaucrats and special interest groups, the new assessment system probably will find ways to assimilate conflicting organizing principles. After all, the policy design of the reform act is a hybrid of market ideas and regulatory reforms, not pure free-market principles by any stretch of the imagination. (A free market would have no need for governments to produce performance information!) Nevertheless, such coexistence of apparently conflicting emphases may in the end prove satisfying neither to the market enthusiasts, nor the education establishment. Already, one thoughtful commentator asserted that 'the design wasn't bad, but its realization has seriously distorted the design. We are being left with a monster of an external assessment system' (Nuttall 1989).

Conclusion

In this analysis three different uses of performance reporting have been reviewed. They are illustrative rather than exhaustive in what they can tell us, to be sure. Many other examples might be found, and they undoubtedly would help specify more clearly the conditions under which performance reporting works effectively and what its pitfalls are.

Yet the three cases do take us a considerable distance in this process of understanding the complexities of performance reporting. First of all, we have seen that performance reporting is best understood in a larger political context of policy design and policy settlement. On the design side, the precise goals of performance reporting can be very different and must fit into policy designs which support those goals. If performance reporting is an instrument of state oversight and responsibility, as its principal thrust is in South Carolina, then other state oversight policies must reinforce it in the policy design. These other policies need not be exclusively mandates, but their purpose is clearly to facilitate *state* initiative to improve local performance. The specific elements of policy design may vary in accordance with this principle. Politically, this places the state's credibility and resources on the front line. For the most part, these dynamics have worked well in South Carolina due to a combination of circumstances: South Carolina's clear need to improve its schools based on any objective reading of the data, its perceived need for economic development, its conservative political tradition stressing consensus and business values, and the skills of two successive governors. All help explain the success of the policy design and policy settlement.

Illinois illustrates the political pitfalls of a policy design which employs performance reporting as a tool for citizen political action. The modest accomplishments of the report card might have been predicted from the academic literature on citizen participation reviewed earlier in the chapter. This is not to say that under some circumstances such a locally-driven, decentralized approach can not work. Yet the ingredients have not been there in Illinois, where the educational establishment attempted to cripple implementation of the report card and has learned to live with it only reluctantly. A decentralized political approach to performance accountability may well require normative support from within the fraternity of school professionals. Such consensus building never occurred in the policy settlement process, and the weak policy design of the reform legislation left state officials with no other levers to nudge greater cooperation out of this recalcitrant educational establishment. Under these circumstances, performance information in the hands of parents and other interest groups has had only the most marginal impact on improving Illinois' public education system.

A still more radical approach to decentralization and performance reporting is being attempted in the UK, where market processes are to be the philosopher's stone of reform, but so far there is little evidence that this approach will quickly convert base metal to gold. The Government recognizes that some regulation of market processes is necessary, but this process of deregulating and reregulating cannot occur overnight and it cannot occur simply. Performance reporting is a good example. Its development has become such a complex political process that it may undermine the Government's goal of improving accountability to the public. To generate a system which provides meaningful performance information to parents at a classroom level and yet links that information to national standards (for parents' use as well as accountability to a broader public) may prove to be a political and technical nightmare. The system cannot be created without strong professional involvement. Yet it is a political reality that those who control the development of such a system of information are unlikely to acquiesce too far in their own undoing. The UK's reform is a bold experiment in the use of performance accountability not yet ventured upon in the USA, but its outcomes must await the passage of time.

The three cases, taken together, suggest how difficult it is to reconcile the conflicting purposes to which accountability reporting can be put, and how arduous is the task of aligning that purpose with a larger policy design and successful policy settlement. In the USA the public wants more accountability, and the new wave of accountability policies adopted by states in the 1980s seem to be moving toward measuring student performance and improving instruction (Pipho 1989). Gallup polls indicate that a majority of Americans favor standardized national testing programs and a standard nationwide examination to get a high school diploma. Yet a majority still favors expanding local influence rather than state or federal influence in determining educational programs (Chira 1989). With such conflicting public sentiments afoot, public policy designs and policy settlements are also likely to reflect confusion.

As stated earlier, no one of the three systems examined here has an exclusive emphasis. Within the dominant approach toward accountability (state oversight, local citizen initiative, or consumer initiative) other approaches are included in varying degrees. Thus, South Carolina encourages some citizen initiative through its local planning requirement despite strong state controls over the accountability process. Consumer initiative, though, is nowhere linked to the accountability system. Illinois places some state control on the format and release of the report card despite its reliance on citizen initiative to use the information for reform purposes. The Illinois State Board of Education, at this writing, has only set an objective to develop a statewide policy on educational choice. The UK, as indicated above, is quite regulatory in setting up what the Thatcher Government views as the proper conditions for consumer market forces to operate effectively. Citizen initiatives to reform local education authorities are not ignored altogether, e.g., the expansion of the role of governing boards, but for the Government the key levers for reform are market-supporting.

The reality appears to be that at least two of these three foci will be part of any accountability design. Some central government regulation cannot be avoided, and frequently either a citizen or consumer emphasis accompanies it. It remains an open question how these instrumentalities are combined to optimal effect. Perhaps all three are needed as mutual reinforcements to induce the educational system to change; even if the three seem logically redundant from the perspective of a rational policy paradigm, this very redundancy may prove to be politically advantageous. While some states have choice plans of one kind or another, their integration with the state's performance accountability system tends to be nonexistent or loose. The UK's 'tight-coupling' of market-related choice arrangements into accountability reporting provides one option in this regard.

Embedded in the controversy is the deeper, often unstated issue, of whether educators, elected officials, or individual parents should have the primary power over access to and uses of performance information. This is a political problem at the heart of democratic theory. Further, what one prefers in theory may not be what works in practice. South Carolina has used the benevolent hand (some would say heavy hand) of state government to reform its public schools. It is now moving toward bottom-up strategies which deregulate some high performing schools, using that same performance information. This example of how performance information can be used to centralize and decentralize in the same policy design illustrates the thicket into which the technology of assessment has taken us.

Like the advent of computer technology and information science generally, performance information greatly expands the potential instruments of social control now available to governments. It is not clear yet whose interests will be served by this information technology, and such answers will have to be worked out politically in many different contexts (with the probability of many different results).

One thing seems certain. Performance information is reshaping the character of educational politics. In the USA until now, the big action in accountability reporting has been at the state level. But if pressure continues to build for greater national reporting of performance information, as has occurred already in the UK, national politics will take on a greater role in shaping the direction of accountability reporting.

Acknowledgement

I wish to acknowledge the support of the US Department of Education, Office of Educational Research and Improvement, which provided support for some of the data collection on this project (Grant 008720288). I also acknowledge the able assistance of Roberta Derlin, a Ph.D. student, in executing aspects of this project.

Notes

1. Whereas testing was once defended as a formative and diagnostic assessment technique, designed to help classroom teachers and administrators improve instruction, in recent decades the focus has been on the summative and evaluative purposes of tests, whereby educational outcomes can be assessed and compared.
2. Then the strengths and problems of accountability reporting, as revealed by the cases, are reviewed. In order to place these alternatives in context, the chapter begins with a discussion of competing, unresolved rationales for accountability reporting.
3. The idea that improved performance information will generate local political action is compatible with two different strands of analysis in political science – citizen participation models and interest group theory.
4. It is useful to place this discussion in an historical context. Educational achievement tests were developed in the USA as a technology for increasing professional knowledge and control over teaching. At the time they were first developed by Thorndike and others, never was it envisioned that they might eventually make it easier for the public to increase scrutiny of professional performance. Many states had adopted statewide testing programs by the 1930s (Travers, 1983), but these still were perceived as devices for improved professional monitoring of pupil performance. The idea that assessment could be used as an arm of state government to hold professionals accountable is of more recent origin. Ironically, the many criticisms of tests coming from within the profession were largely ignored by state legislatures when establishing statewide testing programs. Beginning in the 1960s, demands for 'accountability' by public school officials were escalating, and achievement tests were seen as a hospitable tool for measuring professional performance. At that time, educational critics and reformers were beginning to demand the reporting of test scores not merely by school district but by school as well. Some innovative districts adopted this policy, and eventually this development led to comparative reporting at the school level in some statewide testing programs.
5. For reasons of space, my analysis of accountability reporting in the United States focuses on where most developments until recently have occurred, the state level. Recently, some developments at the national level may prove to be important, such as the use of the 'Wall Chart' by the US Department of Education to compare performance among states, efforts by the Council of Chief State School Officers to achieve comparability in indicators, and use of the National Assessment of Educational Progress (NAEP) to permit inter-state comparisons. These developments are commented upon in the concluding section of the chapter.
6. Administrative Progressives, of course, had not stressed the need for holding professional experts accountable, but on this point Progressives were quite ambivalent and of different persuasions. Those

with more populist leanings favored devices such as initiatives and recalls, which still are strong features of the political landscape in a number of Western states such as California. This wing of Progressivism, which still enjoys support across the political spectrum today, believes that information is power and that its availability to an enlightened citizenry will animate reform of public policy. See Hofstadter (1955) for a basic discussion of these contradictions.

7. A brief description of research methods follows. Field research methods employed include in-person and telephone interviewing with superintendents, principals, state officials, as well as documentary research. In the UK, national officials were included, as well as chief education officers in inner and outer London boroughs and school heads (principals) in those boroughs. Initial work on this project was undertaken in 1988 while the author was a Senior Research Fellow at the US Department of Education's Office of Educational Research and Improvement. In Illinois and South Carolina, 12 school districts were selected in each state. The selection process was based on nominations by state officials familiar with the performance accountability program, followed by phone interviews to verify this information. Officials were asked to nominate districts where the response to the reform has been typical of most districts in the state, those where a positive response to the performance reporting process led to reforms in policy or practice, or efforts in this direction; as well as districts where little or no change occurred. Respondent districts included variation in terms of urban, suburban, and rural dimensions, and district wealth. Additional information on samples and methods can be obtained by contacting this author.

References

ALLISON, G. (1971) *Essence of Decision* (Boston: Little, Brown).

BARDACH, E. (1977) *The Implementation Game: What Happens After a Bill Becomes Law* (Cambridge, MA: MIT Press).

BERMAN, P. and McLAUGHLIN, M. (1975) *Federal Programs Supporting Educational Change, Volume IV: The Findings in Review* (Santa Monica, CA: Rand).

CHIRA, S. (1989) 'National standards for schools gain', *New York Times*, 26 December, p. 38.

CORBETT, H. D. and WILSON, B. L. (1988) 'Raising the stakes in statewide mandatory testing programs', in J. Hannaway and R. Crowson (eds) *The Politics of Reforming School Administration* (London: Falmer Press).

CRONBACH, L. J. (1975) 'Five decades of controversy over mental testing', *American Psychologist*, 30(1), pp. 1–13.

CROWSON, R. L. and MORRIS, V. (1987) 'The superintedency and school reform: an exploratory study', *Metropolitan Education*, Fall (5), pp. 24–39.

DAHL, R. (1961) *Who Governs?* (New Haven, CT: Yale University Press).

GINSBERG, R. and BERRY, B. (1990) 'Experiencing school reform: the view from South Carolina', *Phi Delta Kappan*, 71 (7), pp. 549–552.

GINSBERG, R., COHN, E., WILLIAMS, C., PRITCHETT, S. and SMITH, T. (1990) *Teaching in South Carolina: A Retirement Initiative* (Columbia, SC: South Carolina Educational Policy Center, University of South Carolina).

GIPPS, C. (1988) 'The TGAT Report: trick or treat?', *Forum*, pp. 4–7.

GREENSTONE, J. D. and PETERSON, P. E. (1973) *Race and Authority in Urban Politics: Community Participation and the War on Poverty* (New York: Russell Sage).

HAVILAND, J. (1988) *Take Care, Mr Baker* (London: Fourth Estate).

HESS, F. (1990) 'Mobilizing a movement for school reform: Citizen initiative in the Chicago school reform experiment', unpublished paper presented at the annual meeting of the American Educational Research Association.

HOFSTADTER, R. (1955) *The Age of Reform: From Bryan to FDR* (New York: Knopf).

LINDBLOM, C. (1968) *The Policy-making Process* (Englewood Cliffs, NJ: Prentice-Hall).

LOWI, T. (1969) *The End of Liberalism* (New York: W. W. Norton).

McDONNELL, L. and ELMORE, R. (1987) 'Getting the job done: alternative policy instruments', *Educational Evaluation and Policy Analysis*, 9 (2), pp. 133–152.

MEIER, K. J. (1985) *Regulation: Politics, Bureaucracy, and Economics* (New York: St Martin's Press).

MICHAELSEN, J. B. (1981) 'A theory of decision making in the public schools: a public choice approach', in S. B. Bacharach (ed.) *Organizational Behavior in Schools and School Districts*, (New York: Praeger).

NISKANEN, W. A. (1971) *Bureaucracy and Representative Government* (Chicago: Aldine-Atherton).

NUTTALL, D. (1989) 'National assessment: will reality match aspirations?', unpublished paper delivered at the Conference 'Testing Times' organized by Macmillan Education.

OFFICE OF EDUCATIONAL RESEARCH AND IMPROVEMENT (1988) *Creating Responsible and Responsive Accountability Systems: Report of the OERI State Accountability Study Group* (Washington, DC: US Department of Education).

ORLAND, M. E. and STEVENSON, D. L. (1990) 'Structuring the environment of schooling: State performance accountability systems', unpublished paper presented at the annual meeting of the American Educational Research Association.

PANCRAZIO, S. (1990) 'Building an accountability system in Illinois', unpublished paper delivered at the annual meeting of the American Educational Research Association.

PETERSON, P. E. (1976) *School Politics: Chicago Style* (Chicago: University of Chicago Press).

PIPHO, C. (1989) 'Accountability comes around again', *Phi Delta Kappan* 70 (9), pp. 662–663.

PRESSMAN, J. L. and WILDAVSKY, A. (1973) *Implementation* (Berkeley, CA: University of California Press).

SIMON, B. (1988) *Bending the Rules: The Baker 'Reform' of Education* (London: Lawrence & Wishart).

TASK GROUP ON ASSESSMENT AND TEACHING (1987) *A Report* (London: Department of Education and Science and the Welsh Office).

TIMAR, T. B. and KIRP, D. L. (1989) 'Education reform in the 1980s: lessons from the states', *Phi Delta Kappan*, 70 (7), pp. 509–10.

TRAVERS, R. (1983) *How Research Has Changed American Schools: A History from 1840 to the Present* (Kalamazoo, MI: Mythos Press).

TRUMAN, D. (1951) *The Government Process* (New York: A Knopf).

TUCKER, H. and ZEIGLER, L. H. (1980) *Professionals and the Public: Attitudes, Communication, and Response in School Districts* (New York: Longman).

VERBA, S. and NIE, N. (1972) *Participation in America: Political Democracy and Social Equality* (New York: Harper & Row).

WILDAVSKY, A. (1979) *Speaking Truth to Power: The Art and Craft of Policy Analysis* (Boston: Little, Brown).

ZEIGLER, L. H., JENNINGS, M. K. and PEAK, G. W. (1974) *Governing American Schools: Political Interaction in Local School Districts* (North Scituate, MA: Duxbury).

11   *The politics of Australian curriculum:*
the third coming of a national curriculum agency in a
neo-pluralist state

R. J. S. Macpherson

National curriculum development agencies have had a chequered history in Australia. Twice in the last two decades Commonwealth (federal) governments have established major agencies ostensibly devoted to the enhancement of curriculum, and twice they have been wound down. The first Curriculum Development Center (CDC) was established in the mid-1970s. It was an expression of the Whitlam era, and featured reformist ideals and relatively generous budgets. The second CDC was a more cautious and pragmatic attempt by Hawke to revisit those ideals in the 1980s, but in vastly more constrained ideological and economic circumstances. Over the last year a third attempt has been mounted; this time to establish a ministerially-sponsored private company.

This chapter shows that the cyclical nature of federal interest is related to the changing economic and political conditions in which federal politicians and officials (who lack any constitutional responsibility) have recurrently sought a role for the Commonwealth in mainstream curriculum policymaking. The most recent initiative appears to have benefited from the support of an oligarchy comprising the Commonwealth and state Ministers of Education and their senior officials. This suggests that a dual polity has emerged with the new oligarchy located beside the more traditional representative structures; an explanation that is reasonably consistent with a neo-pluralist theory of state.

Introduction

In order to trace the complexities of the national curriculum agency history in Australia, an interpretivist (Morgan 1980) and longitudinal approach was adopted. As Fuhrman (1989) argued, there is a 'the need to view policies as part of the wider setting in which they are initiated and implemented, and to observe their progress over time'. A literature review was supplemented by the triangulated views of well-placed informants at state and federal levels who were prepared to speak freely on a non-attributable basis. However, such is the recency of the events described, and the methodological limitations involved, only a provisional position can be presented.

To interpret the third coming of a national curriculum agency, it was decided to classify the assumptions held by key informants about nature of curriculum policy-making in public service agencies. Different theories of state assume that the political steerage of the policies of public institutions, such as schools and school systems, is achieved in five fundamentally different ways (after Dunleavy and O'Leary 1987:329–341).

- Pluralist theories locate power with citizens who vote, influence party politics, and lobby through interest groups, and hence changing coalitions account for the variations and the multiple directions in the policies of public utilities.
- New Right theories also locate power with citizens, but insist that gross imperfections in public choice-making make it difficult for institutions of state,

0268–0939/90 $3.00 © 1990 Taylor & Francis Ltd.

however demand-responsive, to avoid creating unanticipated effects.

- Elite theories assume that public services are controlled by socially or economically dominant elites who are adept at manipulating the ostensibly liberal democratic process of policymaking.
- Marxist instrumental theories similarly locate power with an elite, but with a capitalist elite that seeks to integrate its purposes with those of governments in order to monopolize public policymaking.
- Neo-pluralist theories assume that a dual polity operates: on one hand public institutions offer multiple points of access to horizontal and vertical policy articulation processes, while on the other, these and other structures endow elites with polyarchical epistemic and process privileges.

The first half of this paper therefore attends to two central issues; the mediating influence of the general context and how political activity contributed to the establishment and abolishing of two national agencies. The second half details and interprets the third initiative in recent times.

I. The Commonwealth's search for power

A conflicted context

A basic feature of the politics of Australian education is that the Commonwealth's (federal) constitution does not mention education. It was generally accepted in 1901, however, that education was a residual power of state governments and territory officials. Since constitutional amendments have only marginally increased the powers of Commonwealth governments to determine education policy (Birch 1975), current practices make it clear that alternative means of federal intervention have been developed (Harman and Smart 1982).

One such means of accruing power to the Commonwealth, at cost to 'states' rights', has been by resort to the High Court. A series of judgements between 1920 and 1940 significantly changed the balance of powers between federal and state governments. The Uniform Tax Case of 1942 finally gave the Commonwealth sole income-taxing rights. Ever since the negotiation of budgetary arrangements between federal and state authorities (Birch 1987) has provided one basis for sharing policy steerage in education.

When demand and the costs of education accelerated in the post-Second World War years, and outstripped what the States, given their limited tax base, could provide, other responsibilities gradually accrued to the Commonwealth (Smart 1978:1–32). By the early 1960s, the demand-based pressures for federal involvement became a federal election issue, and Prime Minister Robert Menzies was obliged or able to promise direct Commonwealth funding for school science laboratories. This reintroduced 'state aid' for church schools, established the precedent for federal aid to go directly to state government schools (that had hitherto been solely serviced by the states and territories), and further enhanced federal influence.

Menzies' $10 million initiative expanded over the next decade, and eventually became a $650 million project of comprehensive school aid co-ordinated by the Commonwealth Schools Commission (CSC) during Prime Minister Gough Whitlam's Labor administration (1973–75). The CSC was a statutory body set up following the Karmel Report (1973) to advise the federal Minister every three years on the needs of all schools in Australia and to distribute resources. Organized on the principles of representative democracy, the CSC's powers to advise and to administer policy through funding priorities became paramount and symbiotic with the (constitutionally non-existent but) presumed reserve powers of the federal Minister.

The CSC's educational agenda mirrored the social philosophy of the Whitlam administration. The CSC Reports made special reference to the needs of disadvantaged groups and to the need to devolve decision making to allow for community participation; the former agenda implied targeted resources whereas the latter meant changing the way that state-directed systems governed and administered schools. It was consistently assumed that education was a major and appropriate vehicle for the implementation of social policy, and moreover, that federal agencies could achieve significantly greater social equity in Australia by altering schooling. In sum, between 1973 and 1981, the CSC was at the apogee of its powers; it charted and implemented major policy directions in Australian education despite the absence of constitutional authority.

The coming and going of the first national agency

It was in this halcyon political climate that the first national curriculum agency was established; the Curriculum Development Center (CDC). An Interim Council began operations in 1973, and the CDC became a statutory body in 1975. It helped federal and state authorities and interest groups concerned with curriculum in both government and non-government schools to consult and develop joint ventures. Federal legislation gave the CDC considerable power. It became a major vehicle for curriculum reform, and in co-operation with many states, promoted School-Based Curriculum Development (SBCD).

A number of CDC and other CSC projects allowed schools to apply directly for SBCD funds which disturbed the traditional state-based patterns of power related to resource distribution, governance, and administration. One result was turbulence in the interplay between Ministers and senior officials in federal and state governments. These grants from the CDC and the CSC, therefore, did more than raise questions about legitimate authority of systems over schools and the levels of state expertise on curriculum matters. They gradually increased the disproportionate policy leverage that federal governments had over 'new money' programme policy, particularly as state education budgets found it harder to cover anything more than basic commitments such as salaries. This added heat to the traditional territorial disputes between federal and state ministers and their respective teams of senior officials (Spaull 1987:199). Indeed, the CDC's high profile in these federal–state conflicts made it vulnerable to wider political and economic forces. Its political exposure was demonstrated when Whitlam's federal government lost office.

A number of Whitlam's social policies had proved unexpectedly expensive. The public were also troubled by an extraordinary rate of change, some inept ministerial performances, and ideological divisions in Cabinet. In mid-1975, faced with a rapidly deteriorating economic situation, all expenditures had to reviewed, and those in education had to be limited to about 9% of total Commonwealth outlays (Smart 1978: 121–128). The government then lost its majority in the Senate, and when the Opposition blocked supply in the Senate and the Governor General intervened, Whitlam's government fell.

It is generally agreed that Prime Minister Malcolm Fraser's incoming Liberal Coalition administration inherited major economic and social problems, and soon encountered and created others. The late 1970s and early 1980s saw inflation rise steeply, a decline in commodity prices, a drought seriously affecting the agricultural sector, and an outdated industrial base unable to arrest deteriorating terms of trade. Turbulent industrial relations compounded the nation's problems. Fraser sought general economies, but given the budgetary favour shown to the private sector (Smart 1987), cuts to public education soon encountered bitter hostility. Nevertheless, some cuts were made. In April 1981, the report of the Commonwealth Review of Government Functions, the so-called 'Razor Gang', recommended the abolition of the first CDC. Its activities were wound down and relocated into a new Curriculum Development Branch within the Commonwealth Department of Education. Special support continued only in those areas deemed to be of national significance.

Fraser's government fell in 1983 in an acrimonious political climate. Incoming Labor Prime Minister Bob Hawke had campaigned using the symbolism of social democracy and national unity. However, as Smart (1987:19) pointed out:

> whilst much of the educational rhetoric of the Whitlam era remained in Labor's platform, the reformist zeal, and the determination to use education as an engine for social reform had largely evaporated. Under Hawke, Labor has moved right becoming a much more cautious party of the middle ground – the politics of electoral pragmatism and consensus have replaced the Whitlam politics of idealism and reform . . . anxiety about the budget deficit has dictated that 'sound economic management' overrides all other priorities.

With Treasurer Paul Keating, Hawke set about stabilizing the economy. Consistent with the policies of the Australian Labor Party (ALP), a Prices and Incomes Accord was forged with the Australian Council of Trades Unions. This helped lower inflation and to set the scene for longer term structural changes in the industrial and agricultural sectors, the deregulation of the financial sector, a reduction of tariffs, and the general contraction of federal government spending. On the other hand, the underlying current account deficit did not improve, interest rates remained high, the labour market remained highly regulated, and more recent signs have suggested that the economy has moved gradually into recession (Burrel and Webb 1989:1, Tingle 1990:19).

The second coming and going of the CDC

Hawke had promised, prior to attaining power, to restore the CDC. And so, in June 1984, the Commonwealth Schools Commission Amendment Bill repealed the Curriculum Development Center Act 1975, and relocated the CDC as one of four divisions in the Schools Commission. The second CDC's functions were to advise the minister on curriculum policy and materials development and to promote quality teaching, learning and materials across state boundaries through funding projects, research reports, publications and marketing.

Three major changes, however, were immediately apparent. Concern for the specific needs of disadvantaged groups had been given the same priority as seven other 'Educational Policies of the Commonwealth Government' (Boomer 1985); namely curriculum, credentialing, teacher–student–parent interaction, teacher renewal and support, school structure and organization, co-operative links, and public support for education. The second change was a very obvious concern to create trusting relationships with 'the states'. Third, absent were the comparatively generous budgets of the Whitlam era and the ideological fervor. Overall, an economic rationalism tended to underscore this second attempt by the Commonwealth to become a full partner in national curriculum policy-making.

The second CDC, however, was no less vulnerable than the first to forces in the wider context. In brief, when the CSC was abolished in 1987, the CDC function was relocated into a new mega-Ministry; the federal Department of Employment, Education and Training (DEET). DEET had been created in 1987 in the months following Hawke's re-election. The CDC was gradually wound down in the DEET and eventually abolished in June 1989. These events can be explained, but again, most effectively in terms of the wider economic and political context.

The mid-1980s in Australia was a time when commonwealth–state resource agreements and relationships were being renegotiated. In 1984 the federal education portfolio was deeply troubled when asked for retrospective evidence in the quality of education that justified the 50% increase in federal per pupil expenditure between 1973 and 1983 (Smart *et al.* 1986). Hawke's Minister of Education, Senator Susan Ryan, was forced to mount defensive inquiries. One, the Quality of Education Review Committee (QERC) chaired by Professor Peter Karmel (1985), sought to establish value-for-money indicators and to identify links between education and the labour market. It can now be seen that the QERC process triggered a fundamental reconstruction of policy powers. The Chairperson of the CDC's Council, Connors (1988:26–27), provided a bitterly disappointed insider's interpretation:

> What the Commission [CSC] failed to deliver was the public support of government school parent and teacher organizations. . . . A united Commission would certainly have been a financial embarrassment to the Hawke government; a divided Commission ensured that it was a political embarrassment as well. . . . The resignation of Peter Tannock from the chairmanship in January in 1985 gave the government its chance to start redefining the role and functions of the Commission in ways designed to transform it by degrees from a political embarrassment into a political irrelevance.
> This was achieved by the progressive transfer to the Department of Education of responsibility for major Commonwealth funding programmes for schools; isolating the Commission from governmental processes; squeezing the Commission's administrative resources; and destablizing the Commission secretariat, particularly those working with the major programmes the Commission had been identified with for over a decade.

Tannock's resignation also allowed Hawke to debud an ugly sectarian rose:

> Under Fraser, the Schools Commission came increasingly to be viewed by the ALP Left as a creature of the private schools. This perception was reinforced by Fraser's appointment as Chairman, of Dr Peter Tannock, an educationalist closely identified with the Catholic education sector – and further reinforced when two representatives on the Commission of the public school teachers and parents dissented from the majority recommendations of the Commission in 1984 – largely on the grounds that the funding recommendations were biased strongly in favor of the private schools sector . . . Fortuitously for the government, Tannock resigned and was ultimately replaced by Garth Boomer – a significantly lower profile and less experienced bureaucratic strategist. In the interim, the recommendations of the QERC Report and a Commonwealth Public Service review of the Commission led to decisions by Hawke and Ryan to transfer the administrative staff, responsibility and funds for the 'big ticket' Schools Commission programs into the Commonwealth Department of Education. In one fell swoop, the Schools Commission was effectively neutered – albeit under the pretext of enhancing its capacity to concentrate on its primary function of giving policy advice!! (Smart 1987:42–4)

While the detail of these interpretations might be disputed, the facts are that the Hawke government regained the initiative in 1987 with three interconnected strategies; it established the new DEET to obtain greater coherence in youth and education policies, reviewed and rationalized the roles of all associated statutory bodies, and separated and reallocated policy advisory, policy making and policy implementation powers. Instead of the CSC, national interest groups were offered a new venue to advise the Federal Government on the funding and co-ordination of education; the National Board of Employment, Education, and Training (NBEET). Four representative councils were established; the Schools Council (SC), the Higher Education Council, the Employment and Skills Formation Council, and the Australian Research Council (ARC).

Where had policy-making been transferred to? Most of the key action eventually went to the Australian Education Council (AEC). The AEC is a forum comprising federal and state Ministers of Education assisted by a standing committee of Directors General of Education or their equivalents in tertiary, further and higher education. The chair rotates annually and the Commonwealth Minister is the chairman of the AEC for 1990. To the extent that this group pool their powers and act in a concerted manner to dominate direction setting in education, they constitute an oligarchy.

The formation of the AEC's oligarchic powers appears to have its antecedents in the 1987 post-election restructurings at Federal level noted above. In addition to the strains over funding criteria, to Federal doubts over productivity, and to anxiety over shifting centers of power, state Ministers and officials were beginning to smart under their increasingly marginal role in educational policymaking. They adopted a traditional tactic; they cast doubts on the cost benefits of Commonwealth support to the state systems. It is significant that these latter tensions were then eased to a degree when Hawke and Ryan began using the AEC as a forum to develop general agreements and bilateral understandings on resource distribution.

However, despite this emerging rapprochement, criticism of the CDC persisted. It seemed to retain its role as a symbol of all that was held by states to be wrong with federal–state relationships. There was:

> a widely-based concern expressed by the States that the CDC should guard against exceeding its functions in the shaping of curriculum projects and packages used by school systems in the States. Recently, New South Wales has led the campaign against the excessive influence of the CDC. It has argued, in the AEC, that national priorities in curriculum should only be established after consultation with the school authorities, that efforts in implementing agreed national priorities should be the shared responsibility of the CDC and the State, and that curriculum initiatives of the CDC that are not clearly established as a national concern should be questioned by the States. (Spaull 1987:265)

Conciliation was then offered by a Federal policy document, *Strengthening Australia's Schools*. The Hon. John Dawkins (1988) called for a co-operative approach to raise the quality, relevance, and effectiveness of schools on the principal grounds that Australia was under going major social and economic adjustment. Four priorities were stressed: the need for a common curriculum framework; the need for regular assessment of the effectiveness and standards of schools; the need to improve the quality of teaching; and the need to increase the number of young people completing secondary school. Kennedy (1989:119) accurately observed that, 'coming from a Commonwealth Minister, they represent one of the strongest statements ever made by the Commonwealth on school level education.'

It was also clear that federal Minister Dawkins was confident that his unprecedented set of policy claims were not going to be rejected by those who actually possessed constitutional authority on such matters; his fellow Ministers in the AEC. Dawkins' declared intention was to develop 'a national approach to policymaking' to straddle public, private, and state boundaries, specifically by 'building agreements on shared fundamental purposes'. However, the process was not given to the representative agency he had helped design in Canberra, the NBEET, but to much less representative group, the AEC, which is located in Melbourne. Instead, the NBEET and the DEET were tasked to tender policy advice to the Commonwealth Minister, who in turn, thereafter, presented 'the Commonwealth position' at the AEC.

The AEC-based national strategy will, therefore, inevitably reorder the politics of curriculum. Part of its manifest aim is to have the Commonwealth assist states to develop a common curriculum framework with key components; major areas of knowledge, content, and sequences of basic skills, criteria for determining content in major subject areas, criteria for assessing the achievement of objectives, criteria for curriculum design and teaching practices, and mathematics and science courses that reflect technological advances and the need for more balanced participation (Kennedy 1988). Another aim is to rationalize the distribution of powers. For example, the NBEET has far fewer powers than the CSC, and, unlike the AEC (which is a national agency), it will remain a

Commonwealth agency serving the federal government. It is also notable that other organizations that had troubled state ministers and senior officials over the years were similarly redirected and repowered to serve the newly required degree of concerted federal–state action (Kennedy 1990:6–7).

In passing it should be noted that these federal–state accommodations also helped calm the federal education portfolio by the end of 1989. This significant achievement was also electorally well-timed. Education was effectively rendered a non-issue for the February–March federal election campaign in 1990, and Hawke's Government was returned for a record fourth term, albeit with a reduced majority. Dawkins retained the Employment, Education, and Training portfolio.

Before turning to the detail of a 'third coming', it is important to realize that the transfer of powers to the AEC oligarchy is consistent with broader data on organizational trends. In 1980, benchmark accounts of the school education policy processes in Australian states and territories were provided by the Australia–United States Comparative Study Project (Harman and Wirt 1980). Six themes were identified (Harman and Wirt 1980:x–xi):

- there was surprising variation among the states and territories in managerial style, and in the dominant values of the political system and its constituencies;
- there was a trend to greater participation by interest groups other than by professionals;
- while the symbols of decentralism were evident, state controls were still far more pervasive and unchallenged than in the USA;
- issue emergence and policy authorization generally remained with the professionals in state education departments and other government agencies, and in the teachers' unions;
- central power was often diffused among branches of departments and other statutory bodies making rapid change difficult to achieve; and
- attempts to broaden responsibilities at school level had encountered resistance from fearful or indifferent parents, reluctant teachers and administrators committed to routines.

The indicators in recent times are remarkably different, namely that:

- the 'potential for [increased interstate] partisanship appears more likely', and is associated with 'the relative decline of the influence on the AEC of the Directors-General, the 'ministerialization' of education and the relative youth of modern Ministers (average age, late thirties) compared with their senior officers (and compared with Ministers of the earlier periods) (Spaull 1987:312);
- federal and state governments have turned from representative committees to committees of inquiry comprised of appointed, independent and expert outsiders to generate data and policy recommendations (Dunn 1989);
- attempts to facilitate participative democracy have been supplemented by new managerial incentives and responsibilities at all levels in order to create the conditions for proactive leadership (e.g., Scott 1989);
- corporate managerialism, instrumental values and pragmatic political action have become a feature of portfolio management in all states (Beare 1989); and
- policy and accountability processes in education have been restructured in all states in the 1980s to challenge the unanticipated effects of 'provider capture' and to raise the responsiveness of institutions (Macpherson 1989a, 1989b, 1990a, 1990b).

On the other hand, neither the fidelity nor the coherence of these new managerial policies during implementation should be presumed. Kennedy (1989) identified two outstanding problems; the adequacy of provisions for the disadvantaged, and the willingness of teachers around Australia to adopt the curriculum practices to be promoted by the national agency. Much will therefore depend on the acceptance of the services provided by the

AEC-sponsored agency whose emergence is now to be examined. What is no longer questioned, in these times of economic rationalism (Birch and Smart 1989), is that the Commonwealth has acquired partnership status, at the very least, in national curriculum policymaking.

II. The emerging patterns of power

The AEC reorganizes and sets the agenda

In June 1988, the AEC established a Working Party on Co-operative Structures to consider the purposes, governance, and management of national agencies. The AEC Secretariat, the Australian Council of Educational Research (ACER), the Australian Schools Cataloguing and Information Service (ASCIS), and the Technical and Further Education National Center for Research and Development (TAFE R&D) were to be reviewed in order to explore the possibilities of amalgamation and rationalization. Interim reports to the AEC meetings in July and October 1988 led to two decisions based on location and performance criteria; to leave the AEC Secretariat and the TAFE R&D much as they were. Conversely, the special meeting of the Ministers held on 27 July 1988 focused on initiatives relating to *Strengthening Australia's Schools*.

Two outcomes of this meeting had special relevance to curriculum. Two curriculum mapping exercises were agreed to. These were to be under the management of the Conference of Directors General and were to be undertaken by the Directors of Curriculum in each state and territory. In addition, there was a recommendation that there be some rationalization of existing organizations that provided services to the states and territories. This included the Australian Council of Educational Research, the Curriculum Development Center, and the Australian Schools Cataloguing and Information Service.

There were also a number of other significant issues discussed at the meeting. These included: the proposition that there should be national goals for schooling; the basis for future Commonwealth funding arrangements for school level education; basic skills testing and programme evaluation (Kennedy 1990:6–7).

The final report of the Co-operative Structures Working Party was made to the April 1989 AEC meeting in Tasmania. There were five key recommendations made:

- since the ACER had a perceived independence and a unique research function, it should not be amalgamated with a national curriculum development agency or the ASCIS;
- the Council of the ACER was too large (27) for practical purposes and should be rationalized;
- the Ministers should establish a private company to be called the Curriculum Corporation of Australia (CCA) and to provide the services traditionally associated with the CDC and the ASCIS;
- from the outset, the CCA was to be considered a more co-operative venture than the CDC to ensure that the States retained and felt strong ownership; and
- the CCA's operating capital would be assembled by combining the resources of the existing ASCIS, a core per capita grant from each state, and the savings achieved by winding up the CDC.

This advice was offered and received on different bases. The Schools Cataloguing Service, for example, had been incorporated as a private company jointly owned by the Ministers of Education, the National Catholic Education Commission, and the National Council of Independent Schools Associations. Given these diverse interests, the ASCIS Board found it difficult to agree with the Co-operative Structures Working Party's recommendations.

The ACER is also a private company, and it has a Council comprised of senior, highly experienced and independent-minded educationalists. It also has a forceful Director of equally high international and professorial standing. On the other hand, the advice from the AEC's Working Party had to be considered with respect since Ministers make substantial annual core grants to the ACER and allocate major annual research contracts in education; to the extent that an estimated 70% of the ACER's income comes from government sources. It was therefore some time before the Working Party's advice was acted on, and then, as it will be shown below, transposed into two partly unco-ordinated counter-agendas.

The most immediate reaction to the recommendations, however, threatened the fabric of the AEC itself. The Working Party's advice was not accepted by the (then) Liberal Coalition Minister from New South Wales (NSW), Dr Terry Metherell. Unlike his state and federal colleagues, most of whom are ministers in Labor governments, he declared his unwillingness to help fund what he saw as 'additional bureaucratic structure at the federal level'. Further, to respect his concern, Metherell asked that there be a structural distance established between the AEC and any national curriculum agency.

There was, at the time, suspicion in NSW that the Hawke Labor Commonwealth government was trying to 'offload unwanted ex-CDC staff onto the states' or to 'sell off a federal lemon'. Further, as the state with the largest school system, the reallocation of significant per capita funds would have been innopportune when the NSW Premier Nick Greiner was struggling to control a ballooning state deficit. Moreover, Metherell had just initiated major changes in NSW with Dr Brian Scott's management review and Sir John Carrick's inquiry into curriculum. It is also possible that Metherell's position on these matters in 1989 was informed by his experiences in 1981, when, as Senior Private Secretary to Fraser's Federal Minister of Education, he helped Minister Carrick apply the Razor Gang cuts to the orginal CDC.

It should not be assumed that the NSW Minister's position was markedly different than that of his senior officials. There were a range of reasons for general solidarity. First, as noted above, NSW and other states' officials have a historical predisposition of 'keeping Canberra at arm's length'. Second, the traditional rivalries between Sydney and Melbourne underpin some resentment at the way national education bodies not located in Canberra appear to concentrate in Melbourne. Third, such is the comparative size of the NSW public education system, its Minister and officials virtually control access to about one third of the potential Australian school education market. Since they were guaranteed access to any later Curriculum Frameworks materials, by virtue of their involvement in the AEC Curriculum Mapping exercise noted above, and since the details of profit shares from the CCA had yet to be negotiated, saying aloof at that point allowed NSW to preserve its advantageous market position.

Some aspects of Metherell's objections were shared by Ministers and by senior officials from other states. There were, for example, residual fears about federal interventionism into 'states rights'. There were, in this regard, concerns that the joint 'Curriculum Mapping' exercise underway to establish commonalities could yet be used to impose a national core curriculum. Others claimed to have 'never embraced' the CDC, noting that it had been 'a remote organization' producing 'federal materials'. Some states (Victoria is an example) have been implementing relatively new curriculum frameworks, and were understandably reluctant to repeat the trials and tribulations of such an exercise in a national context.

Some remembered the CDC practice first initiated in the early 1980s of meeting regularly with Directors of Curriculum from Education Departments. These meetings were, ironically, reputed by some to sustain the problems they were intended to resolve. According to various legends, CDC personnel tended to be 'offensively innovative' while directors tended to be very determined and 'protectionist' people leading large curriculum development 'empires of their own'. Some recalled how the CDC materials had been used to serve parochial poitical ends. Other outcomes were reported to include bitter boundary problems, damaging inter-state comparisons, and resistance myths such as 'the states know best'. However, despite these claims, the meetings of Directors have continued, which, in general, points to their continuing usefulness.

Even though most states have dramatically contracted their curriculum agencies in recent years in search of economies, a number of senior officials saw this as scant justification for putting precious resources back into formal infrastructure, particularly federal infrastructure. They tended to argue instead for the devolution of purchasing power to schools and for the encouragement of private enterprise by gifted teachers and professional organizations, much as implied by the Scott Reports (1989, 1990) in NSW.

Other objectors raised a possible danger of co-locating the mooted CCA with the national research agency; curriculum development could become assessment-driven, or increasingly reflect the 'academic' interests of the ACER Council, rather than 'the needs of kids' as defined by States. There were, therefore, many skeptics at AEC meetings in late 1989 who privately expressed the wish that the CDC 'had never happened', and who indicated that they did not want 'a rerun of the CDC tragedy'. More profoundly, an immediate upshot of Metherell's position was that the AEC felt a loss of legitimation and certainty over the CCA proposals. Reflection, however, then stiffened the resolve of the other Ministers. Special measures were devised to implement the Working Party's recommendations.

The third coming

An Interim Planning Committee (IPC) was established comprising the nominees of Ministers (less NSW) and the national councils of Catholic and Independent educators. The Ministers involved nominated their Directors General, and in the case of DEET, the Secretary. An Interim Chief Executive Officer of the CCA was appointed on contract in May 1989, but from 'outside' the AEC to accommodate the NSW position. An ex-Director-General was asked to establish a private company using the Working Party's guidelines and to appoint an executive director. While this Interim CEO was a retiree, and was therefore no longer officially connected to the AEC, he had been closely associated with the first CDC, and later, an AEC-nominated member of the second CDC Council in 1985. It therefore appears that the accommodation of the NSW objections was largely symbolic, and was accomplished in a manner that also signalled the determination of the other Ministers to proceed.

The advertisement for an 'Executive Director' for the 'Curriculum Corporation of Australia' (*The Australian*, 7 June 1989) offered a salary of approximately A$70,000 plus a detailed package depending on proposed length of contract, relocation costs, etc. The scale of the proposed enterprise was also clarified; it would have a core grant and a trading budget of between A$5 and A$6 million. The structure advertised defined the Executive Director as the executive officer to the Board of Directors, a member of the Board's

Executive Committee and an executive officer to the Executive Committee. As the full-time senior officer of the new company, the appointee was to be responsible for the establishment of structures, staff selection, and future development of the company. Some applicants were short-listed and interviewed in July, but none were considered appropriate. It was then decided to raise the salary and to readvertise.

The new advertisement drew an expression of interest and a novel proposal from the Director of the ACER that set the two different counter-agendas noted above running. He suggested that the AEC consider giving the ACER and the CCA conjoint leadership with separate organizational identities, and that his own name might be considered for the role. The detail of this affray is important for how it revealed the meta-values of two conflicting theories of state.

There is evidence to suggest that while three Ministers immediately gave strong support to the proposal, and that it quickly attracted general support from other Ministers, it came as a surprise to some ACER Council members and raised opposition from a number of senior officials. As the surprise, in some cases, deepened into concern, and then into degrees of resistance, the ACER Council requested the AEC to make a formal approach to them on the matter. It then appears that informal communications, that occasionally verged on lobbying, created enough political 'noise' in and about the ACER and the AEC to threaten longer-standing arrangements and understandings.

To be judiciously specific, a number of ACER Council members felt that any joint appointment would give the Ministers and their officials a new and inappropriate degree of access to the national research agency's policy and operations. Others went further and interpreted it as a substitute for an earlier strategy, that is, when the Directors General had failed to have one of their number elected to the ACER Executive. Hence, while the ACER Director's proposals was geneally endorsed by the AEC, it proved very controversial for the ACER Council.

The chair of the ACER Council, Professor Karmel, accepted the need for an internal restructuring, began consultations to that end, and thereby put the AEC's formal approach on ice for some months. The issue, however, lost none of its potency. When the new and slimmer ACER Council first discussed the question by teleconference in October 1989, such were the range of deeply held views, it was decided to leave the matter until the Council could meet 'in person'. Finally, at the pre-Christmas ACER Council meeting, it was decided to convey to the AEC that there was insufficient support for the conjoint leadership proposal, while leaving open for a short period the possibility of the mooted agency sharing their new building about to be located on the Monash University campus.

As indicated above, the ACER Councillors are people of strong character. They tended to take independent and critical positions. Some saw it as inappropriate for the Directorship of the ACER to become a half-time task. Others saw the value of integrating the research role of the ACER with the policy research, advisory, and materials production services of a national curriculum agency. There were arguments for co-location and co-operation rather than structural integration. Interpersonal agendas played their part. The turning point for most appeared to be the supposed dangers in an even closer relationship with Ministers and with Departments. A dual appointment, it was successfully argued, would embody a conflict of interest. The appointee would be answerable to the ACER Council as well as to Ministers of Education. It can therefore be deduced, with a reasonable degree of certainty, that the members of the reconstituted ACER Council were reluctant to share their power over their Director or to enter into arrangements that could dilute their control of the ACER's policies, resources and service.

Put another way, the ACER Council's view of itself, as an exemplar of traditional representative governance in education, could not be reconciled with the oligarchic powers of the AEC.

The CCC (neé CCA)

The delays created by these debates and the final outcome generated some practical problems now being resolved. The agreement in principle by the Ministers (less NSW) had included staffing structures, and at the direction of the Interim CEO of the CCA, with the agreement of the IPC, the AEC Secretariat initiated staff selection processes before the directorship question had been finally settled. For example, the national advertisement for a 'Deputy Director' of the 'Curriculum Corporation of Australia' gave a closing date of 3 November, offered a negotiable salary to professorial level on a 3–5 year contract, and indicated that the CCA would 'incorporate the functions of the agencies known as the Curriculum Development Center and the Australian Schools Catalogue Information Service and will have co-operative links with the Australian Council of Educational Research.' Informal discussions were held with some applicants and senior officials. Once the official ACER Council position was known, however, these processes had to be put into abeyance.

The AEC went ahead to formalize the standing of the company, although an entrepreneur had already registered a shelf company using the advertised name. The Memorandum of Agreement, dated 6 December 1989, therefore used the unwieldy title 'Co-ordination Curriculum Corporation' (CCC). There is hope that the Melbourne lawyer reputed to have registered the CCA might yet be persuaded to relinquish his rights to the title. In the interim, the articles of the CCC specify the Ministers of Education (federal, state, and territories, less NSW) and the national Catholic and Independent councils as subscribers.

The Interim Planning Council was reconstituted as the Board of Directors for the CCC, and the CCC Board then invited a senior official of the Australian Capital Territory (ACT) Schools Authority (now the ACT Department of Education) to manage the establishment of the CCC. This will involve completing legal arrangements, organizing premises, transferring assets and staff from the ASCIS and DEET, arranging bank accounts, and building a market position through publishing contracts; all much as in earlier years. There are other explicit links between the first and second CDCs and the new 'Curriculum Corporation'. While the organizational base has changed, and there is a substantially different power and budgetary context, the manager, before moving to the ACT Schools Authority, had been a Deputy Director of the first CDC. Above all, the advertised role of the CCC coheres with CDC service traditions.

There are doubts held about its future of the CCC. The NSW Minister continued to insist that the CCC was not an AEC activity, and thus regularly triggered counter-comment. While many others saw NSW as being 'out in the cold', Metherell and his officials tended to see NSW as being 'well out of a mess'. On the other hand, such rhetoric could have been indicating forward bargaining positions, and the other Ministers were no less determined. The Manager of the 'Curriculum Corporation' therefore, moved ahead with considered and brisk momentum.

It was noted above that the federal Minister is Chairman of the AEC for 1990. This will add considerable support to CCC activity and to its political profile. There are, however, continuing policy differences between Ministers and their senior officials on curriculum structures. There are also a range of reserved positions being taken by Directors of Curriculum at state level. There is also evidence that the contested history of earlier CDC ventures is being reworked to serve factional interests. Overall, there is, therefore, the strong possibility that the CCC could retain its role as a 'political football' in the AEC, unless the CCC Board and Manager can lower the saliency of its role in the politics of curriculum. This will not be easy since ambiguities persist with regard to role. For example, can the CCC take over the Curriculum Mapping Exercise, even though NSW is co-ordinating the Mathematics section of the initiative? More generally, can the CCC avoid being held accountable for failing to meet vaguely defined and shifting expectations? Recall that the control of the curriculum is held by ideologues to be the ultimate prize in education. The CCC will be presumed by many, perhaps unfairly, to control access to the fundamental structures in Australian school curriculum. The 'Curriculum Corporation' will, therefore, attract the focused attention and the sharpest criticism of the most committed educators in Australia.

Tentative conclusions

Interpreting the emergent CCC as a mechanism of state is a complex matter. Its establishment has been shown to be one outcome of a complex interaction of forces, not the least of which was a federal Minister's determination to forge a new oligarchy in the AEC to give the Commonwealth a new and full partnership role in curriculum policy-making. The complexities were shown to be derived from a range of sources: constitutional ambiguities; historical events and ideological commitments; electoral contingencies; pressures in other portfolios; structural determinants of participation, issue emergence and actions; political strategies; economic forces; interaction between determined people; emerging constituencies; the integration of youth and education policies; and the development of a new national oligarchy.

It was also shown that the AEC has become the most important policy forum for the negotiation of curriculum policies in Australia. The negotiations over the national 'Curriculum Corporation' were dominated by the collective interests of federal state Ministers and senior officials. It also appears that representative institutions, such as the NBEET (in general terms) and the ACER, could increasingly be concerned with policy mediation rather than with determining strategic matters to do with curriculum.

The third coming of an Australian national curriculum agency was only possible because it was sponsored by a major coalition in the AEC as part of their wider and gradual acquisition of policy steerage over government school education. This suggests that, in general terms, a dual polity has emerged with the AEC process located beside the more traditional representative structures. Indeed, the philosophical tensions between oligarchic and democratic perspectives were most graphically illustrated in responses to the attempt to provide the ACER and the CCA with conjoint leadership. There is, therefore, at least one other important question to be attended to. Does this generally neo-pluralist interpretation of events have an adequate epistemological basis?

The first point is that only a provisional claim can be made given the methodological limitations noted above. It is, nevertheless, strengthened when evaluated using the criteria of non-foundational epistemology (Walker and Evers 1982, Walker et al. 1987, Evers 1987). In this exercise it meant identifying the coherence between experience, data, and beliefs about the politics of Australian curriculum in general, and about the politics of establishing the CCC in particular.

While the facts of the emergent matter are not all in by any means, an important touchstone appears to be the existence of a dual polity; it was repeatedly evident in overlapping accounts, in structural changes, in actual practices, and in the organizational meta-values exposed by the conjoint leadership affray. Further, when the theoretical frameworks of participants were imputed from their interpretations of the politics of curriculum, they appeared to have diverse and yet clustered characteristics that cohere with neo-pluralist theory.

There were few Marxist instrumental perspectives used. There were no class theories used by these elite informants, as might be expected, and yet some argued hard for state intervention and arbitration (on such issues as equity) as an appropriate component of the politics of curriculum. An ethic of principled opportunism was proposed by others.

Another minority used New Right ideas to suggest that greater freedoms would optimize the effectiveness of public choice-making and raise the responsiveness of institutions like the 'Curriculum Corporation'. Ironically, in the light of their stand-off position on the CCC, these ideas tended to come from NSW. While Marxist instrumental and New Right theories had a polar relationship in ideological terms, both explained the politics of curriculum primarily in economic metaphors and shared an assumption that capitalism is facing a legitimation crisis. Such common ground, however, seemed to offer an inadequate basis for developing touchstone theory, and so was retained as a major feature of the context.

Although the data does not permit definitive findings, there did appear to be far greater potential for common ground between elite theory and neo-pluralism. It was patently too simplistic to conclude that the politics of curriculum were controlled by Ministers and officials. On the other hand, the AEC elites, the Ministers and their officials, were clearly very influential given their access to information and technocratic government, and in this case study, demonstrably more influential than representative institutions and the Guardians of democracy in education; the 'academics'. It also appeared to be the case that the moving political and economic context prevented any group manipulating the processes of governance for any lengthy period. There were, conversely, many explanations that presumed that professionalized elites were using state and federal structures with multiple hierarchies. It appeared, for example, that these polyarchies helped shroud policy processes from the gaze of citizens. The 'Curriculum Corporation' and other agencies of the AEC could become exemplars in this respect since they are tending to be exposed only to market forces, to Board review and to input from state and federal officials and ministers. The CCC Board, for example, limits 'public' representation to four national organizations; one nominee each from parent, teacher, Catholic and Independent bodies.

When these components are assembled as touchstone for a theory of state in the politics of Australian curriculum, it implies that corporatist and technocratic mechanisms of state are being serviced by professional elites to sustain both traditional 'representative' and new oligarchic structures, and that this dual policy (embedded in a variegated polyarchy) seeks to reconcile both representative activity and state responses to economic pressures.

The weight of the evidence suggests that the politics of Australian curriculum is increasingly being centered on the AEC. If these oligarchic trends continue, especially if the recession deepens significantly, it is predicted that the governance of curriculum will more and more become a matter of national and Ministerial determination. It can also be anticipated that oligarchic political practices will result in a greater standardization of the quality, scope, detail and prescriptiveness of curriculum. The greatest potential checks on these trends are, however, not economic; they are political. A number of Labor state governments appear particularly vulnerable to recessionary politics and many state-commonwealth relationships remain fragile and eminently contestable.

Note

This paper was also intended to further research into the politics of Australian education. It was presented to the Inaugural Meeting of the Politics and Policy Studies in Education Special Interest Group at the 1990 Australian Association of Researchers in Education Conference at Sydney University.

References

BEARE, H. (1989) 'Educational administration in the 1990s', paper presented to the ACEA Conference, Armidale, 24–29 September.

BIRCH, I. K. F. (1975) *Constitutional Responsibility for Education in Australia* (Canberra: ANU Press).

BIRCH, I. K. F. (1987) 'The courts as policy-makers in Australia', in W. L. Boyd and D. Smart, *Educational Policy in Australia and America: Comparative Perspectives* (New York: Falmer), pp. 77–99.

BIRCH, I. K. F. and SMART, D. (1989) 'Economic rationalism and the politics of education in Australia', in E. E. Mitchel and M. E. Goertz (eds), *Education Politics for the New Century* (London: Falmer), pp. 137–151.

BOOMER, G. (1985) *Curriculum Development Centre: Role and Operations* (Canberra: Commonwealth Schools Commission).

BOYD, W. L. (1987) 'Balancing public and private schools: the Australian experience and American implications', in W. L. Boyd and D. Smart, *Educational Policy in Australian and America: Comparative Perspectives* (New York: Falmer), pp. 163–183.

BOYD, W. L. and SMART, D. (eds) (1987) *Educational Policy in Australia and America: Comparative Perspectives* (New York: Falmer).

BURREL, S. and WEBB, R. (1989) 'Fresh signs of economic slowdown', *Australian Financial Review*, 7 February, p. 1.

CONNORS, L. (1988) 'The rise and fall of the Schools Commission: the case of federal intervention in primary and secondary schooling', in J. Sarros and H. Beare (eds) *Australian Contributions to Educational Management: Some Commentaries by Chief Education Executives* (Applecross: ACEA), pp. 23–29.

DAWKINS, J. S. (1988) *Strengthening Australia's Schools: A Consideration of the Focus and Content of Schooling* (Canberra: AGPS).

DUNLEAVY, P. and O'LEARY, B. (1987) *Theories of the State: The Politics of Liberal Democracy* (Basingstoke: Macmillan).

DUNN, S. S. (1989) *Public Accountability in Australian Education*, Occasional Paper No. 11, Australian College of Education (Canberra: ACE).

EVERS, C. W. (1987) 'Philosophical research in educational administration', in R. J. S. Macpherson (ed.) *Ways and Meanings of Research in Educational Administration* (Armidale: UNE Press), pp. 53–77.

FUHRMAN, S. H. (1989) 'State politics and education reform', in J. Hannaway and R. Crowson (eds) *The Politics of Reforming School Administration* (New York: Falmer) pp. 61–75.

HARMAN, G. S. and SMART, D. (1982) (eds) *Federal Intervention in Australian Education: Past, Present and Future* (Melbourne: Georgian).

HARMAN, G. S. and WIRT, F. M. (1980) 'Foreword', in M. Hogan and P. West, *Making Policy in a Changing Context: The Education Policy Process in New South Wales*. Monograph No. 2, The Education Policy Process at State Level: The Australia–United States Comparative Study (University of Melbourne: CSHE).

KARMEL, P. (Chair) (1973) *Schools in Australia* (Canberra: AGPS).

KARMEL, P. (Chair) (1985) *Quality of Education in Australia* (Canberra: AGPS).

KENNEDY, K. (1988) 'The policy context of curriculum reform in Australia in the 1980s', *Australian Journal of Education*, 32(3), pp. 357–374.

KENNEDY, K. (1989) 'National initiatives in curriculum: the Australian context', *British Journal of Educational Studies*, 37(2), pp. 111–124.

KENNEDY, K. (1990) 'Strengthening Australia's schools as a blueprint for national efforts at curriculum reform', paper presented to the ANZAAS Conference, Hobart, 15–17 February.

MACPHERSON, R. J. S. (1989a) 'Interpreting the restructuring of New South Wales school education as philosophy-in-action, a search for meaning and immortality and as genetic engineering', paper presented to the AARE Conference, Adelaide, 28 November–2 December.

MACPHERSON, R. J. S. (1989b) 'Radical administrative reforms in New Zealand education: the implications of the Picot Report for institutional managers', *Journal of Educational Administration*, 27(1), pp. 29–44.

MACPHERSON, R. J. S. (1990a) 'The reconstruction of New Zealand education: devolution and counter-pressures to effective school governance', in H. Beare and W. L. Boyd (eds) *Restructuring Schools: An International Perspective on the Movement to Transform the Control and Performance of Schools* (New York: Falmer, forthcoming).

MACPHERSON, R. J. S. (1990b) 'Creating Administrative Policy: Philosophy-In-Action?' *Australian Education Researcher*, 17(2), pp. 1–16.

MORGAN, C. (1980) 'Paradigms, metaphors and puzzle-solving', *Administrative Science Quarterly*, 25, pp. 605–622.

SARROS, J. and BEARE, H. (1988) *Australian Contributions to Educational Management: Some Commentaries by Chief Education Executives* (Applecross: AGEA).

SCOTT, B. (1989) *Schools Renewal: A Strategy to Revitalize Schools Within the New South Wales State Education System* (Milson's Point: Management Review, NSW Education Portfolio).

SCOTT, B. (1990) School-Centred Education: Building a more Responsive State School System (Milson's Point: Management Review, NSW Education Portfolio).

SMART, D. (1978) *Federal Aid to Australian Schools* (St. Lucia: UQP).

SMART, D. (1987) 'Reagan conservatism and Hawke socialism: whither the differences in education policies of the US and Australian federal governments?', in W. L. Boyd and D. Smart (eds) *Educational Policy in Australia and America: Comparative Perspectives* (New York: Falmer), pp. 19–46.

SMART, D., SCOTT, R., MURPHY, K. and DUDLEY, J. (1986) 'The Hawke Government and education', *Politics*, 21 (1), pp. 63–81.

SPAULL, A. (1987) *A History of the Australian Education Council* (Sydney: Allen & Unwin).

TINGLE, L. (1990) 'Crash through or crunch?', *The Weekend Australian*, 19–20 May, p. 19.

WALKER, J. C. and EVERS, C. W. (1982) 'Epistemology and justifying the curriculum of educational studies', *British Journal of Educational Studies*, 30(2), pp. 321–329.

WALKER, J. C., in association with Duignan, P. A., Flynn, P., Francis, D., Ikin, R., Macpherson, R. J. S., Maxwell, B. and Wade, B. (1987) 'A philosophy of leadership in curriculum development: a pragmatic and historic approach', in J. C. Walker, (ed.) *Educative Leadership for Curriculum Development* (Canberra: Act Schools Authority).

12 'Nations at risk' and 'national curriculum': ideology and identity

Ivor F. Goodson

This chapter focuses on the phenomenon emergent in several countries of a new 'National Curriculum'. Primarily the chapter draws on the experience of the United Kingdom. In this case study the focus is on the antecedents of the national curriculum and the arguments and groups through which promotion has taken place; the structures, rhetorical, financial and political, which have been established or co-opted to support it; and finally the content, form, pedagogical assumption and ideological projects embedded within it.

In this chapter I focus on the phenomenon emergent in a number of countries of 'national curriculum'. My primary evidence is a case study of the evolution of the national curriculum in the UK. In the case study I focus on the antecedents to the national curriculum and the arguments and groups through which it has been promoted, the structures, rhetorical, financial and political, which have been established to support it, and finally the content, form, and pedagogical assumptions embedded within it.

As in other countries, the national curriculum debate in the UK has been precipitated by a widespread, and largely correct, perception that the nation is threatened by economic decline. Rhetorically then, the national curriculum is presented as a part of the project of economic regeneration. Behind this broad objective, however, two other projects can be discerned. Firstly, the reconstitution of older class-based British traditional subjects, and secondly, a reassertion of the ideology and control of the nation-state.

A good deal of recent historical work has furthered our understanding of the origins of state schooling and curriculum. The common feature uniting the wide range of initiatives by states to fund and manage mass schooling was, these scholars argue, the endeavour of constructing a national polity; the power of the nation-state, it was judged, would be unified through the participation of the state's subjects in national projects. Central in this socialization into national identity was the project of mass state schooling. The sequence followed by those states promoting this national project of mass schooling were strikingly similar. Initially there was the promulgation of a national interest in mass education. Legislation to make schooling compulsory for all followed. To organize the system of mass schools, state departments or ministries of education were formed. State authority was then exercised over all schools – both those 'autonomous' schools already existing and newly proliferating schools specifically organized or opened by the state (Goodson 1987, 1988).

If the central project behind the initiation of state schooling and state-prescribed curriculum was nation-building, this may explain the response to certain moral panics which are currently evident. Above all is the new sense of panic over the 'nation at risk' – the title chosen for the major US report on education in 1983. The perception of national crisis is common among western nation-states. Often the matter is presented as essentially economic: certain nations (e.g., the USA) are falling behind certain other nations (e.g.,

0268–0939/90 $3.00 © 1990 Taylor & Francis Ltd.

Japan) in terms of economic prosperity. But behind this specific economic rationale lie a range of further more fundamental issues which render 'nations at risk'. The globalization of economic life, and more particularly of communications, information and technology, all pose enormous challenges to the existing modes of control and operation of nation-states. In this sense the pursuance of new centralized national curriculum might be seen as the response of the more economically-endangered species among nations. Britain provides an interesting case of this kind of response.

Behind the myths projected by the current UK government and echoed by some of the more sympathetic newspapers and media, the UK economy remains under-capitalized and in many instances, hopelessly uncompetitive. So much for the economic basis of the 'nation at risk'. But perhaps even more significant are the tendencies towards globalization of economic and social life. In the UK case this is rendered particularly acute by the impending full-scale integration into the European Community in 1992. Symbolically the Channel Tunnel will connect UK life with that in Europe. The 'island nation' will quite literally be opened up to subterranean entry. The fear of the nation being at risk no doubt explains the hysteria behind so much of the Thatcher government's response to European integration. Pervasive in this response is the sense of a loss of control, a loss of national destiny and identity. The school curriculum provide one arena for reasserting control and for re-establishing national identity.

The move towards a national curriculum in the UK can be traced back to the late 1970s. The key date in UK postwar educational history was Prime Minister James Callaghan's Ruskin College [Oxford] Speech in 1976. Here economic decline and an accelerating sense of national decline (the UK had joined the EEC in 1973) were attached to the decline in educational standards which it was argued had been fostered in comprehensive schools by the use of more 'progressive' methods. Callaghan's speech called for a 'Great Debate' on the UK's educational policies. Following this initiative, in 1977, a Green Paper, *Education in Schools: A Consultative Document*, was issued. The arguments for a common 'core' or a 'protected' element emerged. The principal points of concern appear to be:

(i)   the curriculum has become overcrowded; the timetable is overloaded, and the essentials are at risk;

(ii) variations in the approach to the curriculum in different schools can penalize a child simply because he or she has moved from one area to another;

(iii) even if the child does not move, variations from school to school may give rise to inequality of opportunities;

(iv) the curriculum in many schools is not sufficiently matched to life in a modern industrial society.

Not all these comments may be equally valid, but it is clear that the time has come to try to establish generally accepted principles for the composition of the secondary curriculum for all pupils. This does not presuppose uniform answers: schools, pupils, and their teachers are different, and the curriculum should be flexible enough to reflect these differences. But there is a need to investigate the part which might be played by a 'protected' or 'core' element of the curriculum common to all schools. There are various ways this may be defined. Properly worked out, it can offer reassurances to employers, parents, and the teachers themselves, as well as a very real equality of opportunity for pupils (Fowler 1988: 38).

The emerging 'consensus' that there should be a 'core' curriculum was further promoted in the period after the election of a Conservative Government under Margaret Thatcher in 1979. The 1980 consultative paper, *A Framework for the School Curriculum*, argued that:

In the course of the public and professional debate about the school curriculum a good deal of support has been found for the idea of identifying a 'core' or essential part of the curriculum which should be followed by all pupils according to their ability. Such a core, it is hoped, would ensure that all pupils, whatever else they do, at least get a sufficient grounding in the knowledge and skills which by common consent should form part of the equipment of the educated adult.

Thus expressed, the idea may appear disarmingly simple; but as soon as it is critically examined a number of supplementary questions arise. For example, should the core be defined as narrowly as possible, or should it, for the period of compulsory schooling at least, cover a large part of the individual's curriculum? Should it be expressed in terms of the traditional school subjects, or in terms of educational objectives which may be attained through the medium of various subjects, appropriately taught? The difficulties and uncertainties attached to the application of the core concept do not mean, however, that it may not be a useful one in carrying forward the public debate about the curriculum to the point at which its results can be of practical benefit to the schools (Fowler 1988: 59–60).

These difficulties notwithstanding from this point on there was a fairly consistent drive to establish a core curriculum. Following the Conservative Party's third election success in 1987, this curriculum was established as a new 'national curriculum', comprising the 'core subjects' of mathematics, English, and science, and the 'foundation subjects' of history, geography, technology, music, art, and physical education.

Alongside this specification of subject titles was a panoply of major new central powers over the school curriculum. The Secretary of State for Education and Science now has responsibility for specifying attainment targets, programmes of study, and assessment procedures for each specified subject area. It should be noted that these are powers for very detailed prescription indeed, these are not the powers of merely a general overview. Written into the parliamentary legislation is the obligation to assess pupils on the curriculum studied at the ages 7, 11, 14, and 16. In addition, a National Curriculum Council and a School Examinations and Assessment Council have been set up to advise on the research, development, and monitoring procedures required.

The styling of the new curriculum specifications as 'national', the composition of subjects included, and the wide ranging new power for governmental agencies suggest three levels of inquiry in coming to understand this new initiative. First there is the need for further inquiry of the theme with which we began: the relationship of these curriculum initiatives to national economic regeneration and national identity. Second the focus on a small number of traditional subjects raises the question of the social antecedents of this choice: we need to analyse the social and cultural, as well as political, choices which underpin the new national curriculum. Third the initiative needs to be scrutinized in terms of the changing modalities of government control which are so clearly pronounced.

The national curriculum and national identity

The national curriculum has been initiated with pronouncements casting national regeneration in terms of links to the economy, industry and commerce, in particular the so-called 'wealth creating' sector. Yet in practice the balance of subjects in the national curriculum suggest that questions of national identity and control have been pre-eminent, rather than industrial or commercial requirements. For example, information technology has been largely omitted, whilst history has been embraced as a 'foundation subject', even though it is quite clearly a subject in decline within the schools.

The reasons for favouring history whilst omitting more commercially 'relevant' subjects are intriguing. On the face of it, this pattern of prioritizing might seem encouraging: sponsoring liberal education and humanist study over more narrow utilitarian concerns, favouring education over training. Regrettably this does not seem to be the case. History has, I believe, been chosen to revive and refocus national identity and ideology.

The recent National Curriculum History Group Interim Report provides information on the new curriculum proposals for school history. Firstly the report confirms that prior to the revival initiated by the incorporation in the national curriculum, history was a subject in decline: 'It now has a tenuous place in the primary curriculum and it is under threat in a growing number of secondary schools, both in terms of the number of pupils taking it, and as a coherent, rigorous and free-standing course of study' (National Curriculum History Group Interim Report). One of the reasons for the progressive decline of history has been the growth of social studies and sociology. The latter subject is a very popular examination subject, but has been omitted in the national curriculum in favour of reviving history. The questions remains as to why has history been so favoured.

The Interim Report provides some evidence on this issue for the national curriculum in history will have some distinctive features. At the core will be UK history which overall will take up 40% of the timetable. 'This figure, however, is slightly misleading because children at key stage one infant level will study UK history almost exclusively, while pupils in the early years of the secondary school will study it as a core subject for just one-third of the time earmarked for history' (National Curriculum History Group Interim Report). The focus of the national curriculum on British history in the formative early years of schooling indicates a wish to inculcate at an early stage a sense of national identity. This desire for a major and increased UK dimension in history has plainly come from within the Government. We are told for instance that:

> The issue which has hitherto aroused the most controversy is the Minister's insistence that the group should increase the proportion of British history for secondary pupils. At the moment, the group is planning to devote only one-third of the syllabus to British history as a compulsory subject for 11- to 14-year-olds. This figure rises slightly to two-fifths for 14- to 16-year-olds. Mr MacGregor wants British history to be taught for at least 50% of the time devoted to history in secondary schools (*Times Educational Supplement, 18 August 1989: 4*).

John MacGregor, newly appointed by Premier Thatcher as the Secretary of State for Education and Science, is clear therefore on where the Government's priorities lie. Certainly the revival of UK history seems unrelated to any strong desires among history teachers themselves, where many disagreements have been voiced. These disagreements have even been voiced inside the select curriculum working group: 'At the heart of these disagreements on historical knowledge, British history and chronology, is the lingering fear among some numbers of the group particularly those who are teachers or educationists that the history curriculum will be dominated by rigid external testing and rote learning of famous dates in British history' (*Times Education Supplement*, 18 August, 1989: 4).

National curriculum and social prioritizing

The styling of the curriculum as 'national' begs a number of questions about which nation is being referred to, for the UK is a nation sharply divided by social class. One of the shorthands for Conservative criticism of what the French Prime Minister has called the UK government's 'social cruelty' has been a reference to the danger of creating 'two nations'. This refers to the UK phenomenon of there being two recognizably different constituencies or nations inside the UK's borders: one nation which is rich and secure and often resides in the so-called 'Home Counties' of southern England, and the other nation which is less well-endowed, primarily working class, and lives in that 'other country' beyond southern England. In truth, of course, the UK comprises a range of identifiable groups; there are in fact more than two nations.

Hence, in examining the national curriculum as a social construction, it is important to establish whether the different groups which comprise 'the nation' are being treated equally, or whether a process of social prioritizing can be discerned.

The pattern of secondary schooling has a long history but a crucial watershed was the 1902 Education Act and the subsequent issue of the Secondary Regulations in 1904 (Board of Education 1904). At the turn of the century a number of alternative versions of secondary schooling were vying with each other. The well-established grammar schools carried the highest status and catered for the more elite social groups through a traditional classical curriculum, but increasingly the school boards administering local schools were providing education for secondary age pupils. In these schools a more vocational curriculum, covering commercial, technical and scientific subjects, were provided for a predominantly working class clientele.

The 1902 Education Act and the Secondary Regulations therefore arbitrated between these two traditions. Ryder and Silver (1970) have judged that the 1902 Act ensured that 'whatever developments in secondary education might occur, it should be within a single system in which the dominant values should resemble those of the traditional grammar school and its curriculum' (J. Ryder and H. Silver 1970). Likewise, Eaglesham judged that (1967):

> These regulations were the work of a number of officials and inspectors of the Board. It may be argued that they gave a balanced curriculum. They certainly effectively checked any tendencies to technical or vocational bias in the secondary schools. They made them schools fit only for a selected few. Moreover they proclaimed for all to see the Board's interest in the literary and classical sides of secondary education. For the future the pattern of English culture must come not from Leeds and West Ham but from Eton and Winchester (Eaglesham 1967 p. 59).

And summarized in this way: 'Secondary education was in 1904 given so academic a curriculum that it suited only a few' (Eaglesham 1967 p. 60). In this manner the settlement of 1902–4 chose the historical legacy and curriculum aimed at certain groups over that aimed at other groups and legislated that this model should constitute the secondary school curriculum. The 1904 Secondary Regulations outline clear guidelines:

> The course should provide for instruction in the English Language and Literature, at least one Language other than English, Geography, History, Mathematics, Science and Drawing, with due provision for Manual Work and Physical Exercises, and in a girls' school for Housewifery. Not less than $4\frac{1}{2}$ hours per week must be allotted to English, Geography and History; not less than $3\frac{1}{2}$ hours to the Language where one is taken or less than 6 hours where two are taken; and not less than $7\frac{1}{2}$ hours to Science and Mathematics, of which at least 3 must be for Science (Board of Education 1904).

The division of secondary schooling between grammar schools and other schools pre-eminently for the working class, the elementary schools, and subsequently secondary modern schools, survived into the period following the Second World War. Opposition to the selective examination for deciding who went to grammar school, the so-called 11-plus, grew, and some experiments in comprehensive or multilateral schooling began in the 1950s. In 1964 a Labour Government was returned, and immediately began dismantling the existing divisive system and introducing comprehensive schools.

The implications of this change for the curriculum were substantial, and a range of curriculum reform projects were initiated through the Schools Council for Curriculum and Examination founded in 1964. Whilst the comprehensive schools initially derived their main curriculum areas from the grammar schools, these reform projects sought to seriously apply the logic of comprehensive school reform to curriculum reform. For plainly without curiculum reform organizational reform was of severely limited significance.

Rubinstein and Simon (1973) summarize the climate of educational reform in 1972 following the raising of the school leaving age to 16, and the rapid growth of the comprehensive system:

> The content of the curriculum is now under much discussion, and comprehensive schools are participating actively in the many curriculum reform schemes launched by the Schools Council and Nuffield. The tendency is towards the development of the interdisciplinary curricula, together with the use of the resource approach to learning, involving the substitution of much group and individual work for the more traditional forms of class teaching. For these new forms of organizing and stimulating learning mixed-ability grouping often provides the most appropriate method; and partly for this reason the tendency is towards the reduction of streaming and class teaching. This movement in itself promotes new relations between teachers and pupils, particularly insofar as the teacher's role is changing from that of ultimate authority to that of motivating, facilitating and structuring the pupils' own discovery and search for knowledge (Rubinstein and Simon 1973: 123).

The belief that rapid curriculum reform, with a range of associated political and pedagogical implications, was well under way was commonly held at this time. Kerr asserted in 1968 that 'at the practical and organizational levels, the new curricula promise to revolutionize English education' (Kerr 1971).

But at precisely the time Kerr was talking new forces were seeking to defend, and if possible re-invigorate, the old grammar school subjects. These were presented as the 'traditional' subjects. In England the 're-invention' of 'traditional' subjects began with the issue of the first collection of Black Papers (Cox and Dyson 1971). The writers in this collection argued that teachers had been too greatly influenced by progressive theories of education such as the integration of subjects, mixed ability teaching, inquiry and discovery teaching. This resulted in neglect of subject and basic skill teaching, and led to reduced standards of pupil achievement and school discipline; the traditional subject was thereby equated with social and moral discipline. The rehabilitation of the traditional subject promised the re-establishment of discipline in both these senses. The Black Papers were taken up by politicians, and in 1976 the Labour Prime Minister James Callaghan embraced many of their themes in his Ruskin College Speech. Specific recommendations soon followed. In 1979, for instance, following a survey of secondary schools in England and Wales, Her Majesty's Inspectorate (HMI) drew attention to what they judged to be evidence of insufficient match in many schools between the qualification and experience of teachers and the work they were undertaking: later in a survey of middle schools they found that when they examined, 'the proportion of teaching which was undertaken by teachers who had studied the subjects they taught as main subjects in initial training . . . higher standards of work overall were associated with a greater degree of use of subject teachers' (HMI 1983).

In the Department of Education & Science (DES) pamphlet *Teaching Quality*, the Secretaries of State for Education listed the criteria for initial teacher training courses. The first criteria imposed the following requirement: 'that the higher education and initial training of all qualified teachers should include at least two full years' course time devoted to subject studies at a level appropriate to higher education.' This requirement therefore 'would recognize teachers' needs for subject expertise if they are to have the confidence and ability to enthuse pupils and respond to their curiosity in their chosen subject fields' (DES 1983).

This final sentence is curiously circular. Obviously if the pupils choose subjects then it is probable that teachers will require subject expertise. But this is to foreclose a whole debate about *whether* they should choose subjects as an educational vehicle. Instead, we have a political *fait accompli* presented as choice. In fact the students have no choice except to embrace 'their chosen subject fields'. The political rehabilitation of subjects by political dictat is presented as a response to pupil choice.

In *Teaching Quality*, the issue of the match between teachers' qualifications and their work with pupils first raised in the 1979 HMI document is again employed. We learn that 'the government attach high priority to improving the fit between teachers' qualifications and their tasks as one means of improving the quality of education' (DES 1983). The criteria for such a fit is based on a clear belief in the sequential and hierarchical pattern of subject learning. All specialist subject teaching during the secondary phase requires teachers whose study of the subject concerned was at a level appropriate to higher education, represented a substantial part of the higher education and training period and built on a suitable A level base.

The belief in subject specialization is best evidenced where the issue of non-subject based work in schools is scrutinized. Many aspects of school work take place outside (or beside) subject work studies of school process have indeed shown how integrated pastoral and remedial work originates because pupils, for one reason or another, do not achieve in traditional subjects. Far from accepting the subject as an educational vehicle with severe limits if the intention is to educate all pupils, the document seeks to rehabilitate subjects even in those domains which often originate from subject 'fall-out'.

> Secondary teaching is not all subject-based, and initial training and qualifications cannot provide an adequate preparation for the whole range of secondary school work. For example, teachers engaged in careers or remedial work or in providing group courses of vocational preparation, and those given the responsibility for meeting 'special needs' in ordinary schools, need to undertake these tasks not only on the basis of initial qualifications but after experience of teaching a specialist subject and preferably after appropriate post-experience training. Work of this kind and the teaching of interdisciplinary studies are normally best shared among teachers with varied and appropriate specialist qualifications and expertise (DES 1983 para. 40 p. 11).

The rehabilitation of school subjects has become the mainstay of Government thinking about the school curriculum. In many ways the governmental and structural support offered to school subjects as the organizing device for secondary schooling is reaching unprecedented levels. Hargreaves has judged that 'more than at any time previously, it seems, the subject is to take an overriding importance in the background preparation and curricular responsibility of secondary school teachers.' But the preferred policy sits alongside a major change in the style of governance of education for Hargreaves argues that,

> ... nor does that intention on the part of HMI and DES amount to just a dishing out of vague advice. Rather, in a style of centralized policy intervention and review with which we in Britain are becoming increasingly familiar in the 1980s, it is supported by strong and clear declarations of intent to build the achievement of subject match into the criteria for approval (or not) of teacher training courses, and to undertake five yearly reviews of selected secondary schools to ensure that subject match is being improved within them and is being reflected in the pattern of teacher appointments (Hargreaves 1984).

The associated issue of increasingly centralized control is also raised in a DES publication on *Education 8-12 Combined and Middle Schools* (1984). Again, the rehabilitation of school subjects is rehearsed in a section on the need to 'extend teachers' subject knowledge'. Rowland has seen the document as 'part of an attempt to bring a degree of centralized control over education'. He states that *Education 8-12* may well be interpreted by teachers and others as recommending yet another means in the trend towards a more schematicized approach to learning in which the focus is placed even more firmly on the subject matter rather than the child. He adds cryptically that 'the evidence it produces, however, points to the need to move in quite the opposite direction' (Rowland 1987 p. 90). His reservations about the effects of rehabilitating school subjects are widely shared. Another scholar has noted that one effect of the strategy 'will be to reinforce the existing culture of secondary teaching and thereby inhibit curricular and pedagogic innovation on a school-wide front' (Hargreaves 1984).

The various goverment initiatives and reports since 1976 have shown a consistent tendency to return to 'basics' to re-embrace 'traditional' subjects. This government project which spans both labour and conservative administrations has culminated in the 'new' national curriculum. The comparison with the Secondary Regulations in 1904 shows the extent to which a patterning of schooling has been reconstituted in this new political settlement called the national curriculum.

1904	1987
English	English
Maths	Maths
Science	Science
History	History
Geography	Geography
Physical Exercise	Physical Education
Drawing	Art
Foreign Language	Modern Foreign Language
Manual Work	
Domestic Subjects	Technology
[Music added soon afterwards]	Music

The similarity between 1904 and 1987 questions the rhetoric of 'a major new initiative' employed by the government, and points to some historical continuties in social and political purpose and priorities. The 1904 Regulations embodied that curriculum historically offered to the grammar school clientele as opposed to the curriculum being developed in the Board Schools and aimed primarily at the working classes: one segment or vision of the nation was being favoured at the expense of another. In the intervening period more equalitarian impulses brought about the creation of comprehensive schools where children of all classes came together under one roof. This in turn led to a range of curriculum reforms which sought to redefine and challenge the hegemony of the grammar school curriculum.

Seeking in turn to challenge and redirect these reforms and intentions the political right has argued for the rehabilitation of the 'traditional' (i.e., grammar school) subjects. The national curriculum can be seen as a political statement of the victory of the forces and intentions representing these political groups. A particular vision, a preferred segment of the nation has therefore been reinstated and prioritized, and legislated as 'national'.

The historical continuities evident in the national curriculum have been commented on in a number of places. For instance, the *Times Educational Supplement* stated that 'the first thing to say about this whole exercise is that it unwinds 80 years of English (and Welsh) educational history. It is a case of go back to Go' (*Times Educational Supplement* 18 August 1989). In writing of the National Curriculum Project, Moon and Mortimore commented:

> The legislation, and the much-critized consultative document that preceded it, present the curriculum in needlessly rather restricted terms. Thus the primary curriculum was put forward as if it were no more than a pre-secondary preparation (like the worst sort of 'prep school'). All the positive aspects of British primary schooling so valued by HMI and the Select Committee of the House of Commons and so praised by many foreign commentators were ignored.
>
> The secondary curriculum, in turn, appears to be based on the curriculum of a typical 1960s grammar school. We would not take issue with the subjects included, but we believe that such a curriculum misses out a great deal. Information technology, electronics, statistics, personal, social and careers education have all been omitted. Yet, surely, these are just the areas that are likely to be of importance for the future lives of many pupils? (Moon and Mortimore 1989 p. 9).

The national curriculum then can be seen as a response to a 'nation at risk' at two levels.

Firstly there is the general sense of the nation-state being in economic decline and subject to globalization and to amalgamation in the wider European Community. There the response is paradoxical. Nation-building curricula are often favoured over commercially 'relevant' curricula. The solution therefore may exacerbate the problem. Further economic 'decline' may follow leading to even more desperate attempts to reassert national identity.

Secondly, given that the UK is clearly a divided nation, investigation of the national curriculum allows insights into precisely *which* nation is at risk. It would seem it is the elite and middle class groups which were perceived of as 'at risk'. For it is this group that have the greatest historical connections to the 'traditional subjects': these subjects have been revived and reinstated in the national curriculum.

The perception of nations at risk and social groups at risk has further provided one source of support for developing the powers of central state over the school curriculum. This is the third level at which the national curriculum is significant. In the central project of rebuilding the nation-state, the issue of re-establishing national identity and ideology has been dealt with but there remains the issue of rebuilding the power of the nation-state itself.

National curriculum and national power

In postwar Britain the national state's powers over education were increasingly devolved to local education authorities (LEAs). This made the schools more responsive to the local 'communities' than to 'the nation'. In addition the teachers' unions were able to assert a growing influence over issues of curriculum and assessment reform. As we have noted, this led some comprehensive schools to develop more comprehensive curricula which moved beyond the 1904-style academic curriculum 'suited to only a few'. The national state's loss of control, specifically loss of control over curriculum, therefore led to patterns of prioritizing which went a long way from the political settlement enshrined in the 1904 Regulations: the so-called traditional subjects. This loss of control therefore threatened those groups which had benefited from this political settlement. The social prioritization so well-established in the early twentieth century was plainly under attack. In short, the 'nation' as represented in these privileged groups was 'at risk'.

Of course reasserting the primacy of curriculum as a vehicle for the education of the elite and custodial classes entirely fits a version of nation-building. These leadership and professional groups are precisely those who will rule and administer the nation – it is consistent to remake the curriculum in their image and reconstruct schools as mechanisms for the selection of this national meritocracy.

But the form of this national reconstruction at the level of curriculum, of course, reflects the existing perception and situation of the 'nation'. Plainly at this point in its history the UK nation-state reflects the postwar period of precipitous decline. Since 1945 the large aspirations of the nation-state as a major imperial power, a major player on the world stage, have had to be severely redefined. A particularly problematic aspect of this imperial angst had been how to deal with the plurality of other cultures. This concern is often wished off into the field of 'multicultural studies' but is of course integral to nations of identity and democracy. Alongside this ideological decline has been a savage experience of economic decline. In both of these aspects of decline the British establishment, the elite and the professions, have been implicated. As a result any campaign to reconstruct and revive the nation would have to respond to this experience of precipitous decline. The particular version of nation-building through curriculum is therefore likely to reflect this perception.

The definition of a central curriculum could in fact take a number of forms, but there are two major directions. One version would specify a common set of goals and objectives and certain amount of common content. In this version the teachers and students are allowed some flexibility and a degree of accommodation with local conditions and concerns is both expected and encouraged. This version of central curriculum would have resonated well with the experience of the UK educational system in the twentieth century.

A second version of central curriculum would prescribe in detail what is to be taught, learned and tested. There would be little allowance for choice on the part of teachers and students. One caricature of this version would be the mythical French Minister of Education who could look at his watch and say what every child in France was studying at any given time. This version of common curricula would go against the grain of twentieth-century UK experience.

That the 1987 UK national curriculum in fact represents the second model of central curriculum says a good deal. It reflects the response of a political establishment that has experienced more than four decades of precipitous and accelerating political and economic decline. In such circumstances the replay of paranoid fears within the domain of the school curriculum seems an understandable, if indirect, response.

The unprecedented expansion of powers over the school curriculum has not gone unnoticed or unchallenged. The Cabinet's intention in the report on history has led the Historical Association, an august and conservative body representing history teachers, to question whether the government has any 'constitutional right' for such detailed intervention.

The major expansion of state power over the curriculum and over assessment leads to a parallel diminution in the teachers' power and therefore has associated implications for pedagogy. At one level the new power over curriculum and the battery of tests represent a substantial push to make the details of teachers' work accountable to the state. The experience of the 1960s where teachers were judged to have superior expertise in assessing the educational needs of their pupils has been rapidly dismantled.

Much of the commentary on the new national curriculum has been sympathetic and optimistic about the results of the expansion of state power. For instance, *The Times* carried an editorial on the passing of the 'True Education Bill', which argued 'most important, a national curriculum, accompanied by attainment targets and tests at key ages, will ensure that a large proportion of young people leave school literate, numerate, and more broadly educated than they are now'. Standards in short, will rise. That is because 'teachers will have a clearer idea of what is expected of them' (*The Times*, 22 October 1989).

In short, greater accountability (and less power over definition) leads to clearer objectives and better work habits. This is a crude simplification employing an almost-Taylorist optimism about a strategy for tackling a most complex enterprise. Lessons from previous historical episodes must be treated with considerable caution for we are not comparing like with like. Yet so clear have been the experiences of teachers and taught in the face of previous nineteenth century government interventions in matters of curriculum and assessment that the pious simplifications behind *The Times*'s viewpoint should be severely scrutinized.

A major experiment in state control of school curricula was conducted in the years 1862 to 1895. The teachers were made subject to a system of 'payment by results'. In short the teachers' pay was linked to pupils' results in school examinations. E.C.A. Holmes, a school inspector at the time, has left a detailed commentary on the results of this experiment. He notes that from 1862 to 1895 'a considerable part of the Grant received by each school was paid on the results of a yearly examination held by H.M. [Her Majesty's] Inspector on an elaborate syllabus, formulated by the Department and binding on all schools alike'. The results of this mechanism were clear. 'On the official report which followed this examination depended the reputation and financial prosperity of the school, and the reputation and financial prosperity of the teacher (Holmes 1928: 103).' The Government therefore had established deliberate and detail control over curriculum and assessment and thereby over the teacher and student. Power was thus established, but what of the 'side-effects' on education? On this Holmes was adamant:

> The consequent pressure on the teacher to exert himself was well-nigh irresistible; and he had no choice but to transmit that pressure to his subordinates and his pupils. The result was that in those days the average school was a hive of industry.
>
> But it was also a hive of misdirected energy. The State, in prescribing a syllabus which was to be followed, in all the subjects of instruction, by all the schools in the country, without regard to local or personal considerations, was guilty of one capital offence. It did all his thinking for the teacher. It told him in precise detail what he was to do each year in each 'Standard', how he was to handle each subject, and how far he was to go in it; what width of ground he was to cover; what amount of knowledge, what degree of accuracy was required for a 'pass'. In other words, it provided him with his ideals, his general conceptions, his more immediate aims, his schemes of work; and if it did not control his methods in all their details, it gave him (by implication) hints and suggestions with regard to these on which he was not slow to act; for it told him that the work done in each class and each subject would be tested at the end of each year by a careful examination of each individual child; and it was inevitable that in his endeavour to adapt his teaching to the type of question which his experience of the yearly examination led him to expect, he should gradually deliver himself, mind and soul, into the hands of the officials of the Department, the officials at Whitehall who framed the yearly syllabus, and the officials in the various districts who examined on it.
>
> What the Department did to the teacher, it compelled him to do to the child. The teacher who is the slave of another's will cannot carry out his instructions except by making his pupils the slaves of his own will. The teacher who has been deprived by his superiors of freedom, initative, and responsibility, cannot carry out his instructions except by depriving his pupils of the same vital qualities. The teacher who, in response to the deadly pressure of a cast-iron system, has become a creature of habit and routine, cannot carry out his instructions except by making his pupils as helpless and as puppet-like as himself.
>
> But it is not only because mechanical obedience is fatal, in the long run, to mental and spiritual growth, that the regulation of elementary or any other grade of education by a uniform syllabus is to be deprecated. It is also because a uniform syllabus is, in the nature of things, a bad syllabus, and because the degree of its badness varies directly with the arc of the sphere of educational activity that comes under its control (Holmes 1928: 103–105).

Holmes provided more details of the working of a system of state prescription of syllabus and control of examinations:

> It was preordained, then, that the syllabuses which the Department issued, year by year, in the days of payment by results should have few merits and many defects. Yet even if, by an unimaginable miracle, they had all been educationally sound, the mere fact that all the teachers in England had to work by them would have made them potent agencies for evil. To be in bondage to a syllabus is a misfortune for a teacher, and a misfortune for the school that he teaches. To be in bondage to a syllabus which is binding on all schools alike is of all misfortunes the gravest. Or if there is a graver, it is the fate that befell the teachers of England under the old *régime* – the fate of being in bondage to a syllabus which was bad both because it had to come down to the level of the least fortunate school and the least capable teacher, and also because it was the outcome of ignorance, inexperience, and bureaucratic self-satisfaction.
>
> Of the evils that are inherent in the examination system as such of its tendency to arrest growth, to deaden life, to paralyse the higher faculties, to externalize what is inward, to materialize what is spiritual, to involve education in an atmosphere of unreality and self-deception I have already spoken at some length. In the days of payment by results various circumstances conspired to raise those evil tendencies to the highest imaginable 'power'. When inspectors ceased to examine (in the stricter sense of the word), they realised what infinite mischief the yearly examination had done. The children, the majority of whom were examined in reading and dictation out of their own reading-books (two or three in number, as the case might be), were drilled in the contents of those books until they knew them almost by heart. In arithmetic they worked abstract sums, in obedience to formal rules, day after day, and month after month; and they were put up to various tricks and dodges which would, it was hoped, enable them to know by what precise rules the various questions on the arithmetic cards were to be

answered. They learned a few lines of poetry by heart and committed all the 'meanings and allusions' to memory, with the probable result – so sickening must the process have been – that they hated poetry for the rest of their lives. In geography, history, and grammar they were the victims of unintelligent oral cram, which they were compelled, under pains and penalties, to take in and retain till the examination day was over, their ability to disgorge it on occasion being periodically tested by the teacher. And so with the other subjects. Not a thought was given, except in a small minority of the schools, to the real training of the child, to the fostering of his mental (and other) growth. To get him through the yearly examination by hook or by crook was the one concern of the teacher. As profound distrust of the teacher was the basis of the policy of the Department, so profound distrust of the child was the basis of the policy of the teacher. To leave the child to find out anything for himself, to work out anything for himself, to think out anything for himself, would have been regarded as a proof of incapacity, not to say insanity, on the part of the teacher, and would have led to results which, from the 'percentage' point of view, would probably have been disastrous (Holmes 1928: 106-108).

In fact the experience of this episode of state intervention had long-lasting effects. In 1944 when the Government was drawing up the influential Education Act of that year James Chuter Ede, parliamentary secretary to the Minister, said in a speech to the house:

> ...there is not one curriculum for every child, but every child must be a separate problem for the teacher. The teacher is the servant of the State, and I hope that no one will say that the State should lay down the curriculum of the schools. Some of us were brought up under the old payment-by-results system, and were the time earlier, I could amuse the House with descriptions that some of my Hon. friends know would be no caricature of the way in which State control of the curriculum prevented the development of a wise and sound system of education (Chitty 1988 p. 322).

Holmes and Chuter Ede then warn us of some of the dangers that attended a 'national curriculum and assessment' strategy. But the implications for teachers and particularly pupils are of profound concern. The development of attitudes of 'mechanical obedience' strike at the very heart of the 'democratic' system of governance. This matter assumes great importance at a time when there is widespread comment in the UK about the absence of constitutional rights and the consequent possibility of substantial erosion of 'traditional' rights by more authoritarian government whether of the right (as at the moment) or of the left. The link between national curriculum and mechanical obedience therefore highlights a major problem with regard to the education of pupils with the capacity to be functioning citizens in a democracy. I find the following statement about 'the erosion of British liberty' particularly chilling in this light: 'Britons have been schooled to think of themselves as subjects, not citizens; as people with freedoms granted by government, not with right guaranteed against government interference' (Broder 1989 p. 7).

Seen in this light the political project underpinning the national curriculum assumes a further dimension for the hidden curriculum of the national curriculum is a reassertion of the power of the state in nation-building. This Project is diametrically opposed to the alternative project of educating pupils, from a plurality of cultures, for active citizenship in a democracy. The history of mass mechanical obedience as a bedrock for nation-building is well known, but it leads not to democracy but to totalitarianism.

Conclusion

The introduction of the national curriculum in the UK has been linked to the problems of national economic decline and a belief that curriculum co-ordination will aid a project of national economic regeneration. Behind the rhetorical priority given to economic revival, two other agendas have been discerned.

First, the reconstitution of a traditional subjects-based curriculum. These traditional subjects evoke a past 'golden age' when schooling was selective and people 'knew their station'. A number of empirical studies have pointed up the links between traditional subjects and social class. In both *School Subjects and Curriculum Change* and *The Making of Curriculum*, I have detailed these well-established historical connections (Goodson 1987, 1988). The obsessive presentism of many of the current government initiatives has successfully obscured this deeply-embedded connectedness which is of course relevant to the present and future of the UK as a class society.

In developing this commentary for a global audience, it is important to note the distinctiveness and strength of UK class politics. For instance, in the USA at the moment a debate is underway about defining a national curriculum comprising traditional subjects. However, the intention, at least one important intention, is to provide rigorous academic subject-based courses of study covering curriculum content and form which will appeal to *all* children. Hence, the pattern of state and class-formation in the USA mean that a national curriculum initiative will have sharply different resonances to those in a somewhat obsolescent class-based society like the UK. (This is not, of course, to say that an initiative in the USA will not have powerful implications for matters of class, race and gender). Moreover, the patterns of civic culture, citizenship education and constitutional rights are sharply different in the UK from the USA: So that once again a national curriculum will be likely to affect the two societies differently.

The second agenda in the UK is one of establishing new modalities of control over schooling on behalf of the nation-state. These new modalities will allow detailed control to be exercised over the school curriculum, both in terms of content, form and assessment. In the UK case this would seem a late and somewhat desperate attempt at nation-building, both in terms of nation-state governance and the partial propagation through curriculum of national ideologies, selective memories and images. It would seem possible that declining nations in their post-imperial phase have nowhere to go but to retreat into the bunker of the school curriculum. In this case, in particular, there may well be some lessons for the USA.

References

BOARD OF EDUCATION (1904) *Regulations for Secondary Schools* (London: Board of Education).

BRODER D. S. (1989) 'Mrs Thatcher and the erosion of British liberty', *Manchester Guardian Weekly*, 141 (5).

CHITTY, C. (1988) 'Central control of the school curriculum, 1944–87', *History of Education*, 17 (4), pp. 321–334.

COX, C. B. and DYSON, A. E. (eds) (1971) *The Black Papers on Education* (London: Davis Poynter).

COX, C. B. and BOYSON, R. (eds) (1975) *The Black Paper 1975* (London: Dent).

DEPARTMENT OF EDUCATION & SCIENCE (1983) *9–13 Middle Schools: An Illustrative Survey, The Times*, 22 October 1989 (London: HMSO).

DEPARTMENT OF EDUCATION & SCIENCE (1983) *Teaching Quality* (London: HMSO).

DEPARTMENT OF EDUCATION & SCIENCE (1985) *Education 8–12 in Combined and Middle Schools: on HMI survey* (London: HMSO).

DEPARTMENT OF EDUCATION & SCIENCE (1989) *National Curriculum History Group Interim Report* quoted *Times Educational Supplement* 18 August 1989 (London) p. 4.

EAGLESHAM, E. J. R. (1967) *The Foundations of Twentieth-Century Education in England* (London: Routledge & Kegan Paul).

FOWLER, W. S. (1988) *Towards The National Curriculum* (London: Kogan Page Ltd).

GOODSON, I. F. (forthcoming) *Subjects and Schooling: The Social Construction of Curriculum* (London: Routledge).

GOODSON, I. F. (1987) *School Subjects and Curriculum Change* (London: Falmer Press).

GOODSON, I. F. (1988) *The Making of Curriculum* (London: Falmer Press).

HARGREAVES, A. (1984) *Curricular Policy and the Culture of Teaching: Some Prospects for the Future* (Mimeo: University of Warwick).

HOLMES, E. C. A. (1928) *What Is and What Might Be* (London: Constable & Co. Ltd).

KERR, J. (1971) 'The problem of curriculum reform', in R. Hooper (ed.), *The Curriculum Context, Design and Development*, (Edinburgh: Oliver & Boyd), pp. 178–200.

MOON, B. and MORTIMORE, P. (1989) *The National Curriculum: Straightjacket or Safety Net?* (London: Colophon Press).

ROWLAND, S. (1987) 'Where is primary education going?', *Journal of Curriculum Studies*, 19 (1), pp. 87–90.

RUBINSTEIN, D. and SIMON, B. (1973) *The Evolution of the Comprehensive School 1926–1972* (London: Routledge & Kegan Paul).

RYDER, J. and SILVER, H. (1970) *Modern English Society, History and Structure 1850–1970* (London: Methuen).

13   *Systemic school reform*

Marshall S. Smith and Jennifer O'Day

This analytic essay draws on research about the effectiveness of current education policies as well as observations about developing policy systems in a number of states. The chapter begins with several observations about policy and school-level success, examines current barriers to school improvement and proposes a design for a systemic state structure that supports school-site efforts to improve classroom instruction and learning. The structure would be based on clear and challenging standards for student learning; policy components would be tied to the standards and reinforce one another in providing guidance to schools and teachers about instruction. Within the structure of coherent state leadership, schools would have the flexibility they need to develop strategies best suited to their students. The systemic school reform strategy combines the 'waves' of reform into a long-term improvement effort that puts coherence and direction into state reforms and content into the restructuring movement.

Introduction

The past decade has seen a blizzard of reports, federal and state legislation, and local efforts designed to stem the 'rising tide of mediocrity' in US education. Two US presidents have announced goals, tens of governors have anchored their campaigns on educational improvement, and hundreds of thousands of educators and citizens have spent countless hours in reform efforts across the nation.[1] Moreover, investment in education in real dollars has increased, not only from government sources, but from dozens of foundations, some of which have refocused their priorities to allocate funds to education, as well as from major corporations, which have donated millions of dollars to local schools and districts (Hawkins 1990).

Yet, for all of this effort, evaluations of the reforms indicate only minor changes in the typical school, either in the nature of classroom practices or in achievement outcomes (Fuhrman *et al.* 1988, Clune *et al.* 1989, Mullis and Jenkins 1990). For the most part, the processes and content of instruction in the public school classrooms of today are little different from what they were in 1980 or in 1970 (Cohen 1989 and Cohen in this volume, Cuban 1990). While realization of these disappointing results has prompted cries for greater effort and more money from some quarters, many analysts attribute the meagerness of the results to the very nature of early reform efforts, which they characterize as 'top-down' and 'more of the same'. Initiated by forces outside the schools and mandated by state governments, 'first wave' reforms sought mainly to expand or improve educational inputs (longer school day, increased requirements for graduation, better teachers) and ensure competency in basic skills (graduation tests, lock-step curricula, promotional criteria) (Stedman and Smith 1983; Firestone *et al.* 1989). That they did little to produce meaningful gains in learning may not be surprising since they did little to change the content of instruction, to directly involve teachers in the reform process, or to alter the reigning notions of teaching and learning (Cohen 1990, Carnegie Forum 1986, David *et al.* 1990).[2]

0268–0939/90 $3.00 © 1990 Taylor & Francis Ltd.

Largely in response to these deficiencies in early reform legislation, a 'second wave' of change efforts began building in the middle to late 1980s. This second wave of reform calls for a fundamental rethinking and restructuring of the process of schooling, not a mere bolstering of the existing one. Decentralization, professionalization, and bottom-up change are key concepts, as reformers focus on the change *process* and on active involvement of those closest to instruction (Carnegie Forum 1986, Elmore 1988, Elmore and associates 1990). In this 'new' conception, the school building becomes the basic unit of change, and school educators (teachers and principals) are not only the agents, but also the initiators, designers, and directors of change efforts. In addition to an emphasis on process, student *outcomes* are also key in this new approach. The principle underlying many of the second wave themes – from school-site management to teacher profes- sionalism to parental choice – is the notion that if school personnel are held accountable for producing change and meeting outcome objectives, they will expend both their professional knowledge and their creative energies to finding the most effective ways possible to do so, relevant to the specific conditions in which they work.

Although the second wave is young and as yet involves only a handful of districts and schools, it has already produced an avalanche of ideas, strategies, and structures. Those involved report optimistically that state as well as local leaders of these initiatives 'have succeeded in stimulating new ways of thinking about change inside schools and about leading, managing, and supporting restructuring efforts' (David *et al.* 1990: 39). Unfortunately, the very strength of this new approach may also be its shortcoming. While reliance on school-based initiative (even that stimulated by states) may be more likely to produce significant changes in classroom practice than have edicts from above, a strictly school-by-school approach makes it difficult to generalize such changes from the small number of initially active schools to the well over 100,000 educational institutions in cities, suburbs, and rural areas across the country. Indeed, analysts have found that in general the schools and teachers who are active in the restructuring movement are those who already have a history of reform experience and interest (David *et al.* 1990).

A second problem is related to the first. Although restructuring literature stresses the critical importance of developing complex problem-solving and higher order thinking skills in our youth, achieving this goal requires a major reorientation in *content and pedagogy* as well as in the structure of the educational enterprise. Perhaps more importantly, it requires a reconceptualization of the knowledge and skills we expect our children to learn, and of the teaching and learning process. This in turn will require that existing elementary and secondary teachers learn, and learn to teach, considerable amounts of new material in the physical and social sciences, humanities, and mathematics. Such a reorientation is not likely to happen on a widespread school-by-school basis among educators who have themselves been schooled in a philosophy and settings that embody fact-based conceptions of knowledge, hierarchical approaches to skill development, and a near total reliance on teacher-initiated and teacher-directed instruction. Site-based management, professional collaboration, incentives, and choice may be important elements of the change process, but they alone will not produce the kinds of changes in content and pedagogy that appear critical to our national well-being (Fuhrman *et al.* 1989, Elmore and associates 1990, Clune 1990, this volume).

The purpose of this chapter is to address these issues of the generalizability and the content of productive and enlightened school reform. We will argue that what is needed is neither a solely top-down nor a bottom-up approach to reform, but a coherent *systemic* strategy that can combine the energy and professional involvement of the second wave reforms with a new and challenging state structure to generalize the reforms to all schools within the state. We assume, along with current restructuralists, that if we are to significantly alter student outcomes, we must change what happens at the most basic level of education – in the classrooms and schools. However, we see in this process a more proactive role for the centralized elements of the system – particularly the states – one which can set the conditions for change to take place not just in a small handful of schools or for a few children, but in the great majority.

Our discussion is divided into four parts. First, we present a picture of the organizational goal of the reforms: a successful school. This is followed by an analysis of the administrative, governance, resource, and policy barriers to effective schooling in the USA. In the third section, we pose a strategy for transforming the system at all levels – but primarily at the state level – so that it will facilitate rather than inhibit the improvement of schools on a broad and continuing basis. Finally, we relate this strategy to other issues and proposals currently under discussion in the educational reform movement.

A successful school

If our goal is to improve student outcomes and we believe that to accomplish this goal we must change what happens in the school itself, one obvious place to begin a discussion of strategy is with a picture of the kind of schools we would like to see in the future. While personal images of the 'successful school' will differ considerably in detail, both research and common sense suggest that they will have certain characteristics in common. These include, among other things, a fairly stable staff, made up of enthusiastic and caring teachers who have a mastery both of the subject matter of the curriculum and of a variety of pedagogies for teaching it; a well thought through, challenging curriculum that is integrated across grade levels and is appropriate for the range of experiences, cultures, and learning styles of the students; a high level of teacher and student engagement in the educational mission of the school – not just for the high achievers but the vast majority of students; and opportunities for parents to support and participate in the education of their children (Purkey and Smith 1983).

Beyond – or perhaps underlying – these resources available to the student, the most effective schools maintain a schoolwide vision or mission, and common instructional goals which tie the content, structure, and resources of the school together into an effective, unified whole (Coleman and Hoffer 1987, Purkey and Smith 1983). The school mission provides the criteria and rationale for the selection of curriculum materials, the purposes and the nature of school-based professional development, and the interpretation and use of student assessment. The particulars of the vision will differ from school to school, depending on the local context; indeed, one of the goals of 'choice' advocates is to enable individual schools to establish unique identities and purposes (Chubb and Moe 1990, Elmore 1986). However, if the school is to be successful in promoting active student involvement in learning, depth of understanding, and complex thinking – major goals of the reform movement – its vision must focus on teaching and learning rather than, for example, on control and discipline as in many schools today (McNeil 1986). In fact, the very need for special attention to control and discipline may be mitigated considerably by the promotion of successful and engaging learning experiences. For these experiences and this focus to be fully successful, however, new research suggests that they must embody a different conception of content and different pedagogical strategies than those in conventional use (Resnick 1986, Lampert 1988, Peterson 1987).

Finally, the literature on effective schools has found that successful schools have not only a vision but also an atmosphere – or 'school climate' – that is conducive to teaching and learning. Minimally, this means freedom from drugs, crime, and chaotic disruptions within the school and a sense of mutual respect among educators and students (Purkey and Smith 1983, Coleman and Hoffer 1987). More positively, it means the construction of a school workplace for teachers and students that both contains the resources and embodies the common purpose and mutual respect necessary for them to be successful. This same literature as well as that on school restructuring further suggests that the common vision and positive school climate can best be promoted by a system of shared decision-making and shared responsibility where the instructional staff, in particular, have an active voice in determining the conditions of work. This might involve shared control not only over how the school is organized in time and space to advance learning and teaching, but also over such things as the hiring of new staff and the expenditure of school discretionary funds.

While other commonalities may exist among successful schools, let us assume that these characteristics – a schoolwide vision and school climate conducive to learning, enthusiastic and knowledgeable teachers, a high quality curriculum and instructional strategies, a high level of engagement, shared decision-making, and parental support and involvement – taken together form the core of the successful school. The obvious question then becomes, why aren't more of our schools like this? Certainly we can all think of a handful, or probably more, of schools that exemplify this quality of education – that have coherent and challenging instructional programs, that genuinely engage all or at least most of their students, and that promote high achievement in their students. Yet these remain the exception rather than the rule in US education.[3] Their very existence represents tremendous commitment, expertise, and effort on the part of school and perhaps district personnel. Moreover, even with all that effort, the stability and future of such schools are at base quite fragile. Changes in principal, staff, school population or district policy may serve to undermine a hard-built but nonetheless tenuous foundation. The question remains: why are these schools so exceptional and so vulnerable?

It is our contention that systemic barriers in the organization and governance of our educational institutions inhibit such schools from developing in most areas and serve to marginalize and undermine successful schools when they do emerge. We also argue that even the very best of these schools are not accomplishing what they could do if (a) the organizational environment were sufficiently supportive; and (b) the instructional content were truly directed toward complex thinking and problem-solving. In the next section we discuss the systemic barriers to effective schooling in the USA. Then, in the third section, we present one possible strategy for developing the supportive organizational environment and challenging content needed for the next generation of students.

Systemic barriers to educational change

Most traditional explanations of poor schooling in the USA focus on low standards and inadequate resources. Yet the history of school reform demonstrates that even when standards are raised and more or better resources are allocated, little lasting change occurs in the classroom (Cuban 1984, 1990, Elmore and McLaughlin 1988). Recognizing this, some critics argue that the teaching profession itself is inherently conservative and resistant to change, or that the increasing diversity of the US student population makes broad-based achievement gains unattainable. Of course, such reasoning ignores the exciting examples of creative and successful schooling situated in unfriendly environments among students most often identified as 'at risk' for school failure. We present here a somewhat different perspective on school improvement. We argue that a fundamental barrier to developing and sustaining successful schools in the USA is the fragmented, complex, multi-layered educational policy system in which they are embedded (Cohen 1990, Fuhrman 1990).

This system consists of overlapping and often conflicting formal and informal policy components on the one hand and, on the other, of a myriad of contending pressures for immediate results that serve only to further disperse and drain the already fragmented energies of dedicated and well meaning school personnel. On the formal policy side, school personnel are daily confronted with mandates, guidelines, incentives, sanctions, and programs constructed by a half-dozen different federal congressional committees, at least that many federal departments and independent agencies, and the federal courts; state school administrators, legislative committees, boards, commissions and courts; regional or county offices in most states; district level administrators and school boards in 14,000 school districts (with multiple boards and administrative structures in large systems); and local school building administrators, teachers and committees of interested parents. Every level and many different agencies within levels attempt to influence the curriculum and curricular materials, teacher in-service and pre-service professional development, assessment, student policies such as attendance and promotion, and the special services that schools provide to handicapped, limited English-proficient and low-achieving students.

We do not mean to imply here that structure and regulations are not necessary ingredients for a well-functioning public system. Indeed, we believe that they are absolutely necessary both to create a coherent environment within which schools and school professionals can best perform their jobs and to protect and promote the interests of those most needy in the society. Properly developed and organized, a consistent set of guidelines could create a nurturing structure within which schools could legitimately be held accountable for providing effective education to all students. Indeed, all of the energy currently generated and used by the multiple levels and responsible parties of our educational governance system would be wonderful if it were coordinated (even loosely) and focused on a set of coherent, progressive, long-term strategies to achieve challenging common goals and outcomes.

Unfortunately, it isn't. While there is considerable communication, there is little purposeful coordination. The policy generation machines at each level and within each level have independent timelines, political interests, multiple and changing special interest groups, and few incentives to spend the time and energy to coordinate their efforts. And in the same sea as this governmental octopus are independent for-profit and not-for-profit corporations generating curriculum materials, tests, and teacher and administrator training programs – corporations whose bottom lines are to stay in business or to represent their respective interest groups, not to maximize quality for the majority of students.[4]

The structural convolutions of the formal and informal policy systems are only the beginning, however. Political pressures on new administrators and elected officials to produce measurable or at least memorable results in short periods of time lead to a 'project' mentality. A new classroom management system, an in-service day on the 'left and right brain', a new 'laboratory' filled with computers but little appropriate software, a tougher attendance policy, a new evaluation and accountability office and policy are all familiar concepts to the nation's teachers. Federal and state legislatures often have a similar mentality; there seems to be great political capital in developing 'new' approaches and programs portrayed to address major social problems. Similarly, universities and corporations get into the act – 'adopt-a-school' programs, gifts of computers, time off for employees to teach in schools, all are points of light that blink on and off. Some of these efforts are wonderful, but most are short-lived 'projects', soon to be replaced by a different 'concept', a new panacea. Though many have a significant effect on the particular school for a short period of time, few leave much of a lasting trace. To many long-term employees of the schools they are properly viewed as marginal and political.

Where does this uncoordinated energy, this short-range perspective, and this multiplicity of purpose lead? On the one hand, they help to produce the overall 'mediocrity' in US education that was criticized by so many observers in the early 1980s. Indeed, the fragmented policy system creates, exacerbates, and prevents the solution of the serious long-term problems in educational content, pedagogy, and support services that have become endemic to the system. Our teachers are badly trained, our curricula are unchallenging, and our schools are inhospitable workplaces. Many of these problems have been the target of periodic reform measures, including those passed in the last decade. Although generally identified as problems of quality or quantity in resources, these deficiencies ultimately must be attributed to the lack of a coherent strategy for allocating the resources we do have or for overcoming problems in both quality and quantity when they arise.

A second result of the fragmentation we have described is to fortify the basic conservatism that exists in any very large governmental system. By and large, educational practice in this country is not very different from what it was half a century ago (Cuban 1990). Teachers 'close their classroom doors' and teach as they were taught. The multiple influences and short-term policy perspective create a protective confusion that allows conventional practice to prevail. When change occurs on a large scale basis it is incremental and reinforces the existing condition. The first wave of reform in the 1980s, for example, can be viewed as 'intensification' of current practice (Firestone et al. 1989). The emphasis was on extending the school day, on increasing course requirements, and on greater amounts of testing. The changes were quantitative, not qualitative, in nature.

Similarly, the sweeping movement toward 'basic skills' in the late 1960s through the early 1980s emphasized the teacher-directed, skills-oriented, rote and factually-based curriculum and pedagogy that now dominate schooling in the USA (Smith and O'Day in press). One might argue that the basic skills movement is an example of a successful reform – one for which there was a generally common vision and relatively common practice, a reform which was therefore able to permeate the entire system. This movement, however, was 'successful' precisely because it reinforced the already existing norms of the system, because the teachers were comfortable with the content, because the pedagogical implications were known, because the teacher development institutions did not have to change, because the curriculum materials were easy to develop and market, and because the prevailing assessment instruments were generally appropriate. This comfortable situation allowed many of the different policy components of the system to line up in support of the movement – commitment to the movement did not threaten their domain. In effect, the basic skills movement represented an affirmation of the most conservative elements of the system.

In sum, we have argued that fragmented authority structures and multiple short-term and often conflicting goals and policies have created dual conditions within the present educational system: mediocrity in resources and conservatism in instructional practice. Before suggesting how the system might overcome these problems, we think it important to elaborate how the conditions are reflected – and in fact reinforce one another – in each of the major components of the educational system.

Curriculum

Although varied somewhat in topic and form, the curricula typically found in American schools share certain characteristics. With notable exceptions, today's typical school curriculum contains little depth or coherence, emphasizing isolated facts and 'basic skills' over opportunities to analyze and solve problems (Goodlad 1984, Cohen 1989). Teachers and students alike find the curricular materials uninteresting and unimaginative; and both students and their future employers complain that school learning bears no connection to real-life experience or problems. It is not surprising that such curricula lead to a pedagogy that rarely demands active involvement from the learner: there are relatively few hands-on activities or group activities, few opportunities for cooperative learning, little and generally unimaginative use of computer technology, and little tolerance for activities that do not have a 'right' answer or that demand sustained and imaginative problem-solving.

In part, the poor quality of US curriculum and instructional practice can be attributed to the fragmented policy system described earlier. Consider the development and selection of instructional materials as just one example. Diffuse authority structures and multiple goals within the system foster mediocrity and conservatism both in the publishers' supply of curricular materials and in the demand generated by local educators. On the supply side, publishers respond to the lack of consistency and the market-driven approach to materials development in two ways. First, they attempt to pack all the topics desired or required by different locales into the limited space of the typical textbook. As a result, in content areas like science, literature, and social studies, textbooks end up merely 'mentioning' topic after topic, covering each so superficially that the main points and connections among them are often incomprehensible to the student. In addition, and again particularly in history and social studies texts, publishers deal with conflicting demands and controversial issues by watering down content, evading sensitive areas, and choosing the least common denominator among the various viewpoints. This approach often leaves the student with so little information or context that he or she is unable to construct his or her own analyses or form his or her own judgments (Tyson-Bernstein 1988, Newmann 1988).

These criticisms are not new and a few publishers have made attempts to incorporate greater depth of material and internal coherence into their textbooks. The sad thing is that in the absence of a consistent demand for such change from the majority of educational consumers – i.e., state and local educators – these attempts will remain isolated and short lived. Nor is such consistency in consumer demand likely, given the current fragmentation of the system. Educators must respond to the same conflicting demands and lack of common goals as do publishers. This fact leads many districts, schools, and teachers to unintentionally support and perpetuate mediocrity in content by choosing curricula that are comfortable (familiar), easy to work with pedagogically (fragmented, factual, simple), and that lead to the most manageable classrooms (again, fragmented, factual, easy to monitor).

Indeed, as ironic as it may seem, this situation has actually contributed to the development of a common instructional practice and, as described earlier, a common basic skills curriculum. Many analysts and curriculum scholars have attributed the instructional focus on basic skills to a 'factory model' of schooling, which emphasizes control and easy monitoring of students, and to rigid hierarchical models of learning (e.g., McNeil 1986, Peterson 1989). Such models, they argue, are clearly outmoded, inconsistent with what we know about how people learn, and unable to lead to the type of thoughtful educated citizenry we require. However, while educators and observers have recognized the inadequacies of these models and the curricula they engender and have written extensively about them, the fragmentation of the policy system makes substantial, widespread change in instructional practice and the curriculum virtually impossible.

What is particularly disturbing is that, with regard to the higher-level cognitive goals now proposed, these basic skills models may further disadvantage those students already at risk in our schools. While an emphasis on isolated facts and skills in unlikely to foster complex thinking skills among students generally, less-advantaged students often lack a surrounding environment that helps them fill in the gaps and draw the connections necessary to construct complex meaning in such situations (Peterson 1986). The problem is exacerbated in lower income areas where poor quality curricula combine with low expectations, with the result that many of these students are locked into failure.[5]

Of course, among the over *one million* classrooms in the USA, there are many exceptions to this general pattern. Innovative teachers or schools may experiment with particularly creative and promising curricula and instructional practices, often with considerable success. But as we observed earlier, most innovations find little support within the system and become marginalized or die out altogether. The same is true for large-scale curriculum reform movements such as the 'new math' or the science and social studies curricula spawned by Sputnik. In part, this is because programs developed in one sector (e.g., curriculum) are rarely linked to the extensive necessary changes in other sectors (e.g., the content of wide-scale assessment instruments, in-service and pre-service teacher development).[6] And we know that if teachers do not understand or do not support particular curricular changes, those changes are unlikely to take hold in the schools.

Professional development

Despite program after program to improve the quality of teacher education, the preparation of educational personnel in the USA remains wholly inadequate. Typically, neither pre-service nor in-service professional development programs are of high quality or are well coordinated with the demands and needs of the K–12 system.

> Few elementary school teachers have even a rudimentary education in science and mathematics, and many junior and senior high school teachers of science and mathematics do not meet reasonable standards of preparation in those fields. Unfortunately, such deficiencies have long been tolerated by the institutions that prepare teachers, the public bodies that license them, the schools that hire them and give them their assignments, and even the teaching profession itself (AAAS 1990: 13–14).

The average elementary school student in the USA receives only 20 minutes per day in science instruction (Raizen and Jones 1985). And, in mathematics, where school regulations require specific minimum amounts of instructional time, the content and form of instruction used by most elementary school teachers minimizes the demands on their understanding of mathematics. For example, whereas many students in other industrialized nations receive introductory instruction in algebra and geometry in grades K–8, few of our students are so challenged (Crosswhite *et al.* 1985, McKnight *et al.* 1987). This should not be surprising – teachers, like everyone else, tend to shun tasks that they feel unable to perform well. Essentially, many elementary and secondary school teachers do not have the confidence in their understanding of science and mathematics to enable them to do a creative job. This pattern is repeated for literature, history, and writing throughout the K–12 grades.[7]

These are not new criticisms. Yet, they persevere. Why? For pre-service professional development there are a variety of proposed reasons. One is that the quality of prospective teachers is weak and declining. Teaching is a low prestige and low paying profession, and women, who once saw teaching as among their few professional alternatives, now have occupational opportunities that did not exist in the past. According to this theory, the solutions are to increase the standards for certification while simultaneously paying new teachers higher salaries, thereby encouraging more talented people to enter the profession. A second reason given is that the content and pedagogy of the curriculum in many schools of education are particularly weak. Critics are especially disdainful of courses that focus on pedagogical strategies. One proposed remedy here includes eliminating schools of education and turning away from pre-service pedagogical training altogether, preferring instead alternative routes to certification. A second proposed remedy focuses on reforming teacher education by limiting teacher training in schools of education to only graduate programs (Holmes Group 1986, Darling-Hammond with Green 1990).

Both these criticisms have some truth and the proposed solutions may have some limited merit. Typically, however, the solutions address the quality of teachers and teaching without consideration of the overall context. For example, raising beginning teachers' salaries to be more competitive with other professions does appear to attract higher scoring candidates and to increase their length of stay in teaching (Murnane and Olsen 1989, 1990). However, while such increases may enlarge the pool of prospective teachers somewhat, they do not guarantee that incoming faculty will have the kinds of knowledge and skills required in today's schools. Moreover, if the demand is for teachers with particular knowledge or expertise – such as science and mathematics – across-the-board salary increases turn out to be a very costly solution that may not sufficiently alter the supply in the desired direction (Levin 1985).

With regard to the second set of proposals, eliminating schools of education and pre-service pedagogical training in favor of alternative certification strategies has unknown merit – we do know that pre-service pedagogical training is even more extensive in other nations than ours, nations such as Japan where students achieve at higher levels than in the USA (McKnight et al. 1987). Concentrating teacher training at the graduate level might be a strategy to raise the prestige of teachers, but judging from existing data, it offers little promise of a major change in their effectiveness (Smith and O'Day 1988). Finally, none of these strategies addresses the lack of content knowledge of many prospective teachers.

An alternative approach to the problems in professional development emphasizes the lack of fit between what prospective teachers are taught and are expected to know, on the one hand, and the knowledge and skills they need to perform their jobs, on the other. This disjuncture between teacher knowledge and teaching practice begins with the entrenched condition of teaching in the nation's post-secondary system. Most of the nation's teachers learn the content of the disciplines in the arts and sciences schools apart from the schools of education within colleges and universities. The courses offered in these settings are not designed for people who will need to teach the disciplines to elementary and secondary students in the future, and they are typically taught in a lecture style, fact-oriented fashion that works only because the students know they need to pass the course to move their life ahead. In many of the larger post-secondary institutions, courses in mathematics, science, and history typically have examinations with short answer questions that can be graded by machine, while literature courses require papers of only a page or two. Thus, neither the content nor the pedagogy of the higher education institutions serves to prepare future teachers well. This is a particularly difficult problem to address because there are no incentives for professors in many colleges and universities either to alter their teaching approach or to teach courses designed to meet the needs of future K–12 teachers.

The colleges and universities are not solely to blame for this situation. As many critics have pointed out, the licensing and certification systems used by the states typically represent a weak attempt to ensure that prospective teachers have the knowledge of content and skill in pedagogy to do an effective job in the classroom. Indeed, there is often little planned relationship between the content and skills required of prospective teachers and the curriculum of the schools. Part of this, of course, is due to the fact that there is no common curriculum beyond the emphasis on basic skills. The most widely used examination, the National Teachers Examination, has no predictive validity. Its face validity is predictive on the argument that its content is derived from current practice and is broad enough in scope to be representative of practice in all of the states in the Union. However, basing the content on current practice is inherently conservative, for it reinforces and legitimizes contemporary mediocrity. Moreover, creating a test with a content so broad (and consequently, shallow) that it is not inappropriate for any state or district surely makes it practically valueless for all of the states and districts (Smith and O'Day 1988, Haertel 1987).

The in-service professional development situation is little better than the pre-service training. One reason for continuing education is the requirement that individual teachers have to obtain a certain number of graduate credits over a period of time to maintain their job and to receive salary increments. After tenure is reached, obtaining a few credits every few years is often the only educational hurdle teachers must clear to keep their positions. Because of scheduling problems and a lack of coordination between higher education institutions and K–12 school systems, the courses teachers take for individual development and advancement are typically badly coordinated with the demands of the teachers' jobs. Their content often depends more on the intersection of the teachers' schedule and the interests of professors in the local higher education institutions than on the needs of their K–12 students.

Other professional development experiences are organized by the school or district and are generally more closely attuned to the specific needs of the schools. These sessions, however, are severely limited in scope and duration, frequently lasting a day or less only once or twice a year. Only rarely are they of sufficient depth and scope to give teachers the experience necessary to make major changes in their approach to instruction. Too often, these experiences are focused on a new innovation or technique which bears very little relationship to the curricula of the schools. Even when the development activity is directly related to the introduction of a new curriculum, the training generally suffers from a lack of depth and time. Perhaps as a consequence of these badly organized experiences, conventional professional development programs show few positive and lasting effects. And, even more damaging to prospects for productive change, the federal, state, and local budgets for in-service professional development are tiny and extremely vulnerable to budgetary constraints (Guskey 1986, Little et al. 1987, McLaughlin 1990).

We do not want to leave the impression that there are no productive in-service experiences. The reports from tens of thousands of teachers who have been to NSF summer institutes in mathematics and science, from the many teachers who have participated in groups such as the Bay Area Writing Project, and from many of the teachers who have used teacher centers all over the nation attest to the power that in-service experiences can have on individual teachers. One key to making these experiences successful has been that they are focused on content that is relevant to the teachers' classrooms and on ways of presenting that content; another is that they are often of sufficient length to be a powerful intervention. Unfortunately, in many instances of powerful individually-oriented in-service experiences, the teachers return to an environment that is not particularly supportive of new curricula or methods of teaching.

This has led some schools to develop an alternative strategy in which the entire faculty of the school or of a particular department in the school will participate collectively in an in-service training experience of their own choosing, based on their particular curricular needs. There is some evidence that such a strategy, which combines the attributes of collective decision-making by the teachers with a focus on relevant content, has a positive effect on student achievement (Purkey and Smith 1983).

Accountability assessment systems

Accountability assessment systems in the USA suffer from a variety of problems. One is that many of our policymakers and educators are hoplessly confused about the purposes of testing in the schools. Different parts and levels of the system use the same assessment instrument for different and often conflicting purposes. In this chapter we are most interested in the use of assessment as an instrument of accountability to gauge the quality of schools and school systems, not in the more directly pedagogical uses of tests to diagnose, assess, and guide the progress of individual students, or in the use of tests to evaluate particular programs or projects. Each of these uses is important, but it is critical to keep the distinctions among them clearly in mind for, more often than not, the same instrument or instruments should not be used for multiple purposes.

Another problem is that the lack of a common curriculum within most states and many districts makes it impossible to construct a broadly-used, valid accountability assessment instrument. If the content of the curriculum purposefully varies across jurisdictions, so logically should the assessment instrument that is intended to assess how well the school or district meets their curricular purposes. Though there is no commonly adopted curriculum, most states and school systems are heavy users of one or more of a small set of norm-referenced, multiple choice, standardized tests – tests that each purport to be appropriate for most variations of curriculum.[8]

A final issue is that many school people take seriously their school's and district's performance on the standardized tests and use it as a gauge of the quality of their instruction. Schools often use individual test performance for student placement, while districts and states use aggregate student performance for school and system accountability. Thus, the tests have high stakes, not only for students but also for teachers, schools, and system administrators. As a consequence, teachers – generally with encouragement and even pressure to do so – will frequently adjust their teaching to improve test scores, not by teaching the subject matter in more creative and productive ways but by tailoring their instruction to the form and nature of the standardized tests (Fredericksen 1984).

Such an influence might be productive if tests were constructed to measure complex thinking and problem-solving and thus served to move curriculum and instruction in the direction of developing these skills. Of course, this would require that teachers know and be able to teach the content and skills assessed by the tests. Indeed, challenging tests or examinations used for accountability purposes might be a particularly powerful intervention if teachers had the content and pedagogical knowledge, the curriculum materials, and the support services that would enable them to 'teach to the challenging tests'. In the absence of such knowledge and materials, however, the gap between the content of the tests and the capacity of the teachers to teach the content could be extraordinarily frustrating and possibly counterproductive.

At present there seems to be little overall conflict between the capacity and pedagogy of the teachers and the content of the tests. In general the most commonly used assessment instruments, like textbooks and other curricular materials, are designed to reflect the least common denominator in a fragmented and ill-structured system. Standardized, norm-referenced tests are developed to be so broad and general that they can assess learning across a wide range of curricular purposes. Their form emphasizes broad coverage of unconnected facts, and the ability to work very quickly on multiple choice, limited time-span, unrelated problems that have only one right answer. It is therefore not surprising that apparently substantial and progressive changes in curriculum produce little effect on such tests or that scores may be more accurate indicators of social class background than of what is actually learned in the classroom (Hawley 1984, Fredericksen 1984, Resnick and Resnick 1985, Archbald and Newmann 1988).

Over the past 20 years many states have tried to address these inadequacies by adopting a second form of assessment instrument: criterion-referenced, minimum competency examinations. While these tests are developed with a clear curricular conception, they typically contain many of the same problems in form as the standardized norm-referenced tests, and they have the additional problem of focusing only on very low level skills and standards. Thus, they cannot appropriately be used to assess the overall curricular aim of a school, if the school has one. Instead, for very low-achieving students, schools often focus their instruction on the content of the minimum competency tests, thereby reinforcing their already low aspirations for these students.

The main point here is that both types of tests exist, in part, because of a lack of coherence in the curricular policy of state and district school systems. Standardized norm-reference tests, with their general all-encompassing nature, are used for accountability purposes because there is no common set of curricular goals among schools and systems; criterion-referenced, minimum competency tests are based on such restricted and elemental sets of curricular goals that it is easy to imagine that all districts and schools could meet their demands, as has been the case in Florida and Virginia. Moreover, both tests, when used for accountability, serve to reinforce an instructional emphasis on facts and skills rather than problem-solving and performance in meaningful situations. The multiple choice and timed format reinforces quickness and recognition rather than thought and recall. These tests thus fortify the tendency of the system to be conservative and mediocre. Indeed, with a few exceptions, such as the Advanced Placement exams, the International Baccalaureates, and the New York Regents, there are no widely-used examinations in this country which either clearly assess curricula in a rich form or stand as a serious intellectual challenge for the student.

Support services

A critical element of the second wave of reform is the issue of how to enhance the professionalism of teachers. Sykes (1990) argues that professionalism will be enhanced as teachers are given more and greater control over resources within their schools.[9] Certainly, it will be impossible for major changes in the quality of schooling to take place if the quality of teacher workplaces continues to be as shabby as now.

This issue has a variety of dimensions. First, there are few resources and services in the system to develop, support, or maintain professional creativity and commitment. Few schools have libraries for teachers, few offer time off for reflection and development of new ideas for teaching, few provide serious support for new teachers, few provide the means by which teachers can experiment with new ideas. On a more mundane level, many schools –

particularly those in areas with high concentrations of poor people – are terrible workplaces. Teachers have no space to meet and talk with other professionals, no or very little access to telephones, few if any photocopiers to reproduce class materials. When papers, books, and pencils are missing, teachers must go without or supply these materials from their own resources, often receiving little respect or reinforcement from their supervisors for their efforts. Generally teachers do not have a private place outside of the classroom to meet with parents, and there is no place for parents to meet and talk or to wait during the school day.

The extraordinary thing about these conditions is that it would take very little money to overcome them in most of the schools in the nation. The only really costly item would be time off for reflection and development of new ideas. The remainder primarily require creative and energetic leadership on the part of principals and central office staff. Unfortunately, instead of basing their actions on what will maximize the quality of schools and on principles of good administrative behavior, principals and district administrators often fall back on rules and regulations to rationalize the status quo.

Frustrated high expectations for creative work in such a difficult environment lead many educators to focus on survival. Ironically, the fragmentation of the system actually assists in this effort by operating as a kind of filter, protecting teachers from some of the otherwise deafening policy noise. Of course, policy demands do get through, often in a form that is both incoherent and divorced from the needs and context of the teacher. It is not surprising, under these conditions, that many teachers simply close their classroom doors and do their own thing. Nor is it surprising that even widely acclaimed reform efforts have little long-term effect on classroom practice. Educational institutions have truly become 'loosely coupled' systems in which instructional practice is only weakly tied to organizational policies, and the system as a whole remains conservatively bound to the processes and content of the past.

If the new reform movement is to have a lasting effect on what happens in the classroom, it will thus have to overcome the current fragmentation of the system and provide a coherent direction for change and the resources to accomplish those changes. The next section discusses one possible strategy for such systemic reform.

A strategy for systemic reform

We suspect that there are many possible paths to a coherent, productive, and progressive educational system. The one we present here seeks to combine the vitality and creativity of bottom-up change at the school site with an enabling and supportive structure at more centralized levels of the system. While recognizing that change must occur at all levels of the system and that the ultimate goal is to transform what happens at the school and in the classroom, we have chosen for the purposes of this paper to focus most of our attention on the role of the state apparatus in this process. We do so for several reasons.

First, most of the current restructuring literature focuses exclusively on the school and district levels of the system. When states are mentioned at all, it is usually in the context of providing waivers from various regulations currently in force. Yet, if we wish to influence more than a few schools or districts at a time, the state is a critical actor. Second, during the past 20 years, most states have gradually amassed greater authority and responsibility over their educational systems as their share of the educational budget has risen, as the economy and productivity of the state have been seen to be more and more dependent on its educational system, and as issues of equity and fairness in the distribution of resources and services among districts became an important part of the nation's agenda.

Finally, the states are in a unique position to provide a coherent leadership, resources, and support to the reform efforts in the schools. States not only have the constitutional responsibility for education of our youth, but they are the only level of the system that can influence all parts of the K–12 system: the curriculum and curriculum materials, teacher training and licensure, assessment and accountability. In addition, the states, at least in theory, could productively affect the way in which the state system of higher education might operate to help the K–12 educational system. Finally, because of the size of the markets they represent, the states are also in the best position to effectively leverage other aspects of education that are outside the system itself, such as textbook and materials development.

We do not mean to suggest that such leadership will come easily to all or even to most states. The nation's tradition of local control had often led to passive, conservative behavior by state departments of education. Party politics and conflicting agendas in state legislatures and governors' offices often impede collective action. And states differ considerably in their technical capacity to implement many of the suggestions we make below. Yet there is a basis for optimism. More and more, policymakers are beginning to understand the interconnectedness of the system, and cooperative endeavors such as the Council of Chief State School Officers and the Educational Commission of the States provide mechanisms for sharing technical resources among states of varying capacity.

A unifying vision and goals

In order for a state to fulfill this unique role – that is, for it to provide a coherent direction and strategy for educational reform throughout the system – it must have a common vision of what schools should be like. Any vision will have a variety of facets. One straightforward conception is that all of our children should be able to attend a 'successful school', in the terms we described earlier. Another view of the vision suggested here is that schools within a state should operate within a coherent set of policies and practices that encourage and support a challenging and engaging curriculum and instructional program. State vision statements would clearly go far deeper than these general statements.

It is important to emphasize that underlying any coherent conception will be important sets of values. We see two such sets of values as particularly significant. One set is the collective democratic values critical to our society: respect for all people, tolerance, equality of opportunity, respect for the individual, participation in the democratic functions of the society, and service to the society. A second set has to do with the tasks and attitudes of the teacher and learner – to prize exploration and production of knowledge, rigor in thinking, and sustained intellectual effort. We believe that these values already exist in a latent form in the minds of most Americans, and especially teachers, when they think about the educational system. But they need to be awakened and to permeate and guide the system and the schools. Held in common, these values can help nourish and sustain over time environments in the schools that can intellectually stimulate and engage ALL children in the way that we should expect. The crisis rhetoric that has prompted many of the recent reforms often has not been productive in this regard. It has instead fostered project-oriented, 'magic bullet' solutions that satisfy immediate political ends, without substantively changing the core of the educational process. The new reforms must cut deeper; to do so they need to be derived from a deeper system of shared beliefs.

Broad conceptions and values, however, will not be enough. We need goals that can be communicated and measured if we are to mobilize the political support necessary to sustain the reforms over time. A carefully selected set of goals and a related system of indicators would give those within the system and the general public a sense of purpose and direction and a basis on which to evaluate progress. Some of the goals could address desired changes in the nature or quality of educational inputs, such as the quality of the teaching force or of the curriculum used in the schools.

Other (and we argue more powerful) goals would be those related to students. Statewide student outcome goals may be an extension and particularization of the national goals developed recently by the governors. They could cover more than academic achievement, including such things as ensuring school readiness, developing students' self-worth and promoting collective responsibility. We believe that the goals should focus primarily on the core functions of the system; that is, on teaching and learning. To meet the demands of the future, however, they must go well beyond the 'basic skills' goals of the 1960s, '70s and early '80s. They must provide a standard that challenges the public and the educational system to prepare our youth to grapple thoughtfully with those problems that defy algorithmic solutions and to be skilled and confident learners in school and later on. Moreover, the goals and indicators must address not only the average level of opportunity and student achievement in the state but also the variation. Justice requires that the goals of the state promote equality as well as quality.

Given an agreed upon direction for reform, we suggest a two-pronged approach for attaining the established goals. The first prong of the strategy is to create a coherent system of instructional guidance, the purpose of which is to ensure that all students have the opportunity to acquire a core body of challenging and engaging knowledge, skills, and problem-solving capacities.[10] Implementing this will require overcoming the fragmentation of the system through coordinating three key functions affecting instruction: curriculum, pre- and in-service teacher training, and assessment. The actual coordination of these functions, we argue, can best be handled on the state level, but it must be linked to the second prong of the strategy: an examination of the responsibilities and policies of each level of the governance structure so that all levels operate in support of each other and of the implementation of the reforms.

A coherent system of instructional guidance

The first step in developing a coherent system of instructional guidance is to work toward agreement on what students need to know and be able to do when they leave the system. The second is then to maximize the probability that all or most students will acquire the desired capacities by ensuring at the very least that they have the opportunity to do so – that is, by ensuring that students are exposed to the requisite knowledge and skills through the highest quality, most appropriate human and material resources possible. For the statewide instructional guidance system to work would thus require coordination among state curriculum frameworks, the more specific curricula of the schools, pre-service and in-service professional development and teacher certification, and system level assessment and monitoring mechanisms. Each of these aspects of the system is discussed briefly below.

Curriculum frameworks: The basic drivers of the instructional guidance system would be curriculum frameworks which set out the best thinking in the field about the knowledge, processes, and skills students from K–12 need to know. The frameworks would be developed for at least the core curriculum areas: reading and language arts, English, mathematics, science, social studies and history, foreign languages and the arts. The frameworks must provide a viable and compelling alternative to the 'basic skills' fact-based orientation that is the norm in US schooling today. They should emphasize depth of understanding, knowledge construction through analysis and synthesis of real life problems, hands-on experiences, and the integration of content and pedagogy. Highly-qualified teams of teachers and disciplinary experts should develop the frameworks which should then be continually updated and reviewed by similarly qualified expert panels. Possible prototypes for such frameworks are already being developed in mathematics by the National Council of Teachers of Mathematics (NCTM), the Mathematics Board of the National Research Council (NRC) and the National Assessment of Education Progress (NAEP), in the sciences by the American Association for the Advancement of Science (AAAS), in reading by NAEP, and in these and other areas by the departments of education in several states.

It is important to distinguish the notion of core curriculum *frameworks* from the more specific curricula actually taught in the schools and classrooms. The purpose of the frameworks is neither to legislate a particular pedagogy nor to specify short-term curricular scope or sequence. Rather, the frameworks should set out desired intellectual curricular themes, topics, and objectives in sufficiently long-range chunks (e.g., four-year blocks) to allow for a maximum of flexibility and creativity at the local level while still establishing the clear instructional direction and goals for the system as a whole. One aspect of this flexibility may be to open the door for more depth in areas of local choosing. For example, if the elementary science framework is organized around 30 great ideas in science, each student by the end of the eighth grade may be expected to have a general acquaintance with 15–20 of these with some greater depth in the remaining 10–15. Schools may choose the areas for deeper coverage based on local conditions, resources, and interests.

California is illustrative of a state that has already developed quite progressive curricular frameworks in a number of areas. These frameworks set out the expectations that teachers, business people and professionals in the field (historians, scientists, mathematicians) have for the content that K–12 students should all learn. Unlike the minimum competency requirements of the 1970s, these expectations reflect the problem-solving and higher-order thinking requirements proposed by the many recent reform reports. The frameworks do not detail a day-to-day, a week-to-week, or even a month-to-month curriculum for teachers to follow. Instead, for the most part, they describe the knowledge, skills, and attitudes expected of students at the end of certain periods of time, such as fourth, eighth, and eleventh grades.

The frameworks should provide a structure within which to organize the other important educational components. Teacher professional development programs, in-service and pre-service, and teacher licensing standards should be designed to insure that the teachers are well prepared to teach the content set out in frameworks. Textbook and curricular material used in the schools should be congruent with the curriculum frameworks. Test instruments used to assess pupil progress and to hold schools and teachers accountable should reflect the content of the frameworks. In short, the frameworks should provide a way of organizing a coherent instructional guidance system.

Two critical conditions are necessary to ensure that the system works to help provide high quality instruction. The first condition is that the frameworks are of the highest quality possible and that they are continually and carefully improved. The frameworks should embody an integrated, challenging, and engaging conception of the subject matter of the schools. If they are of sufficiently high quality, we believe that they would command the respect and enthusiasm of capable teachers. The second condition is that local school personnel are given the freedom within the framework to interpret and implement instructional strategies that most effectively meet the needs of their students. As with the International Baccalaureate, the state frameworks would set out the general content and skills that students need to know, but it would remain the job of local school personnel to decide how best to organize and teach the material.

School curricula: The states must provide sufficient support to ensure that schools and districts have both the flexibility and support they need to construct strong and locally responsive curricula within the structure provided by the state content frameworks. Schools must have the ultimate authority to select and/or revise and develop curricular materials best suited to their students and teachers. However, the state has both the responsibility and the potential leverage to ensure that there is an adequate supply of high quality textbooks and other materials that are in line with both the letter and the spirit of the state curriculum frameworks, so that teachers in every school or district do not have to reinvent the wheel for every subject and every grade.

There are a number of mechanisms available to the state to stimulate the supply of high quality instructional materials. One is to establish a statewide adoption system that emphasizes both quality and coordination with the frameworks. States would then – either singly or in conjunction with other states with similar frameworks – stimulate and/or require textbook publishers to meet those guidelines. A number of states already use this approach, but in our view they need to be much tougher and more rigorous than they are now; textbook manufacturers can and should be held to higher standards of quality and coherence. The state could also try to stimulate a cottage industry to provide imaginative innovations for teaching the core concepts, popularize particularly successful local endeavors, and encourage the development and use of technological software – computer, video, and multi-media – in support of the frameworks. The local districts could choose from among these resources although schools and districts could also be free to select or develop alternative curricular materials as long as the outcome objectives are being met.

Professional development: States must ensure that both new and practicing teachers have the content knowledge and instructional skills required to teach the content of the frameworks. This means, for example, that elementary school teachers will need to know well *and* know how to teach the mathematics, literature, science, reading, and history that are set out in the curriculum frameworks for K–6 or K–8 students. At the high school level teachers must know well *and* know how to teach the content set out in the frameworks in the subject matter areas they are expected to teach. The key here is that the curriculum frameworks operate to structure what we minimally expect teachers to know and be able to teach as well as what we expect students to learn. In most states this would require drastically reforming the pre-service and in-service professional development systems. These systems must provide an adequate foundation both in the content set out in the subject-matter frameworks and in a variety of pedagogical strategies for facilitating student acquisition of that content.

Pre-service professional development: The low quality of pre-service teacher education has proven to be one of the most intractable problems in the entire educational system. Critics find lacking both the subject matter training, generally the responsibility of schools of arts and sciences, and the pedagogical and professional training, the responsibility of schools of education. Prospective elementary teachers are seen as underprepared in the disciplines and badly served by non-rigorous pedagogical and professional training. Prospective secondary teachers are viewed as too narrowly trained in their content fields and as having only limited opportunities to obtain training in instructional strategies. For both elementary and secondary prospective teachers, the supervision of practice teaching is seen as weak. Finally, in general, the teaching of undergraduates is seen as unimaginative and pedantic, thereby providing a poor model for the future teachers.

Over the past decade a substantial number of schools of education have initiated changes in their curriculum and requirements, but few have succeeded in establishing their programs as exemplary courses of instruction. Beyond the individual campuses the formal attempts to improve the quality of teacher training typically depend on the regulation of inputs. Neither state regulation of required courses nor the efforts of independent program certification agencies like NCATE has had much effect on the content or form of pre-service education.

The most optimistic signs of improvement of teacher preparation come from efforts of the teacher preparation profession, such as the Holmes group. These ventures have had success in raising the quality of discussion and in encouraging member institutions to conduct self-examinations and often to alter their programs to provide more rigorous training in the content and pedagogical areas and in practice teaching.

To date, however, teacher preparation reforms proposed by the professional groups and most others have conformed to the traditions of many higher education institutions. They have thus been fiercely independent of educational reforms at the K–12 levels. We know of no major national reform effort that has deliberately addressed the substantive needs of teachers beyond listing general course and degree requirements. Even in a state such as California, where there are well specified curriculum frameworks for grades K–12, there is little formal linkage between the content of the frameworks and the state's requirements for teachers.

Given this independence of higher education from K–12 education, we suspect that the main leverage for improving pre-service education is likely to come not from attempts to regulate pre-service higher education requirements but from the state's authority to screen and credential new teachers. In the context of the systemic reforms proposed here, the goal is to ensure that teachers come out of teacher preparation institutions with at least the knowledge and capacity to teach well the content set out by the state frameworks.

The cleanest way to do this from a policy perspective is to establish what teachers need to know and be able to do and then to assess for licensing purposes their ability to use this knowledge and competence. We are not suggesting a higher passing level on the current or future NTE. We are suggesting a strong, progressive, carefully developed performance assessment, one based primarily on the state's K–12 curriculum frameworks and designed to evaluate the prospective teacher's knowledge both of content and of multiple pedagogical strategies for teaching the content to students of varying abilities and backgrounds. We are also suggesting the establishment of standards that are sufficiently challenging to ensure that those who pass have at least the content and pedagogical knowledge required to be a successful teacher. We come to these suggestions reluctantly, for we would rather rely on the good will and commitment of the higher education institutions and the professional community to reform teacher education than on the blunt instrument of outcome accountability.

Nonetheless, such a strategy continues to place a great deal of authority and professional discretion in the hands of higher education institutions, both the faculties of arts and sciences and of education. Our strong sense is that, if enacted, the strategy would result in increased standards and requirements for prospective teachers. We would expect prospective teachers to have the experience of delving deeply into content through a disciplinary major, while also having a broad enough academic experience to be able to teach competently in the other areas of their future responsibility. We would also expect many institutions to alter their courses and perhaps even their own pedagogical approaches to help insure that their graduates succeed on the new state licensing examinations.

In-service professional development: In-service professional development must be a key component of the overall instructional guidance system for two reasons. First, there is no question that the majority of the current teaching force has been inadequately trained in at least some of the areas of the frameworks for which they would be responsible. Since most of these teachers will remain on the job during and after the implementation of the new frameworks, they will need to acquire the knowledge and expertise necessary to teach adequately the new content. Second, a well-designed professional development system, based on building networks of teacher cadre and trainer–practitioners, can serve another less obvious function in the system. It can foster both the knowledge base and the leadership experience necessary to help empower the teaching force, thus further liberating the initiative and creativity of 'bottom-up' reform.

While the state cannot simply establish such a system, it can encourage its development by influencing both the supply of and demand for in-service programs and materials that are of high quality and meet specifications derived from the curriculum frameworks. Furthermore, the state could work from a systematic, long-range plan to reach and retrain all of the teachers within the state, and to develop and maintain a viable in-service professional development system. We would imagine that a strong system would have a coherent set of opportunities, both for the development and refinement of individual teachers and for working on improvement strategies with groups of teachers such as high school departments or the entire staff of elementary schools.

To influence the supply of quality professional development programs and materials, states can allocate resources either directly into program development or into incentives for independent organizations and sub-units to generate such programs. For example, incentives may be given to universities, museums, libraries, and other non-profit educational groups to develop programs tied to the frameworks or to districts and schools to establish professional development schools, teams of trainers, and so forth. The state could provide incentives and resources to develop a cadre of practicing teachers in the schools who could serve as lead teachers, mentors, and in-service trainers to assist other teachers in mastering the content required by the frameworks. Special funds for professional development should be available for individual teachers and sets of teachers for particularly innovative ideas related to the core curriculum and for areas outside of the core curriculum including human development. Finally, the state could require any professional development programs supported by federal funds to be fully coordinated with the frameworks.

States can also influence teacher demand for and use of professional development opportunities in a variety of ways. For example, if teachers and schools are held accountable for improving student outcomes on assessment instruments that are based on the frameworks, it behooves the teachers to be knowledgeable in the relevant areas of the frameworks and in effective pedagogy. Another available tactic might be to use the state licensing system to encourage professional development. For example, after a set period of time following the institution of the frameworks (e.g., five years), the state might require that all teachers (both practicing and new) pass a state licensing exam based on those frameworks.

This short discussion does not do justice either to the importance of this area or to the substantial institutional changes in schools and universities required to create effective continuing professional development systems within states. A great deal of inertia and skepticism will have to be overcome. Our belief is that productive and substantial improvement is extremely unlikely in the present fragmented and ill-structured policy environment. By contrast, the kind of coherent and systemic reform strategy we have suggested here could provide the structure and purpose necessary for states, universities, and local education agencies to work together to develop a progressive and high quality continuing professional development system.

Accountability assessment: States must construct and administer high quality assessment instruments on a regular basis to monitor progress toward achievement goals for accountability purposes and to stimulate and support superior instruction. The new state assessments, like the teacher training systems and the curriculum, would be based on the state curriculum frameworks. The purpose of the assessments would be to provide information about the progress of the state, districts and schools in achieving the goals established by the state. These data would also be used to hold the various parts of the system accountable and to help stimulate curricula and instruction in the schools to achieve the state's instructional goals.

In most states the approach to assessing student outcomes will have to be completely overhauled if the instructional guidance system is to operate effectively. The rhetoric in the US is that we demand educational accountability of our schools and that student achievement tests are the central measures by which we should hold teachers, principals, and superintendents accountable. In fact, we do a terrible job of holding anyone accountable. In the typical situation, facing falling test scores, our local and state policy makers threaten, cajole, re-emphasize 'basic skills', and adopt a new program as a panacea. Occasionally, a principal or superintendent is removed as a scapegoat, but rarely is the system altered in any significant fashion. In the worst cases, the pressure to demonstrate improvement leads some educational personnel intentionally or unintentionally to manipulate the accountability system. For example, school, district, and state administrators may delude themselves and the public with bogus test scores increases generated by using precisely the same tests year after year.

Much of the reason, we suspect, for this unproductive behavior is that most school people and much of the public realize that it is impossible for assessment instruments to truly serve a monitoring and accountability function unless they measure what the schools are actually supposed to teach. Yet, as we argued earlier, this is not the case in the US. The main accountability instruments used in most places are standardized norm referenced tests, which are purposefully divorced from the curricula of the schools. To a substantial degree this problem would be eliminated in states that adopted the kind of content-driven systemic reform strategy proposed here. The assessment instruments would be constructed to measure student achievement in the content set out in the state curriculum frameworks. In this regard the form of the new assessments, which would replace the old accountability instruments, would be much like that of the International Baccalaureate or Advanced Placement examinations.

Another criticism often raised of current accountability assessments is that schools, teachers, and students become overwhelmed by all the testing. One way to prevent this from happening while also providing for adequate monitoring of the system would be to give the examinations at three levels – say at the fourth, eighth and eleventh grades. The information from these assessments would feed back to the system, and local districts and even schools could be held accountable for the results. Systems and schools could, for example, be responsible for demonstrating either an across-the-board high level of achievement for their students or a steady growth over time in that achievement. Assessment for accountability could also be combined with incentive measures for meeting or surpassing objectives.[11]

It is important to note that the purpose of the examinations will affect the way in which they are administered. If the principal purpose is to hold institutions (schools and systems) accountable, the burden of testing could be reduced by assessing samples of students, rather than the entire population of the three grade levels. If there are student related purposes in addition, however, such as to motivate students to study by making examination results important to their futures, then the entire population of a grade would have to be assessed. The issue of whether to make such examinations have 'high stakes' for students, as they do in many other economically developed nations, is too complicated to address in this paper. High stakes imply that student opportunities would be influenced by their performance on the examinations. This poses major tradeoffs, it seems to us. On the one hand are the gains that might be accrued by having examinations that motivate students to study. On the other hand, the flexibility and second chances that characterize the US educational system might be jeopardized by a system of high stakes student examinations.

Whichever decision is reached by states about the role of the examinations in individual student lives, a major reform in the assessment systems along the lines we have described is critical to education.[12] Assessment instruments are not just passive components of the educational system; substantial experience indicates that, under the right conditions, they can influence as well as assess teaching (Fredericksen 1984). While current standardized and minimum competency tests reinforce teaching toward an emphasis on isolated facts and basic skills, state-of-the-art examinations based on well-designed curriculum frameworks, could help encourage instruction toward higher level goals: depth of knowledge, complex thinking, an ability to respond to problems and to produce results. Examinations, designed to assess the content of the curriculum frameworks, could foster this goal by giving teachers and schools a clear idea of what they should be striving for and a way to monitor their success in getting there. Thus, if students taking a science examination are expected to produce science – that is, to write, to analyze text, to manipulate the necessary tools, to solve problems – teachers are more likely to emphasize these capacities in their classes. This, of course, assumes that the teachers have the necessary content and pedagogical knowledge to do so, but as stated earlier, student assessment can also motivate teachers to seek out relevant knowledge through appropriate professional development opportunities. In addition, allowing for choice among examination questions, as in the current AP examinations, would allow for variation in school program, teacher expertise, and student interest.

A restructured governance system

Much of the current literature on school restructuring and teacher professionalism is based on the notion that centralized policies regarding curriculum and instruction generally serve to undermine the school personnel's sense of authority over their own program. In posing the need for a coherent state system of instructional guidance, we recognize the tension that exists between centralized policy decisions on the one hand and professional discretion on the other. We argue, however, that if states can overcome the fragmentation in the system by providing coordination of long-range instructional goals, materials development, professional training, and assessment, they can set the conditions under which teacher empowerment and professionalization, school site management, and even parental choice can be both effective and broad-based. Indeed, what we propose is an interactive and dynamic relationship between increasing coherence in the system through centralized coordination and increasing professional discretion at the school site.

Thus, while schools have the ultimate responsibility to educate thoughtful, competent, and responsible citizens, the state – representing the public – has the responsibility to define what 'thoughtful, competent, and responsible citizens' will mean in the coming decade and century. One way to picture this relationship is through the analogy of a voyage. The state, through the curriculum frameworks and in consultation with teachers and district personnel, provides a description of the ultimate destination of the journey. Teachers and other school people then have the primary responsibility to chart the course, assemble the necessary provisions and crew, and pilot the ship. Should the state attempt to take over from a distance the steerage of the vessel, it is likely to run aground, never reaching its goal. The state may assist, however, by helping to ensure the availability of high quality provisions, accurate navigational equipment, and a well-trained and capable crew. Such is the intent of the instructional guidance system proposed in the previous section.

The governance structure, then, should define the responsibilities of the various levels in the system in order to ensure that the changes sought in the content and outcomes of instruction are actually manifested in classroom practice. Since the success of this enterprise depends ultimately on what happens in the school, we take the school as the starting point in the governance structure and work backward from there, elaborating the responsibilities at the other levels to support instruction in the school.

Governance at the school building level: Schools obviously have many responsibilities and must meet those responsibilities under a wide range of conditions. Our primary focus here is on instructional guidance to enhance achievement in the areas laid out by the state's goals. In this regard the primary responsibility at the building level would be to develop a stimulating, supportive, and creative environment to maximize student achievement in the areas of the goals. A positive climate and atmosphere, a high level of respect between students and staff, and a set of strategies that help ensure that all students identify with the school in a positive fashion are all important factors in helping to motivate the students and staff. These conditions come from hard work and a shared commitment by the staff to make the school a productive and rewarding workplace where teachers are given the responsibility and support that they need to be effective. The restructuring literature and the older literature on effective schools indicate three practical ingredients that are important in this regard (Purkey and Smith 1983 and 1985, Cohen 1983, Elmore and Associates 1990).

The first ingredient is a staff of well-trained professionals. Under the system proposed here, the school would have the primary responsibility to bring together a staff of professionals who could use their knowledge and experience to follow the best practices appropriate to their students to meet the state goals. This implies that the selection of staff, inservice strategies, curriculum (within guidelines), and pedagogies should be done at the school site in response to local conditions and student needs. School staff should also be responsible for developing a system of goals that are based on the local school conditions within the general framework of the state and local district goals.

A second ingredient for a productive workplace is an internal governance structure that enhances the capacity of teachers to carry out their professional tasks and achieve the goals of the school. These structures will vary from school to school, depending on the content, but research suggests that several aspects of the governance structure may be particularly important. One of these is that teachers should have an important decision-making role. Since they are the closest to the students and have primary responsibility for their learning, the teachers should be in the best position to decide how to design the educational experiences of those students. In addition, it is important to structure teachers' time and responsibilities to allow for collaboration, planning, reflection, and professional development. It is also desirable to allow for flexibility in organizing student learning time, as most effective pedagogical practices (as demonstrated by research) require this sort of flexibility (e.g., smaller units, flexible time allocation for different learning tasks, cross-age tutoring and cooperative learning, interdisciplinary and thematic approaches, and ungraded or multi-grade classrooms). Finally, schools should develop mechanisms for parental involvement in school and in the education of their children (David 1990, Sykes 1990).[13]

Third, schools require hardware and resources for the building to be a productive, professional workplace for teachers and other educational personnel. A place to work and confer with each other and with other professionals, a place to do work quietly, access to phones, computers and library facilities are essential if we wish to attract and retain competent teachers.

While these three conditions are integral to much of the literature on restructuring and 'bottom-up' change and thus are thought to be inimical to centralized authority structures, it is our contention that they in fact underscore the need for systemic reform of the sort discussed here. The three conditions can not be met by schools without support from district and state agencies. Most teachers, at present, do not have the knowledge, skills, and time necessary to do a competent job carrying out their roles in a shared governance system or in jointly developing curricula that are integrated across grades within a school. In-service professional development, higher quality curriculum materials, and enhanced support from the district and state will be necessary. Schools, particularly schools within large districts, operate within a formal and informal network of rules and regulations that can either enhance or diminish the opportunities of the schools to serve their students well. Governance systems at the district and state levels as well as at the school level need to be structured to enhance, rather than detract from, the instructional efforts of the schools. The increased clarity in goals and direction, commonly understood curriculum frameworks, coordinated, high quality curriculum materials, and professional development programs that are part of the state systemic reforms can provide the necessary structure.

Governance at the school district level: In the type of system we advocate here, local school districts would need to establish a clear set of ideas about where they fit into the overall educational structure. This means establishing a balance between school purposes and state purposes without usurping either. The district might establish a set of long-range achievement and other goals that embellish the state goals – progressive districts might add such things as student participation and local service goals. It would be critical for districts to be parsimonious on this score, however, for too many goals can be distracting to schools.

The main responsibility of the local district should be to provide resources and a supportive environment for the schools to carry out their task of educating all of the district's children to meet the state and district goals. One thing that this means is that districts should work to reduce central bureaucracy in areas where centralization is primarily in service of administrative standardization of educational matters. Districts should review and alter as necessary those policies that have educational consequences and that might inhibit innovative and effective school-based instructional approaches. As the schools move to take greater responsibility for establishing their own curricular and instructional strategies, district policies such as uniform class sizes, rigid time requirements for teaching certain subjects and courses, and conformity in the use of textbooks should be eliminated.

A second, important role for districts is to ensure that the most needy under their jurisdiction are fairly treated. The distribution and utilization of common and base budget resources must be equitable across the district and the use of special resources from federal, state and local funds must be integrated and administered in a way that maximizes opportunities for the needy.[14]

For districts to effectively fulfill their roles in this restructured system will require changes in the way the various groups within them relate to one another. Three primary local groups interact to establish much of district policy: the central district administration, the school board, and the union. These groups must work in concert in order to provide adequate support to the schools to work within the structure established by the state goals and instructional guidance system and, simultaneously, to give the professionals within the schools the authority and resources to do their job effectively. This does not mean that the traditional roles of the groups should be forsaken, but it does mean that each of these groups must understand the overall system and strategy and that they must discipline themselves to give their top priority to ensuring the long-range quality of the teaching and learning processes within schools.

One point of necessary discipline concerns the establishment of long term goals and strategies that, together with the state goals, would shape the important decisions of the district. For these goals to operate effectively, the superintendent and the school board must have the will to reject the get-rich-quick 'project mentality' described earlier. That is, they must be able to eschew most of those apparently attractive policies and projects that crop up each year promising short-term results. Similarly, school boards and the superintendent need to work toward strategies that ensure policy continuity rather than disruption and that give schools the steady nourishment that they need to improve; one example of this might be a two- or three-year budget. In general, the efforts of the superintendent and the school board should be directed toward making the educational core of the system work better not just in the immediate period, but over the long haul.

A second point is that the various actors in the district must work to support the efforts of the schools and their staffs in teaching the content of the frameworks and in applying their professional expertise to the specific goals, conditions, and children in their schools. In the case of the unions, this means focusing their attention on a broad definition of workplace conditions. If the union emphasis in contract negotiations is only on increases in salaries and benefits and on requiring standardized practice in schools across a district, it will be very difficult for the district to give the necessary responsibility and autonomy to the school site to allow the school staff the freedom to develop a creative and productive instructional environment. In the case of district level personnel, supporting teacher professionalism and discretion may mean a change in how they carry out their supervisory roles. For example, as the schools and their staffs gain responsibility and authority, district curriculum and instructional supervisors will have to give up much of their apparent authority over curriculum and instructional matters (Purkey and Smith 1985).

This discussion, together with our consideration of school governance, reflects much of the current writing and thinking about 'restructuring schools' (Elmore and Associates 1990). The difference between the typical discussions of 'restructuring' and our formulation is in the role of the state. Where the state is ignored in much of the restructuring literature, we have argued that it is a critical partner in any long-term reform.

Finally, it would be Pollyannaish of us not to acknowledge that many districts will have difficulty in altering their procedures and modes of behavior in the manner we suggest. In some cases the talent is not presently available. In other instances the central administration is simply resistant to significant change. This latter condition is particularly prevalent in many of our large districts. These are important considerations which threaten any major educational reform. Our belief, however, is that part of the reason for the intractability of central bureaucracies in large districts is that the districts lack the coherent vision and direction that might result from the systemic reforms we suggest in this paper. To an extent, then, the state reforms would increase the chances for important changes to occur at the district level.

Governance at the state level: Just as the schools operate within the immediate context of their districts and draw much of their support from them, so too the districts operate within the structure provided by states. The present strength and scope of this structure varies greatly across the nation – from states that have almost total control over funding and that exercise considerable control over the curriculum to states where local control remains prominent. We have presented an argument intended to rationalize and legitimate state authority to create a coherent statewide instructional guidance system. We have argued that the states are in a key position for policy intervention because of their unique position to influence all aspects of the educational system. Since most of this paper has focused on developing a coherent strategy at the state level, little needs to be added here about the content of that strategy.

It is important, however, to make some observations about policymaking at the state level, for the greatest deterrent to an improved school system in the USA may well be the conflicting and politically motivated squabbles at the state level among the variety of agencies which have authority over aspects of the state educational system. In many states there are three independent and aggressive institutions: the state department of education, the governor's office, and the legislature. Each has its separate policy offices and separate, generally loosely structured, agendas. Within the state legislature, alone, there are often two, three, or even more such agendas. The multiple agendas, most of which are political and some of which are substantive, are each typically supported by vigorous lobby groups. The agendas come into conflict over resources and rise and fall in prominence, with the result being that no agenda is well served either in the short-run or in the long-run. Perhaps the most important single change in the educational governance system in many states would be to move the policy debate to a point where it is considering the substantive – and to a lesser extent the political – aspects of alternative, well-formed, and long-term policies and strategies. We obviously believe that the coherent strategy we have argued for deserves consideration.

Systemic change and the reform environment

We have tried to indicate how systemic state-initiated reform and school-based reform (restructuring) could be combined to create something with considerably more chance of succeeding than either type of reform carried out independently. In concluding, we believe it important also to show how this proposed dual reform strategy relates to three other aspects of the present political reform environment.

Educational equity

The educational reforms of the 1980s have been primarily concerned with increasing the quality of education. This concern has detracted attention from the efforts in the 1960s and 1970s to provide greater equality within the educational system, particularly for minorities and the poor. Only recently has there been a partial return to concerns for the less advantaged in our society as the nation has become aware of the growing number of children in poverty and the tragic condition of schools in the nation's inner cities. Our question here is 'what would be the effect of a systemic reform of the sort proposed here on the most needy in our states?'

In another article (Smith and O'Day 1990), we argue that the gains that have been made by African-American and low-income children in reducing the achievement gap have been due in part to a variety of changes in social and economic conditions, including decreasing levels of poverty in the 1960s and '70s, increases in parental education, and desegregation in the nation's schools, particularly in the South. We also argue that the national emphasis on basic skills in the 1960s and '70s contributed to reducing the gap by helping to equalize the quality of education offered to students of different backgrounds. This emphasis was spurred by the Great Society, fueled by the test score decline, and reinforced by minimum competency tests adopted by many states. The basic skills movement focused attention on a factual, skills-oriented conception of knowledge and a view of the learner as a passive receptacle. It fit within the fragmented educational governance structure effortlessly because it was easily understood by politicians and placed little demand on teachers or the system for new learning or special resources. It represented a mediocre and conservative (and therefore politically safe) conception of curriculum and instruction.

The basic skills emphasis is now being challenged in many local districts and states which have instituted reforms emphasizing higher order thinking and a more challenging curriculum. While these proposed reforms are exciting and promise higher levels of learning and more complex skill development for those students involved in them, it is important to recognize that they could also place minorities and the poor at a new disadvantage because the less powerful in the society are typically the last to benefit from state and district generated reforms – if they benefit at all. Districts and schools with large numbers of poor and minority students often have less discretionary money to stimulate reform, less well-trained teachers, and more day-to-day problems that drain administrative energy.

We concluded in the earlier paper that, in this context, a state- or nationally-based instructional guidance system would provide greater opportunity for ensuring that a change toward this new conception of the curriculum and instruction is available to all groups, more or less equally. Unless the curricular reforms are buttressed by a coherent state system that links teacher training, teacher certification, the curriculum, and testing together into a structure within which we can legitimately hold schools and districts everywhere accountable, we will surely enlarge the differences that continue to exist between the quality of instruction available to rich and poor, minority and majority. And unless we have common curricula and a common set of expectations for all children, with both the resources and the local flexibility to meet those expectations, the achievement gap will again swell.

Choice

Over the past few years there have been a substantial number of school choice plans suggested and implemented in the nation (Elmore 1986). Most recently, the idea of a full-blown voucher system has be revived (Chubb and Moe 1990). We do not hold out great hope that there will be dramatic improvement in the quality of the system from choice plans. The reason for our pessimism is that the 'reform' will change only the governance and financing of the schools – the quality of the potential teachers, the curriculum, and the assessment instruments will not be addressed.

Others have argued and will continue to argue that a market system in education generated by choice among schools will operate to change these factors. At best, this is a problematic and long-term hope. At worst, it belies the ever-ready survey data that show that most parents are pleased with their schools, and that many parents value the convenience of a nearby school more than they are disturbed by a report of poor teaching in it. Moreover, it seems clear that even in a 'fair' system of choice, the more advantaged in the society will have the extra opportunity – to travel further to a chosen school, to gather more information about the possible choices, and to have more time to evaluate the quality of each option. Finally, a full-choice system runs the risk of schools being established by entrepreneurs, interested in making money rather than in improving the quality of children's education.

Though we do not believe all of the problems of a full-choice system would be ameliorated by a systemic reform of the sort proposed here, we do suggest that this strategy could provide a structured environment to help control many of the negative aspects, and even enhance the positive aspects of a full choice model.[15] The state curriculum frameworks would establish a protective structure that would help ensure that all schools were attempting to provide a challenging and progressive curriculum. The teacher training reforms and the stimulation of curriculum materials by the state would help make high quality resources available to the schools. Perhaps of most importance, the state examinations based on the curriculum frameworks would provide valid data about student outcomes to help parents and students make their choice among schools.

This would leave school personnel free within the structure provided by the curriculum frameworks to create the most effective school possible. Their responsibilities would include designing and implementing the curriculum and instructional strategies of the school, establishing the role of extra-curricular activities, and creating the climate of the school including that manner in which the students are treated and motivated. Our sense is that it would be these characteristics as well as average examination scores that would be most important to parents in selecting schools for their children. The systemic reform would provide an environment within which there could be substantial variation among schools on these conditions, but which at the same time would engender across schools a structure of common and challenging curricular goals and expectations.

Teacher professionalism

A common criticism of state reforms, particularly curricular reforms, is that they diminish the sense of professionalism, and, therefore, the effectiveness of teachers by restricting their autonomy and authority to control the content of instruction in their classroom (McNeil 1986, Sykes 1990). In certain circumstances – when centralized, required curriculum is detailed, oppressive, and mediocre, as it is in those states that have mandated a mundane conception of basic skills – we suspect the effect on teachers is very stifling.

But what we are arguing for here is something very different from this common conception of a centralized curriculum. As we imagine them, the curriculum frameworks would not spell out the day-to-day, week-to-week, month-to-month, or even necessarily the year-to-year curricula for the schools. They would set out bodies of knowledge and skills with which students should become familiar and competent over fairly large blocks of time, such as four years. This would require teachers and groups of teachers within the schools to design and organize their own curricula and instruction in such a way as to maximize the achievement of their youngsters. The system that we are suggesting would give far greater responsibility and autonomy to the teachers, individually and collectively, than do, for example, the Advanced Placement curriculum frameworks.

Moreover, part of the power of a coherent system, such as the one we have proposed, is that the knowledge and skills contained in the framework become the basis for that 'expert knowledge' component of professionalism that has proved so elusive for teachers (Sykes 1990). The 'restructuring' literature has addressed the need, as have we, of giving teachers authority and responsibility and the resources in their workplace to exercise that responsibility. The specification of content and skills in the frameworks provides a structure within which teachers can acquire the knowledge and skills to become experts in their profession. Too often, we suspect, in areas such as science, history, and mathematics, the field of knowledge is so daunting that teachers – especially elementary school teachers – will learn and teach only the very minimum requirements. As their lack of expertise is exposed, this reduces both the teachers' respect for themselves and the respect they receive from others. In the context of the frameworks, however, the field of knowledge is defined and, we believe, thereby more manageable. Moreover, the requirement that the teachers know and be able to teach the content of the frameworks before they can be licensed would give them the incentive to master the material.

Understanding the content of the frameworks and knowing how to teach it would lead to two important conditions conducive to enhancing the professionalism of teachers. The first is simple – such knowledge would set tomorrow's teachers apart from almost every one else in society. Few in our society know anything about plate techtonics, or the importance of 'error' in science, or Bayes Theorem, or could write a coherent three-page essay about the economic determinants of the American revolution – indeed, this lack of generalized knowledge in such areas is the very problem the recent reforms are trying to address. Even fewer know how to effectively teach these concepts and skills, either to children or to adults.

Knowing how to teach the content and skills of the framework would lead to the second condition. Professional dialogue about common problems in the profession is part of the mysticism and the excitement of being a professional. If all teachers in a state are expected to teach the challenging material set out by the frameworks to all, they suddenly have a common field within which to share professional information and strategies. Just as the surgeon shares a secret knot she has developed, so will the elementary school teacher share his strategy for teaching children about the pull of gravity on the tides.

Our conclusion, thus, is that the professionalism of teachers will be enhanced by the systemic state reform strategy that we have proposed. Of Sykes's (1990) four components – authority, regard, resources, and knowledge – we have addressed three, authority, resources and knowledge. Our belief is that regard from others will follow the attainment of the other components but that it requires, first, regard from within. We believe further that such self-regard will best be nurtured in a system that both defines and fosters teachers' knowledge and thus their ability to perform competently the task of their profession.

Conclusions

We have argued that a chaotic, multi-layered, and fragmented educational governance system in the USA has spawned mediocre and conservative curricula and instruction in our schools. The state reforms of the early and middle 1980s have not had a significant effect on the quality of education, and the present restructuring movement, though promising, does not seem destined to have an impact on very many of the over 100,000 schools in the nation. We have proposed a dual strategy to promote an increase in the quality of education for all schools. The strategy draws on the authority and responsibility of the state to provide a systemwide structure of educational goals and content within which all schools and districts might 'restructure' to maximize the quality of their curriculum and instruction.

The state would design and orchestrate the implementation of a coherent instructional guidance system. The cornerstone of the system would be a set of challenging and progressive curriculum frameworks. The frameworks would be developed through a collaborative process involving master teachers, subject matter specialists, and other key members of the state community and would be updated on a regular basis to reflect our changing understanding of the teaching and learning process. The frameworks would provide a substantive structure for a dynamic curriculum that requires active and sustained learning by students. The state would be responsible for establishing a set of challenging student achievement goals, based on the frameworks. Teachers and other local school professionals would be responsible for designing and implementing the curriculum and pedagogical strategies for their schools within the overall context of the state frameworks, to best meet the needs of their particular students. The frameworks would also provide a substantive structure for teacher professional development and for student assessment. In order for teachers to be able to teach the content embodied in the framework, they would need to be systematically exposed to it during pre-service and continuing professional development experiences and should show command of the material and the ability to teach it before they receive a state license to teach.

These actions would require the state to exercise some long-needed leadership to alter and improve the state higher education professional development systems. In addition, the state would hold the local schools and school districts accountable for making progress toward attaining state student achievement goals by employing very high quality examinations developed, using the state curriculum frameworks as templates. Finally, the states would provide technical assistance to communities needing assistance in implementing and meeting the state goals. We have provided some detail on approaches and tactics that states might use to accomplish these aims, but we are mindful that a great deal more than we have suggested would be required to implement the kind of coherent and high-quality strategy that we have proposed.

A state-initiated instructional guidance system would establish a framework within which schools might implement high quality educational programs. Such a system alone, however, is not enough. To alter the curriculum and instruction in schools will also require that the educational governance system be coordinated in its efforts to give local schools the resources, freedom, and authority to provide high quality instruction for their students. The state has constitutional responsibility for ensuring educational quality and opportunity throughout all of the districts within its boundaries, and it has authority to influence parts of the system (such as pre-service teacher training) that are totally out of the purview of local education agencies and schools. Local school people have the responsibility and opportunity to make professional judgments and to implement effective ways to educate their students. The trick is to establish a governance structure where the strengths of the two are maximized to provide the best possible education for all children. We have proposed a number of changes in the orientation of the present governance system to meet this end. In essence, we have suggested putting coherence and direction into the state reforms and content into the restructuring movement.

Acknowledgements

The authors thank Elissa Hirsh for her assistance in preparing this paper. Work on the paper was supported in part by the Center for Policy Research in Education, a consortium of the Eagleton Institute of Politics at Rutgers University, the University of Wisconsin at Madison, Michigan State University, and Stanford University, under grant number G-0086-90011 from the Office of Educational Research and Improvement, at the US Department of Education. The views expressed do not necessarily reflect those of the sponsoring agencies.

The ideas in this paper have been influenced by the authors' interactions with a wide variety of people, but especially by discussions with our colleagues in the Center for Policy Research in Education (CPRE), Martin Carnoy, William Clune, Daivd K. Cohen, Richard Elmore, Susan Fuhrman, Michael Kirst, Henry Levin, Milbrey McLaughlin, Janice Patterson, Andrew Porter, and Gary Sykes. We have also profited from discussions with Jane David, Mike Cohen, Bill Honig, Alan Ginsburg, Albert Shanker, Gordon Ambach, and Marc Tucker. Finally, David K. Cohen, Charles Kolb, Ramsay Selden and David Tyack all gave us insightful comments on an earlier version of this paper. Naturally, none of these thoughful people necessarily share all of the ideas in this paper or are responsible for our errors of fact or logic. A brief form of some of the ideas in this paper were shared with the Advisory Council for the Science and Engineering Education Directorate of the National Science Foundation over two years ago (Smith 1988). NSF recently released a Request for Proposals to states to design and implement systemic state reforms in support of science and mathematics education (Rothman 4, April 1990). A brief description by Bill Honig of the California reforms, which are similar in some respects to the reforms proposed here, appeared in the *Education Week* (Honig, 28 February 1990). Finally, many of the ideas suggested here have been contained in talks made by Smith (e.g., AERA April 1990).

Notes

1. Darling-Hammond and Berry (1988) estimate that states considered over 1000 pieces of legislation on teacher policy during the first five years of the reforms; see also Firestone *et al.* (1989).
2. A few states are exceptions to these generalizations. South Carolina (South Carolina Board of Education 1989) and California (Honig 1990), for example, both report important recent gains in student achievement, attributed to the reforms. In both of these cases, the state has made a concerted effort to influence the instructional process within the schools.
3. Researchers and journalists who have observed many US schools are struck by the deadening mediocrity of most. See, for example, Powell *et al.* (1985) and Sizer (1984). The first report of the Project 2061 effort *Science for All Americans* describes instruction in science in US classrooms in the following way: 'The present science textbooks and methods of instruction, far from helping, often actually impede progress toward scientific literacy. They emphasize the learning of answers more than the exploration of questions, memory at the expense of critical thought, bits and pieces of information instead of understandings in context, recitation over argument, reading in lieu of doing. They fail to encourage students to work together, to share ideas and information freely with each other, or to use modern instruments to extend their intellectual capabilities' (AAAS 1989: 14).
4. Take mathematics and science education as just one example. At the federal level, one independent government policymaking body establishes the specifications for a national test of mathematics achievement which is then developed by an independent private non-profit organization for administration within most of the USA; another independent agency administers over $250 million in project funds to improve mathematics and science education at the state and local levels; still another agency administers a $200 million federal program to states to improve mathematics and science education. The laws governing these various efforts (which are only a sample of federal government activity) are written by different subcommittees and committees in Congress, governed by regulations that contain little reference to the other federal or even to state programs, and administered by civil servants who rarely talk to each other. (There is now a federal coordinating body chaired by the Secretary of still another government agency, the Energy Department, which has almost no expertise or direct involvement in the educational system.) At the state level, in each of the 50 states, there is at least one, and often multiple, agencies producing independent efforts to improve mathematics and science education, efforts driven by literally tens of different and independently developed state laws. And almost every state has a state assessment or set of assessments designed to measure progress in mathematics and science achievement – assessments that are not only independent of the national assessment effort but of national, state and local curriculum efforts as well. Finally, the mechanisms and requirements for teacher certification in many states operate with almost total independence from other state educational laws, and the authority for overseeing the quality of teacher training typically rests with the state higher education system, which often has little interest in changing itself to meet the needs of the K–12 system. Add to this the supplementary and often conflicting guidance that local school teachers receive from their own district and school coordinators, and from local universities and businesses, and the fact that the basic textbooks and materials in most classrooms are developed entirely independently from all of the federal, state, and local guidance, and we begin to see why many teachers are skeptical of attempts to reform the schools.
5. There is an important irony here. In another paper we argue that the nation's 'common basic skills curriculum' has led to a dramatic reduction in the achievement gap between African-American and white students over the past 20 years. While the achievement distribution for white students has remained unchanged, African-American student achievement in reading, and to a lesser extent in mathematics and science, has shown steady growth. We posit that the basic skills curriculum has contributed both to the lack of change in white achievement and to the important gains of black students (Smith and O'Day 1990). Our hypothesis, however, is that the next major reductions in the size of the 'gap' will require a change for black students away from an overall emphasis on basic skills toward a more complex and challenging curriculum. The equality problem here, of course, is that this change may occur more easily in more 'advantaged' communities which may lead to future increases in the 'gap'.
6. A wonderful, large-scale example of this phenomenon is the history of the 'new' science curricula generated in the aftermath of Sputnik. These curricula were generally well-financed, carefully-developed and contained exciting state-of-the-art (at that time) content, instructional strategies, and materials. Because of their innovative, challenging and hands-on character, they demanded more of teachers than did the conventional curricula. The curricula were initially supported by extensive, but voluntary, in-service teacher training programs. As a consequence they were initially adopted and

adapted by large numbers of innovative teachers around the nation. Moreover, the evaluations carried out on them showed clearly that they produced superior results to the conventional curricula (Shymansky *et al.* 1983). Yet by the middle 1970s these curricula had all but died out in the US schools. There were few pre-service teacher-training institutions preparing their students adequately to use the materials, and the in-service teacher training efforts had subsided to a trickle, so there were few new teachers beginning to use the materials. Meanwhile, increasing numbers of the teachers experienced in the new curricula left teaching, moved to different schools, or succumbed to the quiet pressures of the system to teach the more conventional material.

7. This discussion should not be viewed as 'teacher bashing', but as a critique of the level of knowledge and skills of almost everyone in our society. Few of us have sufficient understanding to teach the content of the seventh grade mathematics (algebra) in Japan or the geometry and probability for US grades K–8 suggested by the National Council on Teachers of Mathematics, or the science content and skills recommended for elementary school students by the American Association for the Advancement of Science.

8. One reason that this fundamental issue is rarely raised among school people is that there may be a lack of clarity about the curricular goals and purposes within schools and districts. If there are no well-articulated curricular frameworks for a school or district, then it is difficult to perceive the inadequacy of a test which is similarly constructed.

9. Sykes (1990) also argues that teachers need more regard from others in society, greater authority within schools, and a specialized knowledge base.

10. See Cohen 1990 for a discussion of 'instructional guidance systems'.

11. Albert Shanker has recently been advocating a 'schools incentive program' along these lines for successful teachers and schools; see Shanker (1990) for a discussion of this proposal.

12. A number of states (Connecticut, California, Michigan, New York) are already on their way in the development of a new generation of challenging and innovative assessment instruments.

13. One mechanism for parental involvement in the education of their children has gathered a variety of advocates at all levels of the governance system. The idea is that parents and schools would enter into a 'contract' with each other. The contract would be moral, not legal, and would specify the schools' instructional (content, pedagogy, and assessment) intentions on the one side, and, on the other side, the parents pledge that they would commit themselves to insuring that their children attend school on time and regularly, that their children do their homework, and that the parents meet with the teachers a number of times during the year. The focus of this effort would be on the intellectual growth of the children. Such an effort could be particularly important in those schools where there are a large number of lower income parents who feel alienated from the schools.

14. There are important roles for districts which are beyond the scope of this paper to discuss in detail. Among these responsibilities are: administration of federal and state programs in progressive ways; administrative tasks such as student transportation, legal matters, facilities management and building etc. that are most efficiently carried out at the central level; maintaining a system of fiscal, administrative and educational accountability, the latter presumably relying primarily on the state examinations; and the coordination of social services for school age children with other service agencies within the district.

15. However, we would not support any full choice (voucher) system unless it contained four key components. First, the 'state' voucher must constitute full payment for the school – schools would not be allowed to charge extra tuition beyond the value of the voucher. Second, over-subscription to a school would be resolved by lottery. Third, transportation would be provided for the needy. Fourth, there would have to be an aggressive and publicly-sponsored system of providing information about the available choices among the schools. In the context of the reforms that we suggest one more component would be necessary. The schools in the voucher system would all be assessed with the state examinations based on the state curriculum frameworks and the data would be made publicly available to assist parents and students in their selection of schools.

References

AMERICAN ASSOCIATION FOR THE ADVANCEMENT OF SCIENCE (AAAS) (1989) *Science for All Americans: A Project 2061 Report on Literacy Goals in Science, Mathematics, and Technology* (Washington, DC: AAAS).

ARCHBALD, D. A. and NEWMANN, F. M. (1988) *Beyond Standardized Testing: Assessing Authentic Academic Achievement in the Secondary School* (Reston, VA: National Association of Secondary School Principals).

CARNEGIE FORUM ON EDUCATION AND THE ECONOMY (1986) *A Nation Prepared: Teachers for the Twenty-first Century* (New York: Carnegie Corporation).

CHUBB, J. E. and MOE, T. (1990) *Politics, Markets, and American Schools* (Washington, DC: Brookings Institute).

CLUNE, W. H., with P. White and J. Patterson (1989) *The Implementation and Effects of High School Graduation Requirements: First Steps Toward Curricular Reform* (New Brunswick, NJ: Rutgers University, Center for Policy Research in Education).

CLUNE, W. H. (1990, this volume) 'Educational policy in a situation of uncertainty; or, how to put eggs in different baskets', in S. H. Fuhrman and B. Malen (eds) *The Politics of Curriculum and Testing* (Philadelphia: Falmer Press), pp. 125–138.

COHEN, D. K. (1989) 'Teaching practice: plus ca change...', in P. W. Jackson (ed.) *Contributing to Educational Change: Perspectives on Research and Practice* (Berkeley, CA: McCutchan), pp. 27–84.

COHEN, D. K. (1990) 'The classroom of state and federal education policy', School of Education, Michigan State University.

COHEN, D. K. (1990, this volume), 'Revolution in one classroom', in S. H. Fuhrman and B. Malen (eds) *The Politics of Curriculum and Testing* (Philadelphia: Falmer Press), pp. 103–123.

COHEN, M. (1983) 'Instructional, management, and social conditions in effective schools', in A. Odden and L. D. Webb (eds) *School Finance and School Improvement: Linkages for the 1980s* (Cambridge, MA: Ballinger).

COLEMAN, J. and HOFFER, T. (1987) *Public and Private High Schools: The Impact of Communities* (New York: Basic Books).

CROSSWHITE, F. J., DOSSEY, J. A., SWAFFORD, J. O., McKNIGHT C. C. and COONEY, T. J. (1985) *Second International Mathematics Study Summary Report for the United States* (Champaign, IL: Stipes).

CUBAN, L. (1990) 'Reforming again, again, and again', *Educational Researcher*, 19, pp. 3–13.

CUBAN, L. (1984) *How Teachers Taught: Constancy and Change in the American Classroom, 1890–1980* (New York: Longman).

DARLING-HAMMOND, L. and BERRY, B. (1988) *Evolution of Teacher Policy*. Report of the Center for Policy Research in Education, Eagleton Institute of Politics at Rutgers University and The Rand Corporation, Washington DC.

DARLING-HAMMOND, L., with J. Green (1990) 'Teacher quality and equality', in J. I. Goodlad and P. Keating (eds) *Access to Knowledge: An Agenda for our Nation's Schools* (New York: The College Entrance Examination Board), pp. 237–258.

DAVID, J. (1990) 'Restructuring in progress: lessons from pioneering districts', in R. Elmore and associates (eds) *Restructuring Schools: The Next Generation of Educational Reform* (San Francisco: Jossey-Bass), pp. 209–250.

DAVID, J., COHEN, M., HONETSCHLAGER, D. and TRAIMAN, S. (1990) *State Actions to Restructure Schools: First Steps* (Washington, DC: National Governors' Association).

ELMORE, R. F. (1986) *Choice in Public Education* (New Brunswick, NJ: Rutgers University, Center for Policy Research in Education).

ELMORE, R. F. and associates (1990) *Restructuring Schools: The Generation of Education Reform* (San Francisco, CA: Jossey-Bass).

ELMORE, R. F. and McLAUGHLIN, M. W. (1988) *Steady Work: Policy, Practice and the Reform of American Education* (Santa Monica, CA: Rand Corporation)

FIRESTONE, W. A., FUHRMAN, S. H. and KIRST, M. W. (1989) *The Progress of Reform: An Appraisal of State Education Initiatives* (New Brunswick, NJ: Rutgers University, Center for Policy Research in Education).

FREDERICKSEN, N. (1984) 'The real test bias: influences of testing on teaching and learning', *American Psychologist*, 39, pp. 193–202.

FUHRMAN, S. H., CLUNE, W. H. and ELMORE, R. F. (1988) 'Research on education reform: lessons on the implementation of policy', *Teachers College Record*, 90(2), pp. 237–257.

FUHRMAN, S. H. and ELMORE, R. F. (1990) 'Understanding local control in the wake of state education reform', *Educational Evaluation and Policy Analysis*, 12 (1), pp. 82–96.

FUHRMAN, S. H. (1990) 'Legislatures and education policy', paper presented at the Eagleton Institute of Politics Symposium on the Legislature in the Twenty-First Century, 27–29 April, Williamsburg, VA.

GLASER, R. (1984) 'Education and thinking: the role of knowledge', *American Psychologist*, 39, pp. 93–104.

GOODLAD, J. I. (1984) *A Place Called School* (New York: McGraw-Hill).

GUSKEY, T. (1986) 'Staff development and the process of teacher change', *Educational Researcher*, 15 (5), pp 5–12.

HAERTEL, E. H. (1987) 'Validity of teacher licensure and teacher education admissions tests', paper prepared for the National Education Association and the Council of Chief State School Officers, Stanford University, Stanford, CA.

HAWKINS, E. K. F. (1990) 'The effects of the 1980s reform movement on levels of public education expenditure', Ph.D. dissertation, Stanford University, Stanford, CA.

HAWLEY, W. D. and ROSENHOLZ, S. J., with H. Goldstein and T. Hasselbring (1984) 'Good schools: what research says about improving student achievement', *Peabody Journal of Education*, 61 (4), pp. 1–178.

HOLMES GROUP (1990) *Tomorrow's Schools: A Report from the Holmes Group* (East Lansing, MI: The Holmes Group).

HONIG, B. (1990) 'Comprehensive strategy' can improve schools', *Education Week*, 9 (23), p. 56.

LAMPERT, M. (1988) 'What can research on teacher education tell us about improving quality in mathematics education?', *Teaching and Teacher Education*, 4 (2), pp. 157–170.

LEVIN, H. M. (1985) 'Solving the shortage of mathematics and science teachers', *Education, Evaluation, and Policy Analysis*, 7 (4), pp. 371–382.

LITTLE, J. W., GERRITZ, W. H., STERN, D. S., GUTHRIE, J. W., KIRST, M. W. and MARSH, D. D. (1987) 'Staff development in California', joint publication of the Far West Laboratory for Educational Research and Development (San Francisco) and Policy Analysis for California Education (UC Berkeley).

McKNIGHT, C. C., CROSSWHITE, F. J., DOSSEY, J. A., KIFER, E., SWAFFORD, J. O., TRAVERS, K. J. and COONEY, T. J. (1987) *The Underachieving Curriculum: Assessing US School Mathematics from an Intentional Perspective* (Champaign, IL: Stipes).

McLAUGHLIN, M. W. (1990) 'Enabling professional development: what have we learned?', in A. Lieberman and L. Miller (eds) *Staff Development and School Change: New Demands, New Realities, New Perspectives* (New York: Teachers College Press).

McNEIL, L. (1986) *Contradictions of Control* (New York: Routledge & Kegan Paul).

MULLIS, I. V. S. and JENKINS, L. B. (1990) *The Reading Report Card, 1971–1988: National Assessment of Educational Progress* (Princeton, NJ: Educational Testing Service).

MURNANE, R. J. and OLSEN, R. T. (1989) 'The effects of salaries and opportunity costs on duration in teaching: evidence from Michigan', *Review of Economics and Statistics*, pp. 347–352.

MURNANE, R. J. and OLSEN, R. T. (1990) 'The effects of salaries and opportunity costs on duration in teaching: evidence from North Carolina', *Journal of Human Resources*, 25, pp. 106–124.

NEWMANN, F. (1988) 'Can depth replace coverage in the high school curriculum?', *Phi Delta Kappan*, 69 (5), pp. 345–348.

OAKES, J. (1985) *Keeping Track: How Schools Structure Inequality* (New Haven, CT: Yale University Press).

PETERSON, P. L. (1986) 'Selecting students and services for compensatory education: lessons from aptitude-treatment interaction research', paper prepared for the Conference on Effects of Alternative Designs in Compensatory Education (Washington, DC: Office of Educational Research and Improvement, Department of Education).

PETERSON, P. L. (1987) 'Teaching for higher-order thinking in mathematics: the challenge for the next decade', in D. A. Grouws and T. J. Cooney (eds) *Effective Mathematics Teaching* (Reston, VA: National Council of Teachers of Mathematics).

PETERSON, P. L. (1989) 'Alternatives to student retention: new images of the learner, the teacher and classroom teaching', in L. A. Shepherd and M. L. Smith (eds) *Flunking Grades: Research and Policies on Retention* (New York: Falmer Press).

POWELL, A., FERRAR, E. and COHEN, D. K. (1985) *The Shopping Mall High School* (Boston: Houghton Mifflin).

PURKEY, S. and SMITH, M. S. (1983) 'Effective schools: a review', *The Elementary School Journal*, 83 (4), pp. 427–452.

PURKEY, S. and SMITH, M. S. (1985) 'School reform: the district policy implications of the effective schools literature', *The Elementary School Journal*, 85 (3), pp. 427–452.

RAIZEN, S. and JONES, L. (1985) *Indicators of Precollege Education in Science and Mathematics: A Preliminary Review* (Washington, DC: National Academy Press).

RESNICK, D. P. and RESNICK, L. B. (1985) 'Standards, curriculum, and performance: a historical and comparative perspective', *Educational Researcher*, 14 (4), pp. 5–20.

RESNICK, L. B. (1988) *Education and Learning to Think* (Washington, DC: National Academy Press).

ROTHMAN, R. (1990) '$80 million NSF program to spur reforms unveiled', *Education Week (4 April)*, p. 5.

SHANKER, A. (1990) 'The end of the traditional model of schooling – and a proposal for using incentives to restructure our public schools', *Phi Delta Kappan* 69 (5), pp. 344–357.

SHYMANSKY, J. A., KYLE, W. C. Jr. and ALPORT, J. M. (1983) 'The effects of new science curricula on student performance', *Journal of Research in Science Teaching*, 20 (5), pp. 387–404.

SIZER, T. (1984) *Horace's Compromise: The Dilemma of the American High School* (Boston, MA: Houghton Mifflin).

SMITH, M. S. (1988) Letter to Bassam Shakhashiri, Director of Science and Engineering Education Programs, NSF; available from Dean's Office, Stanford School of Education, Stanford University, Stanford, CA 94305–3096.

SMITH, M. S. (1990) 'Toward a national curriculum', speech given at American Educational Research Association Annual Meeting (Boston); available on audiotape from Teach 'Em, 160 East Illinois Street, Chicago, IL 60611, USA.

SMITH, M. S. and O'DAY, J. (1988) *Research into Teaching Quality: Main Findings and Lessons for Appraisal* (ED/WP1(88)8). Report Prepared for the meeting of the Working Party on the Condition of Teaching, OECD, Paris, France, 40pp; available from OECD; also available as 'Teaching Policy and Research on Teaching', from CERAS, Stanford School of Education, Stanford University, Stanford, CA 94305–3096, USA.

SMITH, M. S. and O'DAY, J. (in press) 'Educational equality: 1966 and now', in D. Verstegen (ed.) *Spheres of Justice in American Schools* (Cambridge, MA: Ballinger).

SOUTH CAROLINA STATE BOARD OF EDUCATION (1989) *'What is the Penny Buying for South Carolina?'*, (Columbia, SC: SCBE).

STEDMAN, L. C. and SMITH, M. S. (1983) 'Recent reform proposals for American education', *Contemporary Education Review*, 2 (2), pp. 85–104.

SYKES, G. (1990) 'Fostering teacher professionalism in schools', in R. F. Elmore and associates (eds): *Restructuring Schools: The Next Generation of Educational Reform* (San Francisco, CA: Jossey-Bass).

TYSON-BERNSTEIN, H. (1988) 'The Academy's contribution to the impoverishment of America's textbooks', *Phi Delta Kappan*, 70 (3), pp. 193–198.

Index